S ERPENT IN THE SKY

The High Wisdom of Ancient Egypt

Praise for *Serpent in the Sky* . . .

" . . . we may have West and his colleagues to thank for opening our eyes to a chapter of the human past of which we had virtually no awareness till now."

—Richard Heinberg, author of
Celebrate the Solstice

"A truly important book and a very readable one."

—Robert Masters, author of
The Goddess Sekhmet

"Without *Serpent in the Sky* comparatively few people would be alerted to the availability of what must be the most fascinating interpretation of the phenomenon of Egypt ever to be placed on paper."

—J. C. Whitacre, M.D.,
Minneapolis Tribune

"The work of R. A. Schwaller de Lubicz has opened our eyes to the true questions of Egypt. This book makes that work compellingly accessible to everyone."

—Jacob Needleman, author of
Lost Christianity and *The Heart of Philosophy*

SERPENT IN THE SKY

The High Wisdom of Ancient Egypt

John Anthony West

QUEST BOOKS
The Theosophical Publishing House
Wheaton, IL U.S.A./Madras, India/London, England

The Theosophical Publishing House
P.O. Box 270
Wheaton, IL 60189-0270

A publication of the Theosophical Publishing House,
a department of the Theosophical Society in America.

*This publication made possible with
the assistance of the Kern Foundation*

A previous edition of this book was published
by Harper & Row, Publishers, Inc. 1979.

Library of Congress Cataloging-in-Publication Data

West, John Anthony.
  The serpent in the sky: the high wisdom of ancient Egypt /
John Anthony West.
    p. cm.
  Includes bibliographical references (p.   ) and index.
  ISBN 0-8356-0691-0 (pbk.) : $18.00
    1. Egypt—Civilization—To 332 B.C. 2. Occultism—Egypt.
I. Title.
DT61.W46   1993
932—dc20   92-56483
                                    CIP

9 8 7 6 5 4 3 2   * 93 94 95 96 97 98 99

This edition is printed on acid-free paper that meets the
American National Standards Institute Z39.48 Standard

Printed in the United States of America by Versa Press

Contents

c.1

Acknowledgments

We would like to thank the following organizations and individuals for their permission to use the illustrations on the pages indicated. Illustrations from *Sacred Science* by R. A. Schwaller de Lubicz (pp. 68, 89, 131), with permission of Inner Traditions International, 1987; Ronald Sheridan Photo Library (pp. 4, 8, 44, 83, 85, 86, 87, 192); Lawrence Berkeley Laboratory (p. 110); Peter Guy Manners (p. 67); Chicago House, University of Chicago, for the photographs of the Sphinx and Kom Ombo (pp. 165, 196, 197); Patrick Dunlea-Jones (p. 213); and Lucie Lamy for her kind permission to use all the other photos in the book that were not taken by the author.

Foreword to the first edition

by Peter Tompkins

In the current joust between materialist and metaphysician, with admirers of the former screaming for blood from the latter, John Anthony West has taken up the banner in support of the Alsatian philosopher R. A. Schwaller de Lubicz. It is the thesis of de Lubicz, lucidly developed by West, that the builders of ancient Egypt had far more sophisticated understanding of metaphysics and of the laws which govern man and this universe than most Egyptologists have been willing to admit.

It is a striking thesis, but unpopular with orthodox scholars who have deliberately ignored it for twenty years, though they proffer no argument against it other than that it contravenes accepted dogma.

R. A. Schwaller — who in 'real' life was knighted 'de Lubicz' by the Lithuanian Prince Luzace de Lubicz for his contribution to the liberation of Lithuania from both the Russians and the Germans at the end of World War I — has mustered an overwhelming argument in favor of the scientific and spiritual development of the ancient Egyptians; but the argument is complex. Assembled over a period of ten years after a sojourn of fifteen years in Luxor (1936-1951), the evidence is based on the incredibly painstaking measurements and drawings of the stones and statuary of the great Temple of Luxor made by his stepdaughter, Lucie Lamy. This material he incorporated into several published works, of which the most important are the three massive volumes of *Le Temple de l'Homme*. Unfortunately, this work came out in a limited edition, is hard to find and is not easy to read in the original French, though an English translation is now at the printers.

Even so, it remains difficult until one has grasped the fundamentals of de Lubicz' philosophy, a task which West renders much easier by carefully digesting the bulk of de Lubicz' work and by consulting at length with Lucie Lamy, an invaluable aid not only because of her intimate understanding of her stepfather's thought but because of her role as trustee for his unpublished works.

In his daring defense of de Lubicz, West battles for a wisdom kept alive through centuries, despite doctors, lawyers, priests and undertakers who wished to dissect it into carrion. With a stylish lance, refined as a novelist and playwright, West also pricks the bombast accumulated about Egypt and other ancient civilizations — that they were mounted by crude and idolatrous priests, primitive and superstitious.

West says he took up the gauntlet in the cause of de Lubicz because he regards de Lubicz' contribution 'as the most important single work of scholarship of this century . . . one which calls for a total revision of modern man's conception of history and of human social "evolution".'

Since the phonetic values of Egyptian hieroglyphs were discovered by Champollion at the beginning of the last century, the writings of the Egyptians have been interpreted by Egyptologists with as little understanding of the thoughts and beliefs expressed in them as have modern academic teachers of English understood the hermetic philosophy enshrined in Shakespeare. As it happens, the data are the same in both.

De Lubicz was well versed in hermetic wisdom, with a solid founding in the religions of the East, passed on through Hindus, Chinese, Buddhists, Theosophists, Anthroposophists, and Yogis. De Lubicz soon found the same wisdom built into the glyphs, statues, and temples of Egypt.

By interpreting the ancient Egyptian hieroglyphs as symbolic carriers of a hermetic message, de Lubicz discovered in Egypt the earliest known source of a Sacred Science which forms the basis of what has come to be known as the Perennial Philosophy, fragments of which have been kept alive among the Gnostics, Sufis, Cabalists, Rosicrucians, and Masons, but primarily by a series of enlightened and clairvoyant masters.

De Lubicz saw in the Egyptian hieroglyphs not only the overt phonetic script deciphered by Champollion but a more hermetic symbolism which conveyed the subtler metaphysical realities of the Sacred Science of the Pharaohs, too fleeting to be ensnared in a network of phonetic writing.

Just as one glimpses the outlines of the human aura, not by looking directly at the body but slantwise, so, argues de Lubicz, one must glimpse the symbolic rather than the overt meaning of the glyphs.

To de Lubicz this duality of Egyptian hieroglyphs made it possible for the priests to address the people at large with one message while addressing initiates with another, just as with the works attributed to the Lance-Wielder from Stratford-on-Avon one could address the pit with an overt and innocuous message and yet perpetuate the politically dangerous perennial wisdom by addressing the Crown and the Privy Council in language sufficiently hermetic to avoid the Tower or axe.

To de Lubicz the various symbolic devices of the ancient Egyptians were designed to evoke understanding by revelation, by instant vision, rather than by conveying information: they were a means of breaking out of the material bonds which limit human intelligence, enabling man to envisage higher and broader states of awareness. For man, says de Lubicz, was originally perfect and has degenerated into what we are, largely by the use of reasoning.

Only at the end of his life did de Lubicz realize what an impediment to his understanding of the laws of this cosmos had been his reasoning mind, that the brain and psychological consciousness acted as a veil between man's innate awareness and cosmic consciousness.

A study in depth of the texts, images, and arrangements of each stone in the Temple of Luxor revealed to de Lubicz that the Egyptians made no distinction (let alone opposition) between a spiritual state of being and one with a material body. Such a distinction, says de Lubicz, is a mental illusion. 'There was for these sages only differing levels of consciousness in which all is one and the absolute one is all.'

In the course of his fifteen years in Egypt, working with the help of his brilliant and sensitive wife Isha, who was also a professional Egyptologist, as well as an accomplished author, de Lubicz found that the complex of Egyptian temples contain a global lesson of which each temple is a chapter where a particular theme of the Sacred Science is developed. Thus no pharaonic temple is the replica of another, but each edifice speaks through its overall plan, its orientation, the layout of its foundations, the choice of materials used, and the openings in its walls.

Sometimes he found the message to be so hermetic it could only be discovered through what de Lubicz calls 'transparency in the walls,' whereby the meaning of glyphs and reliefs on one side remain incomprehensible unless viewed in conjunction with those appearing on the opposite side.

In the Temple of Luxor, de Lubicz found what appeared to be the only hieratic monument which effectively represents an architectural figuration of man, and which includes such esoteric knowledge as the location of the ductless glands, of the Hindu energy chakras, and of the Chinese acupuncture points. He discovered that the astronomical orientations of the Temple, the geometry of its construction, its figurations and inscriptions are made on the human body, represented by the Temple, and are physiologically located. The proportions he found were those of Adamic Man before the fall, or of perfected Man who has regained his Cosmic consciousness.

In its proportions and harmonies the Temple tells the story of the creation of man and his relation to the universe. In West's words, 'It is a library containing the totality of knowledge pertaining to universal creative powers, embodied in the building itself.'

The incarnation of the universe in man, says de Lubicz, is the fundamental theme of all revealed religion: the human body is a living synthesis of the essential vital functions of the universe. It is also the temple in which the primordial struggle takes place between the essential antagonists: light and dark, Yin and Yang, gravity and levity, Ormuzd and Ahriman, Quetzalcoatl and Tezcatlipoca, Horus and Seth. It is a temple to be refined by man through various incarnations into a regal replica of Cosmic Man. Thus, the Temple of Luxor becomes an image of the universe as well as a harmonic synthesis between the Universe, the Temple and Man; the embodiment of Protagoras's dictum that 'Man is the measure of all things.'

To de Lubicz the temples of Egypt also manifest terrestrial and cosmic measures as well as a whole gamut of correspondences with the rhythms of natures, the motions of heavenly bodies, and specific astronomical periods. The coincidence of these relationships between stars, planets, metals, colors, sounds, as well as between types of vegetables and animals, and parts of the human body, are revealed to the initiate through a whole science of numbers.

As early as 1917 de Lubicz published a study on numbers in which he explained that they were merely names applied to the functions and principles upon which the universe is created and maintained, that from the interplay of numbers result the phenomena of the physical world. He also wrote that to understand properly the successive steps of creation one must first know the development of abstract numbers and how the many are derived from the one.

As de Lubicz launches into his science of numbers, West paraphrases and synthesises his text into a coherent and easily assimilated thesis which shows how Plato and Pythagoras derived what they knew of both number and wisdom from the science of ancient Egypt.

Interestingly, West develops de Lubicz' notion that the Egyptian cosmology and understanding of this universe was not endemic to Egypt but came from colonists or refugees from Plato's sunken continent of Atlantis, which could also explain the similarities and identities with the cosmologies of Central America, presumably brought there by other refugees from Atlantis.

While the Egyptologists agree that the Egyptian civilization was complete at its very beginning, with hieroglyphs, myths, mathematics, and a sophisticated system of measure, de Lubicz goes further, showing that it was not a development; it was a legacy.

As an addendum to his analysis of the work of de Lubicz, West devotes a documented argument on the antiquity of the Sphinx to show that it could be the best proof yet of the existence of Atlantis, not necessarily as a physical location, but as a highly sophisticated civilization which flourished thousands of years prior to the beginnings of dynastic Egypt.

Today the philosophy preached by de Lubicz is even more

pertinent than when he first developed it in the 1920s and 1930s, inveighing against nobility of birth and money, in favor of a nobility of work, pointing out that all the rest is smoke, vanity, or gilded misery.

Man, said the young philosopher, was sick and knew it; almost too sick to attack the malady at its roots. Such institutions as family, administration, and religion he considered to be in ruins, though they could have remained sacred had their laws been adapted to the real goals of human existence.

De Lubicz considered collectivism to be 'useful' but 'low level', motivated by egoism, whereas real solidarity was based on an awareness of the responsibility of each man towards all of humanity.

In a world where nothing has value except through quantity, haste, and violence, de Lubicz suggested that man, instead of destroying himself with his destruction of the world, should work to rebuild himself by recovering a harmony with the cosmos, a harmony which has been shattered by a false concept of sin and an adulterated way of conceiving physical science. Philosophy, he warned, had deteriorated to mechanistic physics.

Yet any revolution in the world, said de Lubicz, must be made on a philosophical level rather than a social one, and never by force. 'There is more power,' he declared, 'in a profound conviction, in an awakening of inner light than in all the explosives on earth.'

As a remedy, the youthful de Lubicz proposed a brotherhood which would obey the laws of universal harmony. Its precepts were: to label this world cowardly and moribund; to free oneself from routine; to affirm all truth, approve all freedom, and treat as brothers the strong, the free, and the aware.

Hence the value of de Lubicz' work and of West's analysis of it. What would be the point of keeping alive the tradition of the Sacred Science of the Egyptians if it were not applicable to this life and to afterlife, for those who keep coming to earth in search of a way to immortality?

For the people of Egypt the Pharaonic priesthood maintained the cult of Osiris, one of renewal and reincarnation. For the elite of the Temple it taught the Christ-like principle of Horus the Redeemer, of freeing oneself from the Karma of reincarnation, of a return to Cosmic Man, bodiless yet fully aware.

But since the closing of the Temple at the end of the Pharaonic empire and the beginning of the Christian era, man has been without the essential guide of the Sacred Science as a means of becoming truly human ... and then superhuman.

While the scientist keeps prodding the barrier to the unknown without being able to breach it, the metaphysician keeps warning him that such is his fate, indefinitely; that truth cannot be probed, only known, intuitively, or by revelation.

The lists are drawn. The joust continues.

Foreword to the revised edition

by Robert Masters

Serpent in the Sky, by John Anthony West, is a truly important book and a very readable one. When I first encountered it more than ten years ago, I was impressed by the depth and breadth of both the scholarship and the thinking, as well as by the clear and vivid writing. Now, as I have had occasion to read this exciting narrative again, I am still impressed by those virtues, and I find the book even more stimulating than before. I write this Foreword to the new edition with great pleasure and with the hope that a great many new readers will be reached.

Peter Tompkins, in his Preface written for the first edition, summarized the book's contents and has provided necessary background information. I will repeat as little of it as possible. For this new edition, West has added an account of his book's controversial history and has dropped a bombshell with seemingly very firm scientific evidence that the great Sphinx of Giza is many thousands of years older than is maintained by almost all Egyptologists. That the Sphinx predates Egyptian civilization as we know it has been claimed by many, including West. However, it was West, with his team of scientific workers, who provided the evidence which may require a significant revision of human history.

Serpent in the Sky presents the revisionist and (when known at all) highly controversial work of the late Alsatian philosopher-Egyptologist R. A. Schwaller de Lubicz. Based on many years of meticulous study of the ancient temples and of Egyptian civilization as a whole, de Lubicz presented to the world evidence for an Egypt to which our minds, hearts and souls can feel free and proud to resonate. That is of course what most of us naturally do when encountering the marvels ancient Egypt has bequeathed to us — Goddesses and Gods, Sphinx and Pyramids, Temples and Magic and Mysteries, and all the rest of it. In fact, the makers of those wondrous images and symbols, works of art and metapsychologies, precisely intended such resonance and obviously knew just how to create what would achieve it. And yet, *mirabile dictu,* we have a profession called "Egyptology" whose practitioners seem totally blind or indifferent to what seizes so many of the rest of us. Rooted in an impenetrable materialism, they insist upon a soulless and almost mindless Egypt hopelessly mired in ignorance and superstition. It is because the findings of de Lubicz contradict such notions at every turn that his work has been ignored or denounced by the professional orthodoxy.

De Lubicz's most important work is available only in his monumental, multivolumed *Le Temple de l'Homme*, difficult to read and daunting in its sheer magnitude. One of West's major achievements has been to present the work of de Lubicz with admirable clarity while also reinforcing it with his own brilliance, erudition and finely honed reasoning faculties. As one inclined to suffer fools not at all, West comes armed with the wit and merciless logic of a skilled prosecutor, targeting one after another of the dry-as-dust materialist "experts" who have come to preside over the dismal world of politically correct Egyptology.

Le Temple de l'Homme is regarded by West as ". . . the most important single work of scholarship of this century." West also takes note of any number of almost uncanny correspondences between de Lubicz's understanding of the ancient science and philosophy of Egypt and the understandings and teachings of the saintly mystic and magus G. I. Gurdjieff. Indeed, what de Lubicz learned about ancient Egypt by means of his study of its works, Gurdjieff seems to have learned from some other source. Another example of apparent penetration into the mind and soul of ancient Egypt is that of the curious nineteenth-century poet, scholar and trance visionary Gerald Massey. In three monumental, multivolumed works — *Book of the Beginnings, Natural Genesis,* and *Ancient Egypt* — Massey presented an Egypt in many ways very similar, and sometimes seemingly identical, to that presented by de Lubicz. This was especially the case in Massey's last work, *Ancient Egypt,* published near the end of his life in 1907. The writings and teachings of these three titans — de Lubicz, Gurdjieff and Massey — deserve to be exhaustively compared. It is a fitting challenge for the author of *Serpent in the Sky.*

It was the observation of de Lubicz that the Giza Sphinx has marks of erosion by water not found on any other structure in Egypt. West, with the help of his scientists, confirmed it. As he explains in detail, the conclusion demanded from his findings is that the Sphinx predates dynastic Egypt. He also marshalls much other persuasive evidence for his belief, and that of de Lubicz, that Egyptian civilization was a *legacy,* not a developmental creation. This leads directly into the ancient legend of Atlantis, mentioned by Plato, and which occurs in one form or another in the myths of many times and places. That is to say, the Egyptians were *taught* what they knew, and marvelous knowledge it was — an unparalleled integration of science and art, philosophy and religion. The result was a civilization which excelled in its potentiation of consciousness and actualization of potentials beyond any of which we have knowledge. The case for this is masterfully presented.

Massey, working with his understanding of the Egyptian use of numbers and astronomy/astrology, places the age of the Sphinx at thirteen thousand years, long before the First Dynasty. Interestingly, the American psychic Edgar Cayce arrived at the same figure. In my own researches for my book *The Goddess Sekhmet,* I reached the conclusion that the Sphinx, like the Goddess Sekhmet, is much older than Egypt. Clearly, the two are related — Sekhmet with the head of a lioness and a human body; the Sphinx with its lioness body and its human head. Ancient tradition links them and also proclaims their antiquity, Sekhmet being known to the Egyptians as the *Lady of the Place of the Beginning of Time* and the *One Who Was Before the Gods Were.* I have often pondered the fact that the Sphinx was built in what would only millennia later be a place close to the principal site of the worship of Sekhmet at Memphis. Thus it may be that the Egyptian civilization was *planned and worked out* for thousands of years before it became a reality. Might this mean that the fate of "Atlantis" was known long before it occurred?

Serpent in the Sky is a marvelously fecundating book. Page after page after page stirs the reader's imagination and furthers creative thought. The account of Egyptian civilization is an inspiring one and offers rays of hope that even now our severely wounded and at least half-crazed world will be able to draw upon what once was in order to realize what might be. The human being possesses awesome latent capacities, at present scarcely tapped and rarely recognized, particularly by those in power. De Lubicz and West confirm that it is possible to have a society in which the human potential is encouraged and enabled to flower. The case is made that Egypt, for a very long time, possessed knowledge of how to awaken and use those potentials. And more, in Egypt's *works* which have survived, there may remain the means to reacquire that knowledge. We are all indebted to Schwaller de Lubicz and John Anthony West for recognizing what is possible and working to achieve it.

Preface

When the first edition of *Serpent in the Sky* was published in 1978, the works of the Alsatian mathematician and philosopher R. A. Schwaller de Lubicz (1891-1962) had not been translated from their original French. English-speaking readers had no satisfactory access to his 'symbolist'* interpretation of ancient Egypt.#

Serpent in the Sky was written as an in-depth examination and introduction to Schwaller's radical Egyptological ideas, intended for the general reader. Since it was first published, many of Schwaller de Lubicz's books have appeared in English and are now available. Unfortunately, the key to understanding his work, the massive, three volume *Le Temple de l'Homme* (The Temple of Man) remains available only in French.△

Without access to that, it may well be impossible to grasp the comprehensive, seamless nature of his symbolist interpretation or to appreciate the magnitude of his achievement. Moreover, like certain other great, innovative thinkers (Swedenborg, Boehme, Kant, Hegel, to name a few) Schwaller was not a gifted communicator. His style is abstruse, complex and uncompromising. Few readers, even those familiar with metaphysical/philosophical writing, seem comfortable with raw, original Schwaller (it's a bit like trying to wade directly into high energy physics without extensive prior training). So even with his other works available in English, *Serpent in the Sky* continues to fulfill its original function.

My chief concern was always a clear exposition of Schwaller's ideas and the evidence supporting them. At the same time, I wanted to emphasize the differences between the symbolist and orthodox approaches to Egypt. Schwaller assumed

---

* The name applied to Schwaller's work by both adherents and detractors.
# Except through the novels, *Her-Bak*, and *Her-Bak, Disciple* by Isha Schwaller de Lubicz, R. A. Schwaller de Lubicz's wife. Though intellectually and philosophically stimulating, I find these novels sterile and psychologically one-dimensional. They are novels, yet they fail to convey the emotional and magical sense of Egypt that infuses R. A. Schwaller de Lubicz's magisterial but strictly scholarly oeuvre — for all the difficulties Schwaller's own works present.
△ When the first edition of *Serpent* appeared, plans were afoot to publish a translation of *Le Temple de l'Homme*. These were never realized, but as this is written, I am told that plans are again afoot. With luck, this time, *The Temple of Man* will finally become available to English-speaking readers.

his readers would have a working knowledge of classical Egyptology and would appreciate the differences without having to spell them out himself. In reality, very few readers have more than the vaguest picture of Egypt, the residue of a few dimly remembered lessons in high school or university ancient history courses. In that standard explanation, Egypt is a civilization of amazing architecture, egotistic kings and a servile, superstitious populace. The symbolist view sees Egypt quite otherwise — as a civilization philosophically and spiritually (in certain areas, even scientifically) far more advanced than ourselves, from which we have much to learn.

Indeed, there is probably no other academic discipline in which identical source material (in this case the monuments and texts of ancient Egypt) has spawned two such diametrically opposed interpretations. Without a solid grasp of the specifics, it's difficult to appreciate the gulf that separates the symbolist from the orthodox portrait.

One of the most frustrating aspects of espousing a heretical view in *any* entrenched scientific or scholarly field is the refusal by the establishment to deal with, or even to acknowledge the existence of contrary evidence. From the onset, I was determined not to counter irresponsible scholarship with irresponsible scholarship of my own. So, in presenting Schwaller de Lubicz's symbolist interpretation, I have cited and discussed opposing views at length and in context.

Elaborating upon an ingenious format developed by Peter Tompkins in his *Secrets of the Great Pyramid*, I set up the book to provide a simultaneous running contrast between the two schools — the symbolist interpretation is developed in the main text, while opposing views and other relevant material is immediately accessible in parallel extensive margin notes. Readers are therefore in a position to decide which interpretation is more valid. The opposing selections have been culled from a full spectrum of academic Egyptological sources in several languages. Taken together, they provide an accurate but unavoidably unflattering overview of contemporary Egyptology.*

Symbolist vs. mainstream Egyptology is not just a quibble between opposing scholars over a dead civilization. Much more is at stake. I considered it necessary, therefore, to spell out what Schwaller left mostly implicit: the profound implications his symbolist interpretation of Egypt has upon all modern thought especially on the way we view history and the evolution of civilization.

* See the Afterword for further discussion of this subject.

Ancient Egypt did not exist in a vacuum. We may be certain that other ancient civilizations had their own versions of the same Sacred Science that fueled and sustained Egypt. As our demoralized, violent and de-spiritualized society lurches toward its final undoing, (even at this late date calling the pell-mell, downhill rout 'The March of Progress'), the certainty that a higher order of wisdom was once generally available to humanity becomes a matter of immediate concern.

In preparing this revised edition, I'm pleased to find, after a lapse of fifteen years, that my discussion of Schwaller's ideas and the evidence supporting them needed little tinkering with. New developments on a few scientific fronts justified minor revisions and additions throughout the body of the text. But the ongoing work on redating the Great Sphinx of Giza called for more extensive treatment.

In his book *Sacred Science* (*Le Roi de la Theocratie Pharaonique*) published in 1961, Schwaller de Lubicz observed that the Great Sphinx had been weathered by water, not by wind and sand as was then universally assumed. Reading that line, as I was working on the original *Serpent*, I realized that this observation should be open to geological proof. If proved, it would mean the Great Sphinx was millennia older than the rest of ancient Egypt, which would, in turn, throw all of accepted ancient history and much else besides into considerable and — from my point of view — healthy confusion.

My original detective work, putting together the body of evidence to prove Schwaller's point, takes up the long last chapter of this book. An important archeological/geological survey of the Sphinx early in the 1980's by archeologist Mark Lehner and geologist K. Lal Gauri provided further crucial evidence for the developing theory — even though the scholars responsible for the survey declined to see it that way. This survey prompted an Appendix for the first paperback edition of *Serpent,* in 1987 which is mostly still valid and has been retained.

Since 1990, the theory has been further developed and has taken several quantum leaps toward acceptance. It has been carefully studied by a number of geologists and geophysicists who support it unconditionally. Now, with powerful scientific backing, it has been the subject of heated debate at two major scientific conventions, with Egyptologists and archeologists in one camp and geologists in the other. The controversy has fueled newspaper headlines around the world, as well as magazine articles and television and radio spots.

A full examination of the evidence, the story of the theory's vicissitudes within the academic community, its treatment by the media and the implications of its eventual (if not impending) general acceptance is now the subject of a book, *Unriddling the Sphinx*, coauthored by myself and Dr. Robert M. Schoch, principal investigator on our Sphinx team. It is scheduled to appear in late 1993 or early 1994 (Villard Books/Random House). A second appendix to this revised edition of *Serpent in the Sky* briefly summarizes the most important developments as of summer, 1992.

In the form of an Afterword, I've also added a substantial essay on the general theme of the problems involved in establishing a new order of thought, with a specific focus on the experience to date of trying to obtain a hearing for Schwaller de Lubicz's symbolist interpretation.

Introduction

Serpent in the Sky presents a revolutionary, exhaustively documented re-interpretation of the civilization of ancient Egypt; it is a study of the life work of the philosopher, Orientalist and mathematician, the late R. A. Schwaller de Lubicz.

After two decades of study, mainly on site at the Temple of Luxor, Schwaller de Lubicz was able to prove that all that is accepted as dogma concerning Egypt (and ancient civilization in general) is wrong, or hopelessly inadequate; his work overthrows or undermines virtually every currently-cherished belief regarding man's history, and the 'evolution' of civilization.

Egyptian science, medicine, mathematics and astronomy were all of an exponentially higher order of refinement and sophistication than modern scholars will acknowledge. The whole of Egyptian civilization was based upon a complete and precise understanding of universal laws. And this profound understanding manifested itself in a consistent, coherent and inter-related system that fused science, art and religion into a single organic Unity. In other words, it was exactly the opposite of what we find in the world today.

Moreover, every aspect of Egyptian knowledge seems to have been complete at the very beginning. The sciences, artistic and architectural techniques and the hieroglyphic system show virtually no signs of a period of 'development'; indeed, many of the achievements of the earliest dynasties were never surpassed, or even equalled later on. This astonishing fact is readily admitted by orthodox Egyptologists, but the magnitude of the mystery it poses is skillfully understated, while its many implications go unmentioned.

How does a complex civilization spring full-blown into being? Look at a 1905 automobile and compare it to a modern one. There is no mistaking the process of 'development'. But in Egypt there are no parallels. Everything is there right at the start.

The answer to the mystery is of course obvious, but because it is repellent to the prevailing cast of modern thinking, it is seldom seriously considered. *Egyptian civilisation was not a 'development', it was a legacy.*

Following an observation made by Schwaller de Lubicz, it is

now possible virtually to prove the existence of another, and perhaps greater civilization ante-dating dynastic Egypt — and all other known civilizations — by millennia. In other words, it is now possible to prove 'Atlantis', and simultaneously, the historical reality of the Biblical Flood. (I use inverted commas around 'Atlantis' since it is not the physical location that is at issue here, but rather the existence of a civilization sufficiently sophisticated and sufficiently ancient to give rise to the legend.)

Proof of the existence of 'Atlantis' rests upon a simple geological foundation.

Questions of chronology and cause remain unanswered. And it is still impossible to say how the wisdom of 'Atlantis' was preserved and handed down, or by whom. But its existence is now as difficult to deny as the completeness and coherence of Egyptian knowledge at its inception.

King Chephren, IV Dynasty, successor to Cheops and alleged constructor of the second largest pyramid. This diorite statue was found in a pit in the temple adjacent to the Sphinx, and the building of the temple and Sphinx is attributed to Chephren (but see the final chapter for a detailed discussion of these allegations).

Can a man who looks like this really be a primitive materialist, with a mind still half asleep?

opposite page

Hesire: Vizier to King Zoser, III Dynasty. One of a series of wood carvings from Hesire's tomb in Saqqara. If scholars choose, they may continue to regard the early Egyptians as 'primitive materialists' with minds 'still half asleep', but the layman may think otherwise on the basis of the message implicit in artistry of this order. Hesire seems rather wide awake, unless this is flattery imposed by the unknown artist, in which case, at least the artist must have briefly surfaced from his reveries. The hieroglyphs are already complete, and later Egypt will never succeed in carving them with more power or purity. Still earlier hieroglyphs are no less complete, but in general less well executed. Nothing supports a postulated 'period of development'. But it is possible that guardians of the ancient tradition required a number of generations in which to bring artists and artisans up to this standard.

The Egyptian technique for producing inlaid eyes reached the height of its perfection in the IV Dynasty and was never equalled subsequently either in Egypt or anywhere else. The Egyptians must have taken careful note of reflection and refraction properties of the material used; the result, even in a photograph, is striking; in person it is practically overpowering. Of the examples found to date, more are blue or grey-eyed than brown-eyed. Can this have anything to do with the long, supposedly 'legendary' rule of Egypt prior to Menes by the 'venerables of the North'?

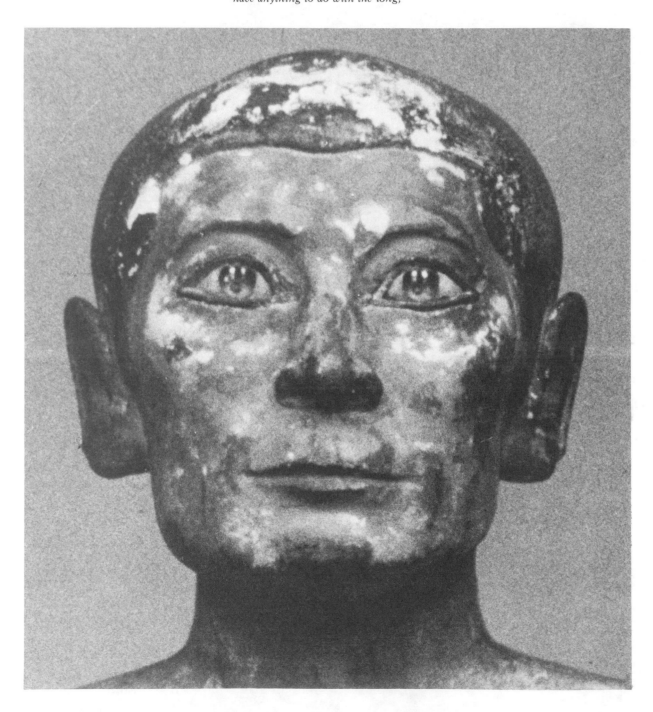

Therefore, it is probably safe to say that in providing this first true picture of ancient Egypt, Schwaller de Lubicz has also provided the key to the study of the wisdom of the earlier 'Atlantis'.

Since I am presenting another man's ideas and work, it is inescapable that these must first pass through the filter of my own understanding, in certain cases perhaps in an altered light. Because Schwaller de Lubicz's work is meticulously developed and always supported by a wealth of documentary illustration and detail, it is impossible to summarise it or even to extract from it, and I have often made use of analogy or metaphor in an attempt to capture the essence of the work without misrepresenting it.

To avoid confusion, and also to avoid the clumsy device of repeatedly distinguishing between pure Schwaller de Lubicz ideas and my own illustrations, opinions and conclusions, it is well to make a general distinction here at the beginning. As a rule, when I write of the knowledge, understanding, language, philosophy and religion of the ancient Egyptians I am presenting Schwaller de Lubicz's ideas in as pure a form as I can, and wherever possible, illustrating with his own diagrams and photos. Whenever I make use of metaphor and analogy, I am exercising journalistic license. Schwaller de Lubicz might or might not approve of my method; there is no way to know.

I have also gone to some lengths to keep a sort of running commentary on the reverberations set up by Schwaller de Lubicz's work in the context of today's world and to continually point out the differences between his interpretation and the generally accepted tenets of orthodox Egyptology. Sometimes I have digressed into essays on art and literature, modern science and philosophy to stress the manner in which Schwaller de Lubicz's work relates to the modern scene.

These digressions and essays are my own responsibility, and reflect an idiosyncratic view that the reader is not obliged to share. My aim is to call attention to Schwaller de Lubicz's vast and neglected work; to arouse sufficient interest in it to inspire its publication in English and its dissemination among those capable of recognising its real significance and of devoting the time and effort necessary to study it in its original form.

To appreciate this radical work, it is essential to understand both the manner in which orthodox Egyptology has been developed and the reasons for its continued prevalence.

Egyptology, along with all modern disciplines devoted to past or alien cultures (anthropology, archaeology, ethnology, etc.), is based upon certain assumptions considered so self-evident they are never stated explicitly, never questioned. Generally speaking, 'authorities' within these fields are unaware that their disciplines are based upon these assumptions.

Bertrand Russell
Wisdom of the West
MacDonald, 1969, p. 10

Philosophy and Science, as we now know them, are Greek inventions. The rise of Greek civilisation which produced this outburst of intellectual activity is one of the most spectacular events in history. Nothing like it has ever occurred before or since ... Philosophy and Science began with Thales of Miletus in the early Sixth Century, BC ... What course of previous events had come to set off this sudden unfolding of the Greek genius? ... Among the civilisations of the world the Greek is a late comer. Those of Egypt and Mesopotamia are older by several millennia. These agricultural societies grew up along the great rivers and were ruled by divine kings, a military aristocracy and a powerful class of priests who presided over the elaborate polytheistic religious systems. The bulk of the population were serfs who worked the land.

Both Egypt and Babylon furnished some knowledge which the Greeks later took over. But neither developed Science or Philosophy. Whether this is due to lack of native genius or to social conditions is not a fundamental question here. What is significant is that the function of religion was not conducive to the exercise of the intellectual adventure.

5

Arthur Koestler
The Sleepwalkers
Hutchinson, 1968, pp. 19, 20

When I try to see the universe as a Babylonian saw it around 3000 BC, I must grope my way back to my own childhood. At the age of four I had what I felt to be a satisfactory understanding of God and the world. I remember an occasion when my father pointed his finger at the white ceiling, which was decorated with a frieze of dancing figures, and explained that God was up there, watching me. I immediately became convinced that the dancers were God . . . Much in the same manner, I like to imagine that the luminous figures on the dark ceiling of the World appeared as living divinities to the Babylonians and Egyptians . . . Some six thousand years ago, when the human mind was still half asleep, Chaldean priests were standing on watch towers, scanning the stars.

Time, June 28, 1976, p. 50

Huge, rich and efficient, the U.S. oil industry has long occupied an ambiguous place in American life. Its dazzling feats of technology in supplying the nation's voracious demand for energy have helped the U.S. to become the most advanced country on earth.

Joseph Needham
In *The Radicalization of Science*
ed. Stephen and Hilary Rose,
MacMillan, 1976, p. 100

The whole anti-science movement has arisen because of two characteristics of our Western civilisation: on the one hand the conviction that the scientific method is the only valid way of understanding and apprehending the universe, and on the other hand the belief that it is quite proper for the results of this science to be applied to a rapacious technology . . . The first of these convictions is held as a semi-conscious assumption by a great number of working scientists; though formulated clearly only by a small number.

1 That man has 'progressed'. There has been an 'evolution' in human affairs.
2 That civilisation implies progress and that the height of civilisation is in direct proportion to the rate of progress.
3 That progress, hence civilisation, began with the Greeks, who invented speculative philosophy and rational science.
4 That science and science-based disciplines are the only valid instruments for arriving at 'objective truth'.
5 That without rational science and speculative philosophy there is no real civilisation.
6 That there is nothing the ancients knew that we do not know, or understand better.

These assumptions (the selected quotes typify the attitude) have been accepted by almost every scientist and scholar for the last two hundred years. They percolate into every aspect of education. No reader of this book will have been taught otherwise at school or university. Yet each of these assumptions is false, or represents a half-truth more insidious than outright falsehood. To demonstrate this according to prevailing academic ground rules is simple enough but time consuming, and would take us too far from Egypt. The reader interested in pursuing the subject is referred to the Bibliography.* (B1, 3, 9, C 11.)

For my purposes, analogy will suffice: the chef makes the restaurant, not the dishwashers. The executive makes the corporation, not the shipping clerks. If the chef is drunk, and the managing director berserk, both restaurant and corporation soon founder.

Modern society is what it is, not because the masses are uneducated, but precisely because of the understanding, beliefs and goals of our leaders — not politicians, but scientists, educators and intellectuals — all of whom are highly educated. Society is shaped by those who control its head and heart. Real physical needs are easily satisfied. It is our desires and beliefs that make the world what it is.

Darwin wields a greater influence than Stalin.

The world is what it is because of progress, not in spite of it. Progress is neither a corollary of civilisation nor vice versa.

'Civilisation', like 'love' or 'freedom', is a word that means something different to everyone.

By 'civilisation' I mean a society organised upon the conviction that mankind is on earth for a purpose. In a civilisation, men are concerned with the quality of the *inner* life rather than with the *conditions* of day-to-day existence. Though there is no commanding logical or rational reason why 'concern with quality' should depend upon 'sense of purpose', human nature is such that without the sense of purpose, it is in prac-

* Bracketed numbers within the text refer to the Bibliography.

Arthur Atkinson
Letters to the Editor
The Listener, Aug. 12, 1976

Surely we can get more satisfaction by facing up to the simple, positive humanist view that man is natural, has evolved by natural processes, and the best we can do is to accept the mystery of existence, seeking what knowledge we can discover about it, but not being conned into 'explaining' one mystery by the introduction of another. Many can still be persuaded that existence must have been planned by somebody. True, our increased knowledge of nature forbids Him to express His pleasure by the rainbow, or His wrath by the thunder any longer, but He still carries on business as usual through some indefinable transcendence. When will we post-Darwinians realise that imputing intelligence to some celestial being or supernatural force is no longer permissible? As a correspondent in the *New Scientist* (July 29, 1976) observes, it ignores the biological nature of intelligence, and the evolutionary processes that have brought it into being.

Only in the absence of religious obscurantism can man get down to the challenging problem of discovering what human needs are and how best to cater for them.

Adolf Erman
A Handbook of Egyptian Religion
Archibald Constable, 1907, p. 255

A time will come when it will appear as though it were for naught that the Egyptians piously and sedulously worshipped the godhead ... for the godhead will return from earth to ᛫ heaven, and Egypt will be left desolate, and the land which was the abode of religion will no longer shelter the gods ... Oh Egypt, Egypt, of thy religion only fables will survive, which will appear incredible to later races, and words only will remain upon the stones which record thy pious deeds. [This prophecy from Pseudo Apuleius, *Asclepius*, xxiii, is quoted by Adolf Erman, a fact even more astonishing than the prophecy itself: for of all the misguided Egyptologists that ever were, none have shown less understanding of ancient Egypt than Erman, none have evinced so deep-rooted a sense of smugness in the accomplishments of modern man. Author's note.]

Herodotus

Concerning Egypt I will now speak at length, because nowhere are there so many marvellous things, nor in the whole world beside are there to be seen so many works of unspeakable greatness.

tice impossible to maintain that essential unwavering concern — a concern which involves the personal determination to master greed, ambition, envy, jealousy, avarice and so on, all those aspects of ourselves that make the world what it is. History is there to bear grim witness: even *with* the sense of purpose man usually fails; without it there is no compelling reason why he should even try. In a true civilisation, men try and succeed.

'Progress' is a parody of civilisation, understood in this sense. Knowledge is a parody of understanding. Information is a parody of knowledge. We live in an age of information, and if we swallow whole the bait of modern education, the thought, art and literature of civilised men is, to us, incomprehensible.

Egypt was a civilisation, and the academic Egyptologist stands helpless in the face of its accomplishment.

It is for this reason that, in all our schools, we are presented with an obvious paradox. We are taught that the ancient Egyptians were a people capable of producing artistic and architectural masterpieces unequalled in recorded history, yet that at the same time they were priest-bound necrophiles, an intellectually infantile race obsessed with purely materialistic concerns for a mythical hereafter; a people slavishly worshipping a grotesque pantheon of animal-headed gods; a people devoid of real mathematics, science, astronomy or medicine, and devoid of any desire to acquire such knowledge; a people so conservative, so opposed to change, that their artistic, political, social and religious institutions remained rigid for four millennia.

Philippe Derchain
*Mythes et Dieux Lunaires en Egypte:
La Lune, Mythes, et Rites*
Source Orientales, 1962, p. 28

It is also remarkable that the exact explanation of the light of the moon was almost found by the Egyptians: 'Khonsu-Io, light of the night, image of the left eye of Amon, rising in the Bahkt (East) while Aton (the Sun) is in the Ankhet (West). Thebes is flooded with their light, for the left eye receives the light of the right eye when they are re-united on the day when the two bulls meet.' The only reservation to be made is that this short text appears to refer to the reflection of the solar light by the moon at the moment of opposition. Whatever it may be, the two latter citations show a clear scientific tendency in the modern sense of the word.

Otto Neugebauer
The Exact Sciences in Antiquity
Harper Torchbooks, 1962, pp. 91, 171

Ancient science was the product of very few men; and those few happened not to be Egyptian ...

The role of astronomy is perhaps unique in so far as it carried in its slow but steady progress the roots for the most decisive development in human history, the creation of the modern exact sciences.

I. E. S. Edwards
The Pyramids of Egypt
Penguin, 1964, p. 52

However primitive and materialist the Egyptian conception of the After-life may seem, it must be conceded that it was responsible for the production of some of the greatest artistic masterpieces in antiquity.

Egyptian religion was not a form of zo-
olatry, or animal worship. The Egyptian
sages recognized animals as 'functional
types' as the embodiments of principles
(recognitions to which, despite our
science, we still pay common verbal
homage: the 'sly' fox, the 'greedy' pig,
the 'jealous' dog, etc. No one would
dream of saying he or she felt 'free as an
elephant' but 'free as a bird' makes sense
to anyone anywhere, though the
elephant is strictly speaking no less free).

In Egypt, the bird represented the
principle of volatility, ultimately
'spirit'. And the Ba, the spirit of a man,
or woman, was drawn as a bird with a
human head, an interesting exception to
a rule that is otherwise only broken by
the figure of the Sphinx — which is not
Egyptian in origin, but older.

Note the two right hands on the
defunct, her role in this case, is entirely
active; two left hands on her Ba.

T. Eric Peet
The Present Position of Egyptological Studies
Oxford, 1934, p. 18

In the eyes of the Greeks the Egyptians possessed a reputation for wisdom. As time goes on and we learn more about the Egyptian mind and its products it becomes increasingly difficult to understand this ... The Egyptian mind was practical and concrete and concerned itself little or not at all with speculations regarding the ultimate nature of things. Theology, for instance, consisted of a mass of myth and legend in which the deeds of the gods, neither better nor worse than those of any other pantheon, were preserved ... The fact is that the Egyptians never disentangled philosophy from the crudest theology.

Somers Clarke and R. Engelbach
Ancient Egyptian Masonry
Oxford, 1930.

Before we can completely account for the extreme conventionality, 'even monotony' of ancient Egyptian architecture, several factors have to be taken into consideration ... The quarrying and working up of the material seem to have been in the hands of the state. It was natural, therefore, that when methods of work had been established, the tendency to a hidebound system common to all bureaucracies should develop itself and become so thoroughly crystallised that we see in Egypt, the same things done in the same way from the earliest dynasties down to the period of Roman occupation, a period of some 3500 years.

A. Badawy
Ancient Egyptian Architectural Design
University of California, 1965, p. 3

Works of sculpture and painting in Egypt are often very similar in composition of detail, and occasionally direct copies of other works, especially during the XXVI Dynasty when achievements from the Old Kingdom were taken as models. Architecture, however, does not show this servile copying, and two buildings are seldom if ever found to have the same characteristics and dimensions ... every pylon or facade and every column or drawing not only bear the stamp of individual design but vary in scale.

But if this picture of priest-bound necrophiles is correct — if there is nothing to be learned from Egypt that we do not already know — why bother with them?

Muhammad Ali spends no afternoons in the local gym watching tankers slug it out. Escoffier never hung about a hamburger joint ferreting out secret recipes. Dostoyevsky did not waste his time sifting through the maunderings of amateurs, yet the Egyptologist cheerfully devotes a lifetime to working out the details of Tutankhamen's laundry list.

It did not start out this way. Actually, what we are witnessing, not only in Egyptology, but in other fields as well, is the senescence and demise of an academic approach based upon faulty premises but at the same time responsible for the development of powerful, if limited, investigative methods. As this approach expends itself in discussions over how many asps killed Cleopatra, a new generation of scholars, free from the prejudices but armed with the methods, begins the process of revitalisation. Schwaller de Lubicz may be regarded as one of the great links between old and new, making meticulous use of the methods and data of his predecessors in order to present a synthesis so new, daring and comprehensive that the youngest of the new school have not yet caught up to him.

To appreciate both the links and the differences between old and new, it is worth looking at a brief, necessarily oversimplified account of the development of Egyptology.

B. Baldwin
Brief Communications
Journal of Egyptian Archaeology 50, p. 181

In his article on this subject (Death of Cleopatra VII, *Journal of Egyptian Archaeology*, v. 47; 113-118) J. Gwyn Griffiths adduces various classical authors for his belief that Cleopatra used two snakes instead of one for her suicide. I should like to challenge some of his interpretations and assumptions.

G. A. Wainwright
'Shekelesh or Shasu'
Journal of Egyptian Archaeology 50, p. 40

In JNES (Journal of Near Eastern Studies) 22 (1963, 167-172) Dr. Wente repudiates my view that the captive chief labelled S3, 3 by Rameses III at Medinet Habu was a Shekelesh. Although he is very definite in his belief, and expresses it forcefully, that the man is a Shasu, there is much and to my mind, definite, to be said in favour of the Shekelesh.

Pythagoras Rides Again

The development of orthodox Egyptology in the historical context

The earliest recorded account of Egypt comes to us from the Greek historian Herodotus, who visited Egypt around 500 BC, when it was already well into its decline. Though much that he wrote has proven true, much is evidently fancy; Herodotus indiscriminately reports as truth tales told to him by an ancient version of tourist guides, whom he mistook for temple priests.

Like so many travellers after him, Herodotus marvelled at the sights. But neither he nor anyone following had access to those responsible for their construction. Throughout history, then, visitors to Egypt have recorded their impressions according to personal interpretation. But the exact nature of Egyptian knowledge, locked as it was in the impenetrable hieroglyphs, could not help but remain a mystery. Modern Egyptologists insist with justice that no possibility of understanding Egypt existed until the hieroglyphs were deciphered.

In the late eighteenth century, Napoleon invaded Eygpt armed with scholars as well as soldiers, determined to solve the mystery as well as to build an empire. Accounts of his discoveries, illustrated with fine, accurately rendered drawings, made Egyptian civilisation known to a European public for the first time and interest ran high as gifted scholars pitted their wits against the hieroglyphs. But it was not until 1822, nearly thirty years after Napoleon's campaign, that a key was found.

Jean François Champollion was convinced, at the age of twelve, that he would decipher the hieroglyphs. He set out to master all the languages, ancient and modern, that he believed would lead to this goal. The solution was provided by the Rosetta Stone, a Ptolemaic relic upon which the same inscription was recorded in hieroglyphs, demotic (a sort of shorthand or vernacular form of the hieroglyphs) and Greek. Working back through the Greek into the hieroglyphs, Champollion was eventually led to the answer or, rather, a partial answer. Egyptology was born.

Prior to Champollion's discovery, many scholars worked upon the reasonable assumption that a civilisation capable of such works must have had a high order of knowledge. Some made sound observations that were subsequently forgotten or neglected in the face of the apparently boastful, repetitive, banal and incoherent nature of the translated hieroglyphs.

The early translations stand in such striking contrast to the works themselves that it is hard to believe so few scholars should have stopped to question the paradox. But it is, of course, impossible to 'prove' a masterpiece. Those who understand, understand. Emotional and psychological factors, more than science, combined to make modern Egyptology.

The pyramids and pyramidology

Of all the monuments of Egypt, the pyramids have always provoked the keenest interest and wildest theories. Generations of Egyptologists have stolidly declared that the pyramids were built for the most trivial and misconceived motives, that their dimensions and proportions are accidents, and that their bulk is no more than an instance of pharaonic egomania. Yet the layman remains unconvinced, and anything smacking of mystery continues to excite attention.

Ancient sources reported that the pyramids, and the Great Pyramid of Cheops in particular, were built to embody in their dimensions and proportions a wealth of astronomical, mathematical, geographic and geodesic data. (Geodesy: the branch of applied mathematics which determines the figures and areas of the earth's surface.)

One of Napoleon's scholars, Edmé-François Jomard, was particularly intrigued by this theory. But while certain of his calculations seemed to bear out the idea, others did not jibe. Accurate measuring of the pyramid overall was then impossible due to the sand and debris around the base, and — as is generally the case in science — those data that supported prevailing orthodox theory were retained, while those that were embarrassing were ignored.

In England, however, Jomard's ideas were taken up by an amateur astronomer, mathematician and religious zealot, John Taylor, who found many astonishing coincidences between the measurements and proportions of the pyramids and the then but recently verified modern measurements of the earth. He could not attribute this to chance. As a fundamentalist, however, Taylor believed in the literal truth of the Bible, and could not bring himself to attribute such knowledge to the ancient Egyptians — a race much abused in the Old Testament (though Moses learned his wisdom at the court of the pharaoh by Biblical account). Given his fundamentalism, Taylor had no choice but to call in direct divine intervention, and the pseudoscience of 'pyramidology' was born.

Colin Ronan
Lost Discoveries
MacDonald, 1973, p. 95

How did the Egyptians build an immense structure like this [the pyramids]? We do not know all the details even now. It is clear from what remains that they used huge limestone blocks, but there are still problems over how they managed to slide one block across another, and of the way in which the walls and ceiling of the inner chamber are supported . . . Obviously they used a block and tackle to lift the blocks, but even so the precise method of getting objects so large and heavy up hundreds of feet without a tall crane to help them is uncertain, while their technique of supporting the internal blocks is completely unknown.

J. P. Lauer
Le Problème des Pyramides d'Egypte
Payot, 1952, pp. 186 and 190

From the astronomical point of view, the single unarguable fact . . . is the extreme care taken in the orientation. The most extraordinary result is found at the pyramid of Cheops, but the precision is scarcely less with Chephren and Mycerinus . . . Such close approximations repeated by many buildings cannot be accidental, and bear witness to certain astronomical knowledge . . .

From the mathematical point of view, the study of the pyramids, and especially the great pyramid reveals very remarkable geometrical properties as well as numerical rapports that deserve attention. But the whole problem that this poses is to establish the extent to which the builders were aware of these properties.

Casing blocks still intact at top of Chephren pyramid give a notion of the appearance of the pyramids prior to their being pillaged of their casings.

Casing blocks of the Great Pyramid of Cheops. Made of dressed white limestone cut to tolerances that today could not be equalled easily or economically, or perhaps at all. The point of the penknife cannot be inserted between two blocks. In the interior of the temple, blocks as finely dressed as this weigh up to 10 tons.

Dr. Kurt Mendelssohn
The Riddle of the Pyramids
Thames & Hudson, 1974, passim

The most obvious reason is believed to have been a religious one, and based on the self-interest of the individual. We know far too little about the spiritual concepts prevailing 5000 years ago to say exactly what motivated the average Egyptian farmer to give his time and labour to pyramid construction . . . [Dr. Mendelssohn supports the view that the problems of policing and guarding would have made it impossible to build the pyramids with forced or slave labour, therefore the work must have been done voluntarily.] We may say that the resurrection of the pharaoh, ensured by a suitable burial, was essential for the afterlife of the common man . . . Altogether one begins to wonder whether esoteric religious concepts were really more important in bringing about the pyramid age than such down-to-earth issues as assured food and a new dimension in neighbourliness . . . After four centuries of fitful attempts at unification and internal strife, the stage

Though Taylor initially found few devotees, his ideas came before the Astronomer-Royal of Scotland, Charles Piazzi Smyth. Smyth set out for Egypt to confirm Taylor's thesis. His measurements on site were by far the most precise to date, and again confirmed the hypothesis that the ancient Egyptians had precise advanced astronomical, mathematical and geodesic knowledge, which was embodied in a magnificent system of related weights and measures, whose remnants were still in wide use the world over in the form of bushels, gallons, acres and other measures.

But, as avid a fundamentalist as Taylor, Piazzi Smyth could not credit the Egyptians with high learning; he, too, had recourse to divinity. Shortly thereafter, another religious enthusiast, Robert Menzies, proposed that the passage system of the Great Pyramid was intended as a system of prophecy from which the date of the Second Coming might be deduced. And at that point, pyramidology became a zealot's playground. Curious as it may now seem, the Anglo-Israelite theory (that the British were descended from one of the lost tribes of Israel) was one upon which many educated Victorians, not

had finally been reached when the gods, Horus and Seth, were finally at peace . . . The stage was set *for the next great step in the development of human society, the creation of the state.* The pyramid was going to provide the means of achieving it.

Once it is realised that the main object of pyramid construction was a work programme leading to a new social order, the religious meaning and ritual importance of the pyramids recede into the background. If anything these man-made mountains are a monument to the *progress* of man into a new pattern of life, *the national state,* which was to become his social home for the next 5000 years.

The state as created by the Fourth Dynasty was the nucleus from which, through an infinite variety of expansions, *mankind has progressed to its present form.* Author's italics. [Dr. Mendelssohn received his Ph.D. in Physics from Berlin University in 1933, an ideal time and place at which to learn that the national state represented the apogee of progress. Author's note.]

Peter Tompkins
Mysteries of the Mexican Pyramids
Harper & Row, 1976, p. 256

As the numbers 1296 and 864 were the key to unravelling the astronomical and geodetic secrets of the Great Pyramid, they may in due course resolve the mysteries of the Mesoamerican pyramids.

Is it a coincidence that a circle of 1,296,000 units has a radius of 206, 265 units and that 20, 6264 is the length of both an English and an Egyptian cubit, that the Hebrew shekel weighs 129.6 grams, and the English guinea 129.6 grains, and the measure of the Most Holy in Solomon's Temple is 1296 inches?

Not only was the number 1,296,000 the numerical basis for astronomical measurements as far back as the records are traceable, it was also the favorite number in Plato's mystic symbolism.

otherwise bereft of sense, spent much time and thought. Pyramidology was a hotly contested intellectual issue.

But in Smyth's ostensibly scientific context, the theory stood or fell upon the validity of the 'pyramid inch', a measure invented by Smyth and manifested in no other Egyptian monument or metric device. When this was disproved by the still more exacting measurements of W. M. Flinders Petrie, the theory was undermined, though enthusiasts continued to read more and more detailed prophecies into the king's chamber. With the advent of the space age, spiritual descendants of the pyramidologists (Erich Von Danikin is the least credible, hence most successful of these) continue to propose new and fantastic uses for the pyramids: they served as landing pads for space ships or were protective baffles for ancient scientists tapping the energy of the Van Allen belt.

Needless to say, these theories are backed by no concrete evidence. But if lack of evidence constitutes the criterion for judging the crankiness of any given theory, then there is one theory crankier than all the fantasising of the pyramidologists and the UFO freaks. This is the theory that the great pyramids were built as tombs, and as tombs only.

In support of this theory there is no direct or indirect evidence whatsoever. While the numerous small pyramids of Middle and Late Kingdom Egypt were clearly and obviously designed as tombs, and have disclosed a wealth of mummies and coffins, the eight 'great' pyramids assigned to the Third and Fourth Dynasties of the Old Kingdom have revealed no sign of either coffin or mummy. The construction of these vast edifices differs in every way from the later tombs. The curious, slanting passageways could not possibly be less conducive to the elaborate funerary rituals for which Egypt was famed. The stark interiors of the 'tomb chambers' stand in vivid contrast to the lavishly inscribed and carved chambers of later Egypt. In addition, the eight great pyramids are believed to have been built over the reigns of three pharaohs (though this is disputed due to the lack of direct evidence attributing these pyramids to specific pharaohs). In any case, it works out at more than one great pyramid per pharaoh, inviting speculation of multiple burials for a king.

Egyptologists, and following them historians, refuse to entertain the possible validity of alternatives to the 'tombs only' theory, no matter how well supported. What, then, is the appeal of this undocumented, unlikely and indefensible hypothesis?

I believe it is that it is prosaic and trivial. In Egyptology, as in so many modern disciplines, all questions are believed to have 'rational' answers. If no evidence is available to provide a rational answer, the customary solution is to trivialise the mystery. In many academic circles triviality is a synonym for reason.

13

Given this passion for trivialisation, the unsubstantiated claims of the pyramidologists had serious repercussions.

Throughout the development of Egyptology, from Jomard on, qualified, serious and sane scholars have challenged the prevailing preconceptions and the widespread determination to regard the Egyptians as primitives. Biot, Lockyer and Proctor, professional astronomers, put forward solid theories attesting to a high order of Egyptian astronomical knowledge. Lockyer — who was derided for proposing that Stonehenge was built as an astronomical instrument — showed how the pyramids might have served practically to gather precise astronomical data.

In many other fields, specialists also attested to high Egyptian knowledge. But the sensational claims of Smyth, Menzies, and their successors stole the spotlight, and allowed orthodox Egyptologists to tar any and all dissenting theories with the brush of pyramidology. The provocative speculations of Lockyer and others were ignored.

Meanwhile, Darwin's theory of evolution had been published.

When Egyptology began, most scholars, as dutiful sons of the Enlightenment, were atheists, materialists or only nominally religious. Most were convinced they represented an apogee of civilisation. But the process was not yet regarded as inevitable and automatic; the most renowned intellects of the time did not yet regard themselves as advanced apes. It was not yet heretical to suggest that ancient people had actually known something.

But as the theory of evolution became dogma, it became (and remains) impossible to attribute exact knowledge to ancient cultures without undermining the faith in progress. Thus, lumped in with the pyramidologists, incapable of supporting sound insight with ironclad proof, the many early Egyptologists who were men of breadth and vision gradually lost ground. In retrospect, this can be seen as inevitable.

L. E. Orgel
Origins of Life
Chapman and Hall, passim, 1973

There are of course enormous gaps in our knowledge, but I believe the origins of life can now be discussed fruitfully within the framework of modern chemistry and evolutionary biology. It must be admitted from the beginning that the way in which condensation reactions occurred on the primitive earth is not understood . . . It is the enormous gap that must be bridged between the most complicated inorganic objects and these simplest living organisms that provides most of the intellectual challenge of the problem of the origin of life . . . We know very little about the chemistry of the organisms that lived on earth three billion years ago . . . The conditions that existed on the primitive earth are very different from those that are usually used by organic chemists. Although many of the constituents of cells can be synthesised in the laboratory, a few of the most important cannot yet be made under prebiotic conditions. It is even harder to join the simple organic molecules together to form polymers similar to proteins and nucleic acids.

Consequently, a great deal of work will have to be done before we can propose a single complete theory of the origin of life and show by experiment that each step could have occurred on the primitive earth . . . We do not understand much about the later stages in the evolution of the code. We do not know whether the structure of the code is an historical accident or not . . . The genetic code is the result of an elaborate series of adaptations . . . Virtually nothing is known about the successive steps in this adaptation . . . We have seen that the idea of natural selection is a very simple one and that it completely eliminates the need to postulate any internal or external 'will' that directs evolution . . . Today, to many biologists, the law of natural selection seems almost a tautology.

Ibid., p. 182

If you read a lot about ribosomes or butterflies and think hard enough about the way they came to be as they are, you will probably find that you are using the idea of natural selection without noticing it — alternatively, you may give up and become a mystic . . . The replacement of 'will' by 'chance' . . . has transformed our view of man's relationship to the rest of the universe.

J. H. Broughton
Letters to the Editor
The New Scientist, Nov. 11, 1976, p. 355

Dr. Richard Dawkins claims too much ('Memes and the evolution of Culture', 28 Oct., p. 208) when he says 'All biologists nowadays believe in Darwin's theory'). There is a sizable minority of equally qualified biologists who reject the theory outright. In the US, for example, several hundred voting members of the Creation Research Society, who must have at least a MSc, and include many biologists, prefer the Genesis account on scientific grounds.

The New Scientist, July 29, 1976, p. 225

The greatest steps in evolution are also the least understood, since the complexities of developing, say, photosynthesis or warm-bloodedness go beyond today's simple mathematical models. So there is still scope for purely qualitative arguments about how these great leaps forward occurred.

Helena Blavatsky was a woman of great personal power and prodigious learning. Her claim was to effect a synthesis of the esoteric traditions of the world, but the result is for some readers more conglomeration than synthesis. Yet, a century later, some of her more outrageous-sounding statements look luminously prophetic, while the initial distrust engendered by her ecstatic and convoluted prose style abates significantly upon rereading.

Without exception, these men were working in the dark. The mystical and metaphysical verities that nourish a true civilisation were, in Europe, obscured, ossified or forgotten (although Fenelon, Goethe, Fechner and a few alchemists had kept their tradition alive). The crude science of the day supported the depressing billiard-ball universe postulated by Laplace.

It was possible then, as it is now, to walk into Chartres Cathedral and to be struck with the unconquerable conviction that, in some way, this is what human life on earth is about. But to explain that conviction, to put it into communicable terms, was impossible one hundred years ago. To 'prove' it is still impossible.

Though corrupt and decadent, the 19th century civilisations of the Orient were flourishing compared to Europe. But they were accessible to Westerners only through the garbled prolixities of Blavatsky, or in books by Western scholars imbued with progressive notions of the Enlightenment and therefore blind to the inner meaning of the words they pretended to communicate.

What is now readily available to every student was then unavailable to the most erudite. It was impossible to study first hand the authentic works of Zen masters, Sufis, yogis, to read the Bardo Thödol, the Tao Te Ching, the Philokalia, the Christian mystics, alchemists, Cabbalists and Gnostics; to compare these to the myths of Egypt; and to recognise above and beyond their differences the bond that unites all these traditions.

At the same time, it was impossible for the majority of men to recognise the true nature of 'progress'. Artists, who in the West especially function as the sensitive nerve ends of society, were less often fooled. Goethe, Blake, Kierkegaard, Nietzsche, Melville, Schopenhauer, Novalis, Dostoyevsky and a few others saw progress for what it was; but these represented a powerless minority. Today, to believe in 'progress' a man must be insane. A hundred years ago insensitivity sufficed.

Seen in historical perspective, Egyptology is an inevitable product of its time. Looking back, it becomes obvious that no single scholar or group of scholars could have discerned the true Egypt one hundred years ago. For that, the advances of modern science were first necessary — as well as the simultaneous availability of the mystical doctrines of the East and the mind capable of applying both these kinds of knowledge to the ruins of Egypt.

Looking back, it is impossible not to admire the Herculean labours of the Egyptologists — their painstaking excavations, the reconstruction of ruins, the collection, collation and classification of data, the gigantic labour of deciphering the hieroglyphs and the scrupulous attention to detail in every field and on every level. At the same time, it is difficult to understand the manner in which these scholars came to many of their conclusions, given the nature of the material at their disposal. A statement made by Ludwig Borchardt, one of the most industrious and prolific of Egyptologists, captures the situation in a single sentence. In 1922, having proved that the pyramids of Egypt were oriented to the cardinal points and sited and levelled with a precision that could not be surpassed today, Borchardt concluded that Egyptian science at the time of the building of the pyramids was still in its infancy.

The Symbolist interpretation of Egypt

Schwaller de Lubicz's vast work, *Le Temple de l'Homme (The Temple Of Man)*, was published in 1957. Though at first glance it seems to present a picture of Egypt wholly at variance with that put forward by academic Egyptologists, detailed examination shows that in certain instances, his work is foreshadowed in the findings of his predecessors. Often, sound work has been allowed to languish while less sound theories gained pre-eminence. In other instances, the past two decades of Egyptology have corroborated Schwaller de Lubicz's theories in significant details in many fields — though without acknowledging him as the source. (This may or may not be deliberate. There is no compelling reason why scholars should not come to similar conclusions independently.)

But above and beyond these similarities, *Le Temple de l'Homme* is unique, for it provides a complete, coherent doctrine fusing art, science, philosophy and religion into a single body of wisdom that can account for the civilisation of ancient Egypt in its entirety. The glaring paradox of primitive, muddle-headed necrophiles producing unparalleled artistic and architectural masterpieces for four millennia vanishes completely in the light of this interpretation. The Symbolist interpretation also accounts quite naturally for the amazing integrity of Egyptian art, architecture and religion throughout its long history — an integrity that, prior to Schwaller de Lubicz, scholars could only ascribe to 'conservatism'. Moreover, as work goes on in the various fields of modern science, in anthropology, archaeology, linguistics, and many other disciplines, new facts keep coming to light, new theories keep being advanced that directly or indirectly relate to the Symbolist picture of Egypt.

Though the unwary reader would never know it from a casual reading of popular scientific journals or from the popular press (even the self appointed 'responsible' press) a real revolution in human thought is already under way (compensating with intensity for what it perhaps lacks in numbers).

The fact has not yet found its way into most school textbooks or even into the heads and hearts of most working scientists and scholars, but science and scholarship have effectively disproved the mechanistic and evolutionary hypotheses motivating so much of its effort.

It is an intriguing and possibly unique situation in human history. Schwaller de Lubicz's work, in the right hands, may play an important role in the shaping of a new society. For although *Le Temple de l'Homme* apparently concerns an ancient and alien civilisation, that civilisation had profound and exact knowledge of the principles responsible for the created universe. It is this knowledge that modern science lacks. For all its success in studying and measuring the mechanisms of phenomena, the principles responsible for this creation are almost as unknown as they were at the onset of modern science. Whether or not scientists and scholars will manage to exercise the necessary faculty of humility, and turn to an ancient and vanished civilisation for instruction, remains to be seen.

Meanwhile, Schwaller de Lubicz's picture of Egypt makes it clear that it was this total understanding of principle, function and process that was responsible for the form and structure of Egyptian society and for all its sacred works.

John Taylor
Science and the Paranormal
The Listener, Dec. 6, 1973

There is also the whole difficulty of reconciling these baffling phenomena, assumed real, with established science. Some scientists have been so disturbed by this that they have become very hostile; others have not been able to watch Geller performing, so as to avoid any chance of their becoming convinced. This 'head in the sand' attitude has let into the paranormal area a number of people who are working to destroy established science. These are people who don't like the present theories of physics or chemistry or astronomy because these don't agree with their deeply held belief in the more extreme paranormal phenomena such as communication with the spirits of the dead or with intelligent beings from outer space.

Such attitudes can only produce a split which will separate the scientific community even more widely from those heavily involved in the paranormal. Since the irrational and the mystical are very popular nowadays it might seem that only science will suffer in this conflict. That would be a disaster: the increasing culture of unreason could well help to lead humanity into another dark age if it is not checked soon enough.

Those who hope to understand the world as *rationally* as possible do not need to be completely downhearted . . . Once a causal explanation can be given, the rational view is saved . . .

Many scientists are now seriously interested in these phenomena, and feel that they contribute useful work. We may hope the picture will be much clearer before too long: when the mists clear away, I trust it will still be a rational world that we observe. [Author's italics.]

R. A. Schwaller was born in Alsace in 1891. Trained in mathematics and chemistry, he was attracted at an early age to philosophical, mystical and religious subjects. He was formally adopted by the Lithuanian prince and poet, O. V. de Lubicz Milosz, for work done on his behalf during World War I, and appended the honorary 'de Lubicz' to his own name. In the 1920s and 1930s he devoted himself to a range of mathematical, mystical, alchemical and scientific studies; to experiments with plants, metals and stained glass; and to attempts to put his ideas into practice with a number of like-minded individuals. But until chance — or more accurately, destiny — brought him to Egypt in 1937, he had no conscious intention of solving the paradox it posed.

Confronted by the Temple of Luxor, he had one of those flashes of deep insight that so often accompany discovery; he was certain that he saw in this immense, asymmetric ruin a deliberate exercise in proportion. He saw in Luxor the Parthenon of Egypt.

This conviction ran directly counter to accepted Egyptologi-

Aerial view of the Temple of Luxor showing clearly its unique asymmetric plan.

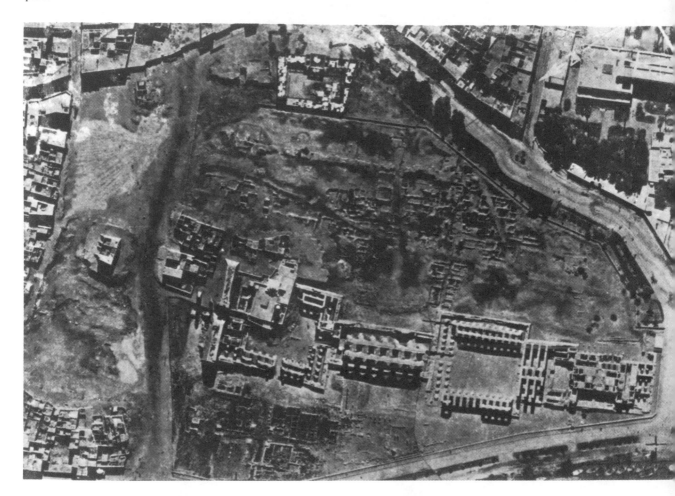

T. Eric Peet
The Rhind Mathematical Papyrus
Hodder & Stoughton, 1923, p. 10

As Plato alone of the Greeks seems to have realised, the Egyptians were essentially a nation of shopkeepers, and interest in or speculation concerning a subject for its own sake was totally foreign to their minds. [Strictly speaking, this is an inaccuracy. Money as such was unknown in Egypt. The more speculative Greeks are usually honored with its invention. Author's note.]

cal theory. Egyptian mathematics was considered a primitive, purely practical affair, concerned with dividing land and apportioning out loaves of bread and measures of corn. The Egyptians were not supposed to have understood the laws of harmony and proportion or known of the existence of irrationals.* All of these were supposedly Greek inventions. (Scholars disputed, and still dispute, not so much the extent of Greek knowledge in these areas, but the extent to which this knowledge was applied.)

* Irrational: not commensurable with natural numbers.

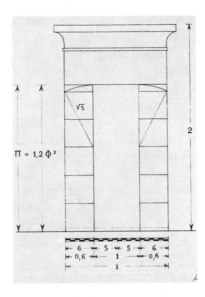

Schwaller de Lubicz's analysis of this Egyptian doorway provides incontestable proof of the Egyptian knowledge of pi. While it might be argued that the 2:1 proportion of height to width could be arbitrary, it is more difficult to call upon coincidence to explain the height of the aperture, which is 1.2 φ² (Phi = The Golden Section) or pi. Is it coincidence that this typical Egyptian doorway resembles the glyph π the Greeks would later choose for pi?

The discovery of the irrational and of the laws of harmony and proportion were attributed to Pythagoras, the disconcertingly semi-legendary mystic and mathematician (ca. 580-500 BC) to whom was also attributed the development of Pythagorean number mysticism: the theory that numbers have *innate meaning*. Although this latter theory has been a subject of some merriment among modern scholars, it is undergoing a strong revival, and understood in context it is a means, perhaps the best means, of understanding the world we experience.

Pythagoreanism in history

Throughout Western history, Pythagoreanism has had a checkered but honorable career.

The Pythagorean brotherhood was founded by Pythagoras to apply his mathematical, philosophical and harmonic theories to the moral and practical spheres of everyday life. Within decades it dissolved, but small groups and isolated individuals continued to regard themselves as Pythagoreans.

Number mysticism became degenerate or diffuse, but Pythagorean principles of rhythm, harmony and proportion continued to exercise an important, sometimes a commanding, influence in art and architecture; these principles made (and make) sense to all those individuals whose personal experience compelled a belief in a fundamental order. Throughout Western history the great creative talents have been explicitly or implicitly Pythagoreans.

Plato, especially in the *Timaeus*, showed himself a Pythagorean, as were the Neoplatonists of Alexandria in the third,

Jules Sageret
Le Système du Monde des Chaldéens à Newton
Librarie Felix Alcan, 1913, p. 66

The cosmology of Philolaus has passed, and still passes, as a heliocentric system, and it is attributed to Pythagoras. This is a legend whose origins are later than Copernicus. And it is important to show how ill-founded it is, for if knowledge of the heliocentric movement goes back to Pythagoras, it is necessary to postulate a long prior scientific development; the history of the evolution of the human spirit would take on an altogether different aspect to that which we have presented up to now.

Morris R. Cohen and Israel Edward Drabkin
Source Books in the History of the Sciences
McGraw-Hill, 1948, pp. 107 and 109

Aristarchus of Samos . . . is best known for his anticipation of the Copernican system . . . The Heliocentric hypothesis of Aristarchus had little success in antiquity. The astronomers . . . generally rejected the heliocentric hypothesis on scientific grounds. [Aristarchus, like Philolaus, was a Pythagorean. Author's note.]

Colin Blakemore
The Listener, Nov. 11, 1976, p. 596

There is even more reason to emphasise the importance of ancient Greek views about the mechanism of mentality, particularly those of Plato and Aristotle. For their opinions and their authority, sanctified and dogmatised by the early Christian fathers, became the unquestionable truth that shackled the mind of man in the Middle Ages and slowed the advance of civilisation to a hesitant crawl.

George Sarton
History of Science
Norton, 1970, p. 423

The influence of the Timaios upon later times was enormous and essentially evil. Many scholars were deceived into accepting the fantasies of that book as gospel truths. That delusion hindered the progress of science; and the Timaios has remained to this day a source of obscurity and superstition.

Marcel Griaule
Conversations with Ogotemmeli
Oxford University Press, 1965 p. 17

Ogotemmeli had nothing against Europeans. He was not even sorry for them. He left them to their destiny in the lands of the North.

M. Ghyka
The Geometry of Art and Life
Sheed and Ward, 1946, p. 118

The link between Pythagoreanism and Medieval and Renaissance Occultism is evident in the following extract from Agrippa's *Kabbala*: Boetius has said: "Everything which since the beginning of things was produced by Nature seems to be formed according to numerical relations, issued from the wisdom of the Creator. Numbers are the nearest and simplest relations with the ideas of Divine Wisdom . . . The power of Numbers in living nature does not reside in their names, nor in the numbers as counting elements, but in the numbers of perceiving knowledge, formal and natural . . . The one who succeeds in linking usual and natural numbers to divine numbers will operate miracles through Numbers.'''

fourth and fifth centuries AD. The early Christian church seems to have evinced no interest, but Boethius, with Rome crumbling about him in the sixth century, gathered together what remained of Pythagorean doctrine and wrote it down before being bludgeoned to death by Theodoric. Though apparently not a Christian, Boethius enjoyed great esteem within the otherwise intolerant church, and Pythagoreanism was never entirely submerged.

Enlightened elements within Islam, probably inheriting the teaching of the later Neoplatonists, kept the flame alive; and it seems possible that it may have survived, more or less underground, in Gnostic, Hermetic and alchemical societies. In any case, it survived (or, conceivably, was reformulated afresh through direct revelation), for it surfaced in full flower in the Gothic cathedrals.

Much mystery still surrounds the building of the cathedrals. The techniques employed were not part of the Christian tradition up to that time; the effect created by the cathedrals was unlike anything earlier, and no one today is certain where the knowledge came from. The cathedral builders appeared in France in the eleventh century. For the next three centuries the movement was widespread over Europe, and whatever was responsible for the guiding spirit seemed to disappear as abruptly as it had appeared. In the later cathedrals (St. Peter's, Rome; St. Paul's, London, for example) the spiritual effect is not the same; everyone notices.

That effect is not the result of accident. Nor is it a concomitant of sheer size: modern structures fail to convey a similar effect, though it may be that the Empire State Building and Waterloo Station do convey a sense of the 'sacred' to technocrats and financiers. The cathedrals 'work', as do the Parthenon and the Taj Mahal, because whoever designed them had precise and profound knowledge of universal harmonic, rhythmic and proportional laws, and equally precise and profound knowledge of the manner in which to employ these laws in order to create the desired effect.

Ibid., p. 153

The meaning of 'symmetry' itself was forgotten and replaced by the modern one.

It was in France that this academic fossilisation developed its worst symptoms. The role of Geometry, the very concept of ordered composition, were attacked, and a manifesto of the *a-geometric* school was launched by Perrault in the following outburst:

"The reasons which make us admire the beautiful works of art have no other foundation than chance and the workers' caprice, as these have not looked for reasons to settle the shape of things, the precision of which is of no importance.'

But Palladio, Christopher Wren, the Adam brothers and Gabriel thought otherwise, and so did the very scientific Baroque architects of Italy, Spain and southern Germany, who incorporated the ellipse and the logorhythmic spiral into the design of their 'metaphysical theatres'.

Ibid., p. 173
The master minds in our Western Civilisation have been, since Plato, the ones who have perceived the analogies, the permanent similarities between things, structures, images. If analogy is found at the base of Dynamic Symmetry, Eurhythmy and modulation, in the arts of space as well as in musical harmony, it also dominates literature, metaphor being only a condensed and unexpected analogy . . . Structure, Pattern, on one side, Metaphor on the other, may lead to Symbol, explicit or veiled, as we have seen in noticing the connection (the 'analogies' in fact) between regulating diagrams and Mandalas, acting on the conscious or the subconscious plane, or on both.

The cathedral age represents the height of European civilisation. The precise knowledge that went in to building the cathedrals was mysteriously lost, or diffused, never again to become a visible living force in the West. But it percolated down through the guilds, through the alchemists, the Cabbalists, Rosicrucians and Masonic orders — with whose work Schwaller de Lubicz was thoroughly familiar.

Looking for phi

Ancient sources claimed Egypt as the original home of geometry. Though biographies of Pythagoras were all fragmentary, secondhand and therefore unreliable, all agreed upon this point: that Pythagoras had acquired much of his learning in the East.

Arguments had long ranged over whether the proportions of the Great Pyramid were deliberate or purely fortuitous. The pyramid's height stands in a precise pi relationship to the perimeter of the base. Pi (3.1416 . . .) is the transcendental that defines the ratio between the diameter of a circle and its circumference. At the same time, pi is related to another, more interesting, irrational, phi, the so-called Golden Section. It had been observed — and ignored by Egyptologists — that not only the Great Pyramid but the other pyramids as well made use of different phi relationships in their construction.

Schwaller de Lubicz therefore set out to discover whether or not phi relationships were built into the Temple of Luxor. If this could be proven beyond doubt, it would corroborate these fragmentary ancient sources and force a reconsideration of the extent of ancient knowledge. If it could be shown that the Egyptians possessed advanced mathematical and scientific knowledge, it would not only prove — as many suspected — that the famous Greek intellectual flowering was but a pale and degenerate shadow of what had been known previously; it might also help substantiate the legend persisting throughout history, and widespread among the people of the world, that great civilisations had existed in the distant past even before Egypt.

In seeing the Temple of Luxor as an Egyptian Parthenon, Schwaller de Lubicz was seeing more than an exercise in harmony and proportion for its own sake. Aesthetics played a secondary role in the sacred architecture of the past. The Greek Parthenon was built to the virgin Athena (*parthenos* means virgin in Greek).

The symbolism of the virgin is widespread and extremely complex, and it operates upon many levels. But its fundamental metaphysical significance is the creation *ex nihilo* — the universe created out of nothing, out of the void.

Sir Alan Gardiner
Egypt of the Pharaohs
Oxford, 1961, p. 57

In some ways the narratives found in the tombs of the nobility and men of lesser degree who had received promotion are less conventional and more illuminating than those reflecting the monarchical activities of the sovereign. But such texts are far from common; of the Old Kingdom mastabas at Giza and Bakkara and Dyn.XVIII rock tombs at Thebes not one in twenty recounts any incidents of its owner's career. On the other hand, long sequences of honorific titles are almost invariable; never was there a race of mortals so enamoured of outward recognition and so given to the flaunting of epithets.

Alexander Badawy
Ancient Egyptian Architectural Design
University of California, 1965, p. 183

From this objective study it is apparent that Egyptian architecture was designed according to a harmonic system based upon the use of the square and triangles ... There is also sufficient evidence about the occurrence of the numbers from the Fibonacci Series in the significant measures in cubits in plans of monuments.

The fact that both the 8 : 5 triangle allied with the square and the Fibonacci Series gives a good approximation of the golden section proves that the Egyptians became aware of the qualities of that ratio at least as early as the Third Dynasty.

Ibid., p. 67

In some cases the dimensions along the axis seemingly express numbers from the Fibonacci Series 3, 5, 8, 13, 21, 34, ... even to as high as 610 cubits (great temple of Amun at Karnak) or closely approximate them, as the result of harmonic design based on the 8 : 5 triangle.

For all its analytical success, science in 1937 was no closer to a solution to the mystery of creation than in Newton's day. But a lifetime's study of mathematics — and particularly the mathematics of number, harmony and proportion — had convinced Schwaller de Lubicz that however distorted and diffuse the teachings of Pythagoras had become, in their pure form they held the key to this ultimate mystery. He was also convinced that ancient civilisations possessed this knowledge, which they transmitted in the form of myth — accounting for the striking similarities of myths the world over, in cultures completely isolated from each other in space and time.

Central to all these interlinked themes was that curious irrational, phi, the Golden Section. Schwaller de Lubicz believed that if ancient Egypt possessed knowledge of ultimate causes, that knowledge would be written into their temples not in explicit texts, but in harmony, proportion, myth and symbol.

Schwaller de Lubicz's first step toward the recovery of this putative lost knowledge was a study of the dimensions and proportions of the Temple of Luxor to find out if significant and deliberate use of measure revealed itself. Schwaller de Lubicz set out to look for phi.

It was soon apparent that his insight had been accurate. But the subtlety and refinement with which measure and proportion were employed demanded a commensurate refinement of technique on the part of Schwaller de Lubicz and his team. In the end, the task occupied fifteen years on the site at Luxor.

Although Schwaller de Lubicz set out knowing more or less what he was looking for, his interpretation does not bring in measure and proportion in order to support a preconceived theory. Rather, the measures and proportions imposed the interpretation. It is also worth mentioning that all measures and data were supervised and checked by qualified professionals: by Alexandre Varille, a young Egyptologist who was won over to the Symbolist approach early on and who, in effect, threw over a safe career in Egyptology to act as spokesman for Schwaller de Lubicz; and by Clement Robichon, an architect, chief of excavations for the French Egyptological delegation in Cairo.

Schwaller de Lubicz claimed that Egyptian civilization was based upon profound and precise knowledge of the mysteries of Creation. The Symbolist interpretation supports this claim with two kinds of evidence; the first linguistic, the second mathematical. In Egypt language and mathematics were simply two aspects of a single scheme. But in order to satisfactorily explain and describe this scheme Schwaller de Lubicz found it necessary to treat linguistics and mathematics separately.

Personal note from Lucy Lamy;
Schwaller de Lubicz's stepdaughter

. . . Isha and Varille worked on the texts.

Everything related to Amenophis III was relevant to his thesis. Varille, for example, was about to put to the test the 'functionaries' whose names did not seem to him to be randomly chosen. Therefore, he and Isha worked over the sense of each letter (or hieroglyph). With Mr. de Lubicz he discussed the philosophical implications, for the text of the Theogamy, for instance, or whatever other religious text.

Isha was working on *Her-bak*, and submitting the day's work to Mr. de Lubicz for commentary . . .

For me: surveying, measuring, drawing, with C. Robichon's help when the tacheometer was needed. Every part of the covered temple was measured, the same for the pavement, stone by stone . . . On specially printed cards, we recorded the dimensions of each of the figures; height of navel, forehead, crown, etc. and compared it with modern human biometry to see what the fundamental bases were for the pharaonic canon.

A propos, here is a little anecdote. At that time, I couldn't yet read the hieroglyphs; it wasn't until 1949 that I began learning them.

One morning, having measured all of an unusual scene, with the king in the company of female character, a rapid calculation indicated that the king, according to the height of his navel, in proportion to his total height, was around 12 years old. At once, surprised and disturbed, I murmured, 'I know in the East one married young, but really, at 12, that seems a bit too young . . .' thinking that woman the wife of the young prince.

I therefore insisted that Varille come to identify the 'woman' accompanying Amenophis III. Burning with impatience, I had to wait for night before we could both get to the temple. Impatiently, I awaited the verdict, for if she was really his wife, that would cast doubt over the whole question of the height of the navel in proportion to the height of the whole figure (providing the key to the age of the figured character) . . .

Slowly, the torch lit up the names of the various characters. Varille let me wait . . .

'Who is it?'

'His mother.'

So, it was thus sound, I could carry on filling out innumerable cards without fear that I was wasting my time . . .

And the day that I was bothered by a measure that seemed to me suspicious! I called Robichon who arrived with all his measuring tapes of compensating metal; one of 50 metres, one of 30, two of 10 and so on. We laid them out over the floor, the metres were all exactly equal, therefore the tapes were correct. Then my *sherit* (the Arab name) was put to the test and stretched out alongside the others. Made of reinforced cloth, it had stretched . . . and the prior work, naturally, had to be done over. So we went back to the place that had given me the warning; a door and a wall. Measured with an accurate tape, the wall was exactly six fathoms long, and the door exactly ten royal cubits, which is what I had anticipated . . .

Varille was at first very circumspect, sounding out the one, and the other (Isha, Schwaller de Lubicz's wife) and myself. He watched for months before 'taking the bait' . . . Clement Robichon was no less prudent, far from it! He confessed to me ten years later, having set a number of traps for Mr. de Lubicz, but seeing that he never fell into them . . .

Varille had already understood that the classical version of the Pyramid texts was deplorably deceptive. It was difficult to admit, amongst others, the too-celebrated 'cannibal text' as belonging to a people as refined and as sensitive from the First Dynasty on. The profound significance of the images had to be divulged by another kind of reading . . . Mr. de Lubicz and Isha began to hold long sessions with him, from which he left completely convinced.

Besides, Drioton was the first to agree, the many texts considered 'historical' were generally but supports of a supra-human teaching founded upon the image of a so-called human history. This world is perishable, the Other is the only true aim of existence, and it behoves one to know, during this life on earth, *how* to achieve it.

The Battle of Kadesh, for example, certainly took place. In the reports, a number of lines specifically define the localities, even the distances between different strategic points, the names of the different army corps, the names of the enemies, in detail.

But apart from these facts which one may take as historically true, there are the interminable 'poems' which are completely stupefying . . . Here are the facts: Rameses II, forewarned of the enormous coalition gathering all of Turkey around the Hittites, then Mesopotamia, upper Syria and the nomadic Bedouin tribes, raised an army and crossed Palestine. In travelling he received intelligence of the enemy's position, and all assured him he would find them at Aleppo. Rameses, too confident of his informers, therefore arrived in Kadesh ignorant of the enemy awaiting him, and hidden behind the hills. His first division pitched camp, and in doing so was encountered disarmed. The three other divisions were driven back over a distance of some twenty miles. By a facile enemy manoeuvre, Rameses found himself cut off from the rest of his troops, and completely alone, as the enemy hurled themselves on the camp massacring at will.

Rameses II then directs a splendid prayer to Amon; Amon incarnates himself in the King, and striking right and left, the King, alone, routs or pitches into the Oront thousands of chariots and soldiers . . .

Historians readily agree that the famous *Poem of Pentaour* narrating this story '*is unfortunately bereft of any historical value*' and Drioton adds, a propos the treaty signed between Rameses II and the Hittites, '*nowhere* (in the poem) *is the essential touched upon; that is to say the respective frontiers of the two countries*'. (E. Drioton, *L'Egypte*, pp. 408-411)

Why then these innumerable representations of this battle, covering the walls of the temples?

And why is the King depicted, menacing with his mace, the 'bouquet of prisoners', some Asian, some African?

'The long lists of conquered Nubian peoples, decorating the pylons and the temples, the reliefs of the King massacring a black prisoner, belong rather to formulae and traditional iconography than to history.' (*Ibid.* p. 377)

Thus, all agree upon the non-historical character of these immense bas-reliefs; but then, once again, why expend so much time and effort only to tell tall stories?

From the classical point of view, the questions remain unanswered.

But from the philosophical point of view, by contrast, one can see the possibility of approaching and understanding these problems. It was this that convinced Varille.

The question of secrecy

Had the Egyptians possessed both their high order of knowledge, and a manner of expressing or encoding it similar to our own, Schwaller de Lubicz's work would have been unnecessary and the paradox of supposed primitives producing artistic masterpieces would have never arisen.

Beyond a certain level, in every one of the arts and sciences of Egypt, knowledge was *secret*. The rules, axioms, theorems and formulae — the very stuff of modern science and scholarship — were never made public, and may never have been written down.

But the question of secrecy is today thoroughly misunderstood. It is generally agreed among scholars that most ancient societies (and many modern primitive ones) reserved certain types of knowledge for select initiates. At best this practice is considered absurd and undemocratic, at worst it is considered a form of intellectual tyranny, by which a class of priestly conmen kept the masses in a state of quiescent awe. But the ancient mind was rather subtler than our own. There were (and are) good reasons for keeping certain types of knowledge secret, including the secrets of number and geometry; a Pythagorean practice that particularly arouses the ire of modern mathematicians.

Five was the sacred number of the Pythagoreans, and members of the brotherhood were sworn to secrecy regarding it on pain of death. We know the secrets existed only because they leaked out.

That Egypt possessed this knowledge is incontestable in the face of the harmonic proportions of her art and architecture as revealed by Schwaller de Lubicz.

But perhaps unfortunately, Egypt was also much better at keeping her secrets than the loud-mouthed Greeks — so very good that Egyptologists refuse to believe she possessed them. Though by definition circumstantial, the evidence that she did so is commanding, and it remains only to understand the valid motives behind keeping this kind (or any kind) of knowledge secret.

In a world of hydrogen bombs, bacteriological warfare and other progressive horrors, it is self-evident that knowledge is dangerous. It is also self-evident that the ancients possessed no technology capable of unleashing such brutal power. However, if we look more closely at the manner in which we are emotionally and psychologically influenced — which in turn makes predictable the manner in which we will react to given situations — we will see that dangerous knowledge lies behind this curious Pythagorean number symbolism.

James Henry Breasted
Ancient Records of Egypt, Vol. I
Chicago, 1906, p. 132

Teti, living forever, high priest of Ptah, more honoured by the king than any servant, as master of the *secret things of work* which his majesty desired should be done . . . [Author's italics.]

A. Badawy
Ancient Egyptian Architectural Design
University of California, 1965, p. 8

Conduct the work, causing to come . . . every prepared one of his workmen, the best of his lay priests, who knows the directions and is skillful in that which he knows . . . Execute *the very secret things, no one seeing, no one beholding, no one knowing his body* . . . [Author's italics.]

Senmut, architect to Queen Hatshepsut
In James Henry Breasted, *Ancient Records*, Vol. II
Chicago, 1906, p. 353

I had access to all the writings of the prophets, there was nothing I did not know of that which had happened since the beginning.

A. Badawy
Op. cit., p. 6

This was not idle talk, for Senmut describes on his stela an archaic text which had been out of fashion for a long time. Some of the writings are described as being on leather rolls, such as the records of annals kept in the Temple of Amun at Karnak during the New Kingdom, or the rolls of the library of the Temple of Edfu.

Marcel Griaule
Conversations with Ogotemmeli
Oxford, 1965, pp. xiv-xvii

But among groups where tradition is still vigorous, this knowledge which is expressly characterised as esoteric, is only secret in the following sense. It is in fact open to all who show a will to understand so long as, by their social position and moral conduct, they are judged worthy of it.

A work of art, bad or good, is a complex vibratory system. All our five senses are constructed to pick up this data in the form of visual, aural, tactile and probably olfactory and sapid wavelengths. The data is interpreted by the brain and provokes a response that — given wide variations among individuals — is more or less universal: no one thinks the last movement of Beethoven's Ninth Symphony is a lullaby.

Accomplished artists know instinctively that their creations conform to law: consider Beethoven's famous statement, made while working on the late quartets, that 'music is a higher revelation than philosophy'. But they do not understand the precise nature of these laws. They arrive at mastery only through intense discipline, innate sensitivity and a long period of trial and error. There is little they can pass on to pupils or disciples. Only technique can be passed on, never 'genius'. But in ancient civilisations, a class of initiates had precise knowledge of harmonic laws. They knew how to manipulate them to create the precise effect they wanted. And they wrote this knowledge into architecture, art, music, paintings, rituals and incenses, producing Gothic cathedrals, vast Hindu temples, all the marvels of Egypt and many other sacred ancient works that even today, in ruins, produce a powerful effect upon us. This effect is produced because these men knew exactly what they were doing and why they were doing it: it was done entirely through a complex of sensory manipulation.

Now, if we look at our twentieth century, we find no masterpieces of sacred art, but we do see countless examples of scientifically proven harmful effects resulting from a misuse of sensory data.

Torture is a misuse of sensory data. Men have known about torture for a very long time. But never before has it been studied scientifically. When it is analysed, it becomes clear that torture takes two forms: sensory deprivation (solitary confinement) and sensory overstimulation (tying someone to the clapper of a bell, the rack, etc.).

It is also well known today — and continuing work reveals ever more subtle and insidious effects — that the stresses and strains of modern life take a real, even a calculable, toll of our emotional and psychological faculties. People go haywire living too near an airport or working in the incessant noise of a factory. Office buildings that recirculate air and make extensive use of synthetic materials create an atmosphere depleted of negative ions. Though undetectable by the senses directly, this is ultimately a vibratory phenomenon on the molecular level, and it has powerful, measurably harmful effects: people become depressed and irritable, tire easily and lose resistance to infection. The subsonic and ultrasonic frequencies produced by a wide variety of machinery also exert a powerful and dangerous influence. Designers today have some knowledge of

New Scientist
May 27, 1976, p. 464

The intriguing notion that weak electric fields can influence animal behaviour is strengthened by a report from two biologists at the Brain Research Institute in Los Angeles ... Precisely what fundamental mechanisms may lie beneath these effects is something of a mystery. The levels of the fields are too low to trigger the fine connections (synapses) between nerve cells ... Chronic exposure to low frequency weak electric fields is steadily increasing, the main sources being power transmission lines and any piece of electrical equipment. There is, therefore, a growing concern about possible health hazards.

G. I. Gurdjieff
All and Everything
Routledge & Kegan Paul, 1949, p. 1156

And it was just then at that period of my existence that I began to notice more than once, that on certain days the forces and degree of my active mentation grew particularly worse . . . and from then on I began to pay attention . . . I became convinced that this undesirable state proceeded with me each time, on the day when our large 'Lifechakan' was in action. ('Lifechakan' approximately corresponds to what on earth is called a 'dynamo'.)

the effects of colors and color combinations; they know those effects can be beneficial or harmful, though they do not know why.

In effect, then, the daily life of city dwellers today is technically a form of mild but persistent torture, in which victims and victimisers are equally affected. And all call it 'progress'. The result is similar to that wrought by deliberate torture. The spiritually strong recognise the challenge, meet it and surmount it. The rest succumb, become brutalised, apathetic, easily swayed; anything or anyone promising relief from an intolerable situation is followed slavishly, and men are easily moved to violence or to condoning violence in what they imagine to be their interests. All of this is brought about by men professing high ideals, but ignorant of the forces they manipulate.

It is incontestable that all of these phenomena work their effects either through the senses directly or (as with un-ionized air and subsonic and ultrasonic sound) through subtler physiological receptors. It is, therefore, clear that they may be reduced to mathematical terms, at least in principle.

The ancients could not have built an H-bomb had they wanted to. At the same time, while the military mind may consider killing people an aim in itself, the ultimate aim of war is not so much genocide as the psychological conquest of the enemy. Brute force alone invariably provokes violent reaction; tyrannies seldom last long when based solely upon military power. But when the enemy is psychologically helpless, the ruler is secure.

We look at our own society and see human beings reduced to slavery by sensory and suprasensory phenomena imposed by men who do not know what they are doing. We can easily postulate a situation in which wiser but equally egotistical men produce a similar effect deliberately, through the knowledgeable manipulation of the senses.

In the cathedrals and sacred art and architecture of the past, we see the knowledge of harmony and proportion employed rightly, provoking in all men who have not had their emotions permanently crippled or destroyed by modern education a sense of the sacred. It therefore takes no great leap in imagination to conceive of the same knowledge put to an opposite use by the unscrupulous. In principle, buildings, dances, chants and music could be devised that would reduce the mass of any given population to helplessness. It would not be difficult for men who knew the secrets, since men who deny that the secrets exist produce the effect consistently in the twentieth century.

And there is a tradition repeated throughout history (though no concrete evidence I know)) that Egypt waned and ultimately fell through the widespread misuse of magic, which is ultimately the manipulation of harmonic phenomena.

This is but one valid reason for keeping certain types of mathematical knowledge secret. There are many others pertaining to the course of development and initiation of the individual: the man found incapable of keeping a simple secret cannot be entrusted with a more complex, more dangerous secret. Finally, we must consider the possibility that our undeniably developed Western intellects are purchased at the price of intuitional and emotional sensitivity; in times past, the misuse of mathematical knowledge might have been more dangerous than it would be today.

In every field of Egyptian knowledge, the underlying principles were kept secret, but made manifest in works. If this knowledge was ever written in books — and there is mention of sacred libraries whose contents have never been found — then these books were intended only for those who had earned the right to consult them. Thus, in writing, we have but a few mathematical papyri intended for students and apparently of a purely practical and mundane nature: they involve problems of distributing bread and beer among X number of people, and so on. Later, I shall briefly show how Schwaller de Lubicz proves that these school exercises are necessarily derived from a high and exact theoretical mathematical knowledge.

In astronomy, there are no texts, but a marvellously precise calendrical system indicates beyond any possibility of doubt that the Egyptians possessed an advanced astronomy. In geography and geodesy there are no texts, but the work of a number of scholars has shown that the siting and dimensions of the Great Pyramid, and of tombs and monuments dating back to the First Dynasty, as well as the whole complex system of Egyptian weights and measures, could not have been achieved without precise knowledge of the circumference of the earth, of the flattening of the poles, and of many other geographical details.

In medicine, again there is the problem of a shortage of texts, and the problem is compounded by technical difficulties in translation. But the available texts allude to a body of unwritten knowledge, while that committed to writing, when studied closely, divulges a profound knowledge of anatomy, pathology and diagnosis.

Finally, and most convincingly, there are no texts relating to architectural techniques. Egyptian murals are rife with depictions of ostensibly everyday occupations. (Actually, they have a deeper meaning as well, but more of this later.) We see carpenters, potters, stick-makers, fishermen, boatwrights, brewmasters — all the trades commonly associated with a developed artisan culture. But nowhere in Egypt is there a scene showing an architect at work. Nothing indicates the manner in which the prodigious monuments of Egypt were planned, designed or executed. A few fragmentary plans laid out carefully on

S. Giedion
The Eternal Present
Oxford, 1957, Vol. 1, p. 491

Schwaller de Lubicz stressed the symbolic implications inherent in the proportional organisation of the whole of a great temple. The graphic analysis in the second volume is of superb precision. One may not be willing to go so far as to compare the meaning of the Christian cathedral with the profoundly different religious outlook of the Egyptians. One may also feel extremely cautious about accepting the idea that different parts of the Luxor temple reflect different stages of human growth: that the proportions of the innermost sanctuary represent those of a *'nouveau né'* [newly born] or that one can find the proportions of an adult skeleton in the entire complex, including the latest additions.

Schwaller de Lubicz' volumes are not normally found in the bibliography of any serious Egyptologist, yet his fundamental point of the relation between symbolic meaning and the use of proportions cannot in the long run be excluded from earnest consideration. His influence upon Robichon and Varille, who were particularly concerned with the cosmic implications of the Egyptian temple, led to a further refinement of Egyptian excavations, and was a contribution to the neglected studies of the symbolism that permeates all Egyptian architecture, down to the setting of every stone.

Ibid., p. 490

In the 1950s the research of Badawy and R. A. Schwaller de Lubicz gave a detailed insight into the proportional organisation of Egyptian buildings . . . Badawy gave a summary of some of his ideas . . . Egyptian complexes such as the large New Kingdom temples which grew by accretion — new parts being added in front of the earlier structures — continued to follow the same pattern of proportions, even if separated by several hundred years. Badawy describes as 'harmonic design' the system based on certain recurrent dimensions occurring in ground plans and sections which can be expressed by a constructional diagram using isosceles triangles and squares. 'Both systems, the arithmetic of Fibonacci and the graphic system of the golden section were combined to achieve harmonic design in architecture according to fixed rules capable of being transmitted by teaching without the help of writing.'

papyri set out in grids prove that plans existed — which comes as no surprise. But not a word of the knowledge underlying those plans. That architectural knowledge existed. There is the architecture to prove it. The technical skill of the Egyptians has always been self-evident. It is now equally evident that this was matched by a profound knowledge of harmony, proportion, geometry and design. And it is clear that all of this knowledge, technical and theoretical, was secret and sacred, and that these secrets were kept.

They were manifested in Egypt's works, where they might produce their effects. Schwaller de Lubicz's work consists in abstracting from the art and architecture the profound mathematical and harmonic understanding responsible for the design of these works, and in delving beneath the confused and complex appearance of the hieroglyphs, mythology and symbolism to the simple metaphysical reality from which all this apparently arbitrary but actually consistent and coherent complexity devolved.

The linguistic thesis

Translation of the hieroglyphs still presents difficulties. In any Egyptological journal, half the articles generally concern unsolved problems of meaning, grammar and syntax. As it stands, the hieroglyphs can be 'deciphered', but it is unjust to say that they can be exactly 'translated'.

Champollion himself did not believe that he had revealed all that the hieroglyphs conceal. But death prevented him from following up his presentiments and subsequent scholars have not done so either, contenting themselves with refinements upon his original work. This failure has resulted in translations that miss the spirit and sense of the texts. But because Egyptologists have not found the metaphysical basis of the whole of Egyptian civilisation, they attribute the incoherence of the texts to primitive and 'unevolved' Egyptian thinking rather than to fundamental shortcomings of their own.

As is so often the case with solved mysteries, once the solution is provided it is difficult to see how it should not have been discovered long ago. But though simple enough to explain and illustrate, the symbolic key to the hieroglyphs requires a kind of thinking that is diametrically opposed to the analytic spirit of modern thought. The analytic mind rebels and refuses to countenance a symbol that contains within a single sign a complete hierarchy of meaning from the literal to the most abstract. But this is what the hieroglyphs do.

Curiously enough, if Egyptologists stuck rigidly to an absolutely literal translation of the texts, the underlying symbolic meaning would almost force itself upon them; but by approaching the texts cerebrally, by trying to turn them into an equivalent of our 'literature', they effectively covered over this inner meaning.

Thus, the sign for 'bird' shows a bird. But the constant use of this symbol in sacred texts suggests that the literal meaning does not tell the whole story. And the ubiquitous symbol for the 'soul' (the *ba*, a bird with a human head) provides the clue

The Pyramid Texts *(or more accurately, The Book of Coming into Light) carved in magnificent hieroglyphs in the pyramid of Unas (Fifth Dynasty) in Saqqara.*

to the symbolic meaning of 'bird'. The sign refers not only to the physical bird, but also to all the functions and properties that are contained within the 'idea' of bird: the ability to fly, to escape from the earth, and hence the principle of volatility which ultimately implies 'spirit'. When, in religious texts, the Egyptians carefully drew scenes of men drawing closed a netful of wild birds, they were not merely reminding the hovering disembodied dead of the pastimes of earth, but performing a magic rite reminding him of the exigencies of the spirit; of the need to capture, to 'draw the net' around the volatile aspects of the spiritual self. The failure to understand both the purpose of myth and its underlying verity contributes to the current unsatisfactory picture of ancient Egypt.

Consonant with evolutionary thought, modern scholars regard myth as either a quaint early attempt by primitives to rationalise the baffling physical world, a romantic effort to escape from harsh, matter-of-fact realities or as a clumsy artistic endeavour to communicate historical and political realities. Even Jung, who often saw wisdom where others saw only superstition, attributed the universality of myth to the workings of a mysterious 'collective unconscious'.

Schwaller de Lubicz comes to a contrary conclusion and substantiates his claim. Myth may be the earliest known means of communicating information related to the nature of the cosmos, but it is also the most precise, the most complete, and perhaps the best.

Myth dramatises cosmic laws, principles, processes, relationships and functions, which in turn may be defined and described by number and the interplay between numbers.

Definitions:

The subjectivity of language is such that readers will invariably put individual interpretations upon many of the constantly recurring key words in this text. In every case, the standard dictionary definitions are so vague as to promote individual interpretation. The following definitions are therefore not intended as comprehensive or conclusive, but they at least serve to define these words as they are intended within the present context.

Action:
the observable consequence of the mystical, unobservable Primordial Scission. Action is 'cause' of the universe. Primordial action is simultaneously 'reaction'. Esoterically, Action is the revolt of spirit against its imprisonment in matter.

Function:
the specificity of action; its role.

Process:
a sequence of action characterised by organised functions.

Pattern:
the schema of process; the manner in which it manifests itself.

Form:
the observable consequence of pattern in time and space; a cat is a vital form; a triangle is an abstract or ideal form.

The mathematical thesis

Schwaller de Lubicz's second thesis is mathematical. Both the deliberate use of harmonic proportions in art and architecture and the numerical basis underlying Egyptian myth compelled him to a detailed reconsideration of Pythagoreanism, and to the construction of a system of thought consonant with the masterpieces of Egypt — with the fact of an empire that lasted four thousand years. But it is a system for which our discursive language provides no convenient label. It is at once philosophy, mathematics, mysticism and theology. To comprehend it rightly, no aspect of it should be studied without simultaneously taking into account its other aspects. In Egypt, the accomplished temple permitted — indeed compelled — this simultaneity. But in order to explain it or describe it satisfactorily in modern language, we must do it piecemeal.

'Number is All', declared the Pythagoreans. To us it seems odd to classify numbers as 'limited, unlimited; odd, even; single, multiple; right, left; male, female; rectangular, curved;

Socrates
Philebus, par. 64

If measure and symmetry are absent from any composition in any degree, ruin awaits both the ingredients and the composition ... Measure and symmetry are beauty and virtue the world over.

F. Le Lionnais
'*Les Grands Courants de la Pensée Mathematique*'
Cahiers du Sud, 1948, p. 76

'Number resides in all that is known, without it we could not think, nor know anything,' wrote Philolaus, the Pythagorean philosopher.

Lancelot Hogben
Mathematics for the Millions
Pan Books, 1967, p. 16

Plato's exaltation of mathematics as an august and mysterious ritual had its roots in the dark superstitions which troubled, and fanciful puerilities which entranced, people who were living through the childhood of civilisation ... His influence on education has spread a veil of mystery over mathematics and helped to preserve the queer freemasonry of the Pythagorean Brotherhoods, whose members were put to death for revealing mathematical secrets now printed in school books.

M. Griaule
Conversations with Ogotemmeli
Oxford, 1965, p. 60

One could not speak of the Lebe in front of the Hogon's wife, of the eight ancestors in front of the priest's wife, of the Nummo in front of a smith, or of anything before fools.

light, dark; good, bad; square, oblong. It seems equally odd to call five the number of 'love' and eight the number of 'justice'. It seems less odd once we consider the thinking that led to these attributions.

The fact that the human mind can discriminate proves that the number two has a different meaning than the number one. The ability to distinguish implies difference, and difference requires two in order to have any meaning. We can, of course, create linguistic traps, and argue that there is no way to prove that language corresponds to 'reality'. From such a trap there is no escape. But if we allow that in some way language does correspond to reality, then philosophically, number becomes imbued with meaning, and numbers are not mere intellectual abstractions.

From the standpoint of everyday experience, we are aware of the universe as an incredibly diverse system made up of a multiplicity of apparent unities. A duck is a unity, made of a multiplicity of cells, each of which is a unity made up of a multiplicity of molecules, each of which is a unity made up of a multiplicity of atoms, each of which is a unity made up of a multiplicity of 'particles' for whose description ordinary language will no longer suffice. Seen one way they are particles, or unities; seen another way, they are modes of behaviour of energy; and it is energy that is now regarded as the ultimate unity underlying the material universe.

The same line of thinking followed into the macrocosmic sphere leads to the same conclusion. The duck is a unity, which is one aspect of the planet earth, which is a unity, which in its turn is part of the solar system, which is a unity, etc ... and on and on to the galaxies which, combined, make up the unimaginable unity we call the 'universe'. Positivists and certain linguistic philosophers may argue that the concept 'universe' is a fallacy, that the universe is an illusion, no more than the sum of its parts. But in that case a duck, or a positivist, is also a fallacy and an illusion, and no more than the sum of its parts.

Multiplicity presupposes unity. Multiplicity is meaningless unless unity also has meaning. Both terms confer a real, not merely abstract, meaning upon number.

It is the manner in which our senses receive information that creates an automatic, often insuperable, problem. Multiplicity assaults our senses on every front, while the unities we call 'duck', 'cell' and 'molecule' are provisional and relative — *and we know this*. We are such philosophically provisional, relative unities ourselves. Philosophically, logically, we may postulate an ultimate unity, but it is impalpable to our senses.

We are obliged to acknowledge the limits of reason, and to acknowledge the necessary reality of realms to which reason has no access. And while reason will not in itself set men going

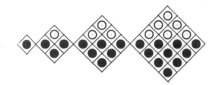

The generation of triangular and square numbers shown schematically can sometimes give an insight into the properties of numbers and the relationships between them that swifter and more 'efficient' modern calculating methods conceal. The Pythagorean ponders rather than memorizes, and understanding does not necessarily follow cumulatively, logically or sequentially. Like the Tao, it seems there one moment, and gone the next. The triangle is the first 'form'; four is the first possible 'analog' of one, and substance in principle; the tetractys is simultaneously ten, four and one. The meaning of the trinity as three-in-one can come leaping to you out of the diagram while remaining forever obscured when expressed in words. But it requires a certain kind of perception, and those lacking it are quick to deride it. It is a foolish sultan who thinks his eunuchs authorities because they speak objectively about love.

along the paths of an initiatic tradition (that is the function of conscience), reason is enough to invalidate skepticism.

It is the senses that make us skeptics. When scientists and intellectuals claim that their atheism or agnosticism is forced upon them by 'reason', they lie. They have simply failed to apply their reason to the relative and provisional data returned by the senses.

What is today called Pythagorean number mysticism is Egyptian in origin (if not older still) and corresponds to the underlying philosophy behind all the arts and sciences of Egypt. In effect, what Pythagoras did was to undramatise myth — a strategy that had the advantage of talking directly to those capable of thinking along these lines.

The work of Schwaller de Lubicz and the independent but complementary work of a few other contemporary thinkers (J. G. Bennett, for example) has made it possible to re-express Pythagorean theory in a way acceptable to our thinking. When we reapply this to Egyptian myth it becomes clear that these curious tales are based upon an understanding of number and the interplay of number, not upon animism, tribal superstitions, priestly feuds, the raw material of history or dreams.

Number: key to function, process and principle

1

One, the Absolute or unity, created multiplicity out of itself. One became Two.

J. M. Plumley
in *Ancient Cosmologies*, ed. C. Blacker and M. Loewe
Allen & Unwin, 1975, p. 24

For them [the Egyptians] the Whole Universe was a living unity ... the Ancient Egyptians could not conceive of anything that was not alive in some degree ... the Ancient Egyptian could speculate that there had been a time when the world as they knew it did not exist ... Every Egyptian Creation story, of which there are three major accounts ... starts with the basic assumption that before the beginning of things there was a Primaeval Abyss of waters, everywhere, endless, and without boundaries or directions. This was unlike any sea which has a surface, for there there was neither up nor down ... only a limitless deep — endless, dark, infinite ...

Ibid., p. 34

As in the cosmology of Hermopolis and Heliopolis we find mention of the Primeval God of the Waters, Nun, and a female counterpart, Nunet. But in the Memphite cosmogony these are said to be the products of the Eternal Mind, Ptah, who manifests himself in many ways and under many aspects. The ancient gods of the other cosmogonies, including Atum, are said to be contained in Ptah. 'They have their forms in Ptah' and are nothing but Ptah. Atum is stated to be the heart and tongue of Ptah, and the divine forms of these are the gods Horus and Thoth.

A. A. MacDonnell
A Vedic Reader for Students
Madras, 1951, X, 129

There was not the non-existent nor the existent then; there was not the air nor the heaven which is beyond. What did it contain? Where? In whose protection? Was there water, unfathomable, profound?

There was not death nor immortality then. There was not the beacon of night, nor of day. That one breathed, windless, by its power. Other than that there was not anything beyond.

Darkness was in the beginning hidden by darkness, indistinguishable, all this was water. That which, coming into being, was covered with the void, that One arose through the power of heat or 'energy'.

Desire in the beginning came upon that, desire that was the first seed of mind. Sages seeking in their hearts with wisdom found out the bond of the existent in the non-existent.

This Schwaller de Lubicz calls the 'Primordial Scission' (Division, Separation). It is forever unfathomable and incomprehensible to human faculties (although language allows us to express what we cannot comprehend).

The creation of the universe is a mystery. But in Egypt this was regarded as the only ineluctable mystery — beyond the Primordial Scission, all is in principle comprehensible. And if it is objected that a philosophy founded upon a mystery is unsatisfactory, it must be remembered that modern science is rife not only with mysteries, but with abstractions corresponding to no possible experience in reality: the zero, which is a negation; infinity, which is an abstraction; and the square root of minus one, which is both a negation and an abstraction. Egypt carefully avoided the abstract.

Tum (transcendent cause), in regarding himself, created Atum out of Nun, the primeval waters.

Heliopolis — appearance of Tum or Atum represents *simultaneously* affirmation (or existence) and negation (breach of primordial unity). Thus Heliopolis reveals the ultimate mystery of Non-Being and Being.

Non-Being is the source. Being is its negation. Tum initiates the divine analysis of the creative act.

He, who is born in the Nu,
When the sky had not yet become,
When the earth had not yet become,
When the two pillars, Shu and Tefnut had not yet become,
Before the gods were born,
Before Death had appeared,
Before the Quarrel (or Combat),
Before the Eye of Horus had been gouged out,
Before Set's testicles had been cut . . .

Jean Yoyotte and Serge Sauneron
La Naissance du Monde
Sources Orientales, 1969

The waters part, the hill arises and is fanned by the wings of the Benou bird [the Phoenix] . . . the waters shuddered. On the primordial mound, about the Phoenix, the light became haloed in its rays and flooding its silhouette until it became a flaming disc rising to the heavens.

In our terms unity, the Absolute or unpolarised energy, in becoming conscious of itself, creates polarised energy. One becomes simultaneously Two and Three.

Two, regarded by itself, is divisive by nature. Two represents the principle of multiplicity; Two, unchecked, is the call to chaos. Two is the Fall.

But Two is reconciled to unity, included within unity, by the simultaneous creation of Three. Three represents the principle of reconciliation, of relationship. (This three-in-one is of course the Christian trinity, the same trinity that is described in innumerable mythologies throughout the world.)

Numbers are neither abstractions nor entities in themselves. Numbers are names applied to the functions and principles upon which the universe is created and maintained. Through the study of number — perhaps *only* through the study of number — these functions and principles can be understood. Generally speaking, we take these functions and principles for granted; we do not even realise they underlie all our experience and that, at the same time, we are largely ignorant of them. We can only measure results, which provide us with quantitative data but not with understanding. We experience the world in

H. R. Ellis Davidson
Ancient Cosmologies,
Ed. Carmen Blacker and Michael Loewe,
Allen and Unwin, 1975, p. 188

The beginning and end of the worlds of
gods and men is a subject which in
Scandinavia as elsewhere invited
speculation. The emergence of an
ordered world out of chaos is
continuously emphasised in the
literature. The original state of
formlessness before creation is not
normally represented by water —
although there is a concept of earth
rising out of the sea — but by a great
abyss, Ginnungagap, which appeared
empty but which was in reality pregnant
with potential life.

Rig Veda

In the beginning there was the
fathomless ocean from which the One
created himself by the immensity of his
energy.

Peter Tompkins
Mysteries of the Mexican Pyramids
Harper & Row, 1976, p. 285

According to Martinex the Maya came to
the mathematical certainty of the
existence of a cosmic consciousness
which they named 'Hunab Ku', sole
dispenser of measurement and
movement, to whom they attributed the
mathematical structuring of the
universe. This divinity they represented
by a circle in which was inscribed a
square, just as did Pythagoras.
The Maya believed that their supreme
divinity functioned through a principle
of dynamic dualism, or polarity ... by
which, through the agency of the four
prime elements, air, fire, water and earth
... the whole material world was
engendered ... To the Maya the earth
was not a corpse, it was neither dead nor
inert, but a living entity immediately
tied to the existence of man.

terms of birth, growth, fertilisation, maturation, senescence, death, renewal. We experience in terms of time and space, distance, direction, velocity.

But contemporary science can account for this only in partial, superficial, quantitative terms. And either it refuses to admit these shortcomings, or to the manifold mysteries it applies meaningless but impressive labels. Eloquent in the emperor's new vocabulary, it insists the mystery is solved. 'Selection pressure', 'survival value', 'interaction between genetics and environment' — analyse any or all of these terms and you will find underlying all the mysteries of fecundation, birth, growth, maturation, senescence, death, renewal. None can be accounted for by the scientific method.

Yet through a restated Pythagorean number mysticism an insight can be gained into their nature. The philosophy based upon Pythagoreanism is called by Schwaller de Lubicz 'the only true philosophy'. This is not arrogance but a recognition of the fact that by this means we can begin to understand the world *as we experience it.*

2

The Absolute, unity, in becoming conscious of itself creates multiplicity, or polarity. One becomes Two.

Two is not One plus One. Metaphysically, Two can never be the sum of One plus One since, metaphysically, there is only one One, which is All.

Two expresses fundamental opposition, fundamental contrariety of nature: polarisation. And polarity is fundamental to all phenomena without exception. In Egyptian myth, this fundamental opposition is vividly depicted in the interminable conflict between Seth and Horus (ultimately reconciled after the death of the king).

The Primordial Scission provokes, postulates, reaction. Modern science is aware of the fundamental polarity of phenomena — though without acknowledging its implications or its necessarily transcendent nature. Energy is the measurable expression of the revolt of spirit against its imprisonment in matter. There is no way to express this fundamental verity in acceptable scientific language. Yet the language of myth expresses it eloquently: in Egypt, Ptah, the creator of forms, is depicted as imprisoned, bound in swaddling clothes.

Polarity is fundamental to all phenomena without exception, but it changes in aspect according to the situation. This fact is taken into account in common language. We apply different names according to the situation or category of phenomena. Negative, positive; active, passive; male, female;

P. H. Michel
*Les Nombres Figurés dans
l'Arithmetique Pythagoricienne?*
Conference du Palais de la Decouvert,
1958, (Ser. D., No. 56) p. 16

American mathematicians Karpinski
and Anning have further shown the
fundamental distinction of the
Pythagoreans to have been justified
between odd and even numbers — in the
way in which they differ in calculating
powers of numbers.

H. Frankfort
Kingship and the Gods
University of Chicago, 1948.

The embodiment of the two Gods [Seth
and Horus] is another instance of the
peculiar dualism that expresses totality
as an equilibrium of opposites.

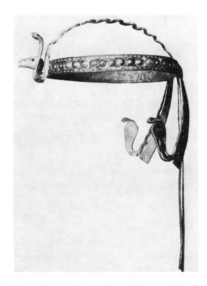

*Tutankhamen's diadem. The combined
vulture and cobra symbolize the
geographical union of Upper and Lower
Egypt, and the spiritual union of the
faculties of discrimination or intellect
(the cobra) and assimilation (the
vulture). The shape of the diadem
perfectly delineates the region of the
brain in which these particularly human
faculties are seated, and it is probably no
accident that the form of the serpent's
body nicely imitates the form of the
division between the hemispheres of the
brain.*

initiating, resisting; affirming, denying; yes, no; true, false —
each pair represents a different aspect of the same, fundamental principle of polarity.

For purposes of clarity and precision, we carefully distinguish among these sets of polarities according to their specific
function within a given situation. And it is true that by doing
so, we may gain in clarity and precision. At the same time we
may — and in science invariably do — lose sight of the cosmic,
all-pervading nature of polarity. In myth, this danger is
avoided. In myth the cosmic nature is intensified, and the individual scholar, philosopher or artist utilises that precise aspect
of the principle that applies to his task or quest, whatever it
may be. Precision and clarity are not purchased at the price of
diffusion.

Two, regarded in itself, represents a state of primordial or
principial tension. It is a hypothetical condition of eternally
unreconciled opposites. (In nature, such a state does not exist.)
Two is static. In the world of Two, nothing can happen.

3

A relationship must be established between opposing forces.
The establishment of relationship is, in itself, that third force.
One, in becoming Two, becomes Three simultaneously. The
'becoming' is the third force, automatically providing the
innate and necessary (and mysterious) reconciling principle.

Here we come to an insoluble problem in both language and
logic. The logical mind is polar by nature and cannot accept or
comprehend the principle of relationship. Throughout history, scholars, theologians and mystics have been faced with
the problem of explaining the trinity in discursive language.
(Plato wrestled manfully with it in his description of the
'world soul'; to all but Pythagoreans it seems gibberish.) Yet
the principle of Three is easily applied to daily life where,
again according to the nature of the situation, we apply a different name.

Male/female is not a relationship. For there to be relationship there must be 'love' or at least 'desire'. A sculptor and a
block of wood will not produce a statue. The sculptor must
have 'inspiration'. Sodium/chlorine is not in itself enough to
produce a chemical reaction; there must be 'affinity'. Even the
rationalist, the determinist, pays unwitting homage to the
principle: unable to account for the physical world through
genetics and environment, he calls in 'interaction', which is a
label applied to a mystery.

Logic and reason are faculties for discerning, distinguishing, discriminating (note the Greek prefix *di-*, meaning two).

But logic and reason will not account for everyday experience: even logicians fall in love.

The third force cannot be 'known' by the rational faculties; hence the aura of mystery hovering about every one of its innumerable aspects — 'love', 'desire', 'affinity', 'attraction', 'inspiration'. What does the geneticist 'know' about 'interaction'? He can't measure it. He infers it, extrapolates from his own experience, and by using a word from which all emotion has been removed, assumes he is being 'rational'. He can define 'interaction' with no more precision than the sculptor can define 'inspiration' or the lover, 'desire'.

The heart, not the head, understands Three. (By 'heart' I mean the complex of human emotional faculties.) 'Understanding' is an emotional more than an intellectual function, and it is practically a synonym for reconciliation, for relationship. The more one understands, the more he or she is able to reconcile, and relate. The more one understands, the more one reconciles seeming incongruities and inconsistencies. It is possible to know a great deal and understand very little.

So, while we cannot measure or know Three directly, we experience it everywhere. From common everyday experience, we can project and recognise the metaphysical role of Three; we can see why trinities are universal to the mythologies of the world. Three is the 'Word', the 'Holy Ghost', the Absolute conscious of itself. Man does not directly experience the Absolute or unity or the Primordial Scission. But the famous mystical experience, union with God, is, I believe, the direct experience of that aspect of the Absolute that is consciousness.

The degree to which one understands Three is a fair indication of the degree to which he or she is civilised. To acknowledge the third force is to assent to the fundamental mystery of creation; at the same time it is a recognition of the fundamental need to reconcile opposites. The man who understands Three is not easily seduced into dogmatism. He knows that true and false in our world are relative — or if seemingly absolute, as in logical systems, then that system itself is but relative, and abstracted from a greater, more complex reality. The failure to understand this results in the curious modern reasoning that declares the part valid but the whole an illusion.

Though the third force cannot be measured or known directly, an enlightened science such as the Egyptian can deal with it precisely. Any manifestation in the physical world represents a moment of equilibrium between positive and negative forces. A science that understands this also understands that by knowing enough about those positive and negative forces it will also, by inference, know about the ineffable third force, since this must be equal to the opposing forces in order to bring about that moment of balance. The ability to make use of this knowledge is one aspect of 'magic'.

M. Griaule and G. Dieterlen
African Worlds (ed. D. Forde)
Oxford, 1954, p. 217

Incidentally, the study of the Bambara had brought to light unexpected cosmologies and metaphysics. There, too, Water and the Word were the foundations of spiritual and religious life.

L. E. Orgel
Origins of Life
Chapman and Hall, 1973, p. 47

Each triplet of nucleotides corresponds either to an amino acid or to a signal to stop translation. Since there are 64 [4 x 4 x 4] different triplets and only 20 amino acids many of the amino acids are represented by two or more triplets.

Ibid., p. 157

The genetic code, from a very early stage in its evolution on, must have been a three-letter code. There is no obvious reason why a two-letter or four-letter code should not have evolved in the primitive earth. However, no transition from an advanced two- or four-letter code would have been possible. Such a transition would have led to a disastrous misinterpretation of all the genetic information that had been accumulated by natural selection.

H. R. Ellis Davidson
Op. cit., p. 188

It has recently been claimed by German scholars that there is evidence for the concept of a mighty creative deity [in Scandinavian cosmology] expressed in symbolic patterns or ornaments . . . Detailed work shows that a favourite motif is a face with an open mouth, which issues a kind of cloud.

In everyday life, recognition of the role of Three is a step toward that most difficult of feats: acceptance of the opposition. A masterpiece of art, indeed creation of any sort, can take place only in the face of commensurate opposition. To the sculptor, the block of wood is his opposition in a very real sense — as every sculptor knows. If his inspiration is insufficient to deal with his block of wood, he will either go out and get drunk or produce an ambitious failure. If the block of wood is insufficient to his inspiration, he will finish with a sense of frustrated ambition. Easy to recognise in principle, the ability to give the opposition its due is one of the most difficult things to put into practice. This is why the principle is expressed and re-expressed in a thousand different ways in sacred literatures of the world. It is this, and not any sense of obsequiousness, that is meant by the Christian dictum to 'love thine enemy'. Try to love thine enemy!

4

Material, substance, things; the physical world is the matrix of all sensuous experience. But material or substance cannot be accounted for in two terms or in three. Two is an abstract or 'spiritual' tension. Three is an abstract or 'spiritual' relationship. Two and three are insufficient to account for the idea of 'substance', and we can illustrate this by analogy. Lover / beloved / desire is not yet a 'household' or even an affair. Sculptor / block / inspiration is not yet a statue. Sodium / chlorine / affinity is not yet salt. To account for matter in principle requires four terms: sculptor / block / inspiration / statue; lover / beloved / desire / affair; sodium / chlorine / affinity / salt.

Thus matter is a principle over and above polarity and relationship. It includes, of necessity, both Two and Three, yet is something beyond the sum of its constituents, as every sculptor and lover knows full well. Matter or substance is both a composite and a new unity; it is an analogue of the absolute unity, with its triune nature.

The four terms needed to account for matter are the famous four elements — which are not, as modern science believes, a primitive attempt to account for the mysteries of the material universe, but rather a precise and sophisticated means of describing the inherent nature of matter. The ancients did not think that matter was actually made up of the physical realities fire, earth, air and water. They used these four commonplace phenomena to describe the functional roles of the four terms necessary to matter — or, rather, to the *principle of substantiality*. (At Four we have not arrived yet at the actual physical stuff we stub our toes against.) Fire is the active, coagulating princi-

Marcel Griaule
Op. cit., p. 73

'The craft of weaving in fact,' said Ogotemmeli in conclusion, 'is the tomb of resurrection, the marriage bed and the fruitful womb.'

It remained only to speak of the Word, on which (he said) the whole revelation of the art of weaving was based.

Ibid., p. 19

The words that the Spirit uttered filled all the interstices of the stuff: they were woven in the threads, and formed part and parcel of the cloth. They were the cloth, and the cloth was the Word. That is why woven material is called *soy* which means, 'It is the spoken word'. *Soy* also means 'Seven', for the Spirit who spoke as he wove was seventh in the series of ancestors.

Ibid., p. 212

The Number 4 is moreover, the number of femininity, that is, of fertility. Ogotemmeli had often said that the ideal pair was composed of two females and consequently had the same sign as the creative word.

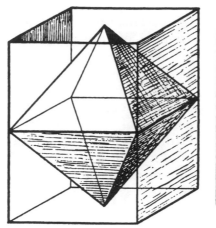
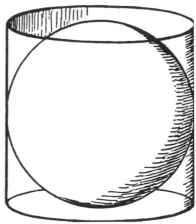

Form is intimately related to function. The octahedron or double pyramid is the most compressed or densest form. It occupies the smallest percentage of the volume that encloses it, while the sphere occupies the greatest. So the densest forms of matter, minerals and crystals, tend to octahedral or related forms; volatiles and gases expand to fill a sphere. The octahedron is the imprisoned fire of the 'seed', the materialized aspect of the sphere, which is symbolically spirit. Among their many functions, the great pyramids of Egypt served as models of the northern hemisphere, and the choice of the pyramid shape was based upon symbolic as well as geodesic and architectural considerations.

W. G. Lambert

Ancient Cosmologies, Ed. C. Blacker and M. Loewe
Allen and Unwin, 1975, p. 34

The idea that everything goes back to the prime element water occurs in sources Greek, Egyptian, Palestinian, Syrian and Mesopotamian.

Lancelot Hogben
Mathematics for the Millions, Pan Books, 1967, p. 169

Another class of good omens was that of triangular numbers. A story about these shows you how different was mathematics as cultivated by the Pythagorean Brotherhood from the mathematics which the Greek merchants and craftsmen could use ... In Lucian's dialogue a merchant asks Pythagoras what he can teach him. 'I will teach you how to count' says Pythagoras. 'I know that already,' replies the merchant. 'How do you count?' asked the philosopher. The merchant begins, 'One, two, three, four ...' 'Stop!' cries Pythagoras, 'what you take to be four is ten, or a perfect triangle, and our symbol.' Seemingly, the audiences of Pythagoras wanted charades. He gave them brighter and better charades.

Tao Te Ching
Translated by D. C. Lao, Penguin, 1963, p. 102

When the best student is taught the Tao, he practices it assiduously. When the average student is taught the Tao, it seems to him there one moment and gone the next. When the worst student is taught the Tao, he laughs out loud. If he did not laugh it would be unworthy of being the Tao.

ple; earth is the receptive, formative principle; air is the subtle, mediating principle, that which effects the interchange of forces; water is the composite principle, product of fire, earth and air — and yet a 'substance' over and above them.

Fire, air, earth, water. The ancients chose with care. To say the same thing in modern terms requires more words, and none stick in the memory. Active principle, receptive principle, mediating principle, material principle — why bother with such abstractions when fire, earth, air and water say the same and say it better?

In Egypt, the intimate connection between Four and the material or substantial world was applied in symbolism. We find the four orientations, the four regions of the sky, the four pillars of the sky (material support of the realm of the spirit), the four sons of Horus, the four organs, the four canopic jars into which the four organs were placed after death, the four children of Geb, the earth.

Unity is perfect, eternal, undifferentiated consciousness.

Unity becoming conscious of itself creates differentiation, which is polarity. Polarity, or duality, is a dual expression of unity. Thus each aspect partakes of the nature of unity and of the nature of duality — of the 'One' and of the 'Other', as Plato put it.

Thus each aspect of primordial, spiritual duality is itself dual. The primordial Scission creates a twofold antagonism, which is reconciled by consciousness. This double reaction, or double inversion, is the basis of the material world. If we understand nothing of this fourfold process, we understand little of the world of phenomena — which is our world. Symbols, studied in the correct manner, make these processes clearer than words. The square inscribed in a circle represents passive, potential matter contained within unity. The same process is shown in action, as it were, in the cross — which is rather more than two sticks of wood upon which an upstart Jew was

Death mask of Tutankhamen. The crossed arms and crossed flail and crook serve the same symbolic purpose as the Christian Cross: the cross of Matter. And both Pharoah and Christ represent Cosmic Man, He who may transcend the cross of the flesh; Five, Number of 'Love' to the Pythagoreans, Number of Eternity, that is to say, beyond Time... Note the elaborate number symbolism expressed in the flail with its triple lash and sets of seven knots or beads. This is typical of Egyptian thinking. Ornament or design is seldom if ever arbitrary. Study of the numbers commanding the patterns usually reveals the symbolic thinking underlying that choice.

Direct evidence of Egyptian knowledge and use of the 3,4,5 Pythagorean triangle is rare, but this relief from the tomb of Rameses VI is an instance of it.

nailed. This is the cross of matter, upon which all of us are pinned. Upon the cross, the Christ, the cosmic man, is crucified. By reconciling its polarities through his own consciousness, he attains unity.

It is this same principle of double inversion and reconciliation that lies behind all religious Egyptian art and architecture. The crossed arms of the mummified pharaoh — who (whatever his personal traits may have been) represents successive stages of the cosmic man — holds the crossed scepter and flail of his authority. Schematically, the point where the two arms of the Christian cross intersect represents the act of reconciliation, the mystical point of creation, the 'seed'. Upon a similar scheme, the exalted, mummified pharaoh represents the same abstract point.

The cross and the mummified pharaoh thus symbolise both Four and Five.

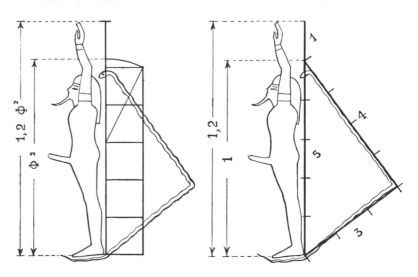

5

To the Pythagoreans, Five was the number of 'love' because it represented the union of the first male number, Three, and the first female number, Two.

Five may also be called the first 'universal' number. One, that is unity, containing as it does all and everything, is strictly speaking incomprehensible. Five, incorporating the principles of polarity and reconciliation, is the key to the understanding of the manifested universe. For the universe, and all phenomena without exception, are polar in nature, treble in principle.

From the roots of Two, Three and Five all harmonic proportions and relationships can be derived. The interplay of these proportions and relations commands the forms of all matter, organic and inorganic, and all processes and sequences of growth. It may be that in the not too distant future, with the aid of computers, science may come to a precise knowledge of these complex interactions. But it will not succeed in doing so until it accepts the underlying principles which the ancients knew.

It may seem odd to saddle numbers with gender. But reflection upon the functional role of numbers quickly justifies such a procedure. Two, polarity, represents a *state* of tension; Three, relationship, represents an *act* of reconciliation. Female numbers, the even numbers, represent states or conditions; the female is that which is acted upon. The male is that which is initiative, active, 'creative', positive, (aggressive, rational); the female is correspondingly receptive, passive, 'created' (sensitive, nuturing). This is not a tract advocating universal male chauvinism; the universe is polar, masculine/feminine by nature. And it is probably no accident that in countless phenomena of the natural world, we find this relationship between odd numbers and masculinity, even numbers and femininity. Genital organs are usually treble. Female mammals of all species have two (or multiples of two) breasts. In an accidental universe, there is no reason why such uniformity should prevail.

So Five, to the Pythagoreans, was the number of love, but given the innumerable connotations of that much abused word, it is perhaps preferable to call Five the number of life.

Four terms are necessary to account for the idea of matter, or substance. But these four terms are insufficient to account for its creation. It is Five — the union of male and female — that enables it to 'happen'.

And it is an understanding of Five in this sense that is responsible for the peculiar reverence in which Five has been held in so many cultures; this is why pentagram and pentagon have

Hieroglyphics of Horapollon
Tr. by J. B. van der Walls and J. Vergote
Fond. Reine Elisabeth, Brussels, 1943, p. 54

When they wanted to portray the god of the universe, or destiny, or the number 5, they painted a star.

been sacred symbols in esoteric organisations (and why it is so ironic to see it currently used as the basis of the plan of the world's largest military headquarters). In ancient Egypt, the symbol for a star was drawn with five points. The ideal of the realised man was to become a star, and to 'become one of the company of Ra'.

As we apply the functional roles of number to familiar conditions of everyday life, we can gain insight into the manner in which they operate more easily than we can by technical description. Roles change and become more complex within functions. Man/woman is a polarity. But the same man and woman, linked by desire in a relationship, are no longer the same; and when the three-term relationship turns into the tetrad of affair, or household, the parties to it again change functionally — as all lovers, husbands and wives know full well. The parties involved play both active, masculine, initiating and passive, feminine, receptive roles *simultaneously*. The lover is active toward his beloved, receptive to desire; she is receptive to his advances, but provokes desire. The sculptor is active toward the block of wood, receptive to inspiration; the block of wood is receptive to the chisel, provoking inspiration.

This kind of thinking underlies the vital philosophy of Egypt.

Broadly speaking, contemporary philosophy falls into two main camps. One, characterised by logical positivism and its rather more sophisticated descendants, concentrates upon logic and a scientific methodology. The other, typified by existentialism in its various forms, concentrates upon human experience in a personal or social context. Neither school incorporates Pythagorean thinking, with the result that the positivists have developed a rigorously consistent analytical tool unrelated to human experience, while the existentialists have made useful observations about experience, but cannot fit them into a consistent or convincing structure. The Pythagorean approach reveals a structure and system underlying experience.

The philosophy of ancient Egypt is not philosophy in our sense; there are no explanatory texts. It is nevertheless a real philosophy in the sense that it is systematic, self-consistent, coherent and organised upon principles that can be expressed philosophically. Egypt expressed these ideas in mythology, and it is not until that mythology is studied as the dramatisation and interplay of number that its coherence reveals itself.

From his study of the Hebrew Cabbala, Chinese yin-yang philosophy, Christian mysticism, alchemy, the Hindu pantheon and the latest work in modern physics, Schwaller de Lubicz recognised a common Pythagorean bond uniting all. However different the means or modes of expression, each of these philosophies or disciplines concerns the creation of the world, or matter, out of the void; each recognises that the physical world is but an aspect of energy, each — excepting modern physics which, by concentrating on the material aspect of the problem, can avoid its philosophical implications — recognises that 'life' is a fundamental universal principle, and not an afterthought or an accident.

The number of 'love', the number sacred to Pythagoras, the number symbolised by pentagon and pentagram, which commanded the proportions of the Gothic cathedrals, played a crucial but subtler role in Egypt. Apart from the hieroglyph of the five-pointed star, we find no overt instances of five-sided figures.

Instead Schwaller de Lubicz found the square root of Five commanding the proportions of the 'Holy of Holies', the inner sanctuary of the Temple of Luxor. In other instances he found the proportions of certain chambers dictated by the hexagon generated from the pentagon. In others, crossed 8 x 11 rectangles, the four-sided generators of the pentagon from the square, commanded the proportions of wall murals symbolically related to those functions represented by Five.

Egypt also made extensive use of the Golden Section which, from the Primordial Scission, commands the flow of numbers up to Five. The pentagram, made up of Golden Section segments, is the symbol of unremitting activity; Five is the key to the vitality of the universe, its creative nature. In mundane terms, Four accounts for the fact of the sculptor's statue, but does not account for the 'doing' of it. Five terms are required to account for the principle of 'creation'; Five is accordingly the number of 'potentiality'. Potentiality exists outside time. Five is therefore the number of eternity and of the principle of eternal creation, union of male and female — and it is for this reason, and along these lines of thought, that the ancients came to hold Five in what looks to us like a peculiar reverence.

6

Four terms are needed to account for the principle or idea of 'substance'. Five terms are needed to account for 'creation', for the act of becoming, the event. But five terms are insufficient to describe the framework in which the event takes place; the actualisation of potentiality.

That framework is time and space.

We may call Six the number of the world, in this sense. Five, in becoming Six, engenders or creates time and space.

The functions, processes and principles relating to One, Two, Three, Four and Five may be called spiritual or metaphy-

To the Pythagorean, the geometric forms associated with a number and the manner in which that number interacted with others provided the keys to its inner significance, a significance that manifested itself in the physical world in terms of function, process and pattern. There is today a growing interest among mathematicians in Pythagorean ideas, but the popularisers of science continue to deplore it as an ancient superstition, though the physical world manifests itself to these savants as to everyone else in terms of function, process and pattern. Function, process and pattern are comprehensible only through the study of the philosophy of number.

Hexagon and circle are intimately connected. A hexagon is formed by cutting the perimeter of a circle six times with its radius. The circle symbolically represents the Absolute, or undifferentiated unity. Six is intimately connected to all matters of time and space. The relationship between six and nineteen is not immediately apparent but reveals itself in the generation of hexagonal numbers: 1+6+12 = 19. The Egyptian decision to base a grid upon nineteen squares was based upon an understanding of the complex role played by nineteen in all questions of manifestation in time and space. Pythagoreans do not consider it a coincidence that nineteen should so frequently crop up in celestial measures and cycles: synodic returns of the moon follow a nineteen-year cycle; nineteen and multiples of nineteen determine many measures involving the planet Jupiter. (cf. Temple de l'Homme, R. A. Schwaller de Lubicz, Vol. 1., 472 ff.)

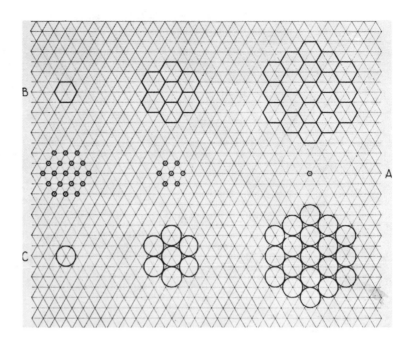

sical. In any case, they are invisible. We cannot actually see or even visualise a polarity, a relationship, principial substance or the act of creation. But we live in the world of time and space and, unfortunately for us, it is this overpowering sensory interpretation of time and space that conditions what we call 'reality', a reality that is but one aspect of the truth. Our language, with its tenses of past, present and future (not all languages have these tenses) reinforces the illusory picture drawn by the senses. From time immemorial, scholars, philosophers and thinkers have stubbed their brains against the problem of time and space, seldom realising that the language in which they hoped to solve the problem was itself ordered in such a way as to support the evidence of the senses.

In ancient times, the problem was probably less acute than it is today. Language is the principal instrument of expression of the intellectual faculty. When men were less dependent upon their intellects, and in all likelihood had more highly developed intuitional and emotional faculties, they were more susceptible to experiences that transcend time and space, and were able to accept the provisional evidence of the senses at its true value.

We seem to experience time as a flow. Space seems to us that in which things are contained. But when we subject these impressions to rational analysis, we end up with apparent absurdities, or else are constrained to go along with the positivists and conclude that our questions are incorrectly phrased and therefore meaningless. We are still left with the overpowering impression of time as flow, logically without beginning or

end, and equally logically without a 'present', since past and future are ceaselessly merging into one another. If we regard space as that which contains, we are constrained to postulate infinite extension or, if the universe is finite, an infinity which begins at its limits. Neither solution is satisfactory, and again we are left with the indelible impression that space contains things, 'space' itself remaining a mystery. Nothing in science or philosophy can resolve this problem.

But the study of the symbolism of numbers and of the functions and principles numbers describe, allows us to grapple with it on a sound intellectual basis. It is no substitute for the mystical experience, which alone carries with it the unalterable emotional certainty that is 'faith'. But at least it enables us to see simultaneously both the 'real' nature of time and space and the conditional aspect of it returned by our sensory apparatus. It also allows us to reconcile the apparently irreconcilable standpoints of Eastern mysticism, which holds that the world of the senses (and with it time and space) is illusion, and wholly a mental construct, and Western empiricism, which takes sensory data at face value despite the insoluble philosophical and scientific problems that this raises.

Both views are correct, depending upon the standpoint taken. In terms of the material world, time is real. Time is real as far as our bodies are concerned. We live and die. In terms of the spiritual world, time is not 'illusion' in the sense of falsely perceived reality. Rather, time does not exist. To the Absolute, to transcendent unity, there is no time. And all initiatic religions teach that the goal of man is reunion with the Absolute, with God, with the realm of 'spirit'. Therefore, an important aspect of all these teachings is the insistence upon the necessity to transcend time; for it is time which holds us in bondage to the material world.

But since our bodies are bound to time, and our needs, pleasures, pains and desires so closely bound to our bodies, it is difficult to instill within ourselves the unshakable determination to act upon the necessity to transcend time — even after we

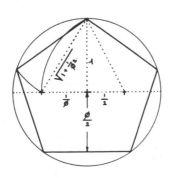
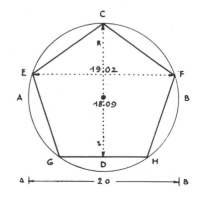

The 18:19 ratio emerges out of the geometric play involved in generating the pentagon within the circle. The pentagon and pentagram, figures sacred to the brotherhood of Pythagoras, are intimately connected to phi, the Golden Section, itself both the cause and the result of what Schwaller de Lubicz calls the Primordial Scission. Note the circle with radius value equal to one, representing unity. The diagonal formed by division into two gives the first Golden Section relationship, generating both the pentagon and the subsequent 18:19 ratio.

have paid lip service to it. Hence the elaborate disciplines and rituals of Yoga, Zen and other forms of Eastern and Western religions.

The study of number symbolism will not in itself enable a man to transcend time, but by clarifying the issue, by demonstrating the manner in which time and space play their roles in the grand universal scheme, number symbolism may help us see them in their true light, and perhaps help to make the need for transcendence that much more urgent.

The framework in which creation takes place is time and space, which requires six terms to define them. Creation does not take place within time; rather, time is an effect of creation. Things do not exist within space; things *are* space. There is no time except that which is defined by creation; there is no space except that which is defined by volume. The material universe is an interpenetrating hierarchy of energies at different levels or orders of density, to which our senses have but limited access.

A science that attempts to explain the universal order in terms of human sensory experience, or through machines which are but quantitative extensions of human senses, is bound to travel further and further from a comprehensive understanding. This situation we see today, as specialities proliferate, and though lip service is paid to the undeniable interaction among the various fields, the specialists involved have no clue as to how or why these interactions take place. The interminable wrangle over whether the universe is ultimately material or ultimately spiritual goes on.

In Egypt and other ancient civilisations the situation was the opposite. In the vitalist philosophy there could be no distinction between mind and matter: both were understood as aspects of a single scheme. Only the Primordial Scission was unknowable; all else devolved from this event in terms of functions, principles and processes, and these were comprehensible in terms of number and communicable (in Egypt) in terms of the Neters (the so-called 'gods') whose attributes, gestures, size and position altered according to the role played within any given situation. (We do the same in less systematic fashion in modern language. We know — though we might not be able to 'prove' it — that the role of the 'man' in a polarity is not the same as the 'lover' in a relationship.)

Six, the number of the material world and therefore of time and space, is the number chosen by the Egyptians to symbolise temporal and spatial phenomena. Six served the Egyptians, as it does us, for the basic temporal divisions: twenty four hours in a day (twelve of day, twelve of night), twelve months of thirty days each in the year, plus five days in which 'the Neters were born'. This is neither accident nor coincidence, but a nat-

W. M. O'Neil
Time and the Calendars
Manchester University Press, 1975, *passim*

The selection of twenty-four hours as the subdivision of the day is quite arbitrary. The Chinese, for example, used twelve sub-units of the day, and the Hindus came to use 60 sub-units ... *no natural event breaks the day* ... into twelfths, twenty-fourths, sixtieths or any other fraction ... The Babylonians, at an early stage, used twelve equal fractions of the day from sunset to sunset ... The Chinese divided the day into twelve equal *shih* periods. However, as the Babylonians divided the *beru* into sixtieths and that fraction into further sixtieths, the Chinese divided the *shih* into eights ... The Chinese also divided the day into hundredths. [Author's italics.]

ural corollary of the functional role of Six. (In celestial mechanics, discussions of motion employ a six-dimensional space — three for the position and three for the velocity of each particle or planet.)

Volume requires six directions of extension to define it: up and down, backwards and forwards, left and right. So in Egypt the cube, the perfect six-sided figure, was used as the symbol for actualisation in space; the cube is the symbol for volume. Pharaoh sits squarely upon his throne, which is a cube (sometimes he is sculpted emerging from a cube). Man is placed unmistakably in material existence. Nothing could be clearer than this instance of conscious recognition of the role and function of Six. But to recognise it ourselves, we must be able to think as the Pythagoreans did.

Six is also symbolised by the hexagon, by the Seal of Solomon and by the double trigrams of the Chinese *I Ching*, each of which represents a different approach to Six and illustrates a different aspect, although these aspects are ultimately complementary. (The cube is the result of Six; the Seal of Solomon and double trigrams are Six in action.)

In Egypt, Schwaller de Lubicz found that the dimensions of certain specific halls of the Temple of Luxor were determined by the geometric generation of the hexagon from the pentagon. This is a symbolic expression of the materialisation of matter from the spiritual creative act. At the same time it is an actual expression of materialisation. The temple both symbolises and is time and space, in strict conformity to the relevant laws.

Giorgio de Santillana and Hertha von Dechend
Hamlet's Mill
Gambit, 1969, p. 222

The cube was Saturn's figure, as Kepler showed in his *Mysterium Cosmographicum*; this is the reason for the insistence on cubic stones and cubic arks.

R. A. Schwaller de Lubicz
Le Temple de l'Homme, Vol. III
Caracteres, 1957, p. 17

Every construction, no matter how simple it may be, has a soul because it has Volume. Volume is the indefinable substance-Spirit arrested in Space. It is alive, it is specific, it is Number, therefore Music.

7

Five terms are required to account for the principle of life, for the creative act, the 'event'. Six terms describe the framework within which the event takes place. But six terms are insufficient to account for the process of coming-into-being, of becoming.

In the material world, we generally experience this process in terms of growth. But when we come to relate the functional significance of Seven to everyday experience, we begin to run out of analogical steam. At Five, the correspondence between the sculptor and the cosmic 'act' was precise. At Six we hover on the edge of metaphor. Our sculptor, at Six, was not creating time and space. He was himself already *in* time and space, and was creatively sculpting. The 'volume' of his statue was pre-existent in the block of wood (though we might say, from the point of view of the statue, that the sculptor was re-enacting

Seshat, also called Sefhet, which means seven, is the female counterpart of Thoth, therefore mistress of measure, and always attends the foundation ceremonies of the temples. Her emblem is the seven-petaled flower. Seshat is found on the earliest inscriptions. Thus it is clear that the correspondence between seven (harmony) and measure was known to Egypt from the onset.

the role of God and creating time and space since the statue *qua* statue did not exist before).

At Seven, however, our analogy becomes pure metaphor. In no material or biological sense does the sculptor's statue 'grow'. We grow. An apple grows. But the 'growth' of the statue is purely metaphorical. (It may not seem entirely metaphorical to the sculptor who, by carefully observing the progress of his creation from idea or 'germ' to completion, may gain an insight into the principle of 'growth'.)

Seven terms are needed to account for the phenomenon of growth. Growth is a universal principle observable (and measurable) in all realms of the physical world, excepting the most microcosmic — we cannot observe or measure the growth of an atom or molecule.

Like all the principles and functions described up to now, all of which contribute to our experience of the world as it is, 'growth' cannot be accounted for scientifically. There is nothing in the behaviour of the hydrogen atom that makes predictable the growth of a kitten into a cat. But, as with all functions and processes, scientific ignorance is masked under jargon. Things grow because 'mechanisms' fortuitously initiated over the course of 'evolution' have proven 'growth' to be a factor conducive to 'survival'. This fatuous circumlocution is called 'rational thinking'.

It is interesting to remark that, up to this point, in relating number to function, we have been able to show why the numbers Two, Three, Four, etc. and not others, apply to polarity, relationship and substantiality, but we could not easily find concrete physical examples to substantiate the correlations: we can find no physical proof that a lump of salt, as material, is predicated by the meaning of Four. A skeptic might call the universal application of Six to time and space measuring systems arbitrary.

When we come to Seven, however, we can no longer relate it directly to our experience — we cannot of ourselves initiate 'growth'. But in the physical world we find a multitude of instances in which Seven manifests itself in growing or active systems.

Growth is not a continuous process. It takes place in discrete steps, in quantum jumps. Children seem suddenly to 'shoot up'. And so they do. Bones do not grow continuously; they grow in length for a period, and then in breadth. At certain (numerically determined) periods growth proceeds apace. In between there is little growth.

Seven terms are needed to account for the principle of growth, and it is remarkable how often seven or multiples of seven command the actual steps or stages and sequences of growth — even more remarkable in view of the fact that science dismisses Pythagorean thinking and does not look for such correspondences. The data accumulate anyhow.

Phenomena tend to completion in seven stages, or are complete within their specific stage. There are seven tones in the harmonic scale. It is the harmonic scale, and the human function of hearing, that give us direct access into the process of growth, of creativity manifesting itself. It is for this reason — not chance or superstition — that led the Pythagoreans explicitly, and the Egyptians implicitly, to employ the harmonic scale as the perfect instrument for teaching and demonstrating the workings of the cosmos.

Consider a string of a given length as unity. Set it vibrating; it produces a sound. Stop the string at its midpoint and set it vibrating. It produces a sound one octave higher. Division in two results in an analogue of the original unity. (God created Adam in his image, and it took Him seven days, or discrete stages, to carry out His work.) Drawn schematically, the divided vibrating string illustrates the principle of double inversion that pervades all of Egyptian symbolism — and that just now is being investigated by subatomic physicists as a fundamental characteristic of matter.

Between the original note and its octave there are seven intervals, seven unequal stages which, despite their inequality, the ear interprets as 'harmonious'.

We cannot describe or define harmony in rational or logical terms. But we react to it — and to its absence — instinctively. This reaction is characterised by an unmistakable sense of 'equilibrium'.

The notes of the musical scale devolve from the division of One into Two. These notes represent moments of rest in the descent of unity into multiplicity. The created universe may be said to 'occur' between One and Two, and harmony evokes in us an instinctive awareness of (even a longing for) the unity from which harmony derives. Harmony is the recall to unity. And art that is based upon harmonic principles arouses in us a sense of unity and of the cosmic or 'divine' order.

In the world that we experience, all unities represent states of dynamic (but provisional) equilibrium; they are stages in the return to unity, oases in the chaos that unchecked multiplicity implies.

An atom is a moment of equilibrium. So is a cat. Equilibrium is a state in which positive and negative forces are balanced. Modern science, with its doctrine of entropy and negative entropy,* expresses the principle without recognising its functional significance. The Western astrological zodiac (product of the primitive imagination!) expresses the principle both precisely and completely. Libra, the Balance, is the seventh sign.

Seven signifies the union of spirit and matter, of Three and Four. One of the forms that traditionally expresses the meaning of Seven is the pyramid, so characteristic of Egyptian architecture — a combination of the square base symbolising the four elements and the triangular sides symbolising the three modes of spirit. The different pyramids are constructed in such a way as to express different functions of the Golden Section.

The pyramid, constructed according to the Golden Section, serves not only symbolically. Practically it is the shape that best serves a host of geographic, geodesic, chronometric, geometric, mathematical, numerical, chorographic and astronomical functions — functions which a number of modern scholars have shown to be incontrovertibly incorporated within the pyramid (specifically within the so-called Great Pyramid of Cheops). Until very recently, Egyptologists have preferred to ignore the relevant data, but there are some indications that a change is imminent.

8

Before discussing the functions and principles inherent in Eight, it is worth interjecting a word of caution regarding number symbolism. As we progress from one number to another, each number not only symbolises and defines the specific function allotted to it, but incorporates all combinations of functions leading to it. For example, polarity, the tension between opposites, is simple and straightforward. But Five not

---

* Entropy: a mathematical idea that is precisely expressable only through mathematics, but is describable as a simile as 'the degree of disordering', e.g., the entropy of the universe will allegedly result in an eventual 'heat death'. Life itself takes place through, or embodies, the principle of 'negative entropy'.

only represents the act of creation; it incorporates Two and Three, the male and female principles, and two sets of opposites — the principle of double inversion — united by the invisible point of intersection. Five is also One, or unity, acting upon Four, or principial material, hence creation.

When we come to Seven, matters become even more complex. Each aspect or combination manifests itself differently. Seven is Four and Three — the union of matter and spirit. It is Five and Two — fundamental opposition united by the act, by 'love'. It is Six and One — the fundamental note, 'do', actualised by Six. That is to say, in time and space it produces its octave tone, which is a new unity.

This new unity is not identical, but analagous, to the first unity. It is a renewal or self-replication. And to account for the principle of self-replication, eight terms are necessary. The old unity is no longer, a new unity has taken its place: the king is dead, long live the king.

In the zodiac, it is the eight sign, Scorpio, that traditionally symbolises death, sex and renewal.

In Egypt, the well-known text declares: 'I am One, who becomes Two, who becomes Four, who becomes Eight, and then I am One again'.

It is Thoth (Hermes to the Greeks, Mercury to the Romans) who is 'Master of the City of Eight'. Thoth, the messenger of the gods, is the Neter of writing, of language, of knowledge, of magic; Thoth gives man access to the mysteries of the manifested world, which is symbolised by Eight.

This brief excursion into the relationship between number

The schematic representation of the fertilised ovum could as well be a biological expression of the ancient Hermopolitan mystery: 'I am One that becomes Two that becomes Four that becomes Eight. And then I am One again.

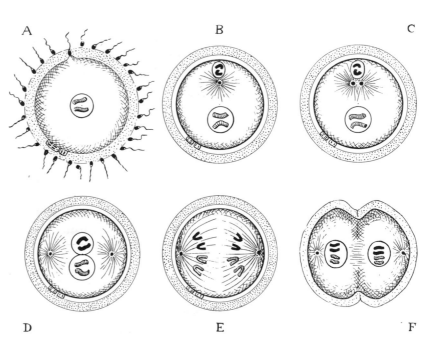

Marcel Griaule
Op. cit., p. 127

When the eight ancestors ... were born
to the first pair, eight different animals
were born in heaven.

Ibid., pp. 18-19

These spirits, called Nummo, were thus
two homogeneous spirits of god (half
man, half serpent) ... the Pair were born
perfect and complete; they had eight
members, and their number was eight,
which is the symbol of speech ... they are
water [in the Western Zodiac, the 4th,
8th, and 12th signs are Water signs] ...
The life force of earth is water. God
moulded the earth with water. Blood,
too, he made out of water. Even in a stone
there is this force.

and function is not meant to be complete or exhaustive.
Rather, it is meant to serve as preparation for the posing of
several questions that can be answered simply Yes or No.

Do we experience the physical or natural world in terms of
polarity, relationship, substantiality, activity, time and space,
growth and sex, death and renewal? Because, apart from polarity, none of these words admit of strict logical definition, are
we entitled to dismiss them as 'arbitrary'?

Number symbolism, related thus to function, provides the
framework that makes the world of our experience comprehensible.

In this introduction we have necessarily touched only upon
the manner in which number relates to the physical world, or
physical experience: the world of being. But number is also the
key to the world of values (which are aspects of will) and the
world of consciousness which, together with the world of physical experience, make up the totality of human experience.
(Readers interested in pursuing these matters will find the relevant books in the bibliography: B9.)

Eight, then, corresponds to the physical world as we experience it. But the physical world as we comprehend it is still
more complex. The interacting functions up to Eight do not
permit of pattern or plan — of the ordering of phenomena.
Nor will an eight-term system account for the source of order
or pattern — for the pattern-maker, as it were. It will not
account for necessity (the principle that reconciles order and
disorder). In order for there to be 'creation' it must first be necessary. Finally, there is the matrix within which all these functions operate simultaneously, which we might call the world
of possibilities.

These higher numerical functions correspond to Nine, Ten,
Eleven and Twelve. The functions corresponding to these
numbers are not a part of our direct experience, but philosophically we can recognise their necessity. Admittedly, these concepts are difficult to grasp — particularly since our education
trains us to analyse, never to synthesise. Nevertheless, these
functions are not abstractions — not in the sense that the
square root of minus one is an abstraction — for they are essential to complete the framework of our experience, even if we
cannot experience them directly.

They are also necessary from a theoretical point of view. As
previously mentioned, in the Primordial Scission One
becomes simultaneously Two and Three. Phenomena are dual
by nature; treble in principle. The vibrating string represents a
fundamental polarity: an impelling, masculine force (that
which strikes) and a resisting, feminine force (the string). The
actual vibrating string represents a relationship: an impelling
force, a resisting force, and a mediating or reconciling force

(the frequency of vibration, which is the 'interaction' between the two poles yet is neither the one nor the other).

The Primordial Scission, in creating duality, creates two unities, each of which partakes of the nature of unity and of duality: Two in this sense equals Four.

The simultaneous creation of Two, Three and Four postulates an interaction between these functions, a cycle, which for its full realisation requires twelve terms. Difficult to express verbally, this twelve-fold cycle is expressed simply, schematically and completely in the traditional zodiac.

Though no actual zodiacs have been found in ancient Egypt, Schwaller de Lubicz provides ample evidence to prove that knowledge of the signs of the zodiac existed from the earliest time, and pervades and directs Egyptian symbolism — once one knows where and how to look for it.

In the zodiac each sign partakes of duality, triplicity and quadruplicity. Naturally, in the newspaper astrology (which scientists and scholars assume to be the only astrology there is) this fundamental aspect of the zodiac goes unnoticed. Unfortunately, most serious modern astrologers, while making intuitive use of the zodiacal signs, scarcely recognise the number symbolism upon which they are founded.

As we shall shortly see, the Golden Section lies at the heart of the Primordial Scission, creating a universe that is asymmetric and cyclical. This cyclical aspect means that multiples of numbers are, as it were, higher registers of the lower numbers.

The physical universe is complete in principle in four terms: unity, polarity, relationship and substantiality. But the full actualisation of all possibilities requires the working out of all combinations of Two, Three and Four. This is accomplished in the twelve signs of the zodiac. The zodiac is divided into six sets of polarities, four sets of triplicities (the modes) and three sets of quadruplicities (the elements). Each sign is simultaneously polar (active or passive), modal (cardinal is that which initiates; fixed or fixing is that which is acted upon; mutable is that which mediates or effects the interchange of force) and elemental (fire, earth, air, water). Polarity is realised in time and space (six times two), spirit materialised (three times four) and matter spiritualised (four times three).

Thus, four terms gives the world in principle. Eight terms gives the world actualised in time and space. Twelve terms gives the world of potentialities and possibilities.

Though this brief resumé touches upon but one aspect of the astrological zodiac, it should be sufficient to suggest that this ancient scheme is in no way founded upon the reveries of ancient dreamers, but is rigorously constructed according to Pythagorean principles. If we hope to understand the physical world we live in (to say nothing of the spiritual world), we must examine the principles and functions that underlie common experience. The symbolism of number allows us to do this.

It was upon this understanding that ancient Egypt and other ancient civilisations operated. Upon this basis and with this understanding it is possible to devise a comprehensive and coherent interrelated system in which science, religion, art and philosophy define and explore specific aspects of the whole, without ever losing sight of each other.

Egyptologists recognise that such a system prevailed in Egypt, but judging that system from their own point of view they miss the point and deplore the fact that in Egypt, 'theology' pervades all aspects of civilisation.

Though it may seem but a small step to the further recognition that Egyptian theology was pervasive because it was based upon the truth, taking that small step demands a full pyschological *volte-face*, and this is by no means easily accomplished. So Schwaller de Lubicz's meticulously presented evidence goes unheeded. In other specialised fields of Egyptology, painstaking, often brilliant work in astronomy, mathematics, geography, geodesy and medicine attests to the refinement and sophistication of Egyptian knowledge. In every case, advances in modern methods reveal former deficiencies and shortcomings and invariably alter opinions on the extent of Egyptian knowledge.

9

Egypt evoked, but never explained. As we have seen, the correlations made between number and function are not arbitrary, and in each case it has been possible to show these correlations employed in the symbols and myths of Egypt. As a general rule, however, we have had to go looking for them, and it is necessary that we first understand the functional significance of number before we know how or where to look. Even the triads of Neters (and trinities throughout the mythologies of other civilisations) are not overt declarations of concern with number, or of an understanding of Three as the principle of relationship. The skeptic could easily argue that the phenomenon of male and female engendering new life is so self-evident that it might easily serve as a symbol without knowledge of its philosophical or Pythagorean connotations.

But a choice of Nine is not at all self-evident, and there can be no mistaking the importance attached to the number Nine by Egypt.

Nine is extremely complex, and practically insusceptible of precise verbal expression. The Grand Ennead (an ennead is a group of nine) is not a sequence, but the nine aspects of Tum

— interpenetrating, interacting, interlocked.

Diagrammatically, the Grand Ennead can be illustrated by that most intriguing of symbols, the tetractys, which was regarded as sacred by the Pythagorean brotherhood.

The tetractys
1 + 2 + 3 + 4 = 10

The tetractys, regarded as sacred by the Pythagoreans, contains within itself the keys to harmony, which in turn govern creation.

4:3 = the Fourth
3:2 = the Fifth
2:1 = the Octave

And the double octave in quadruple ratio: 4:1

Though the tetractys as a symbol seems peculiar to the Pythagoreans, the same Number symbolism is widespread. Hindu mythology speaks of the ' Nine Cobras of Brahma', a parallel to the Grand Ennead arranged around Atum. The Cabbala refers to the Nine Legions of Angels about the throne of the hidden God, 'He whose name is hidden'. The tetractys represents metaphysical reality, Plato's 'ideal world', complete within the framework of a four-term system.

Creation requires five terms. The pentactys represents the manifested tetractys.

The inner triangle is a symbol of the triune nature immanent in unity; it represents the first form: form requires a three-term system; form is the result of the interaction between positive and negative poles. The pentactys depicts principial form surrounded by twelve 'houses', which are the animators of form. This understanding is also common to many ancient civilisations. The Egyptian physiological system is based upon it. 'These canals, by cosmic flux and reflux, conduct the red and white solar energy to the areas where the twelve powers lie sleeping within the organs of the body. Once, every two hours of the night and day, each is activated by the passage of Ra, the sun of the blood, and it then returns to sleep.' Chinese acupuncture is based upon the 'twelve meridians of the body'. Every two hours one or the other of these meridians reaches peak activity. The twelve 'houses' of the astrological zodiac.* express the same understanding in another way. The 'houses' derive their meaning from the interplay of number; they determine the nature of the time, personality or event.

The Grand Ennead emanates from the Absolute, or 'central fire' (in the terminology of Pythagoras). The nine Neters (Principles) circumscribed about One (The Absolute) becomes both One and Ten. This is the symbolic analog of the original Unity; it is repetition, the return to the source. In Egyptian mythology the process is symbolised by Horus, the Divine Son who avenges the murder and dismemberment (by Set) of his father, Osiris.

The tetractys is a rich, many-layered symbol which repays meditation with an almost inexhaustible flow of meanings, relationships and correspondences. It is an expression of metaphysical reality, the 'ideal world' of Plato. Its numerical relationships express the basics of harmony: 1:2 (octave); 2:3 (fifth); 3:4 (fourth); 1:4 (double octave); 1:8 (tone).

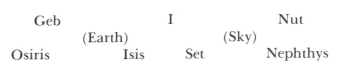

Tum

Shu   Tefnut
(The Dry)   (The Moist)

Geb   I   Nut
   (Earth)   (Sky)
Osiris   Isis   Set   Nephthys

Application or materialisation
of the Four Principles

Osiris = incarnation/reincarnation, life/death, renewal
Isis = feminine aspect of Osiris
Set = principle of opposition, antagonism
Nephthys = feminine aspect of Set

The tetractys may be seen as the Egyptian Grand Ennead made manifest and demythologised. This is not necessarily an improvement, but it is one means for catching a glimpse of the many meanings behind the ennead. (Another is the extraordinary symbol, the enneagram, that Gurdjieff claimed to have rediscovered from an ancient source. Whereas the tetractys shows the Grand Ennead made manifest, the enneagram shows it in action as Seven, the octave, number of growth and process, interpenetrating Three, the basic triune nature of unity. Correspondences between Gurdjieff's work and Schwaller de Lubicz's are striking, though neither knew the work of the other.)

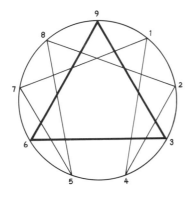

The enneagram

The enneagram is a *universal symbol.* All knowledge can be included in the enneagram and with the help of the enneagram it can be interpreted. And in this connection only what a man can put into the enneagram does he actually *know*, that is, understand. What he cannot put into the enneagram he does not understand. For the man who is able to make use of it, the enneagram makes books and libraries entirely unnecessary. *Everything* can be included and read in the enneagram. A man may be quite alone in the desert and he can trace the enneagram in the sand and in it read the eternal laws of the universe. And every time he can learn something new, something he did not know before.

If two men who have been in different schools meet, they will draw the enneagram and with its help they will be able at once to establish which of them knows more and which, consequently, stands

upon which step, that is to say, which is the older, which is the teacher and which is the pupil. The enneagram is a schematic diagram of *perpetual motion.* . . .

G.I. Gurdjieff, quoted by P. D. Ouspensky,
In Search of the Miraculous (Harcourt, 1949), p. 294

The properties of numbers, the manner in which they behave, was evidence, indeed 'proof', to the Pythagoreans of the divine order. To the modern rationalist, these properties are simply the natural consequences of an abstract system with no inner meaning or cosmic significance. The study of these properties amounts to 'mathematical games and diversions'. Finally, it is up to the individual to choose between the camps, but it is not a choice to be made lightly: upon it hinges, ultimately, the

whole of one's philosophy.

Esoterically, because all numbers are to be regarded as divisions of unity, the mathematical relationship a number bears to unity is a key to its nature.

Both three and seven are 'perpetual motion' numbers. Divided into unity, they divide infinitely.

$1 \div 3 = .3333333333333. . .$
$1 \div 7 = .1428571428571. . .$

Three: the number of relationship, of 'the Word', of the mystical trinity, three-in-one.

Seven: the number of growth, of 'process', of harmony, gives the same recurring sequence of seven when divided into unity. Note the enneagram following this sequence.

Marcel Bessis
Ultra-Structure de la Cellule
Monographies Sandoz, March 1960, pp. 39-40

The centricles [nuclei of the living cell] have in fact a very curious structure: they are little cylinders ... the walls of each cylinder are made up of nine tubules ... A considerable interest devolved from these constations once one knows that these structures of nine elements (or multiples of nine) are re-encountered in all sorts of formations endowed with movement.

Peter S. Stevens
Patterns in Nature
Penguin, 1976, p. 3

When we see how the branching of trees resembles the branches of arteries and the branching of rivers, how crystal grains look like soap bubbles and the plates of a tortoise's shell, how the fiddle-heads of ferns, stellar galaxies, and water emptying from the bathtub spiral in a similar manner, then we cannot help but wonder why nature uses only a few kindred forms in so many different contexts. Why do meandering snakes, meandering rivers, and loops of string adopt the same pattern, and why do cracks in mud and markings on a giraffe arrange themselves like films in a froth of bubbles?

In matters of visual form we sense that nature plays favourites. Among her darlings are spirals, meanders, branching patterns and 120-degree joints. Those patterns occur again and again. Nature acts like a theatrical producer who brings on the same players each night in different costumes for different roles. The players perform a limited repertoire: pentagons make most of the flowers but none of the crystals; hexagons handle most of the repetitive two-dimensional patterns but never by themselves enclose three-dimensional space. On the other hand, the spiral is the height of versatility, playing roles in the replication of the smallest virus and in the arrangement of matter in the largest galaxy.

Cursory as this essay into Pythagoreanism has been, it should be enough to suggest both the extreme complexity and extreme importance of Nine. And given its importance in the metaphysics of structure and pattern, it comes as no surprise to find it made manifest in the structure of the living cell, whose mitosis, it is held by some biologists, begins in the centriole, made up of nine little tubules.

The importance and recurrence of certain numbers, number combinations and forms have long been remarked upon by naturalists, botanists and biologists. As science delves ever deeper into molecular, atomic and subatomic realms, the physical world continues to reveal its innate harmonic and proportional nature in ever more striking and precise fashion. Scientists note these data but because they never subject them to Pythagorean scrutiny, they continue to learn more and more about how the world is constructed, but not about why. Yet these answers seem practically on the verge of imposing themselves, if only the right questions were asked. The form of the double helix and the sequences of amino acids and proteins in basic cell structures and enzymes all follow clearly defined and precise patterns whose proportions and numerical relationships must conceal the reason why these things are as they are. For example, water (H_2O) displays two basic harmonic attributes. Two hydrogens to one oxygen gives the octave; by volume, eight oxygen to one hydrogen gives 8:9, the tone.

Is this 'coincidence'? No one can 'prove' that it is not. And yet these basic harmonic attributes do seem too neatly Pythagorean to dismiss. Remember that in the ancient system 'water' is the fourth element, the primal, principial 'substance' and analog of one, as the octave is the analog of the fundamental. In the physical world water is the support of life. In the metaphysical world of Egypt, Tum creates himself out of Nun, the primeval waters. Creation proceeds harmonically, the octave is the instrument of process, of 'life', and the first note of the octave is the tone. To produce the perfect tone, the string must be proportioned 8:1 — just the ratio of oxygen to hydrogen atoms by volume. And creation *is* volume, which is space.

Schwaller de Lubicz's interpretation of Egypt demonstrates that Egypt understood why the world is as it is; her choice of symbols, as well as countless indications from scientific, mathematical and medical texts, proves that she also knew an astonishing amount about how. Obviously, Egypt had no lasers, electron microscopes or particle accelerators; she could not have specific, quantitative knowledge of the microscopic world. But the curious appositeness displayed by her symbols and texts makes it clear that technology is not the only means for gaining insight into these realms.

Serpent in the Sky

Divine Duality

Language, particularly discursive or descriptive language, is linear and consecutive. In relating numbers to functions I have immobilised them, deprived them of life. This is unavoidable. To know the anatomy of a butterfly we trap it, kill it, pin it down, dissect it. But if we want to understand the butterfly we must never lose sight of the fact that we have sacrificed the living embodiment of a principle in order to ascertain certain facts. These facts make sense only when reapplied to the living butterfly.

The functions definable through number do not operate in isolation. We experience no isolated instances of polarity, relationship or substantiality. The world of our experience is a web of function in simultaneous operation.

Discursive or descriptive language cannot begin to capture the simplest experience without depriving it of life. But the higher languages of myth and symbolism can.

The Neters of ancient Egypt are personifications of function in action. To us an Egyptian frieze or mural may appear peculiarly rigid and lifeless when compared, say, to a Greek frieze or mural. But Greek art is apparently intended as a sensory experience, like our own art. Egyptian art has other intentions. In relation to it, we are like a man with no musical training trying to make sense of a Beethoven score or worse, like students who have learned to read notes but have never actually heard music. Our judgments are no more than reflections and projections of subjective beliefs and desires.

Schwaller de Lubicz shows that the symbolism of the Neters involved both a carefully considered choice and a deep understanding (based upon meticulous observation as well as theoretical consideration) of the nature of the chosen symbol. He supports this contention with a number of examples, one of which I will give here.

At first glance the serpent may seem a perfect model for unity. What could better express singleness than the serpent's undifferentiated length?

In Egypt, however, the serpent was the symbol for duality or, more accurately, for the power that results in duality. And that power is itself dual in aspect; it is simultaneously creative and destructive: creative in the sense that multiplicity is created out of unity, destructive in the sense that creation represents the rupture of the perfection of the Absolute.

When it is realised that the serpent bears both a forked tongue and a double penis, the underlying wisdom of the choice becomes clear. As a symbol of duality, the serpent represents intellect, the faculty by which man discriminates — that is to say, by which we break down the whole into its constituent parts.

But unchecked duality is chaos. Analysis run rampant is just destruction. To merely know without synthesising is to parody God — which is probably why, borrowing the serpent from Egypt, the Book of Genesis uses it as symbol for temptation.

The serpent, seemingly a unity, is dual in expression — both verbal and sexual, dual and divisive by nature.

But duality, and for that matter intellect, is not only a human but a cosmic function. There is a higher and a lower intellect. Thus, symbolically, there is the serpent that crawls, and the higher intellect, that which allows man to know God — the heavenly serpent, the serpent in the sky. The Egyptians knew perfectly well that snakes don't fly. But there is a deep meaning to their placing the serpent in the air under specific circumstances. The winged serpent, common to so many civilisations, was employed in Egypt as well and played a similar symbolic role.

Parallel thinking directs the union of cobra and vulture on the royal diadem worn by the pharaoh, which stands for the union of Upper and Lower Egypt and at the same time symbolises the triumphal union of the faculties of discernment and assimilation, the mark of the perfected or royal man. (Schwaller de Lubicz also demonstrates the connection between the serpent and the sense of smell and shows this symbolism pervading the sanctuary of the Temple of Luxor in which the olfactory sense is symbolised. This in turn relates to the hieroglyph for Neith, Neter of 'weaving', since the action of warp and weft is the Egyptian way of symbolising the 'crossing' that is characteristic of the mental process.)

Thus the choice of the rich and powerful symbol of the serpent for duality divulges both a total understanding of the many aspects of duality in both its creative and destructive senses, and an equally complete understanding of the nature of the animal chosen to represent duality. It is also significant that while in general Egypt provided each animal with a single name, the serpent, in its role of 'separator' (hence obstructor) of the works of Ra, is vilified under a host of different names (perhaps qualifying in some way the specific kind of obstruction or negation). These appear in the innumerable

Peter Tompkins
Mysteries of the Mexican Pyramids
Harper & Row, 1976, p. 387

To Sejourné, Teotihaucan was the place where the serpent learned miraculously to fly, that is 'where the individual, through inner growth, attained the category of a celestial being'.

E. A. Wallis Budge
Hieroglyphic Vocabulary to the Theban Rescension of the Book of the Dead
Kegan Paul and Co., 1911, p. 273

Apop possessed many names; to destroy him it was necessary to curse him by each and every name by which he was known.

rites and texts in which the deceased is supposed to pray to be freed from the protean forms negation takes. Set, the separating fire, in Christian terms becomes Satan, who is famous for his guile; in other words, Satan appears under many guises, and in Egypt under many names.

Phi: the Golden Section

The Neters of Egypt are founded upon number, as are the Egyptian hieroglyphs.

Numbers may be called 'the language of the Absolute', a statement that is not meant as metaphor but as a close analogy, and one that may soon be receiving official corroboration. Advances in linguistics make it ever more apparent that human language is not an 'evolved' system of ape talk, but rather a mysterious totality, the fundamentals of which may be common to all people despite the vast differences between individual languages. More than fifty years ago, the alchemist Fulcanelli declared that certain sounds and combinations of sounds had the same meanings no matter what languages they occurred in (though the original meaning might well have been lost over the ages). Knowledge of these combinations is probably what lies behind the science of spells, chants and incantations — which become superstition when the underlying knowledge is lost and only the outward form remains. In any case, the universality of phonetic significance is receiving some support these days; and all sound is reducible in principle to frequencies — that is to say, to number.

We also experience the world hierarchically, as a hierarchy of values. The most common expression of this is our distinction (however subjective) between better and worse. As human beings we can choose. We can even choose to become behaviourists and maintain there is no choice. In biology the hierarchical order of the organism is recognised: the brain commands a system of organs and glands which in turn command the flow of hormones and secretions. In human institutions, the general commands the captains, who command the sergeants, and so on. This is natural, instinctive compliance with the hierarchical principles that pervade the universe — principles which have always been understood by initiatic and religious systems. (Compare Christianity with its spheres of angels and archangels with ancient Egypt, where there is a hierarchy of Neters.) Though the terminology may seem quaint today, these spheres or hierarchies describe the realms to which our senses have no access, but which are necessary within any comprehensible universal scheme that corresponds to reality and to the principles of organisation in the human sphere.

Organization proceeds from the top down, not from the bottom up. Apparent exceptions to the rule reveal a hidden obedience to it upon closer examination: a working democracy is hierarchy by mandate, and tribal societies have their councils of elders or some other mutually agreed upon governing body. Even communes, insofar as they are at all viable, are originally organised by a distinct organising body.

The restaurant starts with the chef, not with the dishwashers. I write this book with a master plan in mind. I do not go blindly word by word, hoping that sooner or later a sentence will 'evolve'. The sculptor sees the finished statue in the uncarved block.

Instead of presuming that human language 'evolved', it is time to take seriously and literally the statements made by all great ancient civilisations and by many so-called primitive societies: that language was bestowed upon men by the 'gods'. In whatever sense this is meant (by the 'gods' directly or by sages in direct contact with the 'gods'), it tallies with the curious fact that no language has ever been discovered that is not grammatically and syntactically complete. No language has ever been found in an early state of 'evolution'. The most primitive language allows its speakers to convey whatever they want to convey within that society's frame of reference. Languages change, certainly, but they do not 'evolve' — our language is no more 'evolved' than Shakespeare's and in many ways it is degenerate, debased by advertising and the mass media into numbing cliché, or perverted by the priesthoods of science in jargons designed to exclude the uninitiated.

By recognising the universality of hierarchy and remembering that modern physics has shown matter to be a transient form of coagulated energy, we can look afresh at language. Instead of regarding it as an isolated phenomenon proper only to humanity (and in simpler forms to animal species), we can regard it as a human form of communication that also takes place in realms higher than our own. We might then justly regard astrology as the 'language' of solar systems. And the Neters, based upon number, are the 'language' of the Absolute or transcendent cause. Seen this way, it also becomes easier to regard the languages of myth and symbolism in their proper light as languages higher than our own — higher because they are based upon and directly, numerically related to the functions and principles of the higher realms to which they refer.

Analogically, the Neters serve as the consonants of a cosmic language. The vowels are provided by the interactions between the Neters. These interactions are all based upon and related to the functions that result from the Primordial Scission. One of the most important of these we call phi, the Golden Section.

Perhaps the greatest single achievement within Schwaller de Lubicz's reinterpretation is the solution of the ultimate

G. E. Duckworth
Structure, Pattern and Proportion in Virgil's Aeneid
Michigan, 1962, p. 77

Almost a century ago, Fechner demonstrated that by requesting opinions from a large number of persons of both sexes, a rectangle constructed on a Golden Section with its sides 21:34 has a far greater appeal than any other rectangle: it had absolutely no rejections and received 35% of the preferences. The result of this poll has been brushed aside as inconclusive by many writers, who apparently ignore the fact that the two rectangles closest to the Golden Section each received over 19% of the preferences; in other words the Golden Rectangle and the two approximating it received about 74% of the total number of votes; viewed in this light the poll seems significant and implies that the Golden Mean Ratio produces the aesthetically perfect rectangle.

Did Virgil likewise believe that poetic passages or groups of passages bearing this same ratio, exact or approximate, had a mathematically formal beauty which would contribute to the perfection of the structure of his epic?

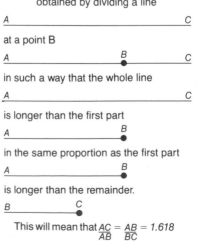

The Golden Section, or φ is
obtained by dividing a line

A _____ *C*

at a point B

A _____ *B* _____ *C*

in such a way that the whole line

A _____ *C*

is longer than the first part

A _____ *B*

in the same proportion as the first part

A _____ *B*

is longer than the remainder.

B _____ *C*

This will mean that $\frac{AC}{AB} = \frac{AB}{BC} = 1.618$

---

meaning of the Golden Section — a problem that has occupied many of the greatest thinkers and artists of history.

When this significance is divulged, the reader may well be puzzled as to why so apparently elementary an explanation should have remained a mystery for so long. Yet the fact is that the solution eluded the genius of Leonardo and of Kepler, of a number of brilliant modern biologists, and of a host of astute artists and researchers in aesthetics. The answer to the mystery's amazing persistence can only lie in the fact that the *cause* of *number*, the Primordial Scission, was never grasped.

Yet it is known that phi controls the proportions of innumerable living organisms, that the spiral of the 'spiral galaxy' is a phi spiral, that the orbits of the planets of our solar system are in complex phi relationships to each other, and that the proportions of Gothic cathedrals and Greek temples are commanded by phi.

Though long before Schwaller de Lubicz's work a number of scholars had noted phi proportions in the pyramids and other Egyptian remains, only in the past few years has this been acknowledged by Egyptologists. Even now, attempts are made to show how the Egyptians might have used the Golden Section without actually realising they were doing so. But the fact is that the Egyptians knew and used phi from the earliest dynasties—as well as the so-called Fibonacci numbers that devolve from phi.

Evidently the Egyptians — and the builders of the Greek temples and Gothic cathedrals and to a certain extent the painters and Neoplatonists of the Renaissance — also knew the significance of phi and the manner in which to employ it effectively; knowledge which they either deliberately kept secret or which was later inadvertently lost. Even those modern artists who have been intrigued by phi and attempted to use it (Mondrian and le Corbusier, for example) did not understand its meaning and met with but partial success.

A line, AC, is divided at B in such a way that AB is to BC as AC is to AB. In other words, the smaller portion is to the larger as the larger is to the whole. The ratio AB/BC is equal to the ratio AC/AB, and this ratio is phi, or 1.6180339 . . .

Expressed in simple mathematical terms this may scarcely seem earth-shaking. But how do we know where to draw the line, where to place point B?

When we show geometrically how we arrive at phi and relate this to the number symbolism as we described it before, we may catch a glimpse of its universal significance.

Phi: consequence of scission

Because the physical universe is 'ideal', or foreshadowed in

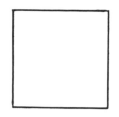

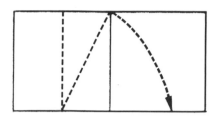

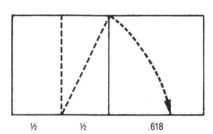

½ ½   .618

four terms, we legitimately symbolise its physical aspect with a square, which represents unity. Remember that Four is an analogue of unity. Unity becomes duality; we divide the square in half. The diagonal of each half brought down to the base line creates phi, the Golden Section. But at this point we run into problems. In one sense we cannot express what we draw. In another sense, we cannot draw what we express. The Alexandrian mathematician, Theon of Smyrna, tried to resolve a similar problem with a mathematical absurdity that is yet a mystical truth. He declared the situation one in which the diagonal of the square was equal to the side. Expressed another way, we may say that One, in becoming Two, divides into unequal parts, and that inequality is both caused by phi and is phi. The rational mind cannot grasp the situation. Because modern education trains only the rational faculties, we cannot help but feel uncomfortable faced by the apparent paradox. Yet we can recognise the metaphysical necessity for the situation. If unity, in becoming duality, was a mere division in equal halves, then any universe devolving from the scission would result in an infinite number of materialised simulacra of the Absolute (whatever that might look like!). In Egypt, recognition of this fundamental inequality is expressed in the hieroglyph for one-half, ╱▭ which clearly shows sides of unequal length. The obvious, rational method of illustrating one-half would be to make the sides equal.

Another way round the problem is to bring in the concept of infinity. (And it is only in this instance that the concept of infinity is legitimate, for only the Absolute is infinite.) When infinity is commonly used in modern mathematical equations, it is a mere abstraction with no foundation in experience, and of course it is unverifiable by science. We therefore commonly find a science that prides itself as based upon experience making use of a mathematics unrelated to experience.

If our square is an infinite square, then both its side and its diagonal equal infinity. (See J. G. Bennett in the Bibliography.)

In school mathematics, phi is treated as just another 'irrational'.* Phi is defined as being equal to $\frac{1+\sqrt{5}=}{2}$ 1.618...

Often the curious prevalence of phi in natural forms is noted, as is its relationship to the Fibonacci series and the manner in which the Fibonacci series also turns up in nature. Sometimes it is studied in some detail for its power in generating proportions.

But phi and other irrationals are still regarded as a special class of number, and it is this point of view that prevents

* An irrational number is a root of an algebraic equation which cannot be expressed as a fraction or an integer, e.g., $\sqrt{2}$, $\sqrt{3}$, etc.

science and mathematics from understanding the significance of the irrational.

The irrational as a function

Phi is not a number. It is a *function*. To regard the irrational as a number, even a special class of number, is to reduce the concept of number to meaninglessness. Number implies the capacity to enumerate, and it is by definition impossible to enumerate with an irrational: we cannot have or imagine 1.618. . . chickens or 3.141. . . eggs.

Phi, pi, and the square roots of two, three and five are all that are required to form all Perfect geometric solids,* and to define and describe all possible harmonic combinations. It is this web of interaction, this vast complex of harmonies, that we respond to as 'the world' — in this case the physical world, which is but one (the tangible, perceivable) aspect of the spiritual world, or world of consciousness. The key to this harmonic world is number, and the means by which number is to be understood is geometry.

Plato regarded geometry as sacred, the Pythagoreans declared 'All is Number', and the heading of the Egyptian Rhind Papyrus promises 'rules for enquiring into nature and for knowing all that exists, every mystery, every secret'.

Because, until very recently, science has concentrated upon asking 'How?' rather than 'Why?', it has lost sight of the reasons behind this reverence for geometry and the interplay of number. Scientists regard mathematics as a descriptive tool which allows them to describe phenomena with increasing accuracy; to the Pythagoreans, mathematics was the symbolic representation of the functions and processes whose results are the phenomena that concern today's science.

Incomprehension of the mentality of the ancients tends to breed a kind of snide contempt, particularly among popularisers of science and mathematics. (The genuinely creative minds within these fields sometimes make statements that reveal them to be Pythagoreans at heart. This is natural, almost inescapable; creation implies synthesis, and the purely analytic mind can never create. Remember E. M. Forster's telling and justly famed admonition: 'Only connect'.)

Unfortunately, it is the popularisers and the authors of school texts who reach the largest audiences, and trends in wrong thinking tend to be self-perpetuating, at least up to that point where even convention can no longer conceal fatal inner

Guy Murchie
Music of the Spheres
Dover, 1961, Vol. 1, p. 30

At an altitude of 2500 miles you can stay up at only 2 miles per second and your orbit can be even freer . . . Getting completely out of the whirlpool is, relatively speaking, a pushover from here. The rule is that from any orbit that holds you continuously above the earth (or above any other gravitating body) all you need do is multiply your velocity by $\sqrt{2}$ to escape the body altogether. Thus if any satellite with an average velocity of 2 miles per second increases it to $2\sqrt{2}$ or 2.8 mps it will just sail off never to return.

---

* A Perfect solid is a solid each of whose faces is identical and is an equilateral planar form, e.g., Triangle, square or pentagon. The five perfect solids are the tetrahedron, cube, octahedron, dodecahedron and icosahedron.

contradictions and inconsistencies. The snowball goes down the hill only until its momentum is expended.

Pythagoras reborn

That point has not yet been reached, but it may not be very far away. In mathematics, and in related fields and disciplines, certain aspects of Pythagorean thinking are enjoying a renaissance. Platonic terminology may still look quaint, but an increasing number of people begin to realise that it refers to realities; that there is an intrinsic, functional difference between 'square', 'rectangular' and 'triangular' numbers; that the laws of harmony are universally applicable to the physical world; and that these are consonant with human experience and demonstrable. And as it becomes recognised that this curious, old terminology conceals truths, it may also become more apparent that much unquestioned modern terminology conceals fiction. Consider 'natural selection', for example, which cannot account for the origin of species without calling in the aid of 'mutation' (which is a mystery); or 'survival value' and 'biological advantage', which are tautologies: what exists, no matter how apparently ill-suited to survive, evidently has 'survival value' and 'biological advantage', no matter that a thousand seemingly more efficient creatures have long since met a mysterious extinction. This is explicable only by again calling in the same tautology: they became extinct because they did not have, or lost, their 'biological advantage'.

Having recognised a need to revise our conceptions of number, geometry and harmony, we can then turn back to Egypt, the source of Platonic and Pythagorean ideas and of a civilisation in which these ideas and precepts ruled for four thousand years.

Harmony, today, is taught only to music students, and then simply as the basis of music, with no suggestion that this purely mathematical arrangement has universal significance. I have already gone into the limitations (from a Pythagorean standpoint) of our geometrical and mathematical education.

In trying to present a panoramic view of the Symbolists' Egypt, I am faced with a problem to which there seems to be no solution. All but a (purely hypothetical) handful of readers will come to Pythagorean thinking as I came to it myself — in a state of pristine ignorance. And it is not that the geometrical, numerical and harmonic bases of Egyptian thought are particularly difficult. They are not — no more difficult than, say, advanced geometry. To a certain cast of mind, they are far less difficult than algebra or calculus. But to understand Egyptian thought, one must proceed step by step. And this step by step procedure must occupy a hundred pages or so of text. Like any geometry, you cannot 'read' the subject, you have to study it. Schwaller de Lubicz's work is in effect unreadable: it is meant to be studied. This book is meant to be read.

I should have liked to present a précis version that would yet convey an insight into the actual operating procedures. But I will only be able to write about the Symbolists' Egypt, selecting specific samples of the documentation to show the kind of evidence this radical reinterpretation rests upon.

The whole of Egyptian civilisation, over the course of its four-thousand-year history, must be regarded as a single ritual gesture, an act of homage to the divine mystery of creation. Unity, in taking consciousness of itself, unfolds into a created multiplicity and thereby into the universe.

Tum, in regarding himself, creates Atum out of Nun, the primeval waters. The 'big bang' theory, which sees the universe as a physical event resulting out of a critical build-up of purely physical forces, is a trivialised, de-spiritualised version of this myth. Egypt created a civilisation upon it.

Christianity expresses the Egyptian revelation as God the Father, God the Son and God the Holy Ghost. And while fundamentalists vehemently affirm the literal truth of the virgin birth, and science as vehemently denies it, in this aspect of esoteric cosmology, the virgin may be regarded as equivalent to Nut, the 'sky', the (necessarily) virgin matrix of principial substance.

The Primordial Scission provokes a situation that can be schematized by geometry. We can show that this single act automatically sets in motion the sequence of whole numbers and of the 'irrationals' (which we represent as diagonals). Irrationals are not to be regarded as numbers, or as a special class of number, but as functions; *diagonals define the interactions between numbers*. And intimately linked to number symbolism and geometry are the various harmonic scales, which may be shown — either geometrically or mathematically — to be derived from the numbers set in play by the Primordial Scission.

Harmony rapidly becomes extremely complex, and perhaps because of this obscures for our senses its fundamental role in the creation of 'form'. It is harmony that is responsible for the specific physical phenomena that scientists call 'reality', but that wiser men realise is but the physical aspect of reality to which our senses have access. We speak of musical 'form'. We know it is the result of harmonies that may be reduced to vibrations — that is to say, to number. But we tend to think of musical 'form' metaphorically, whereas we should regard it literally. Sound *is* volume. From the modern point of view we say sound 'fills' space; it is therefore scientifically 'volume'. From the point of view of the more accurate esoteric science, we would say that sound is volume, and therefore sound *is*

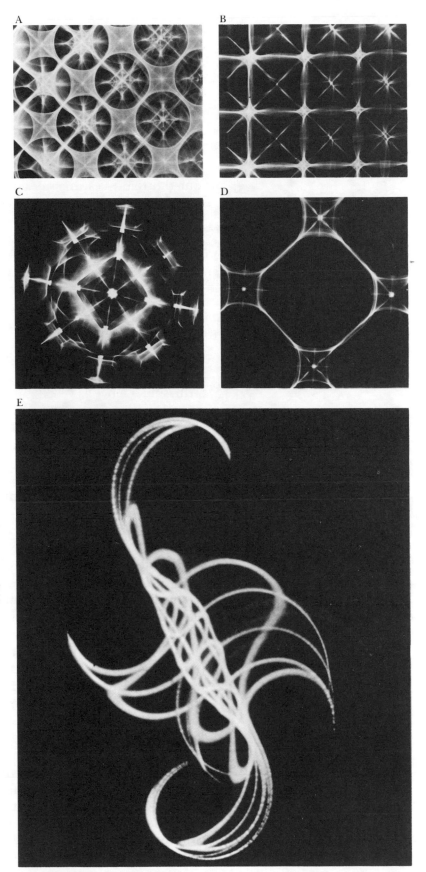

Cymatics, the study of wave forms, illustrates dramatically the relationship between frequency and form. Specific materials subjected to specific vibrations assume specific forms. A given form can only be summoned forth at its corresponding frequency; form is a response to frequency. Form is what we call 'reality' but that reality is obviously conditional — for it is the structure of our organs of perception that is responsible for the ultimate picture. If our senses were differently attuned, reality would assume a very different aspect. We might perceive matter as motion if our senses were quicker; if they were slower, we would be aware of the apparent motion of the sun, and our whole world would appear to be motion.

Vibration is an alternation between positive and negative poles. Metaphysically, it is a manifestation of the revolt of spirit against its imprisonment in matter. In Egypt, Ptah, creator of forms, is shown bound in mummy cloth.

Cymatics gives visual expression to 'In the beginning was the Word' — or more accurately, 'Verb'.

In A, B, C and D, oil of turpentine has been subjected to vibrations and the resulting pattern photographed. The pattern prevails throughout, and can be photographed on a microscopic level. E represents an electron beam subjected to two opposing magnetic fields.

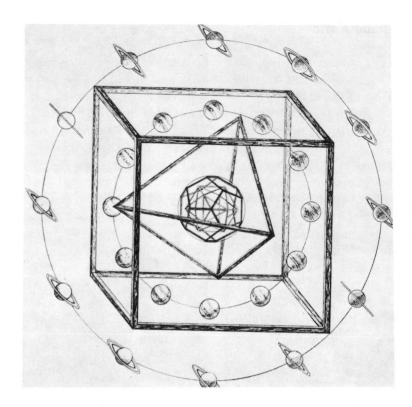

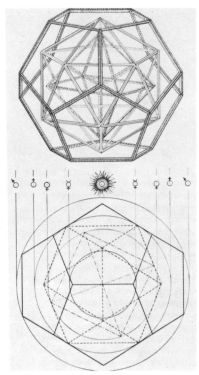

Since modern physicists now understand that matter is not a 'thing' but a state or pattern of energy describable by mathematics, it is clear the Pythagoreans were right in declaring 'All is Number'. They were also right in assuming there to be valid analogies of form and function. But the physical world tends not to respond as precisely as Pythagoreans would like. Kepler tried to work out a relationship between the perfect or 'Platonic' solids and the orbits of the planets. But the planets were not sufficiently co-operative to convince modern astronomers of the validity of the results. Still, the last word has not yet been said; more sophisticated inquiry may yet bear out some of Kepler's insights.

space. In either case, it is volume. It is as literally 'form' as is a cat or a cathedral; all are the result of an interplay of harmonics, ultimately number. The Absolute expresses itself through number (the Neters), and number is the divine language: a cat is a poem or sonata by God — literally.

Form and frequency

Irremediably for the literal-minded, there is empirical evidence demonstrating this direct relationship between frequency and form. The study dubbed by its founder, Hans Jenny, 'cymatics' (the study of wave forms) dramatically illustrates this esoteric dictum. Different kinds of material subjected to specific sound frequencies assume specific patterns and shapes — and these patterns and shapes occur only at these specific frequencies. No one can yet answer why or in what fashion these forms relate to the given frequencies responsible for calling them into being. But the fact that form and frequency are intimately tied is now indisputable.

This throws new light onto certain ancient sayings currently regarded as merely poetic or fanciful. In ancient Egypt, the 'words' of Ra revealed through Thoth (the Egyptian Hermes, or Mercury) become the things and creatures of this world.

Word and world

St. John's Gospel begins, 'In the beginning was the Word, and the Word was with God, and the Word was God.' The Egyptian *Book of the Dead*, the oldest written text in the world, contains a striking parallel passage. 'I am the Eternal, I am Ra . . . I am that which created the Word . . . I am the Word . . .'* Esoterically, the role of 'The Word' would be clearer if Logos were translated as 'The Verb', as it is in French.

The 'Word' (any word) is scientifically a vibrational complex. Though the esoteric meaning of John's powerful but paradoxical sentence has been understood by many Christian mystics, and masterfully explained within a medieval context by Meister Eckhardt, its precise scientific, Pythagorean meaning has been lost. Conceivably it was not understood even by its author; though it is equally possible the choice of poetic over philosophical language was deliberate (witness the dilemma Plato and later Plotinus were in, trying to express these concepts in the discursive philosophical language of the time).

Today, in modern terminology, we can say: at the incomprehensible and, by human faculties, unimaginable but nevertheless expressible and logically necessary instant of the Primordial Scission, the Absolute in becoming conscious of itself created the manifest universe, whose fundamental formative aspect is vibration, a wave phenomenon characterised by movement of variable frequency and intensity between oppositely charged poles. This movement is not to be considered as separate or distinct from the poles but rather as that which by its existence produces or compels the significance of the respective poles, since negativity and positivity require an underlying concept of opposition/affinity in order to render them meaningful; the three aspects or forces thereby are assumed as inherent within the original unity, which is the Absolute or transcendent cause. (This may not be an improvement upon St. John.)

In Egypt, art, science, philosophy and religion were aspects or facets of a complete understanding, and were employed simultaneously: there was no Egyptian art without science, no philosophy that was not religious. Central to this complete understanding was the knowledge that man, through his faculties and physique, represented the created image of all creation. And Egyptian symbolism and all measures were therefore simultaneously scaled to man, to the earth, and ultimately to the solar system.

Egyptologists puzzle without success over the curious system employed in Egypt for weights and measures, and of

* P. Barguet, *Le Livre des Morts*, Ed. du Cert, 1967 (p.123).

C.H. Nims
'Problems of the Moscow Mathematical Papyrus'
Journal of Egyptian Archaeology, 44 p. 65

From English measures, using one archaic term and three from modern cookerybook usages, we can, on the basis of one *hekat* = 1 Imperial British Gallon, give equivalent names for all the fractional measures. The series is: 1 gallon, one pottle = 1/2, 1 quart = 1/4, one pint = 1/8, one cup(ful) = 1/16, one gill = 1/32, one glass = 1/64, one tablespoon(ful) = 1/320 = 1 *ro*, 1 teaspoon(ful) (U.S.) = 1/3 *ro*. Putting at the beginning of the series 1 Hogshead = 100 gallons (British molasses measure. 1749, OED) and one keg = 10 gallons (an arbitrary figure) we could write the answer to Moscow Problem 20, 133 1/3 *hekat* as 1 hogshead, 3 kegs, 3 gallons, 1 quart, 1 cup, 1 tablespoon and 2 teaspoons . . .

course assume that our modern decimal system is an improvement upon all that has gone before. Schwaller de Lubicz is not alone in challenging certain aspects of this assumption. Even within the Egyptological camp, the Egyptologist and mathematician C. H. Nims has pointed out that, if nothing else, Egyptian measures have withstood a severe test of time. Until recently most of these measures were in current usage (under non-Egyptian names) the world over.

Though it may be easier to *calculate* in decimals, it is difficult to *work* conveniently with the measures dictated by this system. The most brilliant scientist cannot easily visualise 117.46 liters. But any peasant can visualise precisely five gallons, two quarts, one pint and four tablespoons.

The mathematician C. Laville (A. 1, vol. 1., p. 209) has discussed the manifold advantages of nondecimal systems. 'Insofar as man has lived taking as guide his organic impulses and his constitutional tendencies, that is to say before the great civilizations have made of him a creature nearly entirely divorced from nature, he employed nondecimal systems. The most elegant of his *artificial* creations was the establishment of 10 as the base for his calculations . . . . The decimal system is in permanent conflict with our natural tendencies, it is out of rapport with our make-up . . . the natural way to multiply is to double, as 2, 4, 8 . . .'

This of course is the system to which Egypt adhered throughout its history. And, incidentally, today we find the new science of cybernetics returning to a binary system of numbers. Computers are binary as well. As is so often the case, what is most advanced in science and mathematics proves to be a return to ancient ways, but with this crucial difference: modern scientists and mathematicians rarely have a vision of the whole of which their specialised knowledge is but a part, and accordingly their 'solutions' are stopgaps in an infinite regress of crises and exigencies. The sages of Egypt knew exactly what they were doing, and why; no aspect of their knowledge is divorced from any other aspect.

Measure, volume and the eye

Egyptian measures and volumes refer both to man and to the earth, and the symbolic means Egypt chose to express her measures reflects her profound understanding of the relationships between the measures themselves and those human faculties that allow man to measure in the first place. Perhaps the most striking and convincing example of this is the eye, Ouadjit.

The eye gives man access to space, to volume, hence to measure. In Egypt, the symbol of the eye is comprised of those symbols that stand for the various fractions of the *hekat*. The

The eye gives access to space, that is to say volume, and therefore to measure. In Egypt, the sections of the eye are the glyphs for the fractions 1/2 to 1/64. The parts total 63/64. [The sum of successive division will always fall short of unity except at infinity, which is perfectly consonant with Egyptian thought: only the Absolute is one.]

 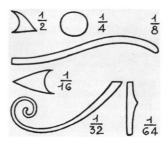

symbols total up to 63/64 (for the sum of a series of fractions of unity will never equal unity).

The symbols for the parts derive from the myth in which the eye of Horus is torn to bits by Set. Later Thoth miraculously reunites the bits.

Apart from the *hekat*, other Egyptian measures are also based upon cosmic considerations. They relate to each other harmonically, geometrically and mathematically. They link man to both time and space. For the sage, they mean perpetual renewal of conscious revelation in the exercise of the tasks of everyday life. For the ordinary man, uninterested in direct spiritual experience and incapable of being sufficiently aroused to work toward that higher state of consciousness variously called 'grace', 'samadhi' and 'nirvana', the unconscious but persistent use of cosmically significant weights and measures assures him of contact with certain aspects of higher realities, no matter that he is unaware of them.

The theological considerations that pervade every aspect of Egyptian thought and practice guaranteed a society in which practically every private and public gesture in some way touched upon deliberately imposed harmonies, from the size of a beer mug to the shape of a pyramid. With us it is exactly the opposite. We are born into dissonances and live out our lives in grotesque surroundings whose forms have been dictated by specious considerations of utility and economy. As mentioned earlier, in the digression on secrecy, the grosser consequences of progress are now becoming susceptible of measurement. The most advanced scientists have now advanced to the stage where their data have forced them to agree with the nineteenth-century artists and poets (such as Blake, Novalis and Melville) who could feel the consequences but could not measure them.

Recognition of the real physical and psychological effects of the ambiance within which people live provokes a number of questions concerning the art and architecture of Egypt.

The desert climate of Egypt has preserved more of its art than any other civilisation has preserved of its own. So it is impossible to say if others were as committed to artistic aims. On the face of it, with the possible exception of the unknown constructors of Machu Picchu in the Andes, no other civilisation has practised art and architecture more skilfully or in comparable magnitude.

Apart from the medical and mathematical papyri our knowledge of Egypt is largely derived from a study of its art and architecture. But since it is clear that the Egyptians were not building to satisfy the curiosity of later scholars, it is essential that we examine Egyptian art and architecture from a fresh point of view to try to fathom her motives for producing it (which are evidently dissimilar to the motives behind our own) and also, if possible, to try to understand the practical consequences of this intense artistic concern.

Art old and new

Generally speaking, the modern world regards art as a luxury. The doctrine of evolution precludes the possibility of objective values beyond that of biological survival, which is not a value in any ethical or philosophical sense, but an inevitable consequence of 'selection pressure'. As an extension of this philosophy, all that contributes to raising the 'standard of living' (up to a certain indefinable point) has a utilitarian value.

Once the demands of utility have been met, there is time for leisure activities, of which art is one — important perhaps, but in no sense essential, certainly not to the survival of the species.

But 'utility' is an emotionally loaded word. In speaking of art as nonutilitarian, there is an automatic connotation of superfluity. Even Schwaller de Lubicz follows the convention of referring to art as nonutilitarian.

But from the Egyptian point of view our concept of utility is naive.

The aim of all human existence is the return to the source. This is the message of Egypt, and of all other initiatic teachings. We are here, according to these teachings, to work to regain that higher state of consciousness that is our birthright. If we fail to fulfill this responsibility, then our biological survival is of no particular importance, and our preoccupation with utility meaningless. Whatever contributes to the acquisition of consciousness is useful. Building a pyramid or a Temple of Luxor is useful. Building an airport, flying to the moon, improving the standard of living beyond what is strictly necessary to satisfy our real physical needs . . . all of that is useless. It is Art that is useful. Progress, all technological advance, is by this definition, a frivolity.

Though it is apparent that man's love of personal wealth and splendor was not absent from ancient Egypt (periodically, a corrupt priesthood and bureaucracy appropriated the riches of Egypt for themselves), over the long course of her history

Egypt was to some extent successful at keeping the lives of her people simple and uncomplicated, while devoting the great proportion of her talents and wealth to the execution of religious art and architecture.

Through the study of Egyptian art and architecture Schwaller de Lubicz was able to recover the wisdom of a self-perpetuating group of initiates ('the Temple') who were responsible for keeping that body of wisdom intact throughout Egypt's history and of manifesting it in her works. It is this, according to Schwaller de Lubicz — and not a hypothetical innate conservatism — that explains the amazing coherence of Egyptian art throughout its long history. The charge can be levelled that the postulated 'Temple' is equally hypothetical. But since Egypt's sciences, language and amazing technical skills were all complete at the very beginnings of her history, then either the Egyptians must have been bold experimenters to have acquired this extraordinary skill and knowledge (in which case, the sudden change to 'extreme conservatism' is inexplicable) or, as Schwaller de Lubicz and many unorthodox sources believe, the wisdom of Egypt is a carry-over from a prior, lost civilization (in which case the mere ability to keep so vast a body of knowledge intact and perpetuating implies a dedicated and deliberate organisation). Certain primitive tribes may be cited as conservative corollaries, but in fact anthropologists do not actually have four-thousand-year histories of any of these tribes. Their myths and legends often indicate changes, times at which their organisation was not what it now is; and most significantly, none of these tribes built an equivalent of the Pyramid of Cheops or of the Temple of Luxor. Their 'conservatism' is not applicable to Egypt.

Egyptian art

To understand Egyptian art, we must first carefully distinguish between it and our own.

In the Western world, 'art' means something different to everyone: it is 'self-expression', 'social comment', 'art for art's sake', 'a means for radicalising the masses' or 'an instrument for providing aesthetic pleasure'. In short, to us, 'art' is but seldom what it is meant to be, and what it has always been: a means of playing upon human faculties in such a way as to provoke a consciousness of superhuman realities — of the realm beyond the senses.

In every great ancient civilisation, art has been used to further understanding, to lead men and women to a higher experience of reality than they might be able to achieve individually left to their own devices. Art is not meant to be 'enjoyed', it is meant to illuminate. In Egypt, we are nevertheless impressed by the harmoniousness of proportion and the orderliness of composition, even though aesthetic satisfaction is merely a side effect, a by-product of the interplay of number (which, utilising complex harmonic principles, evokes in us a corresponding awareness of that harmony).

Unfortunately, this distinction doesn't mean much unless we have personally experienced, even for only a moment, the effects of this higher art. Not many of us have.

We have no civilisation of our own, and therefore very little real art. Since the Renaissance (which was no more a 'rebirth' than the Enlightenment was an 'illumination'), there has been no art in this traditional sense. A few individual men of genius, after immense personal struggle, have broken through into this transcendent realm. Their work conveys the intensity (but never the magnitude) of a Chartres, a Taj Mahal, a Luxor. And while the simplest peasants and artisans feel the impact of these old structures, the greatest modern Western works are inaccessible to the multitudes — and, judging from criticism written by 'authorities', even more inaccessible to specialists. Not everyone can read a Dostoyevsky novel. You may dutifully listen to a Beethoven late quartet over and over, and hear nothing but vigorous scraping until one day something clicks and you know that you are in the midst of a drama in which inexorable cosmic forces are pitted against one another.

The rest of Western art does not succeed — and seldom pretends — to such heights. At its best it is a kind of commendable journalism of acute observations — ultimately a glorification of precisely those aspects of daily life that, according to all initiatic teachings, are worth observing only so that they are recognised as obstacles to be overcome. At its more common worst, Western art is egotism or neurosis, or both.

Generally, Egyptologists and art historians take an ambivalent stance toward the art of Egypt. They recognise the perfection of technique and the magnitude of the works. (The Pyramid of Cheops uses more stone than all churches of England built since the time of Christ; the pyramid complex of Zoser is the largest single-purpose monument ever built by man.) But Egypt is severely taken to task for its 'conservatism', its lack of originality; scholars commiserate with the oppressed Egyptian artist, forced by theological considerations to stifle his creative urge. Occasionally, a gentle voice is raised in protest, calling for us to suspend judgment when faced by the works of a culture as alien to us as Egypt. This sounds generous and tolerant, but it is also nonsense. Unless we happen to be saints or Zen masters we are incapable of suspending judgment about anything that affects us emotionally in any way whatsoever. This is an unpleasant truth to face, and the illusion of an open mind is commonly cherished by the most hermetically sealed minds. The best we can do, faced with an alien culture, is to recognise that we *do* judge, and therefore try to make allowances for our necessarily subjective views.

As for creativity, originality and the vaunted 'freedom of expression' that are allegedly so vital to the artist, they too are largely illusions. More often than not their importance is stressed not so much by artists as by scholars, art historians and aestheticians — who are not themselves artists. It is true that the dogma of 'free self-expression' is thoroughly ingrained in our upbringing, and most artists unthinkingly pay homage to it. But if we look closely at the methods employed by a good modern artist, even by one considered 'abstract', we soon see that, in the absence of a set canon or a theological imperative, the artist seeks, often desperately, to establish a personal 'style'.

But what is 'style'? It is at once an expression of the artist's personality and a personal set of *rules*. And the artist then proceeds to work within that set of rules, exploring every possibility. Without it, he cannot work at all. If he sets out with the intellectual determination to follow no rules at all, then the result — as with John Cage, William Burroughs and other avant-garde practitioners — is chaos, not art. To say that the intention is to create chaos, in order to capture the spirit of the age, begs the issue. For, as chaos, these creations are not particularly disturbing. To create artistic chaos, chaos that drives men to despair in as short a time as it takes to read a book, view a painting or listen to a piece of music, it is necessary to make deliberate use of effective disharmonies: to know which disharmonies will create the desired effect, the artist must first know, or at least feel, the harmonic laws that require breaking.

The desirability of 'artistic freedom' is by no means self-evident. And if we look at art in terms of the result (surely the most valid way to look), it becomes possible to put forward a strong case *against* personal freedom of artistic expression. I shall not develop this case further, however, since there is, in fact, a valid case to be made for it. But the latter is not based upon the usual considerations. It is based upon the inherent specific nature of the activities proper to succeeding precessional ages. That is to say, the ages of Taurus, Aries, Pisces, and shortly, Aquarius, demand (by their nature, by the organic unfolding and development of human faculties) different means and modes of expression.

Meanwhile, it is important not to lose sight of the distinction between art produced under tyranny — the vapid, ideological stillbirths of Communist Russia and China — and art produced under the directives of an esoteric tradition, which bequeaths to us the prodigies of Egypt, the Gothic cathedrals, and the Taj Mahal.

Art, clarity and logic

This distinction made, viewing the notion of 'freedom of expression' with some caution, we are in a position to look afresh at Egyptian art and at the motivation behind it, which also is dissimilar to ours.

Possibly the best approach to this new look is to first examine in some detail the way *not* to look at the art of Egypt. To this aim, it is enough to analyse a single paragraph from a famous magazine article by a renowned archaeologist, N. F. Wheeler. The article, 'Pyramids and their Purpose', appeared in *Antiquity* in 1935.

This article is regarded in Egyptological circles as having put the coup de grace to the then still quivering carcass of pyramidology. The conclusions of the author are all, according to the author, arrived at through the exercise of 'sound archaeological evidence' and 'common sense'.

Wheeler is talking about the artists of the earliest dynasties of Egypt. 'There is no doubt that the Egyptians of the Pyramid Age were a very remarkable people, and that they had developed exceptional technical and artistic skill. They were clear and logical thinkers, systematic in all they did; they were persevering and remarkably accurate in executing plans given them, being in no way satisfied with 'near enough' . . . They were in no way afraid of tackling the most difficult mediums in which to work, and preferred them at this time (the Pyramid Age) to more easily worked materials.'

This is innocuous enough at first glance; if you came across it in a university textbook you would let it slip by unquestioned and unnoticed.

Yet it is a psychological non sequitur, and betrays a perfect disregard for that faculty allegedly responsible for engendering it — that is, 'common sense'.

In what way does 'clear, logical thinking' lead artists to work with difficult rather than easy materials? The end result is to be a statue or temple which will look more or less the same whatever the material employed. The African Bushman, enjoined by some progressive busybody to turn to agriculture, replies : 'Why should we plant when there are so many mongo-mongo nuts in the world?'

That is common sense, a perfect example of 'clear, logical thinking'. Our own brand of common sense would lead us to an identical conclusion. Why make unnecessary work for ourselves?

The obvious technical and artistic mastery of Early Kingdom temples presupposes clear thinking of some sort. But what kind of 'logic' dictates a preference for working with difficult material?

To comprehend the motives of the Egyptians, we must look

away from logic. There we find a number of possibilities.

The first, most obvious one, is that the Egyptians were interested in durability, hence worked in granite and diorite rather than limestone — a choice that perhaps involves a philosophical outlook, not logic.

Seemingly plausible, this possibility is ruled out in the main by a study of Egyptian methods. These granite and diorite statues were often installed in temples built of much softer stone, and the temples themselves were often built upon foundations that were downright shoddy.

Reasoning along Western lines, Egyptologists conclude that these were economy measures. But as Schwaller de Lubicz points out, the fantastic care and detail (therefore expense) with which the rest of the temple was finished precludes an economic motive. So durability alone could not have been responsible.

If logic or durability did not dictate the choice of material, then two choices remain.

The first is that for some reason the Egyptians felt that the artistic end product justified the additional labour. What could that reason be? The Egyptian artist was not free to choose his material or his subject. Thus, it would seem that those in command deliberately chose difficult mediums in order to create difficulties for their artists. As I have mentioned, it is universal law, dictated by the necessities of number, that achievement takes place only in the face of commensurate opposition.

By forcing artists to work with the most intractable materials (and by deliberately avoiding the development of a complex technology to facilitate the task), the sages of Egypt provided their artists with a challenge that gave them an opportunity to achieve a pitch of mastery they might never achieve left to their own devices.

Western artists, even great ones, are seldom thinkers. We often find, when the best of our artists discuss their own work, they have not thought the matter through, while the thinkers and theorizers — who cannot write a novel or paint a painting or compose a symphony — do not and cannot speak out of experience, so that their ideas must be treated with caution. Who would trust a cookbook written by an 'authority' who has never fried an egg?

Art for whom?

The chief beneficiary of art is the artist. He can put into his work only as much as he personally understands. In the exercise of his art, he develops his understanding.

In Western terms, 'communication' is so important an

aspect of art that we can scarcely envisage an art that was not intended to 'communicate', as we understand that word. If a modern writer writes a novel or a play, he fully intends that it should be read or seen. Nevertheless, you may be certain that if you read it or see it and learn something from it, he has learned much more from the doing of it. Still, it is a hit-or-miss affair.

If the Western artist, through a combination of talent and discipline, comes upon an understanding of himself and his motives, he may produce a late quartet or a *Brothers Karamazov*. On the other hand, if he doesn't, he blathers on for the rest of his life about his unhappy childhood or racial problems, and he learns nothing worth knowing.

In Egypt, the anonymous sages were the artists, in our modern inspirational sense. They designed the temples and the statues and the wall friezes. The sculptors, painters and masons were but interpretive artists, this is true. But there is no ignominy in this position. We do not think the violin virtuoso 'repressed' because he must play Beethoven's or Bartok's notes. Moreover, within the restriction of the imposed piece, there is ample opportunity for the exercise of creativity — otherwise all virtuosos at a given level of professionalism would sound the same. And if the virtuoso is a real virtuoso, then he will share in Beethoven's revelation.

The Egyptian artist was precisely in this position, but more fortunate: he didn't have to endlessly play Schumann and 'A Night in Old Vienna' to get at the occasional Quartet in C Sharp Minor. Rather he was constrained to work upon forms imposed by cosmic, harmonic law, and the successful completion of his task ensured the enrichment of his own understanding in those aspects of specific wisdom.

These massive works were designed from the onset to provide insights into the wisdom of the temple, upon every level from the humblest quarryman to the master sculptor, painter and mason.

Leaf through any pictorial survey of Egyptian art and architecture, and you will get some idea of the magnitude and mastery of their works; a moment's reflection will give some insight into the encompassing nature of the activity that must have been required to produce it. Then, if instead of passively accepting the orthodox conclusion that all of this was the product of organised delusion carried out to satisfy priestly and pharaonic megalomania, we look at it as a continuous exercise in the development of individual consciousness, we will be coming somewhere close to what must have been one aspect of Egyptian motivation.

Today, technology deprives the mass of men from deriving satisfaction from work. Sociologists blandly assure us that this is part of the price that must be paid for 'progress'. It is nevertheless true that even under modern conditions a few inventive, heroic souls create challenge out of occupations that contain no inherent challenge. But the mass of men cannot. And this is a contributory cause to the product that is twentieth-century man: devoid of direction, faith or understanding, his head stuffed with facts, his only response to the inevitable stirrings of humanity within him violence, sex, or apathy.

Egypt organised matters otherwise. And in view of her works, it should come as no surprise that ancient Greek

Napoleon's artists' impression of the Temple of Denderah in operation. Given a degree of latitude for romantic imagination, this probably conveys the idea better than any photograph, perspective allowing the artist to do what the camera lens cannot.

sources — written at a time when Egypt was no longer supreme militarily, and was, relative to her former position, decadent artistically — report that the Egyptians were the happiest, healthiest and most religious of races. Since there is no particular reason to suppose these Greek sources were gulling their audiences, there is no reason not to take these reports at face value. And we need only look around us today, at the innumerable but invariably evanescent tyrannies to check if people are happy and healthy, to say nothing of religious,

under such regimes.

Since we cannot actually suspend our judgment, we can at least recognise our incapacity and look at this alien art aware of what we are doing.

We must also recognise that apart from the alien system of hieroglyphs, mythology and the Neters, in no instance can we experience Egyptian art intact. We have perfectly preserved statues, friezes and other individual items, impressive in their own right. But these were always meant to be seen in the context of the completed temple (when they were intended for the public and not for the tombs in which they served symbolic, magical purposes). And this we can no longer experience intact. Extensive as the Egyptian ruins may be, they are still ruins.

The colors have gone, the walls have crumbled, the roofs have fallen. We can only imagine what it must have been like when, on one specific day of the year, and that day only, at sunrise a shaft of light travelled through an opened door down the eight-hundred-foot-long narthex of the temple, throwing into blazing relief a single colossus of white stone — and this in the midst of ritual, chanting and incense, all designed to a single purpose, all formulated according to specific harmonic laws.

Because Egyptian art is not based upon individual inspiration as we know it but upon knowledge, and because that knowledge is written into the ruins in proportion, hieroglyphs and myth (all of which devolve upon the significance of number), we are in a position, following Schwaller de Lubicz, to backtrack, and in our modern piecemeal way, uncover the many-layered aspects of Egyptian wisdom.

We are now a long way from those 'clear, logical thinkers' who preferred to use difficult rather than easy materials. Still, we have not yet touched upon the most important aspect of Egyptian art and architecture: the purpose served by the finished product.

We have at our disposal the extensive ruins of a society that, over the course of four millennia, expended its resources upon art in the service of religion. (Strictly speaking, what Schwaller de Lubicz calls the Egyptian 'Temple' is a more complex and more comprehensive organisation than religion as we understand that word today, but for lack of a more precise word, 'religion' will have to serve.)

Though it is obvious I cannot 'prove' that this organised art served artists as an exercise in the development of consciousness, analogies drawn to statements by the best modern artists make this a plausible assumption: it is in no way essential that art 'communicate' in order to justify itself.

Even today there is a kind of 'art' that is intended to guide the performer along the road to consciousness, though we tend not to think of this as 'art' but rather as exercise or discipline. Into this category of art fall Zen archery and painting, tea-making and the martial arts, and the dances of the Dervishes and of the temple dancers of India and Bali. With the possible exception of Zen painting, these arts are not meant to 'communicate'. Watch a Dervish dance and you get nothing from it. Try to do a Dervish dance and you will be in for a big surprise.

But much of the art of Egypt seems to fall neither into this category nor into the Western category of 'communication'. If we allow that all art that is not mere self-expression is an exercise in the development of consciousness, we still cannot quite account for Egypt.

Art as 'magic'

Certainly Egypt had its dancers, musicians and warriors, and it is virtually certain that they performed these activities Zen-fashion. The Roman writer Lucian talks of Egyptian mimes who expressed the deepest religious mysteries through gestures. Relics of these dance forms are believed to exist in the music played today by the Copts. And it is clear that in all Egyptian painting, careful attention is paid to ritual gestures.

These Old Kingdom ritual dance movements are curiously similar to those practiced today in certain groups devoted to 'inner development'.

But even accepting art and artisanship as legitimate, consciousness-expanding activities, we are at a loss to account for the Egyptian motives for burying all those masterpieces in tombs never meant to be opened. What was the point of it?

To the modern mind, the Egyptian preoccupation with death, funerary rites and the afterlife is unqualified superstition. But if we reflect that the quality of modern life is a direct corollary of the quality of understanding of those who shape it (scientists, educators, media men; to a lesser degree, artists; and to a still lesser degree, politicians and the public itself), we may then be prepared to challenge any and all prevailing assumptions which cannot be substantiated by iron-clad proof. For example, having looked at the evidence offered, we can safely agree with science that the world is round, but in no way are we obliged to accept scientific opinion of such subjects as reincarnation or the journeys of the soul after death — even if science asserts its views with as much assurance as it does concerning the roundness of the earth.

The themes central to the art and architecture of Egypt are reincarnation, resurrection and the journey of the soul in the

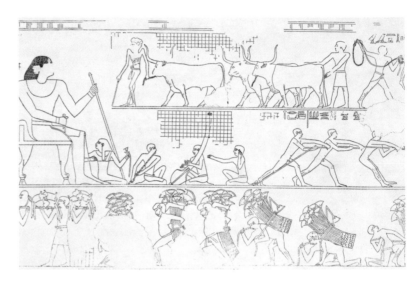

Scenes from daily life which scholars regard as a kind of light relief from the obsessive theology of Egypt. But these scenes are no less spiritual in intent and content. The king, earthly representative of cosmic or 'developed' man, is always concerned with wholly spiritual matters; scenes of arts and crafts occur only on the tombs of nobles and commoners, but symbolise the attainment of the spiritual through the agency of the material. As in those scenes devoted to theology, details have an inner significance and are not arbitrarily chosen.

Ancient Egypt did not have the cinema, but the principle was understood. Note the papyrus gatherer in the bottom register. He is moving through more time than it takes to gather a single bunch of papyrus, since he is young at the beginning and ages in each 'frame'. He has also carefully taken note of the single bent stalk and, as he stands upright, supports it with his hand. This is a symbolic representation of one aspect of the life of Ouk-hotep, vizier to Sesostris I [Twelfth Dynasty, 2000 — 1788 BC], who was evidently a man of supreme accomplishment: 'Unique confidant, Treasurer, Great Chief of the Priests of Hathor, Mistress of Cusa, Scribe of the Divine Books, Master of all Sceptres and Costumes, 'unique of his kind and without rival', he who masters the secrets that only one knows.'

Colin Blakemore
in *The Listener*, 11 Nov. 1976, p. 596

Persistence of the soul beyond mere physical death is an almost universal tenet of religions and philosophies. It is not, I believe, an expression of man's selfishness alone; it is the inevitable cultural formulation of the most basic and most essential requirement of any living thing — the desire to survive. In Darwin's theory, it was amply fulfilled by successful and abundant self-reproduction. To the egocentric Platonists, re-incarnation was needed, too . . . Transmigration of the soul is not,

underworld. The fact is that science knows nothing of these matters. Its beliefs, however strongly held and expressed, are without substance. It is also a fact that these themes are central to the beliefs of other old civilisations, all of which evidently managed their societies far more successfully than ours. Given the state of our ignorance in these areas, we are free to choose between the conclusions of the opposed authorities, neither of which are, or can be, supported by hard evidence; I, for one, would sooner take instruction about the human soul from the constructors of Luxor than from the inventors of napalm.

Bearing in mind that modern physics has shown matter and the physical world to be but a form of energy, there is no commanding reason not to suppose that those abused and misty words 'soul' and 'spirit' may well be meaningful.

To deal adequately with reincarnation, resurrection, magic, symbolism, soul and spirit lies outside the scope of this book. The simple point I make is that our own science is sufficiently advanced to destroy once and for all the rationalist's assumption that these matters are necessarily fictions. There is nothing in physical science that makes reincarnation impossible or even improbable. It is a subject outside the framework of science: it is not measurable. Nor is it possible to measure

however, an idea original to Plato, nor is his the most extreme example of the hypothesis. Pythagoras, who probably founded geometry with his theorem about the dimensions of right-angled triangles, thought that, in a previous existence, he had been a bush. The religious philosophy of the Pythagorean brotherhood seems laughable today.

The ceremony of the opening of the mouth of the deceased with an iron hook. This strange ceremony is also common among the Yakouts of eastern Siberia, a people believed originally to come from Turkey. The ceremony is already found in the earliest texts of the Book of the Dead *[Fifth Dynasty] and the reference to an iron hook is specific — which is curious since iron, though known to ancient Egypt, was seldom used. Why, then, an iron hook? Ambitious young Egyptologists can find more interesting questions to answer than the number of asps responsible for Cleopatra's death.*

the peculiar mental state that settles upon measurability as an ultimate criterion. Materialism is a metaphysical stance: a puerile philosophy and a negative faith, but a philosophy and a faith nonetheless. It is not a logical consequence of science.

Like all other initiatic teaching, Egypt held that man's purpose on earth was the return to the source. There were recognised in Egypt two roads to this same goal. The one was the way of Osiris, who represented the cyclic nature of universal process; this was the way of successive reincarnations. The second road was the way of Horus, the direct path to resurrection that the individual might achieve within a single lifetime. It is the Horian way that is the basis of the Christian revelation and, according to Schwaller de Lubicz, the aim of Christianity was to make this direct path available to all who chose to embark upon it, rather than to a small group of select initiates who, in Egypt, comprised 'The Temple'. In this sense, and in this sense only, has there been 'evolution' in human affairs.

Now when death is regarded not (as with us) as an ultimate dissolution, but rather as a transitional (and crucial) stage of a journey, then the apparent Egyptian preoccupation with death becomes exactly the opposite of what it seems to be. It is, in fact, a preoccupation with life in the deepest possible sense.

Because the principles underlying the universe are everywhere the same, analogy is a more accurate, ultimately a more 'scientific' means for arriving at an understanding of phenomena than mere measurement. This is why all sacred teachings make use of parable, analogy, myth and symbol instead of facts. Facts do not aid understanding.

If reincarnation is a reality, then at death the disembodied 'soul' is in a similar situation to the physical seedling, which requires the dissolution of the husk in order to sprout. Like the seedling, the unperfected but viable 'soul' is in a vulnerable position, easily trampled upon and requiring nourishment specific to its needs. In the case of the soul, though, that nourishment is not physical but spiritual. (Hence the worldwide prevalence of elaborate funeral preparations, rites, prayers, and so on.)

To us, of course, the provision of such nourishment is 'magic', and our education, based as it is (even now, after seventy years of relativity theory and quantum physics) upon materialist Victorian conceits, instils in our minds the notion that magic is a synonym for superstition.

Schwaller de Lubicz defines magic as the manipulation of harmonic forces which may lie outside sensory perception and are therefore beyond the pale of possible measurement.

We live, even today, in a magical world.

Art is magic. Its effect cannot be measured and it cannot be comprehended rationally. To some extent, the methodology of art can be measured, broken down into its constituent harmonics, vibrations, wavelengths and rhythms. But this does not and cannot explain the effect produced, which is magical. A transformation of energy has taken place within us. And only an understanding of the meaning of the numbers that govern the rhythms, wavelengths and so on can account for these transformations. We eat a potato. Before long the energy of the potato may be transformed into the energy of thought. That, too, is magic — the magic of the Neters. Our science can take measurements of the quantitative aspects of the phenomenon; the conversion of the potato into thought, or rage, or anger, is a fact. But to account for the *qualitative* aspects of the transformation of energy, science can only fall back on the chicanery of evolutionary jargon: energy is transformed because organisms that could transform energy had a 'biological advantage' over those who could not. This is an imposition of human thinking upon the putatively blind and accidental forces of nature. 'Advantage' implies goal. According to this theory there is no goal.

The purpose of the prodigious artistic and architectural efforts of Egypt was magical. In the temples that magic was public, designed to work its transformations upon the individuals making use of the temple. In the tombs the magic was directed at the disembodied soul of the deceased. Who are we to say it was superstition, that it was misguided, that it did not work?

Viewed this way, the Egyptian preoccupation with 'death' makes sense, although it is still alien to our own preoccupation, which is not even with 'life' but with standards of living. The buildings, statues and friezes of Egypt were meant to bring both living men and the disembodied 'souls' of the dead into the presence of the Neters.

Symbolic art

Finally, we come to symbolism. The whole of Egyptian art is symbolic.

We take a symbol to be something that stands, without particular precision, for something else. In literature, as with Joyce and Virginia Woolf, for example, it is a subjective system of correspondences that means something to its author and may or may not convey a similar meaning to readers. We may take a symbol to be an arbitrary device representing a concept or collection of concepts — the American flag, for example. To us, a symbol has no meaning unless we already know what it is supposed to stand for. Then it serves as a kind of sign or shorthand.

In Egypt, symbolism was a precise science. We have already touched upon the richly appropriate symbol of the serpent for

The scarab beetle, kheper, *symbol of the morning sun, the sun as transforming principle. The scarab lays its eggs in a ball of dung and eventually the larvae appear, as though by spontaneous generation, having nourished themselves on the ball. The analogy to the sun — disappearing at night and appearing in glory in the morning — is clear. The symbol also relates to the function of the sun. In human terms, man's brain is his sun and his transforming principle. Schwaller de Lubicz notes the similarity in form between scarab and human skull.*

the dualizing power. All Egyptian symbols and the hieroglyphs are similarly profound and appropriate. And it is in the study of Egyptian symbolism that we come to appreciate the keen observational (that is to say 'scientific') powers of the Egyptians.

Their symbols are carefully chosen from the natural world, and the chosen symbol is that which best expresses or embodies within it a function or principle. A symbol thus chosen represents that function or principle on all levels simultaneously — from the simplest, most obvious physical manifestation of that function to the most abstract and metaphysical.

Unfortunately, the symbolism of Egypt, perhaps the single most pervasive and striking feature of its civilisation, is also that one which, to us, is least accessible. Even if, following Schwaller de Lubicz, we are able to penetrate to the inner meanings of individual symbols, the chances are that few of us will ever be able to 'read' a text as it was meant to be read. The nature of the symbols, with their manifold meanings, is such that they cannot be read in the linear, sequential fashion that we read a book today; they demand that heightened state of consciousness that today some people experience after years of meditation practice, in which the whole is perceived as a whole.

Sometimes, if we are lucky, we may experience this with a painting or a piece of music. If you know the experience there is no mistaking it, and you will then know the psychological state required to read an Egyptian text as it must be read, even though you cannot expect to partake of it.

But if this direct experience is closed to us, we can still recognise the untenability of the orthodox view, which sees in Egyptian symbolism (and in all Egyptian methods) nothing but a primitive, cumbersome means of going about things that we go about more easily.

Geb, the 'earth god' torn or separated from Nut, the 'sky goddess'. Scientists find these graphic representations of creation primitive, though sometimes charming. But to account for the fact of creation, the same scientists must resort to the phantasmagoria of evolutionary theory, perhaps the most unfounded corpus of superstition ever to infect the human mind. Egypt dealt with the principles behind the facts. Nut, female, is matrix of creation. Geb, male, is fecundating principle. But creation at this level is spiritual, not actual: the phallus is directed at the umbilical cord. Thus the separation of heaven and earth is simultaneously cause and effect.

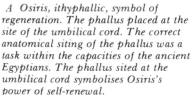

A Osiris, ithyphallic, symbol of
regeneration. The phallus placed at the
site of the umbilical cord. The correct
anatomical siting of the phallus was a
task within the capacities of the ancient
Egyptians. The phallus sited at the
umbilical cord symbolises Osiris's
power of self-renewal.
B Wailing women. Tomb of Ramose.
Note the attention paid to details of
gesture. One gesture is active and is
portrayed with two right hands; one
gesture is receptive and is portrayed with
two left hands. Proof that this is
deliberate is afforded by the figure of the
girl, bottom row, third from left, who
clasps the adult woman with a right and
a left hand.

The Egyptologist, like a good child of the eighteenth century, believes in the credo of facility. A mathematics that is
easier is automatically better; an alphabet that allows everyone
to write whatever he wants is better than a hieroglyphic system
that requires years of training.

We are so used to accepting increased facility as a synonym
for progress that we never question it. It is, however, an arbitrary value judgment.

This concern with facility is called 'common sense'; but actually it is another unthinking genuflection before the altar of
theo-economy, the cargo cult of the West. (Probably, the current worldwide obsession with sport reflects an innate appreciation of excellence, of something performed for its own sake,
the hard way — the challenge that was formerly built in to the
everyday business of living but which has now been wiped out
by technology. The lucky few have an insight into the nature
of the problem and pit themselves against each other or the
clock, while millions watch and get only a vicarious thrill out
of an experience that ought to be their own.)

When we look into Egypt and find certain aspects of their
civilisation unwieldy, conservative or unnecessarily primitive,
we must always remember that their values were not ours. Invariably, when we look closely at their methods, we can see that,
given their aims, the refusal to give up their cumbersome methods, to develop an alphabet or a more advanced technology,
was deliberate, and based upon a deeper understanding of
human nature and of human destiny than we possess.

A

B

C

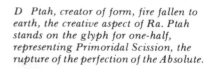

D *Ptah, creator of form, fire fallen to earth, the creative aspect of Ra. Ptah stands on the glyph for one-half, representing Primoridal Scission, the rupture of the perfection of the Absolute.*

D

A *Taming the wild bull. This is no doubt a representation of the method used to actually subdue a bull prepared for sacrifice. At the same time, the wild bull represented untamed inner (usually sexual) power. The actual sacrifice of the bull is a symbolic representation of a necessary inner, spiritual quest.*

B *Hunting scene. Certainly Egyptian greyhounds hunted antelopes in the desert. But the antelope was also one of the many creatures belonging to Set [perhaps because it characteristically flees before the enemy?], so the hunting scenes symbolise one aspect of the victory over the forces of Set.*

C *It does not seem likely that in daily life, the keepers of the kennels exercised their greyhounds and their monkeys simultaneously. But the animal forces within man must be kept reined together. It is of no use to walk the dogs while the monkey pulls apart the orchard.*

A

B

*The net for catching wild birds.
Egyptologists think such scenes no more
than charming representations of daily
life. But when [as at Edfu] the net
contains not only birds but bound
captive prisoners and animals, it is clear
the net has another meaning. In B, the
net is drawn by the king in the company
of three Neters, which seems a curious
way to spend one's daily life, even in
Egypt. Schwaller de Lubicz found that
the net was also based upon extremely
interesting geometrical proportions.
Wild birds are in fact trapped by this
method, but the 'wild birds' here are
symbols of spirit, which man, in the
quest for inner mastery, must trap.*

Summary

Let us now look briefly at specific aspects of Egyptian science,
symbolism, myth and literature as interpreted by Schwaller de
Lubicz and some others. But because this digression into the
meaning and purpose of Egyptian art has taken so long,
because reading is a linear process, and points made thirty
pages back will be already forgotten or obscured, I should like
to summarise the difficulties and disadvantages inherent when
we approach Egyptian art.

1 Egyptian knowledge is a whole. No aspect of it is meant to
   be studied divorced from the rest. Since there is no other way
   for us to study it except piecemeal, we must always bear in
   mind that any conclusions we come to must always be
   related to the whole from which they have been extracted.

2 Egyptian knowledge is always implicit, never explicit. It
   was 'secret' only in the sense that it was not committed to
   writing (unless in the lost Books of Thoth, kept in Hermopolis, mentioned in certain texts). Egypt did not talk about
   its knowledge, but rather incorporated it into its art and
   architecture, allowing it to exercise its effect emotionally:
   Egypt talked to the mind of the heart.

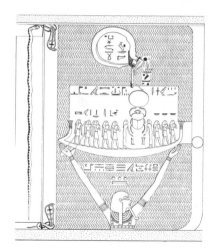

The Boat of the Sun, supported by Nut, the sky (with left hand on right arm, right hand on left arm), steered by 'consciousness' and 'the verb'. Every detail in every Egyptian relief or painting has a precise and considered meaning. Nothing is accident, nothing capricious or superstitious. All details yield their meanings to the symbolic methods developed by Schwaller de Lubicz.

3 Self-expression is not a necessary aspect of creativity.

4 Egyptian art, religion, philosophy, myth, mathematics and science are based upon the abstract and metaphysical but logically inescapable premise of the Primordial Scission. From this naturally devolves the flow and interplay of number, the mediating agency of the Golden Section and related 'irrationals', and harmony. Through a study of number, the irrationals and harmony, man is in a position to understand the whole of creation and all the laws, principles and functions underlying physical phenomena, which are *results*. Our science studies only these results, or, more accurately, measurable aspects of the results. Thus, the living fact is by definition beyond the reach of Western science as it is currently practiced; this science is a mortuary discipline, devoted to dissecting the cadavers of phenomena.

5 Egypt was practical. Art, strictly speaking, is practical. It is practical to organise a society in such a way as to permit, even entice, men to realise their spiritual goals.

6 Though we cannot experience the emotional impact of Egyptian art and architecture, we can at least look at it in its proper context, not as an appeal to aesthetic sensibility nor as an instrument of imposed tyranny, but as a perpetuating exercise in the development of consciousness.

7 Finally, because the methods of Egypt were, broadly but also specifically, magical, the purposes to which Egyptian art and architecture were put must remain unfathomable to us, and will remain so until modern man reachieves a commensurate understanding of the spiritual realities that all Egypt was based upon. What is 'magic' to us to Egypt was science, and in a sense even technology.

Modern science is ignorant of reincarnation and resurrection, but if we can accept the possibility that these concepts correspond to realities, then we must approach the Egyptian treatment as one from which we can only learn, for we have nothing to add.

We are similarly deficient in our knowledge and treatment of symbolism. Each symbol of Egypt was carefully chosen from the natural world as that which best expressed and embodied a gamut of principles and meanings, from the most abstract to the most concrete.

Schwaller de Lubicz sees the whole of Egyptian civilisation as a gigantic, consciously organised symbol appropriate to the stages mankind was then passing through. Therefore, when we look at the separate aspects of Egyptian knowledge, we must never forget that all of it was developed to be applied to a foreordained scheme.

Science and Art in Ancient Egypt

Astronomy

From Napoleonic times to the present, astronomers interested in the development of astronomy have looked into Egypt, and while differing over details, have generally concluded that Egyptian astronomy was more advanced, sophisticated and refined than Egyptologists acknowledge. Schwaller de Lubicz carefully examines and summarises the evidence as it stands, and adds striking insights of his own.

Like all ancient civilisations Egypt devoted much time and energy to a study of the heavens. Historians imagine that a combination of practical agricultural necessity and primitive superstition is sufficient to account for this universal ancient interest.

Egypt observed the heavens with as much precision as us, as far as they went. To a certain extent, information was put to practical use in agriculture, geodesy and the system of weights and measures. But at the same time, the data of astronomy was studied for its meaning: that is to say, it served the purposes of astrology, which is the study of correspondences between events in the heavens and events on earth.

Contemporary evidence that these correspondences exist is exhaustive and indisputable. The amount and quality of direct and indirect contemporary evidence attesting to these correspondences would be sufficient in any other field to establish the matter beyond question. Over the past ten years a gratifying number of scientists, having looked at the evidence, have accepted it. But for many psychological and philosophi-

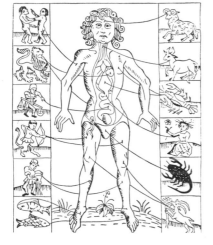

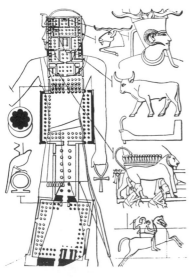

Astrology traditionally assigns the parts and organs of the body to the dominion of the various signs of the zodiac. Though the zodiac as we know it does not seem to have existed in Egypt, Schwaller de Lubicz believed that knowledge of the zodiac and of astrology was what determined the erection and destruction of temples and shifts in emphasis of Egyptian symbolism. In the Temple of Luxor, he found symbols corresponding to zodiacal signs in most of the halls and chambers in which medieval astrology would have assigned them. Most of the reliefs of Luxor are in extremely bad condition or altogether effaced, and the missing signs might well have existed earlier. Similar analogical understanding lies behind the Egyptian attribution of the hours of day and night to the dominion of certain Neters — a practice also common to Chinese acupuncture, and now in the process of substantiation by modern medicine.

Though to date nothing resembling an individual horoscope has been found in ancient Egypt, the commanding evidence for what might be called macro-astrology presupposes an individual astrology of some sort. I cannot prove the Egyptians made the vital connection between the individual and the moment of birth, but since the "birth" of temples was astrologically determined, it can hardly have been otherwise. What is certain is that Egypt understood the correspondence between man and the stars.

This is demonstrated in unmistakable fashion in a single Egyptian drawing whose significance has eluded scholars, (even those interested in proving astrology existed in Egypt) until noted recently and interpreted by the pseudonymous Musaios (Dr. Charles Muses) in *The Lion Path: You can take it with you*, published in 1985.

The figure below comes from the second golden shrine in the Tomb of Tutankhamen. It is one of a row of identical mummiform figures, part of a complex and particularly enigmatic funerary text. But however puzzling the text and the reliefs, the astrological significance of this drawing cannot be misunderstood. Rays of force or energy connect the consciousness of the human individual and the stars; there is no other possible interpretation of this figure. Taken by itself, this little relief is enough to prove astrology existed in Egypt.

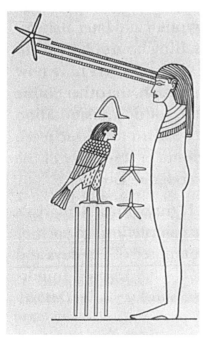

cal reasons, the subject of astrology remains an emotionally charged one, so much so that recently, 186 eminent scientists, including among them nineteen Nobel Prize winners, signed a petition condemning the resurgence of interest in astrology. This perfectly futile but extremely interesting symbolic gesture indicates firstly that the 186 scientists had not looked at the accumulated evidence supporting terrestrial-celestial correspondences, and secondly, that the College of Cardinals presiding over the church of progress no longer feels secure of its position: a few decades ago scientists would not have felt themselves sufficiently threatened to issue an official condemnation. (I.4)

This modern evidence, though compelling, naturally concerns only those astrological correspondences that fall within modern methods of measurement. It is, however, ample to justify the kind of analogical thinking necessary to clarify the uses to which Egypt put astronomy.

As we have seen, starting from the mystical Primordial Scission and proceeding through a study of number, we comprehend physical phenomena as results of interacting functions and processes. To make sense of the welter of impressions communicated by the senses, we classify this information according to scale. Science accepts this classification grudgingly but can hardly do otherwise. Ordinary people act upon it instinctively, immediately and accurately.

The key words to this innate system are 'hierarchy', 'rhythm' and 'cycle'.

The universe is organised hierarchically as are all human institutions.

In the physical world, simpler or 'lower' unities combine to form more complex or 'higher' unities. We distinguish the 'higher' from the 'lower' by a host of unmeasurable but unavoidable qualities: the 'higher' the unity or organism, the greater its degree of sensitivity, sentience, intelligence and, finally, choice. A cabbage is 'higher' than a stone, a dog is 'higher' than a cabbage, a man is 'higher' than a dog. A positivist might argue that 'higher' is a subjective and misleading word in a chance, meaningless universe; but unless he is a very quick-thinking positivist his reaction to running over a cabbage will not be quite the same as his reaction to running over a dog or a child.

Science cannot escape the hierarchical nature of the physical world. (From the standpoint of mathematical statistics alone, this fact precludes the possibility of evolution as a chance occurrence.) Science recognises man as a hierarchical unity (or organism) made up of glands and organs, themselves made up of cells, each of which is made up of molecules, in turn made up of atoms. Each stage (going from atom up) is characterised by a higher degree of sensitivity, sentience, complexity, organisation and autonomy.

. At this point, modern science stops. Restricted by a self-imposed criterion of measurability, it refuses to admit, much less try to study, those higher hierarchies that are analogically, if not logically, required to make experience comprehensible.

Individual man is a hierarchical organism, or unity. He is part of a higher organism or unity: mankind. Mankind is part of organic life, which is part of earth, which is part of the solar system, which is part of our galaxy. Each represents a higher hierarchy or realm, with inferrable higher degrees of sensitivity, sentience, etc.

Meanwhile, we observe that physical phenomena follow an alternating rhythm within a cyclical pattern. Inhale, exhale; wake, sleep; spring, summer, autumn, winter: these alternations are imposed by the dual, polar nature of creation. And the cycle of fertilisation, birth, growth, maturity, senescence, death and renewal is common to all hierarchies. (Though not observable in molecular and atomic realms, it is to a certain extent observable in the higher galactic hierarchies.)

Given the extent to which we can observe hierarchical structure, alternating rhythm and cyclical patterns in the physical world, it is shortsighted and more than a little daft to refuse to assent to the existence of these principles in those areas beyond the senses and therefore inaccessible to direct measurement.

Egypt and other ancient civilisations were never bound by such arbitrary frontiers. It was her astronomy — in the service of astrological understanding — that afforded insight into these higher realms and upon that insight Egypt acted, sometimes directly, sometimes symbolically.

It may be difficult for us, with our narrow, utilitarian concept of society, to understand the results obtained, but we can understand the underlying thinking.

It is a universal characteristic of hierarchical organisation that the 'higher' organises the lower, while the 'lower' disorganises the higher.

The chef organises the dishwashers and waiters into a restaurant. If the dishwashers are refractory (or the chef drunk and tyrannical), they revolt and bring the organisation down. The cancer cell within the body revolts, refuses to obey, seeks to 'express itself' and brings the higher organisation of the body down. But while organisation proceeds from the top down in concept, it proceeds from the bottom up in execution. The book is complete in the author's head before he touches paper; the oak is complete and potential within the acorn. But the book proceeds word by word, and the oak begins with the seedling, and only this part of the process is observable. It is of course this observed process that is used to support evolutionary theory, but as Plato understood perfectly, this is but the mechanical and least interesting half of the story.

These principles of organisation hold in all observable realms. There is therefore no reason why they should not hold in realms difficult or impossible to observe, and there is certainly no reason why, in these realms, exactly opposite principles should prevail.

As we see in the human body, the hierarchies are interacting and interdependent; disorganisation in the lower realms disrupts and may destroy the higher.

So when in the name of progress we rape the earth of its resources, destroy the ecological balance, significantly expend the planet's potential energy (coal, oil, even hydroelectric power), we may well be taking destructive action that could reverberate beyond the earth, even beyond the solar system — for we have no idea what part organic life on earth plays in the grand scheme. A small wound turned septic may go gangrenous and bring the whole system down.

In any case, it is the data of astronomy interpreted in terms of number, cycles and hierarchy that provide insight into higher realms. Egypt organised and administered her civilisation upon this knowledge; it is this that accounts for the structure of her system of calendars, the changes in emphasis in her symbolism, the ascendance of one Neter over another and the shifts of theological hegemony of her various religious centers.

As for the physical means of obtaining the necessary precise astronomical information, Egypt possessed the finest observatories possible prior to the development of modern telescopes. Two English astronomers, Richard A. Proctor and Sir Joseph Lockyer, before the turn of the twentieth century demonstrated the manner in which the pyramids, first in truncated form, then in complete form, could have been used as observatories.

The calendar

The cycles of the moon and sun obviously (and of the planets, solar system, fixed stars and constellations less obviously) correspond to events upon earth. On the most obvious practical level, man must observe these cycles. Any human society that practices agriculture requires some kind of calendar if it is to plan ahead at all.

The whole of Egypt's agriculture depended upon the annual rise and flood of the Nile, and this, Egyptologists think, was the original inspiration for the study of astronomy and the development over many centuries of Egypt's curiously complex, extremely ingenious and very accurate calendar.

But why should those clear, logical thinkers who liked to work with difficult rather than easy materials keep three calendars simultaneously? To make things difficult for farmers?

Egypt worked according to a lunar calendar of alternative twenty nine and thirty-day months, a moving or civil calendar of 360 days plus five additional days (on which the Neters were said to be born), and a calendar of 365¼ days based upon the heliacal return of the star Sirius — exactly the same calendar that regulates our present year.

As far as I know, no one has tried to work out in detail the relationships between Egypt's independent yet simultaneously operating systems. But Schwaller de Lubicz makes an observation that may eventually lead to a complete understanding.

The twenty-five-year cycle corresponded to 309 lunations (a lunation is the period between one new moon and the next). The calculations are

$$25 \times 365 = 9{,}125 \text{ days, and}$$
$$\frac{9{,}125}{309} = 29.5307 \text{ days per lunation.}$$

This in itself reveals extremely accurate observations. Modern astronomy reckons the lunation as 29.53059 days, a difference of about a second. But Schwaller de Lubicz notes the intriguing equivalence of twenty-five years to 309 lunar months. $309 = \frac{(\phi - 1) \times 1000}{2}$ and its choice as the number determining the cycle cannot have been accidental. (A double cycle, which would express the Golden Section, comprises fifty years; $618 = (\phi - 1) \times 1000$. It is interesting that this is the cycle given by the African Dogon as the orbit of the invisible companion star of Sirius, upon which the whole of Dogon astronomy is based.)

As we have seen earlier, phi, the Golden Section, is the function that generates five geometrically. In Pythagorean number symbolism, five is the number of creation, six is the number of time and space. We found this understanding reflected in Egyptian symbolism, and now it appears these numbers play a role, and perhaps may have been the determining factors, of the Egyptian calendrical system. For the various cycles can be reduced to the interplay of five and six and their multiples. And since the Egyptian calendar is recognised as a marvel of accuracy, it is interesting to notice how the facts of astronomy seem to bear out the premises of purely symbolic Pythagorean thinking.

The lunar calendar ran in twenty-five-year cycles of 309 lunations. The year itself was calculated in two ways. There was a 365-day 'civil year' similar to ours. But unlike ours, it was not subdivided into months of arbitrary length in order to make up the 365 days. Egypt counted twelve months of thirty days each (multiples of six, and of six and five) plus five additional days. On these additional days the Neters (or divine principles) were supposed to have been 'born'.

As we know, the actual year is not 365 days but 365¼ days long. We add the extra day every four years, in our 'leap year', which keeps the calendars synchronised.

Egypt, however, kept two calendars running concurrently. The civil or moving year gradually shifted in relation to the fixed or Sothic year. (Sirius = Sothis in Greek, Sopdit in Egyptian). The civil year, losing a day every four years, took 1,461 years (365¼ x 4) to coincide with the Sothic year. The date of this coincidence marked what Egypt called the New Year. It is the Egyptian habit of recording events according to both calendars that allows modern Egyptologists to establish the chronology of Egypt with precision, since the astronomical coincidence of the heliacal rising of Sirius with the summer solstice can be determined within narrow limits. The Egyptian New Year also allows us to establish the date of the founding of Egypt as a unified kingdom, since the first New Year, according to the records, marks that date. Here a complex dispute arises among Egyptologists as to which heliacal rising of Sirius should stand for the date.

There are three possibilities: 4240 BC, 2780 BC and 1320 BC. The last of these is excluded since known Egyptian dynasty lists cannot be incorporated into the time allowed. The second date falls within what Egyptologists believe to be the height of the pyramid era. Known Egyptian history, however, does not fit comfortably into this date either, and the pyramid texts of the Fifth Dynasty kings (ca. 2500BC) repeatedly refer to the inauguration of the 'New' Year, which indicates strongly the prior existence of the double calendar and suggests it was set up in 4240 BC.

Egyptologists are loath to accept this conclusion for the simple reason that they do not want to believe that Egyptian civilisation is that old. Moreover, the establishment of the Sothic year is a sophisticated astronomical process; it predicates the ability to single out of the entire sky the one star that allows for the establishment of a year of 365¼ days. This in turn predicates a long process of refined observational techniques prior to 4240 BC.

Only the eminent German Ludwig Borchardt has accepted the astronomical evidence at face value, and supported 4240 BC as the date for the establishment of the Egyptian calendar. (This is a curious exception, since Borchardt was in every other instance contemptuous of Egyptian science.) Other Egyptologists have tried to reckon Egyptian chronology by non-astronomical means. But the majority acknowledge the importance of the Sothic calendar. Unable to face the implications of its establishment as early as 4240 BC, however, they take 2780 BC as the date.

R. A. Schwaller de Lubicz
Le Roi de la Théocratie Pharaonique
Flammarion, 1961, p. 142

On the ivory tablette of King Den (Ist Dyn.) *the sign of the year* encircles two of these ceremonies, attesting to *the existence at this time* of a perfectly constructed calendar. It is therefore due to this calendar, already functioning *before* 3000 BC, that one is able to recast during the Vth Dyn. the annals of the first kings, year by year, and mentioning months and days.

Even this implies a long history of accurate astronomical observation. Rather than accept this, scholars look for some simple-minded, primitive method by which Egypt might have hit upon the extremely accurate Sothic calendar by accident or trial and error; and in this pursuit all the usual scholarly and scientific rules are waived. Anything goes as long as it allows scholars to go on believing that science started in Greece.

Otto Neugebauer, for example, thinks that by averaging out the periods between successive annual Nile floods, at the end of 240 years the correct figure of 365.25 would be obtained. To support this hypothesis there is no evidence whatsoever. Even apart from the lack of evidence, it is absolutely untenable, for there is no instance of the Egyptians taking averages, and it is extremely unlikely that any given average taken over 240 years would give 365.25 years precisely.

Even if such an average gave the correct figure, there would be no way for the Egyptians to realise that it was correct — *unless they already knew the figure.*

If the figure were obtained by this method, there would be no reason to place such importance upon the heliacal return of Sirius. The annual flooding of the Nile coincides but roughly with Sirius, and varies by as much as sixty days from one year to the next. If the Egyptians had actually counted upon Sirius to herald the rise of the Nile, they would all have drowned long before the First Dynasty.

In order to accurately determine the length of the year as 365.25 days, none of this is necessary. It requires no more than the meticulous observation of the length of shadows. The time taken between the two shortest (or two longest) shadows of the year will give the exact length of the year. Within a few years the figure will be verified and it will be exact. It is the coincidence of the 365.25-day year with Sirius that entails an advanced astronomy.

Less credible than the wildest dreams of the pyramidologists, Neugebauer's unsupported, and unsupportable, hypothesis enjoys the support of many prominent Egyptologists. For science, as everyone knows, began with the Greeks.

However obtained, the Egyptian calendrical system is assumed to be a response to the needs of agriculture.

But a rough lunar calendar is sufficient for agriculture. Egypt worked according to an extremely accurate triple calendar, and the reason for it must lie outside the exigencies of agriculture. When we know that Egypt planned its festivals according to all three calendars, and that certain of these festivals moved in accordance to the calendars, we have one clue to their motives.

The cycles of moon, sun, Sirius and the fixed stars were kept separate because their effects were separate. Festival days were intended to consecrate and make use of these effects at the correct time. Agricultural and fertility festivals followed the lunar calendar. Others followed the civil year, while yet others corresponded to the Sothic calendar.

Having worked out a 365.25-day year, there was nothing to prevent Egypt from thinking up the leap year. But this would have made it impossible to keep track of those dates that depended upon the fixed (Sothic) year and the cycle of 1,461 civil years to one Sothic New Year. This, along with the Egyptian designation of Sothis as the Great Provider, shows that Egypt was thinking in terms of the hierarchy of realms and cycles. For if Sothis as provider simply was a synonym for the flooding Nile, why then shift festival dates? Ancient sources declared that the Egyptians regarded Sirius as another and greater sun. Modern astronomy reveals that Sirius is a double star with one vast low-density half and one smaller, extremely dense half. Schwaller de Lubicz suggests that this looks similar to the nucleus of an atom with its positron and neutron. And it may relate to the 'central fire' of Pythagoras. But its precise cosmic role, as well as its precise role in Egypt, is still a mystery. It is possible that Egypt knew what some modern scholars suspect: that Sirius is the greater sun about which our sun and solar system orbits.

If this is the case, then we may regard cyclical long-term effects analogous to the easily detectable short-term effects of our lunar and solar cycles. The lunar governs fertility and other biological periodicities in a host of lower organisms, and various meteorological phenomena; the solar cycle commands the seasons, with all that that implies. So the Sothic year, according to this kind of thinking, would also have its phases and seasons; and an understanding of their implications would allow a civilisation to take measures to promote and enhance those aspects favourable to its own ends, and minimise those unfavourable. We do not understand those implica-

Marcel Griaule and G. Dieterlen
African Worlds, ed. Daryll Forde
Oxford, 1954, pp. 83-110

The starting point of creation is the star which revolves round Sirius and is actually named the 'Digitaria star'; it is regarded by the Dogon as the smallest and heaviest of all the stars; it contains the germs of all things. Its movement on its own axis and around Sirius upholds all creation in space. We shall see that its orbit determines the calendar.

R. Temple
The Sirius Mystery
Sidgwick & Jackson, 1976, p. 29

Saturn is known [to the Dogon] as 'the star of limiting the place' in association somehow with the Milky Way.

Ibid. p. 258

The Sigui among the Dogon is celebrated every sixty years ... The Egyptians had such a period associated with Osiris [principle of renewal] ... My own predilection, when considering the period of sixty years, is to think in terms of a synchronization of the orbital periods of the two planets, Jupiter and Saturn, for they come together in nearly sixty years ... Stonehenge has sixty stones in its outer circle ... (This) outer circle is the oriental cycle of Vrihaspati ... It is therefore interesting that the Dogon say that sixty is the count of the cosmic placenta ...

The sixty-year cycle also provides a link between the Egyptian Sothic year and the Great Year of the precession of the equinoxes, which bear a relationship to each other similar to the Egyptian civil year of 360 days to the tropical year of 365 days. A precessional 'month' of 2160 years divides into three 'decans' of 720 years each. Two 'great' civil years of 360 days (6 x 60) plus five epagomenal years per 'great' year 2(360 + 5) make up the precessional 'decan' of 730 years. Conceivably, it is this relationship that determined the Egyptian year of 360 + 5 days to begin with; a reckoning which, as far as I know, has not been satisfactorily accounted for otherwise. In any case, 72 Sothic hemidemicycles of 360 years each plus one great epagomenal year (72 x 5 years) make up a precessional year. To construct a pentagon within a circle, it must be divided into 5.72° angles, and thus on a grand scale the Sothic and precessional cycles again reflect the relationships between 5 and 6, and their multiples and powers. The sixty-year Dogon cycle and Egyptian Osirian cycle is therefore a 'day' of the precessional year. Perhaps in this greater galactic scheme, Sirius plays a role similar to that played by Jupiter within the solar system; her Egyptian title of 'Great Provider' perhaps furnishes a clue that further research could elaborate upon. [Author's note.]

Dogon symbol relating the rite of circumcision to the orbit of Digitaria around Sirius. However curious the concept, expressing a simple religious rite in cosmological terms, the diagram bears a resemblance to the 'mouth of Ra', Egyptian symbol of Unity, which itself, either fortuitously or through design, takes the same form as the monochord vibrating along its length and producing its fundamental sound.

S: Sirius
B: Foreskin
A: Knife

The Dogon symbol also may be seen as including, within the trajectory of Digitaria, the treble principle of creation.

Ibid., p. 21

The bright star of Sirius is not as important to the Dogon as the tiny Sirius B, which the Dogon call *po tolo* (*tolo* = star). *Po* is a cereal grain ... whose botanical name is *Digitaria exilis*. In speaking of the *po* star Griaule and Dieterlen call it 'Digitaria'.

Ibid., pp. 24-27, 44

The Dogon also know the actual orbital period of this invisible star, which is fifty years ... The most amazing of all the Dogon statements is this, 'Digitaria' is the smallest thing there is. It is the heaviest star ... The Dogon have four kinds of calendar ... a solar calendar, a Venus calendar, and a Sirius calendar. Their fourth is an agrarian one and is lunar.

The orbit of Digitaria is ... at the center of the world, Digitaria is the axis of the whole world, and without its movement no other star could hold its course.

R. A. Schwaller de Lubicz
Le Roi de la Théocratie Pharaonique
Flammarion, 1961, p. 38

Sirius played the role of great central fire for our sun (which is the Eye of Ra, and not Ra himself) for the Temple ... It took the recent discoveries of astronomy and physics to suggest another role for Sirius, coinciding with what we begin to understand of the atomic nucleus, comprising a Positron (giant star of low density) and Neutron with vastly inferior volume relative to the mass of the atom, but in which the weight is concentrated (the incredibly dense dwarf star).

tions, but it seems Egypt did. Otherwise it is difficult to understand the concern with the Sothic year.

Finally, there is the great cycle of the constellations (a cycle of particular importance to the present), about which we know rather more.

The earth does not spin true upon its axis: we may regard it as a slightly off-center spinning top. If the sky is regarded as a constellated backdrop, then because of the 'wobble' of the earth upon its axis, the vernal equinox each year rises against a gradually shifting background of constellations. Astronomers call this the 'precession of the equinoxes', and the discovery of this phenomenon is generally attributed to the Greek astronomer Hipparchus in the second century BC. Of course, as with all astronomical phenomena, no effective importance is attached to it.

The ancients regarded the matter otherwise. It takes roughly 2,160 years for the equinox to precess through a sign. Thus it takes some 25,920 years for the spring equinox to traverse the full circuit of the constellations. This cycle is called the Great, or 'Platonic' Year. And it is the precession of the equinoxes through the constellations that gives names to the various ages: of Pisces at the moment, which began roughly in 140 AD, of Aries beginning around 2000BC, of Taurus beginning just prior to 4000BC, Gemini around 6000 BC, and so on, with Aquarius coming up shortly.

Though ancient sources affirm that the precession of the equinoxes was known to Egypt, modern scholars have found no direct evidence — although, given their predilection to attribute everything 'scientific' to the Greeks, they have not looked very hard.

It is accepted that the Egyptians divided the sky into thirty-six sectors of ten degrees each, called decans, and that these decans related to the ten-day periods within the 360-day civil year. But the division of the sky into constellations, the invention of the signs of the zodiac and the attribution of significance to the signs is held to be a Greek effort, in this case a misplaced one in which the otherwise wary and rational Greeks swallowed whole a Chaldean superstition and applied their keen astronomical minds to developing it into a system which, albeit mistaken, was nonetheless coherent.

It is true that no zodiacs turned up in Egypt until it fell under Greek domination, nor is there written evidence that Egypt named the constellations or thought them important. But in studying the course of Egyptian symbolism, Schwaller de Lubicz uncovered evidence that, from the earliest dynasties, the precession through the zodiac was what guided the course of Egyptian artistic and architectural policy.

The unification of Upper and Lower Egypt is held to be a purely political affair. Yet the date of the unification, around

Rodney Collin
The Theory of Celestial Influence
Stuart, 1954, pp. 14-15

The diameter of the earth, for instance, is one millionth that of the Solar System; but the diameter of the Solar System is only perhaps one forty-millionth that of the Milky Way. When in our own system we find such relationships it is not between the sun and planets, but between the sun and *satellites* of planets . . . By analogy of scale and mass, we should expect the Solar System to be revolving about some greater entity, which in turn was revolving about the centre of the Milky Way; just as the Moon revolves about the Earth, which in turn revolves about the Sun.

What and where is this 'sun' of our Sun? Several attempts have been made to discern a 'local' system within the Milky Way, particularly by Charlier who in 1916 seemed to have established such a group 2000 light years across and with its centre several hundred light years away in the direction of Argo. If we study our immediate surroundings in the galaxy, we find an interesting gradation of stars, two of which are suggestive from this point of view. Within ten light years we find one star similar in scale to our sun, and Sirius, over twenty times as bright. Between forty and seventy light years distant we come on five much larger stars, 100 to 250 times as bright; between 70 and 200 light years, seven greater still . . . and between three hundred and seven hundred light years six immense giants tens of thousands of times more brilliant. The greatest of these, Canopus, which lies 625 light years behind, in the exact wake of the Solar System, and is 100,000 times more radiant than our Sun, could indeed by the 'sun' of Charlier's local system . . . The most brilliant object in the heavens, after those within the Solar System itself, is of course the double-star Sirius . . . By physical distance and by radiance and mass a Syrian system would seem in some way to fill the excessive gap between the cosmoses of the Solar System and the Milky Way. Indeed, the distance of the Sun to Sirius — one million times the distance from the Earth to the Sun — falls naturally into the scale of cosmic relationships mentioned, and provided nineteenth century astronomers with an excellent unit of celestial measurement, the siriometer, now unfortunately abandoned.

4240 BC, coincident with the establishment of the Sothic Year at that time, also marks the precessional exit out of Gemini and into Taurus. While little is known of this pre-Dynastic Egypt, there is no mistaking the emphasis upon duality, on the separate kingdoms of Upper and Lower Egypt, on the hegemony of the twins, Shu and Tefnut. The temples that have been found emphasise this preoccupation with the dual and have two entrances. In addition, the capitals of both Upper and Lower Egypt were dual cities: Dep/Pe and Nekhem-/Nekhed.

The unification of Egypt took place under the legendary king, Menes (his Greek name). Historians consider this an event of purely political significance. No doubt political changes took place, but at the same time a new era of art and architecture began. Though the question of chronology is complex, even without Schwaller de Lubicz's precessional theory, there are many reasons to favour the 4240 BC date as that marking the foundation of the First Dynasty of the newly united Egypt.

Now the emphasis changes dramatically; the symbolism of Mentu, the bull, becomes the most salient feature of Egyptian art; architecture becomes monolithic, is carried out on a scale never equalled throughout recorded history and performed with a finesse never surpassed. Old Kingdom Egypt radiates a kind of gigantic calm assurance. What little is known of other civilizations of the Taurean age suggests they shared these qualities. It is just possible that the veneration of the cow in India dates from this period. The parallel civilisation of Crete was also consecrated to the bull. And while the case cannot be couched in terms acceptable to the skeptic, the astrological nature of the sign of Taurus (feminine, fixed, earth and ruled by Venus) corresponds neatly with Old Kingdom Egypt. In fact, the Arian and especially the Piscean ages also conform to the nature of their signs, and there are already unmistakable indications that the world is moving toward the kind of forms, concerns and attitudes imposed by Aquarius. (This may be largely constructive or largely destructive, but the nature of its constructivity or destructivity will be Aquarian, and within limits can be foreseen.)

The uses to which Egypt put its symbolism were complex and ever changing. Just as the day, in Egypt, was divided into hours (which were not 'fixed', but varied with the seasons), each of which had its own 'influence', just as the month was divided into days and the year into seasons, so the precessional 'month' was not a constant. In the vitalist philosophy of Egypt, only the Primordial Scission was immutable; all else moved, alternated, flowed . . . and Schwaller de Lubicz finds, within the Taurean symbolism that prevailed for two thousand years, distinct changes of emphasis. So, in the statues and reliefs of the kings of the early dynasties, at a time when the power of the bull was the salient 'influence', emphasis upon the power of neck and shoulders (focus of the bull's power) invest the portraits.

Many of the kings of the Old Kingdom incorporated Mentu, the bull, in their names, and the age of Mentu ended with the Mentuhoteps I to V. In the Temple of Mentu consecrated to Mentuhotep II, the king is shown as an old man. The word *hotep* is generally translated as 'peace', but when subjected to Schwaller de Lubicz's kind of interpretation it takes on a richer significance for *htp* is the reverse of Ptah, creator of form, and refers in this sense to realisation or completion — of which 'peace' is but an aspect. Ptahhotep means 'realisation of (the work of) Ptah'. Mentuhotep means 'realisation of (the work of) Mentu', which in this case seems to be symbolically correct, but historically more like wishful thinking, since the available evidence suggests that the Old Kingdom disintegrated in a shambles with the Mentuhoteps of the Eleventh Dynasty. From this period comes the famous 'Lament of Ipuwer', a document that for all its lacunae, and allowing for all the usual problems of translation, remains one of the most vivid descriptions ever penned of a state of calamity.

If Schwaller de Lubicz's precessional explanation of Egyptian symbolism is correct, a drastic change of emphasis would be predicted around 2100 BC, when the equinox moved into Aries.

That is precisely what the records reveal. Mentu the bull disappears and is superceded by the ram of Amon. The character of the architecture loses its monolithic simplicity. While still within its recognisable tradition, there is no mistaking a change of 'character'. The pharaohs incorporate Amon in the names they assume: Amenhotep, Amenophis, Tutankhamen.

Egyptologists attribute the fall of Mentu and the rise of Amon to a hypothetical priestly feud, with the priests of Amon emerging victorious. There is nothing illogical or impossible about this hypothesis, but at the same time there is no evidence whatever to support it.

The evidence shows a shift of symbolism, from duality under Gemini, to the bull, to the ram. These shifts coincide with the dates of the astronomical precession.

Further corroboration of Egyptian knowledge and use of the precession of the equinoxes, and of the incredible coherence and deliberation of the Egyptian tradition, was deduced by Schwaller de Lubicz from a detailed study of the famous zodiac from the Temple of Denderah. This temple was constructed by the Ptolemies in the first century BC, upon the site of an earlier temple. The hieroglyphs declare that it was constructed 'according to the plan laid down in the time of the companions of Horus' — that is to say, prior to the beginnings of

Paul Barguet
Le Temple d'Amon — Re a Karnak
Le Caire, 1962, p. 2 ff

Montu was known from the Old Kingdom ... [The sacred animal of Montu was the Bull, to whom four temples were consecrated: Thebes, Medamoud, Ermant and Tod] ... One must wait for the XIIth Dynasty for the appearance of Amon as 'King of the Gods' ... The sacred animals of Amon were the Ram and the Nile Goose ... [There is mention of a colossal statue of a ram in the front court of the temple of Amon-Ra at Karnak] ... In one of the halls of the Temple Akh-menu at Karnak, which is part of the temple of Amon, it is written: 'palace of retreat for the majestic Soul, *high hall of the Ram which traverses the sky*'. [Author's italics.]

G. Santillana and H. Dechend
Hamlet's Mill

The preceding Age, that of Aries, had been heralded by Moses coming down from Mount Sinai as 'two horned', that is, crowned with Ram's horns, while his flock insisted upon dancing around the 'Golden Calf' that was, rather, a 'Golden Bull', Taurus.

100

Dynastic Egypt. Egyptologists regard this statement as a ritual figure of speech, intended to express regard for the tradition of the past.

The zodiac of Denderah is depicted in a form more or less recognisable to us, and by the time Denderah was built, the Greek zodiac was universally known, through its transmission by the Greeks and Alexandrians. But Schwaller de Lubicz was able to show that apparent anomalies in the zodiac, and certain hieroglyphs whose meaning had eluded Egyptologists, indicated that Imhotep was not brought in for ritual, but for literal reasons.

The Denderah zodiac marks the entry of the equinox into Pisces. At the same time, its orientation and its symbolism calls attention to the precessional passage into the two preceding ages of Aries and Taurus. The evidence is written into the zodiac.

The circular zodiac from the Temple of Denderah. The zodiacal constellations are arranged in an irregular circle around the center. Note the curious placing of Cancer, well within the circle described by the others, or perhaps intended as the inner point of a spiral.

OUEST D'ORIGINE

SUD VRAI

O.

E.

NORD VRAI

AXE DU TEMPLE

EST D'ORIGINE

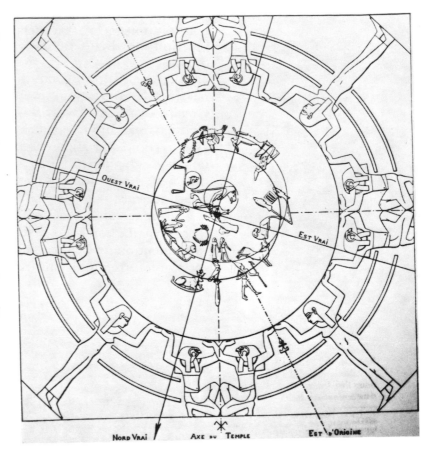

Detail of the round Denderah zodiac. Schwaller de Lubicz thought the signs of the zodiac disposed about an eccentric circle with one center at the pole of the ecliptic (nipple of the female hippopotamus) and the other at the pole star (jackal or dog). This does not seem to me entirely convincing. Note the placement of Libra, for example. But whatever the scheme directing the arrangement, it is certain that the sign of Cancer has been singled out for special treatment.

On the ceiling of the main hypostyle hall of the Temple of Denderah, another zodiac mysteriously begins with the sign of Cancer. This has provoked all kinds of scholarly controversy, but in this case, I think it can be accounted for. The Egyptian New Year began on July 19, at the heliacal rising of Sirius, but within the sign of Cancer. The Temple of Denderah was associated with calendrical and astronomical lore, and it was at Denderah that the Egyptian New Year was celebrated.

Understanding the physical (and spiritual) world in terms of hierarchy, rhythms and cycles leads to a system of analogies and correspondences which, in degenerate form, we still find much in evidence: consider the association in popular astrology with a 'lucky' number, colour, flower, gem, animal and so on.

Because the knowledge that went into the establishment of these correspondences has vanished, it is impossible today to say which are valid. But the principle remains sound: the interplay of number lies beneath the interacting functions whose results are the phenomena of the physical world. Cymatics demonstrates that form is the result of frequency; frequency is the oscillation between opposite poles. It therefore follows that, in theory, it should be possible to erect a rigorous system of correspondences throughout the observable (and inferrable) hierarchical realms — mineral, vegetable, animal, human, planetary, even galactic — since analogies of forms suggest analogies of number and therefore of function.

There is some direct, and much more indirect, evidence accumulating showing the existence of these correspondences, often corroborating old 'superstitions'. Experiments by followers of the German mystic and scholar, Rudolf Steiner, show that solutions of specific metals upon filter paper react to conjunctions of specific planets (iron to Mars, lead to Saturn, tin to Jupiter, copper to Venus). Michel Gauquelin's statistics dramatically prove that there is an overpowering relationship between certain personality types and certain planets (Mars for athletes and soldiers; Saturn for scientists; Jupiter for actors and clergymen). Homeopathy is based upon an affinity or correspondence of specific metal salts with specific organs and ailments.

But if correspondences between form and function are now demonstrable, extrapolating from what is soundly established is fraught with dangers. This was a favourite pastime of the medieval mind, which saw the seven planets mirrored in the seven facial orifices, and then went on from there. To the modern rational intellect, the whole procedure is anathema and therefore, often, in attempting to account for the establishment of certain correspondences in ancient times, an attempt will be made to think medievally, and when this has been performed to the satisfaction of the scholar, this hypothetical reconstruction will be put forward with considerable assurance. For example, as long as there has been astrology, the planet Mars has been associated with war, soldiery, athletics and allied occupations. Trying to imagine how this came about in the first place, the modern scholar notes that Mars is distinctly red. Since blood is also red, he infers that the primitive mind would relate the red planet to the red of blood, and Mars would then become the planet of war. But the fact is that no one has the faintest notion as to how the correspondence was first made, while Gauquelin's statistics demonstrate that in the horoscopes of athletes particularly, but of soldiers and surgeons as well, the planet Mars shows up in one of four 'critical' regions with a frequency that represents odds of many millions to one.

Despite ancient claims of Egyptian knowledge of the precession of the equinoxes, Egyptologists have been hesitant to accept the idea. It was proposed by the astronomer J. B. Biot in the middle of the nineteenth century and strongly supported with evidence from the Denderah zodiac. Biot's figures were never refuted or even disputed, but they were never acted upon. Recently a French Egyptologist, Paul Barguet, in a paper upon the significance of the twelve hours of day and the twelve of night, suggested that these might correspond to the signs of the zodiac. Though this may seem a very small concession in the light of Schwaller de Lubicz's reinterpretation of the entire civilization, in fact in scholarly terms it represents an important step forward. For it is impossible to admit a correlation between the hours and the signs without admitting the existence of the zodiac, which in turn implies knowledge of the precession, and therefore of that high astronomy that

Schwaller de Lubicz and others have supported for so long in vain.

According to Schwaller de Lubicz, Egyptian astronomy was a refined and sophisticated science, and like all ancient astronomy, it was the significance of the data — that is to say, its astrological meaning — that was responsible for its practice, development and the tremendous importance attached to it. These astrological connotations found their way into the Egyptian language, into the symbolism, into the measures and proportions of her architecture and into her medicine (medical papyri often state specific times at which to administer specific medicines or treat specific ailments). Schwaller de Lubicz also cites one further use to which Egypt put her astronomy. If ever accepted, this idea will open an immense and important field of study. It is well known that Egypt was perpetually engaged in taking down her old temples and erecting new ones, often on the site of the old. This is generally attributed to the usual pharaonic egomania. (And in all fairness, even allowing for the symbolic interpretation, the pharaohs were not notable for their modesty.) But Schwaller de Lubicz contends, and supports his idea with much direct and indirect evidence, that in general temples were not destroyed, but rather dismantled carefully and deliberately when their predetermined symbolic significance had passed. The new temple was then constructed and consecrated to whichever Neter the changing cycles of time pushed forward into prominence. These temples were not designed to last forever (when conditions demanded constructing for eternity, the Egyptians were fully capable of doing that) but were designed to last only as long as the particular cycle or stellar configuration demanded. In other words, it was Egypt's astronomy, interpreted for its astrological significance, that guided the entire course of her art and architecture. On a practical level, this means that the sages of Egypt were deliberately and knowledgeably organising the ambiance or atmosphere of an entire civilisation in harmony with cosmic requirements. In principle, it should be possible, through a study of the monuments, their dates, alignments, consecrations, symbolism, proportions and so on to retrieve some of this astrological lore. For it may well be this that lies behind the intriguing but hopelessly inadequate body of knowledge astrologers work with today.

Mathematics

School textbooks and all general interest books by authorities paint a simplistic, unsympathetic view of Egyptian mathematical achievement. Among specialists that low opinion is not unanimously held, nor has it ever been. However, the existence of controversy is never mentioned in those texts or general interest books, and this is misleading.

Most Egyptologists contend that Egyptian mathematics was a practical affair concerned with doling out corn and land. To this end, an unwieldly mathematics was developed, and once settled upon, never improved. This camp is convinced that the Egyptians did not understand the mathematical principles underlying their own method, which is supposed to have 'developed' through trial and error.

But a minority contests this view, and seeks to prove that, while the rules and principles are never stated explicitly, a knowledge of the rules is implicit; in other words, if the rules and principles were unknown, Egyptian mathematics would not be and could not be what it is.

Ideally, I would like to present this argument in such a way as to allow the mathematically-minded to judge for themselves. Unfortunately, a step-by-step presentation requires too many pages, and there is no way to present a summary.

The situation, therefore, may be represented by analogy. It is as if, five thousand years from now, all evidence of Western technology had vanished except for one children's Meccano set and a few bits and pieces of other mechanical toys.

Confronted by such evidence, the great-great-grandsons of modern Egyptologists would argue that twentieth-century technology was a practical, jocular pursuit intended to keep children amused. The descendants of the other camp would disagree, arguing that the very nature of the toys presupposed a complex technology and an intimate knowledge of theory in a number of fields.

All that is known of Egyptian mathematics comes from a Middle Kingdom papyrus intended as an exercise for children, and a few fragments of other texts of a similar nature.

The complete text is called the Rhind Papyrus. It consists of a scroll with some eighty problems and their solutions. Though a Middle Kingdom relic, it is stated to be a copy of an earlier papyrus, but no one can say how much earlier. It is therefore impossible to talk about the 'development' of Egyptian mathematics. Knowing that Egyptian mythology, symbolism, hieroglyphics, medicine and astronomy were fully developed in the earliest dynasties, there is no particular reason to suppose mathematics was a later addition.

The deciphering of the mathematical texts was a formidable task. Apart from the inevitable linguistic problems, Egyptologists were confronted by a mathematical system quite dissimilar to our own, and as though to further complicate matters, the best and most complete papyrus, the Rhind Papyrus, was copied in a magnificent hand by a scribe, Ahmose, who evidently delighted more in his calligraphy than in his mathematical accuracy. There are a number of obvious errors in the papyrus.

Ibid., p. 95

It is hardly worth while to spend much time on a problem which is clearly incomplete and incorrect. All that is to be made out is that the second calculation is the finding of the area of the small triangle whose base and height are marked in the figure 2¼ and 7 respectively. In this problem the multiplier ½ is actually written as it was ½ *setat* ... while there is continual confusion between thousands-of-land, which should be shown in free standing units, and *setat*, which should be placed beneath the rectangle sign.

The first calculation is hopeless, and appears neither to have a meaning in itself nor to bear any relation to the figure. [Lucie Lamy was able to solve this problem, showing it to relate to knowledge of the tetractys and of proportion. Author's note.]

Having established the existence of errors, Egyptologists cannot be blamed for assuming further copying errors in certain problems to which correct answers could not be found. Nevertheless, in re-examining these problems from the proportional, geometric and harmonic bases upon which Egyptian mathematics was actually founded, Schwaller de Lubicz was able to show that problems formerly regarded as intractable or incorrect were not incoherent (even though they may have contained errors), but rather could not be approached by current Western methods.

This difference in approach applies to every aspect of Egyptian mathematics, though obviously the results will be the same: multiplication is multiplication, division is division, and the area of a surface can only be X number of square feet or meters or cubits. We generally teach students the rules, the student then applies the rule to the problem, and in doing so learns to calculate; but *he does not gain an insight into the meaning of the rule itself*; he learns *how* numbers behave, but not *why* they behave that way. The Egyptian student was given the problem and then led through the calculations by the scribe. But the rule was never given; it would seem that it

A problem from the Rhind Papyrus. Above, a transcription of the problem as it appears. Below, the hieroglyphs reversed to conform with our system of reading from left to right. Schwaller de Lubicz's literal rendering of the text illustrates the Egyptian habit of personifying the problem: 'I go down three times into the hekat *(bushel). A third part of me above myself. I leave fully satisfied. Who said that?'*

Schwaller de Lubicz found that all problems of the Rhind Papyrus could be expressed geometrically, as in the lower right hand corner of the illustration. This does not mean that geometric expression preceded the formulation of the problem, but that the Egyptian mathematicians formulated these school problems upon a fully developed knowledge of proportion. For if simple problems of divisions of bread, beer, land, etc. were formulated haphazardly, they would not all be susceptible of geometric expression.

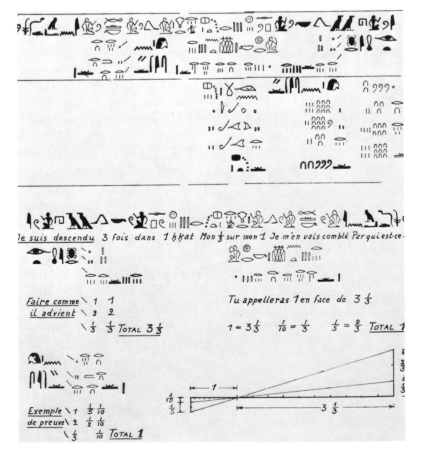

R. J. Gillings
'The Addition of Egyptian Unit Fractions'
Journal of Egyptian Archaeology 51, pp. 95 and 97

A student of the ancient Egyptian exact sciences . . . soon becomes aware of what, at first glance, appears to be quite an 'oddity' in the solutions of the arithmetical problems. This 'oddity' is one of *emphasis*. For example, having due regard to the technique and methods available to the Egyptian scribe, a problem may be presented of some relative difficulty, and one finds explanatory matter, especially in the arithmetic, of the most elementary and simple kind set down in extensive detail, while the mechanism of the most abstruse and closely reasoned argument may be omitted altogether. It is as if the scribe was unaware of any inherent difficulty in it, and so he merely sets down the answer . . .

One can only be amazed at the trouble to which the scribe will go over things which appear to us so elementary; yet elsewhere, with operations on the addition of unit fractions of alarming proportions, he will produce immediate answers with the utmost nonchalance.

William Temple
Nature, Man and God
Macmillan, 1934, p. 149

We discover that the universe shows evidence of a designing or controlling power that has something in common with our individual minds — not so far as we have discovered, emotion, morality or aesthetic appreciation, but the tendency to think in a way, for want of a better word, we may call mathematical . . . Surprise has lately been expressed that mathematics appears to be the only surviving science, for all others are passing into mathematics.

was up to the student to discover the rule for himself. In other words, mathematics was a matter of individual discovery, rather than of successfully executed repetition, as it is with us.

Even the language employed in the papyri serves to promote this sense of vitality, of living interaction. Our school texts characteristically keep the problem and student safely distinct. If seven loaves of bread will be needed to feed nine families, how many loaves of bread will be needed to feed thirty-two families? Egypt personified the problem: 'I descend three times into the *hekat*. One third of myself is added to me. One third of one third of me is added to me, and one ninth of me is added to me. I return fully satisfied. Who said that?' (Rhind Pap. Prob. 37) 'I descend three times into one *hekat*. One seventh is added to me. I come back fully satisfied.' (Prob. 38.)

Our system imposes a task upon the student; the Egyptian system offered him a kind of adventure into familiar grammar school mathematics: multiplication, division of whole numbers and of fractions, arithmetic and geometric progressions and proportions, measure and the calculation of the slope of the pyramid (which employs the triangle of Pythagoras, supposedly unknown to the Egyptians), the rule of three, and the volume of the cylinder.

Although commendable, these would not be considered particularly sophisticated or advanced techniques by today's mathematicians and Egyptologists, who dismiss the lofty opening claim of the Rhind Papyrus: 'Herein lies every secret, every mystery.'

The difficulty in understanding Egyptian mathematics lies in modern man's unwillingness and finally incapacity to see things other than the way he is used to seeing them. Though prior to Schwaller de Lubicz the arguments put forward in favour of Egyptian knowledge of mathematical rules and principles were compelling, even these were based upon an unequivocal assumption of 'progress' in mathematics (as in everything else). It is assumed that Egypt (and all other ancient or so-called primitive societies) are in some way trial runs for the Western twentieth century. So even those scholars who held that Egyptian mathematics was far more sophisticated than was generally recognised judged it from our own point of view, and looked to see if they had the binomial, algebra, the decimal algorithm; in other words, they tried to see how far Egypt had 'advanced' in our direction.

But Egypt had no notion of 'progress'. To evaluate her mathematics we must judge it within the context of Egypt's civilisation, not ours. And secondly, our own all-pervading obsession with progress and 'evolution' has prompted modern mathematicians to regard their speciality in exalted, even sacrosanct terms. Yet for all its facility in mundane spheres and its elegance in scientific spheres, modern mathematics is open to criticism. On the most profound level, modern scientists and philosophers expect to use mathematics to describe the physical world objectively. A mathematical formula is believed to be precise, accurate and immune to subjective interpretations — unlike a merely verbal description.

To modern science and philosophy, the physical world is 'reality'. To diehard materialists, emotional and psychological 'realities' are merely aspects of that physical reality which are (momentarily) insusceptible of measurement.

But at this stage modern man must face a series of paradoxes of his own making. This 'objective' mathematics, for all its success in mechanics, makes use of abstractions that correspond to nothing in experience. The square root of minus one, the zero, infinity are abstractions corresponding to nothing in that physical realm we call 'reality'. And without these abstractions the formulae do not work. In other words, to describe the phenomenal world 'scientifically', science must have recourse to abstraction — which is a euphemism for fantasy.

When science leaves the realm of mechanics and technology and looks into subatomic physics — the science of the basic structure of matter and therefore, necessarily, the science upon which all other science is based — the picture becomes even more complex and intriguing.

Since Einstein's relativity theory it has been known and accepted that matter is a form of energy, a coagulation or condensation of energy. One consequence of this is that, for scientists at any rate, materialism has been a provisionally impossible philosophy, a fact which has done nothing to prevent most scientists from professing it.

Largely in the hope of obtaining ultimate proof of the accidental nature and inherent meaninglessness of the universe (and therefore of their own lives), scientists have pressed ever further into the structure of matter, hoping to find some ultimate material building block upon which all matter somehow depends.

This search, intuitively understood by the brighter of modern physicists as doomed to failure, is now in the process of abandonment even by those psychologically incapable of accepting the consequences of their own discoveries.

Meanwhile, the newest generation of physicists has grown up with the paradox of waves that are particles and particles that are waves. Though no more able to grasp the situation intellectually than were their predecessors, at least some of these new physicists approach the subject free from the emotional legacy of Victorian and Newtonian fallacies.

It is now clear and inescapable that the latest discoveries and theories concerning the structure of the physical universe run strikingly parallel to the view implicit and often explicit in Oriental philosophies — philosophies whose origins, according to accepted evolutionary theory, are lost in prehistory, when our ancestors had just jumped down out of the trees.

The similarities and correspondences have been explored at length recently by Fritjof Capra, a physicist thoroughly familiar with Eastern philosophy and, more important, with its practice. (C4)

It is a great pity that Schwaller de Lubicz is no longer alive to comment on Capra, and that Capra has not read Schwaller de Lubicz, and therefore has not explored the underlying realities of Pythagoreanism. My own competence to comment is limited; I am not a physicist or a mathematicisn and cannot either criticise or commend with authority. Yet, insofar as I can understand it, it seems to me that physicists are on the verge of surrendering that most solidly entrenched of scientific beliefs: the ability of science to discover the 'objective truth' about the universe.

Modern mathematics and ancient metaphysics

In the context of subatomic physics, there are and can be no 'objective truths'. There are only 'processes' and 'patterns of probability'. The stability of 'matter' is an illusion of the senscs. Mathematics can be used with increasing accuracy to describe these patterns, probabilities and processes. But it cannot, in its present form, account for them in themselves. Yet the Pythagorean approach, which Schwaller de Lubicz shows to be the foundation of Egyptian mathematics, can be used to do so.

At least a few physicists are closely studying thc Hindu, Buddhist and Taoist view of the physical universe: that what we call the 'world' or 'reality' is but an aspect of 'mind'. It has no 'objective' reality in its own right, but takes its form and is subject to measurement only through the agency of man's senses. In other words, if our senses were organised differently, the world would also appear differently. It would be 'objectively' different.

But Eastern metaphysical concepts are expressed verbally, not mathematically, and the verbal can never be rigorously scientific in our sense of that word. Insofar as I am able to follow the thinking of modern mathematicians, I believe that there is no way in which this crucial and ultimate realisation can be scientifically expressed; yet the discoveries of subatomic physics are forcing scientists to endorse a metaphysical, unmaterialistic and ultimately spiritual Eastern world view.

At this point, some striking differences between the Eastern and Western methods (and aims) become apparent. For all its sophistication, modern mathematics by its nature will not serve to describe absolutes. The physicist must content himself with ever closer and more precise approximations, which concern only chosen aspects of the whole. Science has decided to look at Ali Baba's treasure through a keyhole; its efforts are expended in improving its viewing equipment and its descriptive language (mathematics). But as all voyeurs know, it is impossible to see the whole room through the keyhole from any given angle, and it is possible to peep at only one angle at a time.

Despite similarities in description, the mystic's methods and aims are different. To the mystic, the voyeuristic approach serves no purpose. The mystic spends his life learning to say 'Open Sesame' and then walks in and makes the treasure his own. For the benefit of others he describes what he sees as best he can, but his object is to get himself through the door. In practical terms, the implications of the two approaches reverberate far beyond the bounds of mysticism, metaphysics and the philosophy of science: the one leads to the hydrogen bomb and the other to the Taj Mahal.

In the world of subatomic physics, time and space in the ordinary sense lose their meaning, and language will not allow physicists to express what they find in terms comprehensible to the rational intellect. Particles that are simultaneously waves can be in two 'places' at the same time, and subatomic events of the 'past' are preceded by events in the 'present'. Matter is not a thing but a pattern of probabilities, the likelihood of which can be statistically determined within a certain degree of accuracy by mathematics. But that is the best that can be expected of modern mathematics.

For all its descriptive power, then, it cannot further an understanding of those key words that pop up again and again in this radical new science: they are 'pattern', 'process' and 'interaction'. Physicists, including even Capra, tend to use these words as though their meanings were self-evident, but they are not: they are as mysterious and as immune to modern scientific explanation as time and space.

Though unable to explain process, pattern and interaction (and apparently unaware of the necessity or importance of doing so), modern physicists put mathematics to work formulating theories that might at least describe them. To date, none of the theories put forward are without drawbacks, yet it is intriguing to find that the most promising seem to relate in striking fashion to fundamentals of Egyptian mathematics and symbolism: creation of matter involves the 'crossing' of oppositely charged particles. The beautiful and elegant pictures taken in bubble chambers with their crosses and spirals seem almost deliberate or conscious representations of the principle of double inversion and of the unfolding spiral action of the Golden Section, the primordial creative principle.

Writing in the 1950s, Schwaller de Lubicz had already noted

Subatomic particle tracks from the 'bubble chamber'. Particles which are not 'things' but rather packets or foci of energy, collide and create these beautiful patterns. The physicist Fritjof Capra rightly sees in this a parallel to the Indian dance of Shiva, which represents the mystical creation. From the point of view of Pythagorean number theory, it is interesting to note the formation at this fundamental state of spirals and the division into four, the 'number' of principial matter.

the way in which advances in physics were proving the validity of the ancient Egyptian and Pythagorean philosophy.

Now, the wisdom of the Egyptian Temple did not survive Egypt intact, or in its original form, but percolated down to our day through more or less underground groups without any apparent central organisation — alchemists, Gnostics, Neoplatonists, Cabbalists, Freemasons, Sufis and others. (As late as 1341, according to Paul Tannery, the Byzantine mathematician Rhabdas was still using the Egyptian system of fractionalisation for the extraction of square roots.* No one can say at what point it vanished completely.) But the art and architecture of Egypt is sufficiently intact to allow us to retrieve much of the original.

In the East, the situation is the opposite. Very ancient traditions have been kept alive to the present day, handed down by a succession of masters. But no art or architecture as ancient as Egypt's remains, and Eastern philosophy and metaphysics, according to most authorities, were not put into writing until relatively recently. It is therefore impossible to know precisely how much of the ancient system is in its original form today, and how much has become corrupted, popularised or purely exoteric.

In an exhaustively detailed architectural study, *The Hindu Temple* (University of Calcutta, 1946), Stella Kramrisch has proven that an understanding of number, harmony and the interplay of number — similar to that prevailing in Egypt — directs the proportions of the Hindu temple. It therefore seems likely that the bewildering proliferation of Indian deities and the profusion of Indian myths embodies a similarly precise knowledge of number as key to function (though at this late date it might well be impossible for scholars to extricate those elements that are based upon knowledge from those that are based upon imagination).

In delving ever deeper into the structure of matter, physicists have had to abandon the absolutes upon which Newtonian modern science was based: the atom as an immutable entity, absolute time and absolute space. These have been replaced by pattern, process and interaction.

How pattern, process and interaction are to be dealt with in the framework of modern mathematics I am unequipped to say. But in a host of organic and inorganic sciences it is quite clear that they conform to harmonic, rhythmic and proportional laws. Form, as we have seen from the study of cymatics, is the result of frequency. Or to put it into esoterically accurate words, form is that aspect of frequency apprehensible by the senses. It is hard to imagine that the subatomic should not be similarly structured.

J. Pecker
L'Astronomie
June, 1975, p. 230

The philosophical problem posed was to learn if this wave associated with particles (electrons or photons) measured (by its intensity) the probability of their presence, without thereby denying quasi-temporal nature and their determinist movement (attitude of De Broglie and Einstein); or if, on the contrary, this discovery implied, on the microphysical scale, a complete renunciation of determinism (attitude of Heisenberg and Bohr). This controversy is not yet ended. Hence the great interest of the current debate, aired here by Prof. Espagnat . . . .

* *Memoires Scientifiques*, Gauthiers-Villars, 1920; Tome IV, p. 13.

R. Espagnat
L'Astronomie
June, 1975, *passim*.

Thus, under one form or another, fundamental quantum principles dominate the world of physics. They have permitted not only progress but also an extraordinary unification of our knowledge. It is not surprising that so powerful a tool breaks through familiar boundaries, that it obliges us to think of the world and of our rapport with the world differently than did our predecessors. And this leads to the second part of this essay; the role of the new mechanics in the development of ideas ... [We must recognise that every shimmer of qualitatively different forms is quantitatively realised through the introduction of *whole numbers*. These whole numbers, which Kepler sought in vain in the orbits of the planets, regulate the orbits of atoms and of molecules. Thus, through a long detour (refined, and stripped of archaisms) an essential component of Pythagorean thought returns to honour.] This is our first instance of the fact that scientific thought is universal thought ... Once the veil is lifted, we are faced ... with surprising perspectives which in fact bring back the questions posed by our ancestors before the spectacle of the world, but at a less ingenuous level.

Among these great questions, we must take note of that of chance....

It has been said that Einstein did not believe in indeterminism, and he is quoted as saying, 'The Good Lord does not play dice'. But this is merely an anecdote. The problem, in his eyes, was not fundamental. The problem that preoccupied Einstein was, above all, that quantum mechanics reopened the equally fundamental concept of 'the object' and forced the revision of all current scientific views upon the relation between subject and object. This problem is unrelated to the casting of dice, and it is more serious.

I believe we should pay attention to the great uncertainties of Einstein and De Broglie, and to the lesser known voices of the younger physicists of all countries, who tell us that formulas no longer suffice; that there must be a reality beyond our senses and beyond our spirit, and that if science hopes to approach it, it may be that special requirements are imposed which lead beyond formulas. Delineating these requirements is difficult and dangerous. And it is a thankless task to set them out in detail, for one obviously risks the arbitrary. But faced with what seems to be an excess of neopositive pragmatism, it is essential that these requirements are formulated, at least as hypotheses to put to the test.

In his detailed and elaborate analysis of the problems of the Egyptian papyri, Schwaller de Lubicz shows the whole of Egyptian mathematics to be founded upon an intimate knowledge of harmony and proportion, of the interplay of number and of the particular functional significance of certain specific numbers and proportions. Moreover, he shows that without exception, all the problems given in the papyri are susceptible of a geometric solution: in every case, the solutions given to the problems can be set out in a geometric form that 'proves' them to be true.

R. A. Schwaller de Lubicz
Symbol et Symbolique
Cairo, 1951, *passim*

For the first time, [exoteric] scientific research arrives by rational means, at the threshold of the door that permits a glimpse into the inner life of matter. It is therefore indispensable to keep in touch with the science of the day, if only in a general way.... The current state of progress, the cause of the profound revolution of scientific thought ... permits the restoration of those principles underlying the real significance of the *symbol*. That which, only yesterday, might have been considered pure philosophical speculation, is today founded upon scientific experiments with revolutionary consequences, of which but few take notice, the rest remaining true to the rational determinism of the nineteenth century.... The granular character within the continuity of the wave, that is to say, the photon, which has the appearance of an isolated quantity within the continuous function of the wave, the discontinuous within the continuous. It is this simultaneity that the 'cerebral' intelligence can no longer grasp, but whose existence is demonstrated by experiment, which the physicist Werner Heisenberg would call 'the Uncertainty Principle' but which, translating psychologically, I would call 'the present moment'.

Within the atom, the constituent unit of matter, the old laws do not apply. They remain valid for matter; but for example, within the atom, Newtonian gravitation plays no role; it is electromagnetic effects which operate. This is a fact, but it asks for further study, for one is once again up against the unknown, called 'affinities'. On the other hand, the chemistry of Lavoisier is happily extinct, since we now know that matter constantly vanishes into energy, and is constantly being created (by transmutation into isotopes). We know that in the upper atmosphere nitrogen is transmuted into a carbon isotope, which then comes to 'nourish' vegetation, which casts — or will cast — a curious light over the vital phenomena of the earth's surface.

Egyptian mathematics is not founded upon trial and error, nor were the Egyptians ignorant of the rules underlying their methods. As Schwaller de Lubicz shows, the key numbers and fractions chosen by the Egyptians to illustrate these school problems are alone enough to dispel this notion.

Even the despised 'cumbersomeness' of the Egyptian system is open to reevaluation, providing we can temper our worship of facility.

It is true that it takes longer to write ᵎᵎᵎᵎ than it takes to write 9. And a simple multiplication or division written out in full, as in the Rhind Papyrus, takes longer to write than the same problem in modern notation. On the other hand, the method employed by the scribe provides an insight into the actual practice of mathematics once the methods have been

T. Eric Peet
The Rhind Mathematical Papyrus
Hodder and Stoughton, 1923, p. 29

The Egyptian system of multiplying by doubling was a slow one, but it was sure; it is astonishing how simply and even how quickly the most complicated multipliers can be constructed by this method.

mastered. In many cases steps have been omitted from the calculations. This indicates that these steps have been carried out mentally. Schwaller de Lubicz points out that a facility for mental calculation has always been strong in Eastern and Semitic races. Even Egyptologists have noted that the Egyptian method of progressive doubling lends itself to speedy calculation, only the notation is unwieldy. But with a bit of practice, very little notation is necessary. If I want to multiply 273 x 359 by modern methods I cannot do it in my head with confidence, and if I don't do it in my head then I must write the whole thing out. But if I do it in Egyptian, a brief acquaintance with the method tells me that I do not need to write out the entire problem with the Egyptian system, which would entail:

$$
\begin{array}{rr}
1 & 359 \\
2 & 718 \\
4 & 1436 \\
8 & 2872 \\
16 & 5744 \\
32 & 11488 \\
64 & 22976 \\
128 & 45952 \\
256 & 91904 \\
\end{array}
$$

I go from the bottom, and see immediately that this is 256 + 16 + 1. Since it is easy to double mentally, I need only calculate in my head, and write down in hieroglyphs the total for these three figures, which can be obtained mentally without great strain. So, in everyday use, the Egyptian method is scarcely more cumbersome than our own; it may even be less so. It is significant that the methods used in modern calculators and computers are closer to the Egyptian than what we are taught in school and use every day. Schwaller de Lubicz quotes other mathematicians who have noted with interest that the most ancient method of calculation in the world is also the most modern. More important, from the Egyptian point of view the method does not betray the imperatives of theology. As Schwaller de Lubicz repeatedly stresses, all Egyptian thought, mythology, science and art devolves from the concept of the mystical Primordial Scission, and any discipline that did not have its roots in this revelation was inadmissible to the Egyptian mind. The mathematical method itself is a practical application of the principle of double inversion, which, as we have seen, is a natural consequence of the division of unity into multiplicity. (One becomes Two, and each half partakes of the nature of the 'One' and of the 'Other'.)

It is this attitude, and not stupidity or perversity, that led Egyptian mathematicians to their curious system of fractions — one instance where theological considerations undoubtedly made difficulties we consider unnecessary. To Egypt, a fraction, any fraction, could only be a fraction of *unity*. It was inadmissible to divide 17 by 7 and arrive at 2 3/7. The Egyptian answer would be 2 + ¼ + 1/7 + 1/28.

Even in this instance, the difficulty is merely one of notation — the (to us) unnecessary time it takes to write out these fractions in hieroglyphs. On the positive side, whatever we may think of the determination to restrict mathematics to theological considerations, there is the undeniable fact that the operations involved in Egyptian calculation were simpler and speedier than our own. Heading each mathematical papyrus that has been found there is a table, similar to our tables of logarithms and square roots, in which all fractions with a numerator of 2 are broken down into constituent fractions with a numerator of 1. This relieves the student or calculator of the one really difficult, time-consuming task. So, in practice, the Egyptian system was no more laborious than ours, and may have been less so.

Meanwhile, commanding the choice made by Egyptian mathematicians in the breakdown of these 2/n fractions, Schwaller de Lubicz finds a systematic application of harmonic principles and a profound knowledge of the interplay of number, and of the particular significance of certain numbers.

His long essay into the underlying intricacies of the Rhind Papyrus is irrefutable. In Egyptological circles it is ignored. One attempt to refute it (M. Meyer-Astruc; *Chroniques d'Egypt*, 35, pp. 120-139) was easily answered by Schwaller de Lubicz himself shortly before his death (*Chroniques d'Egypt*, 37, pp. 77-106). Since that time occasional articles have appeared in the Egyptological journals which, without exactly corroborating Schwaller de Lubicz or citing his work, upgrade the standard image of Egypt's mathematics, and call attention to inadmissible inconsistencies in currently held views.

But there is nothing to commend this cautious advance. The groundwork was done by Schwaller de Lubicz. Any competent mathematician can follow the development of his argument. And without going into intricacies of harmony and Pythagorean number play, there is one glaring, deliberate exception to the rule of Egyptian fractions that, long before Schwaller de Lubicz, should have inspired scholars to look for cogent reasoning behind the whole system.

The exception: 2/3

Fractions with numerators other than 1 are inadmissible. With the exception of 2/3.

Why 2/3? What is so special about 2/3? In the Egyptian fac-

A. Badawy
Op. cit., p. 34

Can we deduce from these facts that the figures of the Fibonacci series were known by the Egyptians and that they played a direct role in the design of their temples? That this was actually the case is proved by the temples at 'Amarna, the sanctuary of the great temple.

Ibid., p. 60

Although the circle was rarely used in Egyptian architecture, its derivative polygons occur in the various columns ... the commonest polygons were the hexagon and the octagon....

There is no way to construct exactly a polygon with seven, nine, eleven or thirteen sides. Yet the Egyptians contrived to design their capitals with nine elements and occasionally with seven.

toring system, 2/3 breaks up easily into ½ + 1/6. If 2/3 is legitimate, then why not 2/5 or 2/29? Was there anything other than caprice behind this curious exception? Such a question seems natural enough to ask, particularly by men whose lives are purportedly dedicated to understanding ancient Egypt. The answer is by no means obvious, and requires a capacity to think along Pythagorean lines — which may be why so few have asked the question.

Esoterically, 2/3 is not actually a fraction — a subtle point mirrored in the hieroglyph itself. The glyph for 1/7 is  but the glyph for 2/3 is  . 2/3 *is not separate from the whole*; the sign indicates an aspect of unity itself, one of the direct simultaneous consequences of the Primordial Scission.

In looking at these signs from Schwaller de Lubicz's point of view, we can catch a glimpse of the extraordinary coherence pervading the whole of Egypt's civilisation. When we write the modern sign 1/7 it evokes nothing but a mathematical quantity. But in Egypt, the symbol for unity, for 1, is , the open mouth, that which emits the 'Word'; this is also the Primordial Scission, the separation of two unequal parts which, mystically, are incorporated within the whole, a simultaneous fusion and fission that cannot be expressed rationally or comprehended cerebrally. The glyph  might be translated as 'One emits seven'. But 2/3 would have to be translated as  'Unity is proportioned as two is to three'.

Viewed as a proportion, as a relationship rather than as a quantity, 2/3 has unique characteristics. The exceptional treatment accorded it in Egypt is fully justified. As we have seen, geometrically and numerically we can express different aspects of the Primordial Scission in different ways. These geometrical and numerical representations form the bases of all subsequent systems of harmony, rhythm and proportion. (In this sense, it is legitimate to say that the truths of geometry are absolute and eternal; it was in this sense that Plato and Pythagoras understood them. Euclid misunderstood them, taking the form — of the triangle for example — as the reality, rather than as the symbol for the reality. And modern mathematicians have blamed Plato and Pythagoras for Euclid's lack of insight, themselves taking a curiously perverse delight in creating unobservable, hence unscientific and imaginary, worlds of n dimensions in which the axioms of Euclidean geometry do not hold.)

One becomes Two and Three simultaneously. Therefore 2/3 is an expression of female to male, of matter to spirit. The whole of the proportion 2/3 may be seen as the 'structure' of Five, the sacred number of the Pythagoreans. And the 2/3 interval on the vibrating string determines the vibration of the perfect fifth, the first harmonic interval, to which all other harmonic intervals relate.

So while it is possible to regard harmony as a purely quantitative phenomenon, it is legitimate to see it as a fundamental moment of rapport between matter and spirit, between female and male.

In Egypt, as Schwaller de Lubicz has shown, the 2/3 proportion also crops up in the system of weights and measures. There is and can be no logical reason for this. From the point of view of facile calculation it complicates matters. Only when its mystical significance is considered does its incorporation become comprehensible. Meanwhile, from our point of view Schwaller de Lubicz's explanation of the significance of the proportion 2/3 is important. Even the formally uncommitted have been subjected to modern education. Though this is little more than an informal gospel of undemonstrable orthodoxies, its persuasive power is considerable. It is difficult to accept Schwaller de Lubicz's word against the self-styled authority of professional historians. For the interested but unspecialised reader, his evidence takes so long to develop, and involves knowledge of so many specialities, that it is difficult to follow, much less judge or criticise.

For this reason, his explanation of the exceptional treatment accorded 2/3 by Egypt is particularly important. It is one of those instances where detailed or specialised knowledge does not matter. Nobody disputes the fact that, in Egyptian mathematics, 2/3 stands as the only exception to a rule that was inexplicable prior to Schwaller de Lubicz. When, through his magnificent reconstruction of the basis of Pythagorean thinking, it becomes possible to explain both the seemingly bizarre rule and the single exception to that rule, then only a kind of deliberate disdain for truth can account for neglecting his work.

Whether or not the study of Egyptian mathematics can be of practical use in our present society I cannot say. It seems unlikely that it should be of any use in tracking down still more hadrons, muons and neutrons. There is surely no point, for us, in a return to hieroglyphic notation. Yet the fact is that subatomic physics corroborates Eastern philosophy, and seems on the verge of physically demonstrating the principle of double inversion which, according to Schwaller de Lubicz, is the basic metaphysical principle upon which physical creation rests. It is possible that a new generation of mathematicians may find clues in those Egyptian school problems to problems as yet unsolved, and seemingly unsolvable. Egypt was not interested in hadrons and muons. Egypt was not interested in 'things', but in principles, patterns, processes — in other words, in life. Her mathematics reflected that concern in its methodology, which performed its tasks without recourse to abstractions that could not be related to human experience. Since modern physics, the cornerstone of our own science, is now recognising the futility of studying 'things' and the underlying validity and importance of pattern, process and principle (and therefore of harmony, rhythm and proportion) it may well be expedient for those qualified to do so to look deeply into Schwaller de Lubicz's elaborate but still preliminary examination of Egyptian mathematics.

Medicine

When the first Egyptian medical papyri were deciphered, German doctors laughed. The Egyptians advised the application of crocodile dung and other unlovely substances to soothe and heal wounds, inflammations and infections. The system was dubbed 'Drekapoteke' (sewage pharmacology) by the bemused Herren Doktoren.

But doctors today do not laugh. It is clear that medicine men five thousand years ago knew some things the medical men of fifty years ago did not know — that the application of these substances was making use of raw, natural antibiotics.

How could Egypt acquire this knowledge? Historians will consider but two related explanations: accident or trial and error (which is systematically organised accident). Accident and trial and error are, like 'coincidence' in other familiar contexts, catchall explanations designed to ease the scholar over intractable problems and dissuade the student from asking embarrassing questions. But when subjected to the kind of scrutiny we applied earlier to those clear, logical thinkers who worked with diorite instead of sandstone, discrepancies appear.

How, in point of fact, might accident lead to the discovery of the natural antibiotic qualities of dung? Can we postulate a wounded soldier, returning home along the river bank? Too tired to pay close attention to where he is walking, he slips in a pile of crocodile dung, which smears over his wounded knee. An unfastidious sort, he neglects to clean the wound. Indeed, he neglects to clean it for several days. But at the end of that time, miraculously, his wound is healed. He reports this to the local shaman who forthwith stops chanting incantations and starts applying dung. Somehow this is unconvincing. (Strictly speaking, crocodile dung was principally used for eye complaints, only Pap. Ebers, 542, recommends it for a wound.) If accident will not satisfactorily account for medical discoveries, then let us look at trial and error. Noting that wounds go septic and heal slowly, Egyptian medicine men decide to systematically look for healing agents. Having only just learned to walk on their hind legs, they have no idea where to begin looking, and apply whatever substance happens to be at hand; pomegranate juice, crushed melon rind, sand, beer, goat's blood, camel

Gustave Lefebvre
Essai sur la Médecine Egyptienne
Presses Universitaires de France, 1956,
p. 197

The bat plays a large role in the pharmacopoeia of ancient civilisations. In Egypt, its blood was used in a pomade applied to the eyelids.... The Chinese ... used its excrement for another eye ailment, night blindness.... Magical remedy, one would think; to cure the eyes, use the droppings of an animal that can see by night. But chemical analysis of bat excrement shows that it contains a greater quantity of Vitamin A than cod liver oil; and we know that Vitamin A cures certain types of night blindness....

Let us be on guard before ridiculing all those remedies whose presence we find disconcerting in the Egyptian apothecary. The part played — a very large one — by magic and superstition should not stop us from paying close attention, and studying with indulgent comprehension a medicine that was not, as it turns out, simply 'demonic' or 'excremental'.

Jurgen Thorwald
The Science and Secrets of Early Medicine
Thames & Hudson, 1962, pp. 84-86

It does not matter how the Egyptians learned the specific effectiveness of certain remedies — the fact remains that they did know them. Perhaps superstition and ideas of sympathetic magic led them to their original choice. A number of these remedies reflect this only too clearly.... However, we may shed some of our respect when we come upon prescriptions calling for ... fly droppings, pelican droppings, human urine, lizard excrement, a child's faeces, a gazelle's dung — and most frequently of all, the excrement of a crocodile.

The use of copper and aluminium compounds seemed to reveal the perspicacity of the Egyptian doctors. And modern medicine even found a rational explanation for the application of fish gall and crushed beef liver for inflammations of the eye ... but the use of filth and excrements seemed a clear token of repulsive barbarism. Medical historians invented the term 'sewerage pharmacology'.... When Dr. Benjamin M. Duggar, Professor of Plant Physiology ... presented the world ... with the new drug, aureomycin, he certainly had no thought of the effect of his discovery upon our valuation of Egyptian medicine .... Investigation soon showed that bacteria living in the human body release their excretory products into the faeces and urine, which therefore are rich in antibiotic substances....

Presumably the Egyptians originally included faeces and urine in their prescriptions because they expected these substances to drive out the demons which caused sickness. But then the substances suddenly produced successful cures — although in many cases they may only have done harm — and produced new infections, since the Egyptians had no idea of the secret of their power. Success depended upon chance .... Many of these prescriptions are astonishingly specific in their recommendations of excretions from particular animals.. ... It is known today that every animal produces different antibiotic substances, and the same is true for mud and various soils....

Bruce Pomeranz,
New Scientist
Jan. 6, 1977, p. 13

From all the results to date, I propose the following hypothesis for acupuncture analgesia: needling activates deep sensory nerves which cause the pituitary (or mid-brain) to release endomorphins (morphine-like brain chemicals); these endomorphins block signals from getting through the nerve chains in the pain pathway carrying messages from spinal cord to the higher brain centres.

sputum. As medicine men, not only are they clear, logical thinkers, they are also conscientious. It is clear to them that there are thousands of substances to apply to wounds, none any more likely to cure than any others. So, as they go through the list over the centuries, they keep records. By the law of averages, these records consist mainly of failures. Thus, over the generations a vast lore of ineffective medicine accumulates, and this knowledge is kept secret and handed down from master to pupil so as to avoid repeating mistakes.

Given sufficient time, all known substances could be tested for their efficiency in healing wounds. But being clear, logical thinkers, these medicine men would soon realise that because a given substance was ineffective against wounds, that did not mean it had no other medical use. Therefore, by a trial and error method, each of the thousands of possible substances would have to be tested against every known ailment. Otherwise, having tried camel dung as a cure for dyspepsia and finding it inefficacious, the ancients might never have hit upon its antibiotic properties against infection. Statistically trained readers might enjoy working out the number of millennia required theoretically to develop an effective medical lore by trial and error. Others may question trial and error as an explanation for ancient medicine and keep open minds to the possibility that the ancients knew what they were looking for, and knew how to find it: they would work through observation of the natural world, insight, intelligence and experiment — in other words by the same methods used today. But in all likelihood they would make additional effective use of prayer, incantation and more highly developed intuitive faculties.

However acquired, Egyptian medicine, more than any other branch of Egyptian knowledge, has gone up in official esteem. But even this rare instance of scholarly generosity leaves much unplumbed, and fails to take many aspects of the situation into account.

Scholars work upon the customary assumption that modern medical science is more advanced in every way than any ancient system. But a cursory glance at the most recent developments proves the contrary. For all its technical sophistication and its knowledge of microscopic detail, modern medical science is far from comprehensive. Over the past few years, all but diehards have had to accept the validity of acupuncture, despite the fact that the Chinese 'meridians' or lines of 'force' are still physically undetectable. And less narrow-minded medical men are now paying serious attention to branches of medicine dismissed as nonsense not long ago: homeopathy, naturopathy, dietary systems, even faith healing.

While it is legitimate to look into Egyptian medicine to see how much they knew of what we know, it is equally important to bear in mind the possibility that Egypt had knowledge that

Colin Ronan
Lost Discoveries
MacDonald, 1973, pp. 83-84

A tomb painting at Beni Hassan dating from about 2000 BC shows an acacia tree. The Egyptians made a chemical contraceptive by grinding together the acacia spikes, honey and dates. We now know that acacia spikes contain lactic acid, a chemical that kills sperm. . . .

The mud of the Nile, dried hard by the sun after the annual flooding had subsided. The Egyptians used this mud as an ingredient in a number of medical preparations, and only recently it has been found to contain natural antibiotics. . . . In Ancient Egypt it was possible to have a pregnancy test at the earliest states and, at the same time, to determine the sex of the unborn child — or so it was claimed. The method used was to take a woman's urine and soak bags containing wheat and barley with it. They found that if the subject was pregnant, the urine would accelerate the growth of the wheat if the child was to be a boy, or the barley if it was to be a girl. Yet such a test is only a comparatively recent innovation with us; not until 1926 was a urine pregnancy test discovered, and it was another seven years before the acceleration of wheat and barley was confirmed by laboratory tests. . . . The Egyptians who went on the caravan routes . . . chewed a root they called the *ami-majos*. They found this gave them extra protection from the sun by reinforcing their skin pigmentation, and modern research shows that the root contains the active organic chemical compound called 8-methoxypsorate.

we do not have. Schwaller de Lubicz's detailed study of the medical papyri, as well as certain hints contained within the papyri themselves, support this latter possibility. And there are a number of problems and mysteries that remain unsolved, some of which are unsolvable.

First, written documents that have survived such as the Smith Papyrus, refer on numerous occasions to knowledge that was never committed to writing. Hippocrates, writing a thousand years later, refers to it. The insistence upon secrecy by so many ancient priesthoods makes an oral tradition so likely that authorities have almost no choice but to accept it as fact. What they imagine to be the value or otherwise of this secret lore is of course another matter. But it would seem fairly obvious that the Egyptians would keep secret whatever they felt most important, or liable to abuse in the hands of the uninitiated.

Second, there are difficulties with translation. Though in most other areas, the majority of hieroglyphs have yielded to decipherment, many signs in the medical papyri are peculiar to those documents and as yet are untranslated. Many are believed to refer to specific medical substances, minerals, herbs and plants, while others are thought to be unknown maladies. It seems unlikely that their meanings will ever be divulged.

Third, there is the difference in approach, and the tendency for modern scholars to discount as superstition all that conflicts with current beliefs. For example, it is clear that Egyptian medicine had a strong astrological element. The papyri advise specific times at which to administer specific recipes. Modern medicine knows nothing of such things. But accumulating evidence from many sources begins to reveal the existence of cycles and periodicities in the incidence of diseases and in their intensities. Under natural conditions, more children are born near the full moon than at any other time. Childbirth also follows a daily rhythm: more children tend to be born in the early morning, providing nature is left to her own course and birth is not induced. It is of course well known that fevers increase at night, and that asthmatics are most likely to suffer an attack early in the morning. By the same token, anthroposophical experiments have shown that mineral salt solutions are sensitive to planetary influences (as is the sap of plants), while the work of the Italian chemist Giorgio Piccardi has shown colloidal suspensions sensitive to influences that seem to be extra-galactic.

But at present, the obvious conclusion to be drawn from such evidence is far from universally accepted, and no one would know how to put it to practical or systematic use if it were accepted. From the extant papyri it would appear that the Egyptians had such knowledge, and knew how to apply it.

Complementary to the tendency to discount all that conflicts with modern belief, there is the practice of failing to study the implications of those aspects of Egyptian practice that we acknowledge as sound. Schwaller de Lubicz's detailed examination of the medical papyri reveals the extensive, profound and all-embracing theoretical understanding of the human body that cannot help but lie behind the practical diagnostic and therapeutic information.

Finally, there is 'magic'. Many of the papyri include magical incantations and magical practices. Sometimes these are incorporated in the texts, sometimes they are written separately. In the Edwin Smith papyrus (F.5) the most complete and informative papyrus yet discovered, one side is concerned with sound, detailed surgical information — except for a single incantation which the doctor is instructed to chant over one specific type of injury. (Looking for a sound reason for this bizarre exception, Schwaller de Lubicz found that with this kind of head injury, the crucial factor was to prevent the patient from falling asleep and losing consciousness. Hence the inclusion of this single incantation, perhaps embodying specific rhythms, designed to focus the patient's attention and keep him awake.)

The other side of the papyrus is written in a different hand, and is wholly devoted to incantations of a general nature against epidemics, and to a recipe for a kind of rejuvenating cosmetic.

Following the logic predicated by evolutionary thought, it was assumed that magic and superstition was the earliest form of Egyptian medicine, and that a body of sound practice evolved over the centuries by trial and error.

This has now been disproved, not by Schwaller de Lubicz, but by orthodox scholars. As was so often the case in Egypt, old documents (whose originals are lost to us) were copied and recopied over the centuries. The copies were faithful to the original, but meanwhile the language itself was changing. And it is therefore possible to date documents with some accuracy by the style employed. Nor is it any longer legitimate to dismiss out of hand those aspects of Egyptian medicine formerly dismissed as 'magic and sorcery'.

Schwaller de Lubicz carefully distinguishes between magic and sorcery:

Magic is a summoning-up and utilisation of *natural cosmic energy* by harmonic means.

Sorcery concerns itself with influencing the psychological ambiance, thus with an energy *emanating from* the complex of human life. Both are valid, both 'work'.

There is both 'white' and 'black' magic, and 'white' and 'black' sorcery; and there are higher and lower forms of both magic and sorcery.

These distinctions may seem superfluous to the rationalist, who will deny the realities of either. In fact magic and sorcery are as rife in our own society as elsewhere, though they are of a low order, almost invariably destructive and always called by a respectable euphemism that hides the true nature of the practice. The voodoo witch doctor sticks pins in a doll and the victim dies. That is sorcery, and anthropologists do not doubt that such sorcery works in the societies that practice it.

But how does voodoo apply to twentieth-century progressive society? The glossy automobile advertisement subtly convinces me that if I buy a new Wombat the pretty blond in the picture, or her equal, will make herself available to me. I buy a new Wombat. The witch doctors of Madison Avenue have taken over my will as surely as their jungle colleagues, without my giving conscious assent. That is sorcery, literally and technically; and I get the blond, too. Sorcery works. It works by influencing the will of the victim, a procedure not susceptible of measurement, but demonstrably effective. In the twentieth century, sorcery is called 'advertising' by the businessman, 'propaganda' by the politician and 'suggestion' by the psychologist. All are sorcery, and nothing but sorcery. It is irrelevant that these modern witch doctors and their bewitched victims do not actually realise what they do, or even how they do it; they do it, and it works.

Magic is also still with us, in its most exoteric form. In this case it is not hidden under euphemism; rather its true nature has been forgotten, obscured or is denied.

A military march plays. I shout and cheer. I am ready to go out to kill for the Fatherland. I hear a ballad of unrequited love. I am moved to tears. I walk into Chartres Cathedral. I am suddenly overwhelmed with an indefinable, inexplicable but prodigious sense of the sacred. It is 'art' that produces these effects — for good or ill.

Art is technically and literally magic. There is 'black' art, 'white' art, sacred art and secular art, but all achieve their effect — if they achieve it — by magical means, by a summons to an innate human capacity to respond to harmony.

Now, when we look back at the 'magic' and 'superstition' of Egyptian medicine it becomes obvious that 'incantation' is a magical phenomenon. Because no one today knows exactly how to pronounce ancient Egyptian, and because we do not have any inkling of the actual techniques used, there is no way to reproduce the incantations that we can with some certainty translate. So on the surface it looks ridiculous when we read the advice to the doctor who is to chant, 'Out, fetid nose! Out, son of fetid nose!'

But if music commonly provokes a physical reaction; if specific vibrations induce organic and inorganic substances into patterns and forms; if, as has been proved, even plants respond

Nick Humphrey
New Scientist
Sept. 2, 1976, p. 486

If humans, like wolves, are mildly suggestible, then hypnosis is simply achieving an escalation of suggestion through positive feedback.... With each new suggestion which is made and confirmed the subject's conviction of his own suggestibility is reinforced still further. It is important, of course, that the suggestions do not fail, for should the subject once start to doubt the hypnotist's power he must begin to doubt the hypnotist's sugestion that he is suggestible — and the circle will be broken.

A. Erman
A Handbook of Egyptian Religion
A. Constable, 1907, p. 148

Magic is a barbarous offshoot of religion and is an attempt to influence the powers that preside over the destiny of mankind.

to sound, it is perfectly conceivable and reasonable to postulate a situation in which men with highly developed intuitive and sensitive faculties would understand objectively the disharmonies and disruptions inherent in specific maladies and diseases.

The body as a whole is an immensely complex vibratory system. Everything (including the atoms that make up the primary molecules) is in a constant dynamic state of flux, flow, rhythm, pulsation, alternation. If we suppose — as with the witch doctors and medicine men of today's 'primitive' societies — that the patient is brought by hypnosis, drugs or other means into a particularly receptive state, it is then quite feasible that incantation would work. The body responds as a whole to sound; why should not specific organs and glands respond to specific sounds? Indeed, the famous 'bedside manner' of certain modern physicians is a far more mysterious and inexplicable phenomenon than chant, though few doctors would deny its existence. By contrast, incantation is pure science.

Needless to say, it is also a science that lends itself easily to abuse in the wrong hands. And there is no way that we can distinguish the science from the superstition when we look into Egyptian magic. But the principle involved is valid, and easily related to common modern experience. And this is but the physical aspect of 'magical' incantation. There are psychological and emotional aspects of it as well.

The Edwin Smith surgical papyrus

This Middle Kingdom copy of a very ancient text serves as the base for Schwaller de Lubicz's inquiry into the actual state of those aspects of medical knowledge that are accepted today as medicine rather than magic. To that end, this papyrus is well suited, for it is obviously intended for doctors who have already undergone training.

It describes forty-eight different types of injuries to the head, face, neck, thorax and spinal column. The outward aspect of the injury is described along with ancillary symptoms that may or may not attend that kind of injury. Treatment or treatments are recommended, or the case is termed incurable. With doubtful cases, the stages of improvement or decline are also described, along with the measures to be taken at each stage.

The translation of the Smith papyrus was a formidable task, not completed until 1930. It is largely due to this document that Egyptian medicine has enjoyed its upsurge of esteem. Medical scientists have acknowledged that the descriptions of the various injuries reveal a thorough knowledge of anatomy and of the body's functions; in most cases the recommended treatments are pronounced sound, and demonstrate sophisticated therapeutic knowledge.

Schwaller de Lubicz's study of the papyrus carries this appreciation a step further.

Severe injuries to the head, neck and spinal column affect specific areas of the brain and the nervous system, producing symptoms in areas of the body that are under the control of the relevant parts of the brain and nervous system. A head injury of one sort may result in incontinence, another in partial paralysis. It is the secondary symptoms that provide the key to the real nature of the injury; the actual fracture or wound is of secondary importance.

These connections were perfectly understood by Egyptian medicine. It is clear that Egypt had a complete knowledge and understanding of the functions of the various parts of the brain, of different nervous systems and of all their interactions.

However rich it may be in detail, contemporary neurology is incomplete. Given its current methods it will never be complete, despite the sophisticated technological tools at its disposal. For its principal mode of investigation is doomed from the start. Moral and spiritual questions aside, tampering with the brains and nervous systems of various animals can never divulge complete or satisfactory knowledge of the intricacies of the human brain. The customary method today is to surgically, electrically or chemically suppress (or stimulate) the activity of some part of an animal's brain to see what effects this may have on its behavior or health.

But the brain is a whole, and information obtained by these means can never account for the complex automatic compensatory action taken (apart from the far greater subtleties of the human brain compared to the brains of animals). It is like trying to understand the importance of the rook in chess by removing (suppressing) that piece. The chess player automatically alters the whole of his game to compensate for the loss. To understand the importance of the rook, it is essential to understand first the principles of the entire game of chess. The same applies to any dynamic unity, and games are useful analogies. Imagine trying to understand the importance of the goalie in football by taking him from the game. Either another player would take his place, altering the tactics of the rest of the team, or the opposing team would run riot.

Egypt understood man as a whole. But because Egypt also understood the universally valid principle of hierarchy, her knowledge of the physical organism was intimately related to her understanding of the greater realms of which man's physical organism is a part.

Man is the sum of the principles that pervade and organise the universe; he is the self-perfecting product of the grand experiment that is organic life on earth, embodying within

New Scientist
Nov. 11, 1976, p. 334

The aspect of visual development that Blakemore and Pettigrew were investigating was ocular dominance — or which eye controls which nerve cells in the visual area of the cerebral cortex. There has been some noisy dispute about some of the effects of early experience. But the effect of monocular vision — keeping one eye of the kitten covered — is not in question. Everyone agrees that in those conditions the covered eye loses control of the columns of cells it would normally influence, and the open eye takes over.

himself the mineral, vegetable and animal kingdoms. His body is the temple designed to permit him to carry out the rite of self-perfection — the only legitimate human goal. All other goals lead to apathy or disaster, as is obvious from any daily newspaper.

Man is a model of the universe. If he understands himself perfectly, he also understands the universe: astronomy, astrology, geography, geodesy, measure, rhythm, proportion, mathematics, magic, medicine, anatomy, art . . . all are linked in a grand dynamic scheme. No aspect can be isolated from another and treated as a separate speciality or field without distortion and destruction. In Egypt, the very language employed in the medical papyri, the nomenclature employed to distinguish the parts of the body, reflects this fabulous capacity for synthesising, for automatically suggesting the intimate links between microcosm and macrocosm.

The parts of the body were in a general way consecrated to one of the Neters, or divine principles — meaning that the function symbolised by the Neter is corporified in that part of the body. (This has leaked down to us in the familiar figure of the medieval astrological man with his organs and limbs assigned to the domination of the twelve astrological signs.) In the same way, the nomes or territories of Egypt were also consecrated to the Neters — for the physical territory of Egypt was its 'body', the temple in which the rite of civilisation was performed. And the words used in anatomy are often the same as those used in religious texts; religious words are related by puns and homonyms to medical words that seem to have no obvious external link, but which when looked at through Schwaller de Lubicz's eyes bear an unmistakable functional relationship. He shows that the very structure of the language was designed to evoke in those using it an understanding of these functional connections.

For example, the word for the innermost nasal recess is *shtyt*, a word that is always used for the innermost sanctuary of a temple; it means 'hidden', 'secret', 'sacred'. What can there be that is 'sacred' in a nasal passage? The name, Schwaller de Lubicz claims, is based upon more than a fanciful physical resemblance, for this innermost nasal chamber has a special significance in the spiritual quest for perfection. This area corresponds to the sixth Hindu *chakra*. (The *chakra* is not a specific anatomical piece or organ, but the site and seat of a complex of activities that are at once physical, emotional, psychological and spiritual.)

This area is connected to the sympathetic and vagus nerves, and when resonated — particularly by the letter M (as in Aum, Muhammad) — aids in achieving that desired state of consciousness that transcends the conditional realities of sensory experience. An exercise in Zen meditation consists of exhaling in a hum that resonates this area. It is therefore not only physically 'hidden' and 'secret', but like the sanctuary of a temple, 'sacred'. These resonating exercises prove that knowledge of the spiritual properties of this physical area are current in various initiatic disciplines; but in Egypt even the word used to describe the area reflected that knowledge.

Modern language proliferates daily into new jargons, making it increasingly difficult to see the connections between fields and to express them. The language of Egypt was designed to an exactly opposite aim, with the names of things often containing clues to their inner relatedness. So, *ais* is the word for the physical mass of brain tissue. And the word *sia* (*ais* spelled backwards) is the word for consciousness; thus language embodies both the connection and the distinction. It obeys that cosmic principle of inversion that lies at the root of creation, which is the calling forth of matter out of spirit.

The brain is not an 'evolved' organ which, somehow, accidentally over the aeons generated a faculty we call 'consciousness'. Rather, it was developed in order to receive and apprehend those aspects of universal consciousness necessary for man to perform his foreordained task — just as the radio does not generate radio waves but receives the waves already there. The nature of consciousness determines the structure of the brain; the nature of sound determines the structure of the ear; the nature of light determines the structure of the eye; the nature of the Neters determines the structure of man, the microcosm, and not the other way round.

Secure in this understanding, the great and true scientists of ancient Egypt were able to be as exact, as empirical, as utilitarian and as meticulously observant as they liked, without allowing themselves to be led into today's labyrinth of analysis.

There cannot be the slightest doubt of the quality of Egyptian observational faculties. Cases 29 to 33 of the Smith papyrus describe minutely the different results brought about by wounds, dislocations, sprains, displacements and crushing of a vertebra of the neck. Even today, without recourse to X rays, it is extremely difficult to determine the exact nature of damage to the neck vertebra. The Egyptians could make these determinations effectively.

Schwaller de Lubicz's study of Egyptian medicine proves that by the highest orthodox modern standards it was highly advanced. Yet it is clear that modern methods of investigation can get at but one aspect of Egyptian medicine, its scientific side. Meanwhile, it is equally clear that Egyptian medicine was as much art (that is to say, magic) as it was science. Even today, people instinctively talk of the 'healing art'. And the secrets of this art that are not lost forever are inaccessible to the uncomprehending analytic mind. But if the testimony of ancient sources has any real value, that testimony invariably refers to the Egyptians as the healthiest race of the ancient world.

Schwaller de Lubicz's study validates this ancient testimony. A generally high level of health is consistent with a civilisation based upon metaphysical realities, in which medicine understood man as a whole ideally in tune with the cosmos. When out of tune, the body was seen as unhealthy or diseased. But because it was intimately connected to the rhythms, harmonies and pulsations of both terrestrial and extraterrestrial spheres, it was susceptible of being brought back into tune by the deliberate summoning-up of the specific harmonic phenomena pertinent to the case.

Myth, symbolism, language, literature

Giorgio de Santillana and Hertha von Dechend,
Op. cit., p. XI

Mathematics was moving up to me from the depths of the centuries; *not after myth but before it.* Not armed with Greek rigor, but with the imagination of astrological power, with the understanding of astronomy. Number gave the key. Way back in time before writing was even invented, it was *measures and counting* that provided the armature, the frame on which the rich texture of real myth was to grow. [Author's italics.]

Ibid., p. 312

Myth can be used as a vehicle for handing down solid knowledge independently from the degree of insight of the people who do the actual telling of the stories. . . . In ancient times, moreover, it allowed the members of the archaic 'brain trust' to 'talk shop' unaffected by the presence of laymen. The danger of giving something away was practically nil.

Ibid., p. 49

All the myths presented tales, some of them weird, incoherent or outlandish, some epic and tragic. At last it is possible to understand them as partial representations of a system, as functions of a whole.

Myth is a whole; it transcribes a fundamental knowledge of the laws of genesis, which apply to everything. Each Neter (or principle) has its application: in medicine and astronomy as in theology, which is the metaphysics of becoming and return.

Why the meaning behind myth should have vanished so completely, why the mythmaking genius should have virtually disappeared from man's makeup is a mystery. But once the universally applicable roles of number, harmony and proportion are glimpsed, the truth of the Symbolist analysis of myth becomes self-evident.

Myth is a deliberately chosen means for communicating knowledge. While it is possible, even probable, that the ancients could not have expressed that knowledge in modern philosophical language, that is no shortcoming. It is we who are at the disadvantage. To make sense of the myth, we must first convert it into a form the intellect will accept; thereafter, it may or may not work upon our emotional center and allow us to arrive at understanding. Myth works directly upon the understanding, and the whole of Egyptian civilisation was organised upon myth.

The religious centers at Heliopolis, Memphis, Thebes and Hermopolis did not represent separate and vying cults, nor a political and social federation. Rather, each reveals one of the principle phases or aspects of genesis.

Heliopolis revealed the primordial creative act, the apparition of Atum through Nun, forming the Grand Ennead of principles or Neters generated by the scission: Atum, Shu/Tefnut, Geb/Nut, Osiris/Isis, Set/Nephthys.

Memphis revealed the work of Ptah, producer and animator of form. Ptah is Atum fallen to earth. He is the coagulating fire, simultaneously cause (of the created world) and effect (of the scission). Ptah is phi, the creative power immanent in Atum but locked in Atum in his fall to earth. Ptah is not free. He is bound by Set, principle of contraction. That is why he is always pictured bound in swaddling clothes, with only head, hands and feet free. And Ptah is also the prototype for the Greek Hephaestus (and perhaps the source of the name), the smith in his subterranean laboratory, his lameness a psychological equivalent of Ptah's bindings.

Ibid., p. 57

But although the modern reader does not expect a text on celestial mechanics to read like a lullaby, he insists on the capacity to understand mythical 'images' instantly because he can respect as 'scientific' only page-long approximations in formulas and the like. He does not think of the possibility that equally relevant knowledge might once have been expressed in everyday language. He never suspects such a possibility; although the visible accomplishments of ancient cultures — to mention only the pyramids and metallurgy — should be a cogent reason for concluding that serious and intelligent men were at work behind the stage, men who were bound to have used a technical terminology.

Sir Alan Gardiner
Egypt of the Pharaohs
Oxford, 1961, p. 130

An act of association which resulted in two Horuses functioning simultaneously made nonsense of this doctrine, but there is no hint that the Egyptians ever felt scruples on this score. In matters of religion, logic plays no great part, and the assimilation or duplication of deities doubtless added a mystic charm to their theology.

At Memphis, Atum of Heliopolis, the unique issue of Nun, becomes Ptah/Sekhmet-Hathor/Nefertum. Ptah is the personification of the creative aspect of Atum. Sekhmet-Hathor is primordial femininity in both its facets; destroyer and matrix. Nefertum (the accomplishment of Tum) is the lotus, the seed bearer, that which effects the interchange of fire and water, of action and resistance, the 'third force' that is always and everywhere necessary as mediator between male and female, active and passive.

Hermopolis revealed the realisation of Ptah's action through Thoth. This is the creation of the manifested universe, which is 'words'. Thebes revealed the reunion of that which had been separated.

The apparent incoherence of the Egyptian myths and Egyptian theology turns out to be a single, interrelated but prodigiously complex system. It is not surprising that, prior to Schwaller de Lubicz, no one had been able to make sense of it. Pythagoreanism in orthodox circles had become no more than a kind of aberrant curiosity, and the Egyptian practice of giving different names as well as different attributes to different aspects of the same Neter is, to us, an inconceivable method of going about philosophy. Yet this practice is perfectly consistent with common psychological experience. We do not doubt for a moment that there is a real difference between the 'man' in a polarity, and the same man who is the 'lover' in a relationship. Nor do we think it confusing that, to a child, its mother is variously nurse, protectress, tyrant, healer (playing active, hence *masculine* roles in the two latter) jailer, teacher and so on. The same woman may be a siren to her lover, a millstone to her husband, an hysteric to her doctor, an ogress to the delivery boy and an indispensable right-hand man to her boss. We have no trouble at all in either separating or combining her various attributes.

The true vitalist philosophy of Egypt recognised the universal validity of this kind of thinking, and applied it to all the levels of the hierarchically organised world. However complex it may appear at first sight, it is both coherent and consistent with experience.

Isis conceived Horus with the phallus of Osiris, who had been dismembered by his relative and implacable enemy, Set. What can this mean? Were the Egyptians going through some kind of Freudian catharsis? Were they reliving savage tribal memories or giving expression to bad dreams? I believe they were expressing in the most concise dramatic form possible the universal principle of regeneration, with the phallus, symbol of fecundating principle unaffected by death and dissolution, acting upon the feminine principle and generating a new cycle. This new cycle was not merely a renewal and repetition of the old cycle, but a transcendent version of it. For Horus will avenge his father Osiris, and after endless battles, defeat Set and live in eternity as the eye of Ra — that is to say, as the observing organ of the divine. The myth is thus simultaneously science and theology, describing a natural process and at the same time furnishing a model for spiritual struggle — for Horus in this context is the divine man, born of nature, who must do battle against Set, his own kin, ultimately defeating him and being reconciled to him. (In Hindu mythology, the battles of Arjuna have a similar meaning.) Set is variously the enemy, the divisive principle, the intellect (whose planet is Saturn), the ruler of time, the destroyer.

The same myth also provides insight into the two paths or ways of 'salvation' — the way of Osiris and the way of Horus. The former is the way of reincarnation, of progressive dissolutions linked only by the generative principle; the latter is the direct path, that of the warrior of the spirit, out to subdue the enemy within himself by his own efforts.

Once the key to the inner meaning of the myths has been revealed, they become marvels of simultaneous completeness and brevity; the more they are studied the richer they become. Any aspect of the myth may lend itself to the most exhaustive scientific or philosophical exegesis. Yet, rooted in the myth as it is, the part can never be mistaken for the whole, nor can its functional significance be forgotten or perverted. To the disciple, myth is an endless source of instruction, while for the incurious majority (past or present), the myth explains reality in a story form that is easily remembered.

Symbolism

Regarding myth, modern scholarship falls into two main fields: that of Jung, Eliade, etc. considerably less barren than the other which sees myth as a wholly primitive means of accounting for the physical world.

When we come to symbolism, we find a free-for-all, with little unanimity of opinion anywhere.

At best, a symbol is recognised as a subconscious representation of archetypal concepts, perhaps as experienced in dreams. At the more common worst, symbols are regarded as arbitrary devices invented by aggrandizing priesthoods to cloak their activities in secrecy and buffalo the masses.

The symbol, in Egypt, is neither. It is a scrupulously chosen pictorial device designed to evoke an idea or concept in its entirety. It is a means of bypassing the intellect and talking straight to the intelligence of the heart, the understanding.

The heart synthesises, the mind analyses. A true symbolism is neither primitive nor subconscious. It is a deliberate means of evoking understanding, as opposed to conveying informa-

A. Deiber
Clement d'Alexandrie
I.F.A.O., Cairo, 1904, p. 22

The symbolic method is subdivided into several sorts; one represents objects by direct imitation, others express them in a figurative manner; while the third is entirely allegorical, expressed through certain enigmas. [Clement, writing in the third century AD, evidently still knew the underlying principles upon which the hieroglyphic system was based. Author's note.]

R. A. Schwaller de Lubicz
'Le Temple de Karnak'
Unpublished paper

The image is neither a rebus nor a cryptogram, it speaks simply as the evocation of an intuition. This can not in any case be transcribed into words without danger — of leading to a concrete notion, be it an object, or a mental abstraction — which may disguise the original intention. When, for example, we take for the word 'horizon' the apparent line separating the land (or sea) from the sky, this visible line is an abstraction, for it is only an appearance; it has no material reality. But in formulating the notion by the word 'horizon' we mentally see this line; we are obliged to see it or the word would make no sense to us. By contrast, the Egyptians *represented* the horizon by the image of the sky between two mountains — thereby evoking the moment of the sun's appearance rising out of the darkness of the morning and returning in the evening. This is a *function*, a vital state. The sign 'horizon' as image is positive, concrete; there is nothing abstract or conventional about it. But what it evokes is an 'intuition', that of the function of 'becoming', of Being emerging from nothingness. For it would again be reasoning, hence concretisation of the intuition were it said: 'the sun was merely concealed from view. . . .

Therefore, when Champollion and the philologists after him declare that the ancients made use of certain images to stand for abstractions, this does not exactly accord with the mode of pharaonic thought, which is concerned with the evocation of intuitions that, for us, are abstractions, but to the ancients were 'states of Being'.

tion. Words convey information (excepting poetry); symbols evoke understanding. Information alone is useless, unless it is transformed into understanding. Thus symbolism is virtually the opposite of what it is believed to be: symbolism, as employed in Egypt, is direct and exact. It is language, and scientific language in particular, that is circuitous and misleading.

Before investigating Egyptian symbolism, it is worth briefly examining contemporary symbolism in order to clarify the distinctions.

Modern symbols in their accepted sense are generally arbitrary. The American flag has its stars and stripes representing the thirteen original colonies and the states. But why stripes for colonies, stars for states? Why are some stripes red, others white, and the field for the stars blue? Clearly, for no objective, functional reason. A flag had to be designed, and Betsy Ross liked the idea of stars and stripes in red, white and blue. The American flag is an arbitrary symbol. It may serve as a focal point for patriots in wartime, but a study of the symbol repays the student with nothing he does not already know.

We do have legitimate symbols, usually bequeathed us from the past, such as the cross. For the most part, the meanings behind these true symbols have been forgotten or distorted; to reenter the spirit in which they were intended it is necessary to go through a rethinking process almost as radical as that required to approach Egypt.

In degenerate and arbitrary form, a vestige of the power of symbolism thrives in one widespread modern practice: the political cartoon.

Though the symbols themselves (donkey, elephant, Uncle Sam, John Bull, etc.) are arbitrary and reveal nothing functional of the party or nation they symbolise, the cartoon can reveal in legitimate symbolic form the totality of a given situation — at least insofar as it appears to the individual cartoonist. As long as the reader is initiated into and accepts the meaning of the symbols, he may discover a surprising wealth of knowledge in a single cartoon. The same situation described in prose might take pages of explanation, reprinting of speeches, analyses of the conflicting opinions, and the end result would still not be the synthesis the clever cartoonist achieves with a few strokes of the pen. In secular terms, the cartoonist illustrates the power of symbolism to evoke and synthesise.

Here analogies between ancient and modern symbolism stop. Egypt's symbolism was sacred, and it was a science — an adjunct to the sacred science of myth. It was a means of reinforcing and elucidating the truths enshrined in myth in certain cases; in other cases it was employed as the chief means for the simultaneous communication of both the essence and the detail of a given situation.

The image is concrete (bird, snake, dog, etc.), and it represents a synthesis, a complex of qualities, functions and principles. Careful study of the symbols usually reveals the reason why the given symbol, and not some other, was chosen. So the bird represents the volatile, or 'spirit'. The stork, which returns to its own nest, hence a migratory bird par excellence, is the bird chosen for the 'soul'. The serpent symbolises duality and dualising power. The dog symbolises digestion, but given the dog's preference for carrion over fresh meat, the choice of this symbol emphasises that aspect of digestion which is the transformation of dead matter into living. So Anubis, opener of the way, presides over the deceased and takes part in the ritual of the weighing of the heart. For death is not an end, it is a *transformation*.

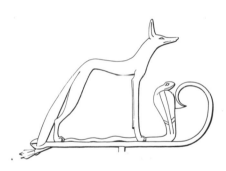

Anubis. At first thought to be a jackal, now generally conceded to be a domesticated dog. Egyptian art, though 'stylised', is always accurate. If the intention had been to stylise the low, skulking jackal, Egypt would not have presented these tall, aristocratic creatures, who nonetheless appear to be a different breed from the ring-tailed greyhounds of the hunting friezes. On Ibiza, where the breed remained nearly pure, both ringtails and bushy, jackal-like tails are found — but more often a long, smooth tail similar to a greyhound's.

Anubis is always connected to the rites of the dead. The dog prefers carrion to fresh meat; it sublimates dead matter to its own living purpose. Hence Anubis, the dog, presiding over the dead, and the 'opener of the way'.

Once the principle is grasped, it becomes impossible to see in those curious animal-headed 'gods' a carry-over from totemistic times.

The intellect cannot fix precisely the extent to which functional analogy is valid, but the symbolism of Egypt made these analogies and possibly, to those initiated into this symbolic language, the knowledge conveyed was as precise as anything we know today.

Peter Tompkins
Mysteries of the Mexican Pyramids
Harper & Row, 1976, p. 165

Like Carlos Castaneda in our day, Le Plongeon learned that the native Indians in his day still practiced magic and divination. . . . Beneath the prosaic life of the Indians . . . in Yucatan, Le Plongeon concluded that there flowed 'a rich living current of occult wisdom and practice, with its sources in an extremely ancient past, far beyond the purview of ordinary historical research'.

As we have seen, the various organs of the body were connected by the Egyptians to the different planets, as were the Neters. Egypt itself (that is to say, civilisation) was regarded as a unity, greater than the individual man, but analogous; and therefore the nomes or states of Egypt played functional roles similar to the roles played by the organs of the body. Each of these nomes was consecrated to one or the other of the Neters. (Schwaller de Lubicz was planning a book examining what he calls 'the sacred geography' of Egypt, but he died before he could realise it.)

It was the symbolism of Egypt that provided the beautifully flexible medium for revealing, within a single consistent system, the wealth of connections and correlations up and down the hierarchies which pervade every sphere of physical, psychical and spiritual life.

I have already discussed briefly the subtle aptness of the serpent as symbol for duality. A complete discussion of the symbolism of the serpent would take a book as long as this one, so in amplifying the earlier comments, I shall restrict myself to certain salient points, hoping to convey an idea of the kind of thinking objective symbolism involves.

In Platonic terms, the division of One into Two creates new elements, each of which partake of the nature of the 'One' and of the 'Other'. Thus, duality is itself dual in nature (it is duality that lies at the origin of 'good' and 'evil'), and this is reflected in many ways in Egyptian symbolism. Duality as the call to unchecked chaos and multiplicity is symbolised by the 'serpent fiend, Apop', who devours the souls of the dead and thus denies them reunion with the source. Duality as higher intellect, duality as primordial creative impulse, is the serpent in the sky — the cobra, symbol of Lower Egypt, which is synthesis, creation.

The symbol for Upper Egypt is Mut (also Nekhebet), the vulture, representing (in all its aspects) gestation, primordial reconciliation.

Cobra and vulture both adorn the royal diadem, the uraeus, which is the crown of pharaoh, earthly symbol of the divine man.

It is neither accident nor politics nor animism that determines the uraeus. The divine man must be able both to distinguish and to reconcile. That dual power resides in man's brain. The diadem itself is modelled on the anatomical structure of the brain.

Down to the minutest detail, Egyptian symbolism incorporates an astonishing combination of aptness of choice and wealth of amplification.

The use of animals as functional types also allowed Egypt to indicate clearly the realm in which the action or event was played out.

Man contains the divine spark within him. Therefore, the transcendent principles are always given human form. There is a subtle yet important distinction between this Egyptian practice and the Greek — which at first glance may seem similar. Greece cut the 'gods' down to human size and depicted them with typically ungodlike behaviour. Egypt started with the concept of divine attributes within man. The gods are not brought down to earth; rather man is raised to the gods. And so, the transcendent gods, those who command creation itself — Tum, Atum, Ptah, Amon, Min (Ra in his generative role) — are always in human form.

The Neters, or functional types, when depicted entirely in animal form, are operating within the terrestrial sphere, within organic life. Shown in human form with an animal head, they symbolise that functional activity within the human sphere. An interesting reversal of the process is the representation of the 'soul', the *ba*, as a bird with a human head — in other words, as the divine aspect of the terrestrial.

In Egyptian symbolism, the precise role of the Neters is revealed in many ways: by dress, crowns, type of symbolic equipment (e.g., flail, scepter, staff, cross of life). Through colour, position, size and gesture, the Neter reveals — to those initiated into symbolic language — a wealth of data at once physical, physiological, psychological and spiritual. And the data are always *in action*.

It is this that constitutes the fundamental superiority of the symbolic science: it illuminates the living process without analysing it, dissecting it and killing it. And yet it can convey precise information or measure if such information is desired. The charge of cumbersomeness may be levelled with a degree of justice — yet what could be more cumbersome than modern education? A whole lifetime goes into studying a single specialisation, and when the specialist has mastered his appropriate jargon, he is incapable of communicating with a specialist in any other field, much less with an artist, philosopher or theologian.

The Egyptian use of gesture is particularly intriguing in that certain aspects of it are so strange and yet so obviously deliberate that it seems almost impossible not to ask questions concerning Egyptian motives.

Gesture has always been, and largely still is, a universal language. People with no spoken language in common can communicate through gesture quite eloquently. Though gestures of affirmation and denial may differ from culture to culture, gestures of giving, receiving, conquest, supplication, adoration, worship and many others are recognisable the world over.

These actions are not merely human; they are in themselves symbolic expressions of functions proper to all realms; gesture

G. Dieterlen
Preface to Marcel Griaule's
Conversations with Ogotemmeli
Oxford, 1965, p. XIII

African techniques, so poor in appearance, like those of agriculture, weaving and smithing, have a rich hidden content of significance. Religious gestures, whether spectacular or secret, and generally uncomprehended by outsiders, show themselves under analysis to be of an extreme subtlety in their implications.

J. Gwyn Griffiths
Journal of Egyptian Archaeology 51,
p. 220

An interesting point emerges with regard to the direction in which the representations face: the men engaged in ritual activity are shown facing inwards, whereas the deity venerated faces outward from the temple. A continuous movement can be observed extending from the temple façade to the back wall of the *sanctum sanctorum* behind the cult statue, and this stream of figures reveals a significant trait of Egyptian architecture in the attempt to accompany one who enters the temple and to lead him eventually to the middle point of the building.

Robert Lafont
Encylopédies des Mystiques
1972 p. 7

A Yakout* shaman, Sofron Zatayev, affirms that customarily the future shaman dies and spends three days in the yurt without food or drink. Formerly one was subjected to a thrice-performed ceremony during which he was cut in pieces. Another shaman, Pyotry Ivanov, told us about this ceremony in detail: the members of the candidate were detached and separated with an iron hook, the bones were cleaned, the flesh scraped, the body liquids thrown away and the eyes torn out of their sockets. After this operation the bones were reassembled and joined with iron. According to another shaman, the dismembering ceremony lasted three to seven days: during this time the candidate remained in suspended animation, like a corpse, in a solitary place.

* Yakout: A people of Eastern Siberia, originally of Turkish origin.

R. O. Faulkner
Ancient Egyptian Pyramid Texts
Oxford, 1969, pp. 13, 14

I split open your eyes for you . . . I open your mouth for you with the adze of iron which split open the mouths of the gods . . . the iron which issued from Seth, with the adze of iron. . . . This King washes himself when Ra appears. . . . Isis nurses him . . . Horus accepts him beside him . . . he cleanses this king's double, he wipes over the flesh. . . . Raise yourself, O King; receive your head, collect your bones, gather your limbs together, throw off the earth from your flesh. . . . The Great Protectress . . . will give you your head, she will re-assemble your bones for you . . . join together your members . . . bring your heart into your body. . . . O King, receive your water, gather together your bones.

A

B

A   The king makes an offering. His role is wholly active: he has two right hands.
B   The king has life and force bestowed upon him by the Neters. His role is wholly receptive: he has two left hands.

is a language proper to the Neters as well as to man.

In the universal code of gesture, the right hand is active, the left passive. The right hand gives, bestows; the left receives. Now, in the Egyptian symbolic scheme, cases arise where the Neter plays a role entirely active or entirely passive. In such cases the Neters are shown with either two right hands or two left hands. (I will be studying this in greater detail later on.)

Language

The hieroglyphic system was complete at the time of the earliest dynasties of Egypt. It continued in use for sacred and religious texts throughout the millennia of Egyptian history, and even beyond: the last recorded discovered hieroglyphs come from the island of Philae, just below the first Nile cataract, and date from the fourth century AD.

Egypt also had a kind of shorthand system of hieroglyphs called 'hieratic', which was used for official communications and other secular matters. Later on, presumably to facilitate economic concerns, a still more cursive script called 'demotic' was employed.

But hieroglyphs were always the language of the Temple. They comprise a symbolic written language based upon principles similar to those governing the symbolism of the Neters and of Egyptian art. The hieroglyphs are both pictorial and phonetic. (This was Champollion's great discovery, which led to the initial deciphering.) Unfortunately, no one knows exactly how they are supposed to be pronounced. This is a matter of more than academic interest. Jenny, in his development of cymatics, invented a machine, the tonoscope, that converted the sounds of speech into visual equivalents. The vowel 'o', when spoken into the tonoscope, came out looking like a perfect 'o'. Given the importance attached by Egypt to chants, spells and a person's name, it is clear that the sound of the words must have had a functional connection with their meanings. This connection is all but lost in modern language, though it lingers on in poetry: the poet agonizes over a choice of words synonymous to the layman. It may be the sound, finally, that is the determining factor. Asked how he determined the form of his free verse, T. S. Eliot replied that he stopped revising 'when it sounds right'. In all likelihood, then, the sounds of Egyptian words (their vibratory structure) had a numerical basis corresponding to their meanings, and this correspondence was not haphazard.

Egyptian was a language, then, in which images contained profound clues to the cosmic meaning of each letter, and this meaning was undoubtedly amplified by the sound of the letter itself. Words were compounded of these letters in a manner incorporating and amplifying the meaning of the individual letters, so that the meaning of a word emerged from the interplay of letters as the meaning of a chord or a musical phrase results from the combination of notes.

Once we see that the language is structured according to these principles, the Egyptian predilection for puns, homonyms, anagrams and other forms of word play is seen as no caprice. Verbal correspondences are not gratuitous.

The problem is to determine when and in what way they are

intentional and meaningful. I have already mentioned *sia/ais*. Here are some further intriguing cases. *Akh* = spirit, or, to become spirit; *khat* = corpse. (And *akh* is used in words of a generally benificent nature, while *khat* written with a different 'h' sign becomes disease and swamp.) *Akh-akh* = to grow green, and stars; *khat-khat* = storm. *Ben* = negation, also the 'primordial stone', that is to say, the first state of matter; *neb* = gold. Gold is traditionally the finished, perfected, end product, the goal of the alchemist. In Egypt *neb* also means master or lord.

Translation of the hieroglyphs is fraught with technical problems. But beyond these technical problems there is a much greater philosophical and theological problem. The sacred texts of Egypt are part of an initiatic religion, and are comprehensible only within that context.

The aim of all initiatic religions is the same the world over and has always been: to guide man from his natural state of consciousness (which is called 'illusion' or 'sleep') to a higher state (called 'illumination' or 'the kingdom'). This higher state, his destiny and birthright, is, within the context of the natural world, 'unnatural'.

It is impossible to construct a rational argument to compel the unwilling and the immune into acknowledging either the existence or the importance of this higher state. It is impossible to 'prove' to the skeptic that this has any direct bearing upon himself or his life. Initiatic writings are therefore comprehensible only to initiates, to those who have at least put one foot down upon the long road. And the further along the road, the greater and deeper the understanding.

The Gospels are initiatic texts; they are handbooks to a higher state of consciousness. But they are seldom regarded as such: the Ayers and the Russells misread them as instruments of oppression and monuments to superstition; while the Billy Grahams and assorted do-gooders read into them an authorisation to mind other people's business. If this kind of egregious misinterpretation is universally applied to the Gospels, the most familiar text in the West, it is hardly surprising that the inner meaning of the alien sacred writings of Egypt should remain concealed. The inevitable consequence of this is that, to Egyptologists, an accurate translation of sacred texts is almost impossible.

But if this lack of understanding is both inevitable and in a sense excusable, there is one aspect of the matter that does not seem inevitable or excusable. This is that, as translated and accepted by Egyptologists, the sacred texts of Egypt are meaningless. Problems of grammar, syntax and meaning aside, there is and can be no justification for the gibberish that is fobbed off as a translation of the intellectual product of Egypt.

There is no such thing as natural gibberish. Even pidgin is grammatically structured. The most primitive tribes possess

Noam Chomsky
In *Psychology Today*
August 1976, p. 51

The study of language offers strong empirical evidence that empiricist theories of learning are quite inadequate. What evidence is now available supports the view that all human languages share deep-seated properties of organisation and structure. These properties — these linguistic universals — can be plausibly assumed to be an innate mental endowment rather than the result of learning. If this is true, then the study of language sheds light on certain long standing issues in the theory of knowledge. Once again, I see little reason to doubt that what is true of language is true of other forms of human knowledge as well.

There is one further question that might be raised at this point. How does the human mind come to have these innate properties that underlie acquisition of knowledge? Here linguistic evidence obviously provides no information at all. The process by which the human mind has achieved its present state of complexity and its particular form of innate organisation are a complete mystery. . . . It is perfectly safe to attribute this to evolution, so long as we bear in mind that there is no substance to this assertion — it amounts to nothing more then the belief that there is surely some naturalistic explanation for these phenomena.

languages that are grammatically and syntactically complete — restricted, perhaps, to the expression of relatively simple concepts, but complete nonetheless. Therefore to render language, any language, into gobbledygook and offer it as a 'translation' is indefensible:

> O King, your cool water is the great flood which issues from you.
> Be silent that you may hear it, this word which the King speaks.
> His power is at the head of the spirits, his might is at the head of the living, he sits beside the Foremost of the Westerners.
> Your *pzn* bread is from the Broad Hall.
> Your rib-pieces are from the slaughter-block of the God.
> O King, raise yourself, receive this warm beer of yours which went forth from your house, which are given to you.
>
> R. O. Faulkner, *Ancient Egyptian Pyramid Texts*, Clarendon Press, 1969
> Utterance 460

Can this really be an approximation of the mental processes of the builders of the pyramids and of the Temple of Luxor? Perhaps, apart from the unwillingness or inability to comprehend the initiatic basis of Egypt's entire civilisation, the immense difficulties encountered in translation so overwhelm scholars that they fail to recognise the garbled quality of their translations?

The fact remains that when seemingly incoherent texts are studied from the symbolic point of view, it is possible to make sense of them. To this end, it is worth looking in detail at a single pyramid text in its various orthodox translations, and then compare them to the same text translated in the light of the Symbolist understanding.

Because this passage is so short, I have included the translations in their original German and French, as well as a rendering of the translation into English:

Spruch (Spell) 316
502a Weggezogen ist der Phallus des Ba bjj. geoffnet sind die Thurflügel des Himmels.
502b Verschlossen sind die Thurflügel des Himmels, der Weg geht über die Feuersglut unter dem, was die Gütter schöpfen.
503a Was jeden Horus hindurch gleiten liess, damit werde auch W. hindurch gleiten gemacht in dieser Feuersglut unter dem, was die Götter schöpfen
503b Sie machen dem Weinen Weg damit W. auf ihm passiere. W. ist (ein) Horus.

The phallus of Ba Bi is drawn back, the shutters to the heavens are opened.

The shutters to the heavens are shut, the way goes over the fireglow under that which the Gods ladle out.

What lets every Horus slip through, thereby will W. also be made to slip through, in this fireglow under that which the Gods ladle out.

They make a way for W. that W may go upon it. W. is (a) Horus.

K. Sethe — *Ubersetzung und Kommentar zu den Altägytptscher Pyramidentexten*. II Band, Verlag J.J. Augustin, Hamburg, 1962

502 Tire ceci (le verrou) (o) Babj! Ouvre la porte du ciel. (O) Hor! (o) Hor, Ouvre a Ra la porte du ciel par la flamme sous l'*iknt* des Dieux.

503 Tu trebuches Hor! Tu trebuches Hor! la ou W. trebucha par cette flamme, sous l'*iknt* des Dieux. Qu'ils preparent un chemin pour W. pour qui W. y passa. W. est Hor!

502 Draw it (the bolt) back, O Babj! Open the door of the sky. O Horus. O Horus, open to Ra the door of the sky by the flame beneath the *iknt* of the Gods.

503 You stumble, Horus! You stumble, Horus! There where W. stumbles by that flame, under the *iknt* of the Gods. That they make ready a road for W. so that W. may pass along it. W. is Horus.

Louis Speleers, *Textes du Pyramides*, Brussels, 1935

502 The phallus of Babi is drawn back, the doors of the sky are opened, the King has opened (the doors of the sky) because of the furnace heat which is beneath what the gods pour out. What Horus lets slip (?)

503 the King lets slip (?) there into this furnace heat which the gods pour out. They make a road for the King that the King may pass on it, for the King is Horus.

R. O. Faulkner, *Ancient Egyptian Pyramid Texts*.
Clarendon Press, 1969

Le phallus de Babj est tiré, les portes du ciel peuvent s'ouvrir, les portes du ciel peuvent se fermer. Ounas a deverouillez (?) le chemin qui passe sur le feu, sous l'*iknt* des dieux. Ce qui fait glisser chaque Horus, Ounas (le) fait glisser a travers ce feu, sous l'*iknt* des dieux; ils font un chemin pour Ounas, afin qu'Ounas y passe, (car) Ounas est Horus.

The phallus of Babj is drawn back, the doors of the heavens may open, the doors of the heavens may shut. Ounas has unbolted (?) the way that passes over the fire, under the *iknt* of the gods. That which each Horus lets slip, Ounas lets slip across this fire, under the *iknt* of the gods; they make a way for Horus so that Ounas may pass along it, (for) Ounas is Horus.

Paul Barguet, *Revue d'Egyptologie*, 22
Ed. Klincksieck, 1970

These translations have little in common beyond a profound incoherence. The radical differences among the interpretations will give the reader an insight into the extreme difficulties facing the Egyptologist. The word that means 'ceci' (this, it) to Speleers is a 'phallus' to everyone else. Horus 'stumbles' in one text, in another 'lets slip' or 'lets slide', and in another is 'let or allowed to slip'. And none can translate '*iknt*' — Sethe and Faulkner fudge around the intractable word. These translations are no better and no worse than those of the rest of the pyramid texts. Four authorities produce four different versions; and each version is nonsense.

Spell 316 is typical of the Old Kingdom texts. It presents the translator with characteristic problems. Once translated in accordance with its inner meaning, it displays a characteristic wealth of esoteric meaning compressed into so few words that for us to grasp it, a substantial commentary is unavoidable. It is worth indicating at this point the broad differences between Old, Middle, Late and Ptolemaic texts, with their different translation problems.

Spell 316 is one of several hundred hieroglyphic texts incised into the walls of the pyramid of Unas, a Fifth Dynasty pharaoh. These, along with similar texts from several other pyramids of the same era, constitute the oldest funerary texts that we have from Egypt.

The individual signs in these texts are often written without the determinative sign that would allow Egyptologists to assign a precise meaning to the individual word. They amount to a kind of symbolic shorthand whose significance would have been perfectly clear to the Egyptians of the Fifth Dynasty but which pose huge problems for us. The problem is further complicated by the compression of complex thought that finds expression in a few simple words. And because material from the Old Kingdom is relatively scarce, there are few variants of the individual texts which would allow scholars to get at difficult meanings through comparison.

Middle Kingdom hieroglyphics are more discursive, more 'intellectual'; there is a wealth of material from this period, and in many cases, it is the ability to read Middle Kingdom var-

Paul Barguet
Revue d'Egyptologie
Tome 22, 1970

Three principal difficulties obliterate the sense of the formulae. The first is the reference to 'the road (which passes) over the fire' a designation which one might consider as applying to something precise; we propose by way of a hypothesis, to recognise there the corridor giving access to the funeral chambers, more exactly the corridor cutting across the zone of granite and cut by portcullisses to free the passages; the fire thus signifying the granite itself.

The second difficulty involves the word, iknt, written without a determinative, and which figures here twice, linked to 'the way (which passes) over the fire'; should it relate to the verb iknt attested only in the Westcar Pap. with the sense of 'scooping (water)' thereby giving the word iknt the sense of 'ladle'? The one would have a relative neuter verb form: 'that which the gods ladle out', and this could express the raising of the granite portcullisses to free the passages. [But perhaps this word iknt in CT VI, 296r-s, which picks up and devlops chap. 320 of the Pyramids: identifying the death of ba-bi, master of the night';] the text gives the 'son of Iknt, the Shadowy, the iknt of N. being that which hides the master of the night'; iknt would then designate something that dissimulates, a hiding place, a well, perhaps, as the little circle that determines the word here seems to indicate. In the absence of a more explicit document, it is impossible to decide between the proposed interpretations.

The third difficulty is raised by the verb sbn 'slip, slide away, slip away, turn about'; here, there can be no other than the factive sense 'let slide' as it is given in the presence of a direct complement; within the totality of the formulae, it must express the pulling of the bolt, or the raising of the portcullisses in their tracks. . . .

iants of older texts that gives the clue to the latter. In the New Kingdom, language becomes still more prolix, and the problems here are often related to a superabundance of signs creating a vast number of nuances of meaning. Ptolemaic Egyptian becomes still wordier, and amounts to a specialty in itself. Scholars steeped in Middle and New Kingdom hieroglyphs cannot readily translate Ptolemaic without further training. If we imagine a Chinese student of English faced with Chaucer, then with Shakespeare, then with Melville, and then with James Joyce, we will get some inkling of the kind of purely linguistic problems facing the Egyptologist.

Formidable as these difficulties are, most could be resolved in principle if the texts could be understood in a secular context. For example, state documents and official letters, written in hieratic, do not sound so very different from their modern equivalents. But to make sense of Egyptian religious texts, it is first essential to realise that all are esoteric and initiatic; they concern resurrection and reincarnation, and they deal precisely with spiritual states.

Spell 316 is presented in four nonsense variants by four learned scholars simply because its esoteric nature is denied. For example, Paul Barguet attempts to read this text as applying to the literal and physical nature of the tomb chamber itself — to the corridors and the raising of the portcullis and so on. This is like reading Christ's parable of the sower and the seed as if it were intended as agricultural advice, or interpreting the parable of the talents as a primitive treatise in economics.

Even a recognition of the true nature of the texts would not ensure a realistic translation. The translator must himself share the Egyptian conviction that resurrection, reincarnation and the journey of the soul after death correspond to realities. Without that conviction, and a degree of understanding of these realities, the texts cannot help but remain perfectly opaque, and any translation will be meaningless.

Apart from the translation of the text, we have also analysed the four translations given above, to show how their differences have arisen, and I have been provided with background material for the notes, without which the esoteric meaning of this short passage would not reveal itself.

Spell 316 is but one of several hundred inscribed in the walls, and though there can be no doubt that these have a sequence and a structure, Egyptologists to date have not been able to discern them. In the translations as they now stand, the numbering of the texts is more or less arbitrary, and it will remain so until someone succeeds in translating them in their entirety upon an esoteric basis.

Spell 316 is found in the corridor leading to the funeral chamber of Unas. In this form, and at this period (Fifth

Dynasty, ca. 2600 BC by orthodox dating), it is found only in the pyramid of Unas. (An inscription in the pyramid of Sesostris I (Twelfth Dynasty, Middle Kingdom) provides a different version of this text.)

The four translated versions reveal the following:

Speleers has kept literally to the Unas text as well as he was able; but certain words are extremely difficult to translate (e.g., *iknt* and *sbn.t.*).

Sethe worked on the Unas and Sesostris texts side by side, completing the first by means of the second, and his version is distinctly different from the original. Faulkner and Barguet have followed Sethe in the main, but each has given an individual interpretation to certain words, phrases and grammatical constructions, and chosen different elements from the longer Sesostris version in the attempt to make sense of the briefer Unas text.

Phrase by phrase, the Unas text reads:

Draw it back, Ba-bi!
Open the two shutters of heaven!
Open for Unas
Above the flame beneath the *iknt*
Of the Neters.

There is no phallus (Sethe); there is no furnace heat (Faulkner); there is no conditional tense (Barguet). But without a prior understanding of what is at stake, the stark phrases have no meaning.

The first key to the text is the significance of Ba-bi. As is so often the case with the complex but vital symbols of Egypt, Ba-bi has both positive and negative aspects. In certain of the Unas texts (*Pyr.* 419, Faulkner) he is called upon to protect Unas. Elsewhere he is at once respected and feared as 'bull of the baboons' and 'chief of the apes'. In other texts (*Pyr.* 1349 of Pepi) he is described as having red ears and violet buttocks. In other texts he is referred to as Ba-ba and as Ba-boui, generally as a baboon (dog-faced ape), sometimes as a dog. In the *Book of the Dead* (Ch. 125) Ba-bi is associated with the 'bolt' that serves as hypostasis, or essence of 'the phallus of Ba-bi'. Finally Ba-bi is called 'guardian of the banks of the lake of fire'; he feeds upon 'the overturned', the fallen, the enemies of Osiris.

As guardian of the lake of fire, he may be found between Chedit (Crocodilopolis, or Fayum) and Naref, (necropole of the nome of Heracleopolis, mythological site of the battles between Horus and Set). Ultimately, he may be understood as a creature of Set, or as certain aspects of Set.

Set represents the contractive force, the coagulating fire, the styptic power of the sperm. It is Set that imprisons spirit in matter; hence the phallic significance. For it is the procreative act that ensnares the 'soul' and imprisons it in human form. Strictly speaking, esoterically, it is incorrect to say, 'Man has a soul.' It should be the other way round: 'The soul has a man.'

Going back to our Pythagorean principles, the Primordial Scission results in duality, and each new entity partakes of the nature of the 'One' and the 'Other'. Set is a principal aspect of the 'Other', and Ba-bi may be a generative aspect of Set, opposed as such to the reunion with spirit, or One. (It is probably more than chance that in Christian literature, Satan shares so many of Set's characteristics under a suspiciously similar name, which in Hebrew means 'adversary'. Satan is also called 'the ape of God'.)

But just as the perfected man reconciles Set and Horus within himself, so Ba-bi's power may be put to constructive or destructive use.

In the abbreviated context of the Unas text the generative or phallic connection is not even implicit, much less explicit. Sethe, and following him Barguet and Faulkner, quite illegitimately draw upon the Sesostris text for their translations. Yet that makes things no clearer. Why should the 'doors of heaven' open when 'the phallus of Ba-bi' is 'drawn back'?

The difficulty here is not only the esoteric meaning of the text, but a fundamental incompatibility of language. In the Sesostris text, the translated text reads literally 'the phallus of Ba-bi is drawn back'. The same sign is employed in the Unas text to give the line 'draw it back'. But in English, German and French there is no connection between 'bolt' and 'phallus'. To say 'the phallus of Ba-bi is drawn back' means nothing whatever, while everyone knows what is meant by 'the bolt is drawn back'. The Egyptian establishes a connection between bolt and phallus that our language will not permit. If we say 'the phallus of Ba-bi is withdrawn' it makes sense, it conveys the idea of a deliberate relinquishment or suspension of the power symbolised by 'phallus'. But if we say 'the bolt is withdrawn' it is just bad English.

In any case, it is Ba-bi who possesses the power to open the doors, or the shutters, of heaven. If a literal translation upon an esoteric basis for the whole sequence existed, it might be possible to explain precisely what is meant. As it stands, an informed surmise is the best that is possible. Draw back the bolt; i.e., the phallus of Ba-bi is withdrawn, hence the power of generation is suspended, which in turn means the need for reincarnation is voided, opening the gates to heaven, the reunion with the Source.

The text then reads:

Draw it back!
Open the two shutters to heaven.
Open for Unas,

Over the flame, beneath the *iknt*.
Of the gods.

Further problems present themselves. The words for 'over' and 'beneath' are formal, but employed as such do not make sense, and the translators try different solutions. ('The way *goes over* the fireglow', Sethe; 'Open to Ra the door of the sky *by* the flame', Speleers; '*Because* of the furnace heat', Faulkner; 'The way that *passes over*', Barguet.)

'*Iknt*' is another difficult word. In other contexts it signifies 'ladling or scooping out', that is to say 'a drawing toward (of something)', in this case by the Neters, or 'gods'. The actual meaning follows upon the understanding of the consequences of a suspension of Ba-bi's power, and the subsequent opening of the two shutters of heaven.

The short phrase describes a double action: a flame or fire that is rising and being drawn upward (toward heaven) by the gods. The flame is 'spirit', the spiritual fire, or 'breath of fire' drawn heavenward by the gods.

'*Seben*' (*sbn.t.*) presents the next problem. *Seben* is variously Horus 'lets slip', Horus is allowed 'to slide or slip through' and Horus 'stumbles'. None of these solutions is satisfactory, yet in this case, the meaning of the word practically imposes itself. The determinative for *sbn.t* (characteristically omitted in the Unas text but understood as implicit) is a little river fish whose peculiarity it is to swim upside down. It is in this position that it is always shown.*

The Nile fish, sbn, *swimming upside down.*

* The reverse of *seben*, *nebes*, is the Christ-thorn or zizyphus tree, whose branches incline to the ground. 'The zizyphus tree bends its head to you' (*Pys.* Text 808, R. O. Faulkner). Thus, *seben* is a fish that turns its face to the sky, *nebes* a tree that bends its head to the ground.

143

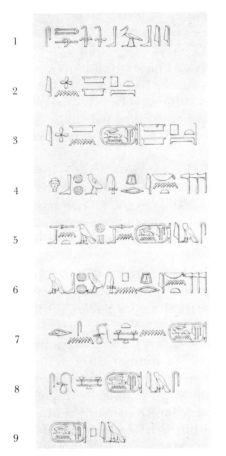

Unas, the dead king, is identified with Osiris, dead, flung to the ground face down (the dead Osiris is often thus portrayed). But Osiris will rise again as Horus, and Unas is asked to follow suit: in death as Osiris, return to eternal life as Horus! *Seben! Seben!* In other words, having fallen to earth, like the little *seben* fish, 'turn your face to the heavens!' 'Arise and return!'

The rest of the text now follows, word for word:

Return! Return, Horus!
That Unas may return,
By the flame drawn up by the gods,
Who make ready the way,
That Unas may pass,
For Unas is Horus!

The text now reveals itself as both sequential and profound. The power of Ba-bi is invoked to open the two shutters to heaven (as opposed, perhaps, to its being used in the generative sense of compelling reincarnation and the return to earth in a bodily existence). The doors open above the spiritual fire that is drawn heavenward, as the breath of the gods. As Osiris, fallen face to the ground in death, Unas is implored to emulate Horus, and like the little fish, turn his face to heaven. And now, like Horus, through the agency of the spiritual fire breathed by the gods, Unas may pass along the way, to live in eternity. For Unas is Horus.

Given the extreme compression of the text and the complexity of the underlying thought, a translation intended for a public interested in esotericism but unable to read the Egyptian might legitimately make use of a degree of poetic license, both to give an insight into the meaning of the text, and to try to capture (insofar as it is possible in translation) a commensurate poetry, sound and rhythm. Spell 316 might read:

Draw the bolt, Ba-bi!
Open the doors to heaven!
Open! For Unas! The doors open:
Over the fire of spirit; the breath drawn by the gods;
Arise, Horus! Return!
That Unas may return,
Borne by the flame, drawn by the gods,
Who clear the way, that Unas may pass.
For Unas is Horus.

Hieroglyphic lines:
1 Draw it [the bolt] back, Ba-bi!
2 Open the two shutters of heaven!
3 Open for Unas.
4 Over the flame, under the iknt *of the gods.*
5 Return, return, Horus!
6 That Unas may return in this flame beneath the iknt *of the gods [i.e., by means of the flame drawn heavenwards as breath of the gods, or divine entities].*
7 Who make ready the way.
8 [That] Unas may pass.
9 [For] Unas is Horus.

(Pyr. of Unas; Ch. 313, Spell 502)

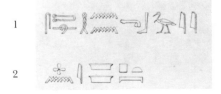

Variations:
1 The phallus of Ba-bi is drawn back.
2 The shutters of heaven are opened.
(Pyr. of Sesostris I, at Lisht)

Before turning to Egyptian literature, another illustration of the importance of sound in Egyptian texts will demonstrate a further difficulty in the rendering of these sacred texts into an equivalent English.

Even though no one knows how Egyptian ought to be pro-

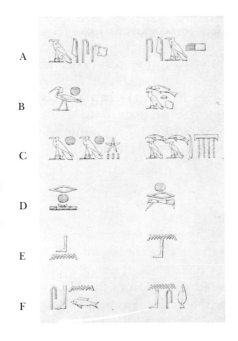

Single hieroglyphs:
A Ais: viscera (of the head), i.e. brain.
Sia: Intelligence, knowledge; v.
recognise, perceive, know.
B Akh: Spirit, spirit-state, be, become a
spirit, glorious, splendid, etc.
Kha: Corpse
C Akhakh: stars.
Khakha: storm.
D Rkh: know, aware of, knowledge.
Khr: fall.
E Ben: Negation, 'it is not' 'there is not'.
Neb: Gold, Lord, Master, All, owner,
every (many variations according to
the determinative).
F Sbn: Fish that turns over on its back
(Synodontis batensoda).
Nbs: Christ-thorn or Zizyphus tree
(Zizyphus spina Christi).
The zizyphus tree bows its head
toward you (the defunct).

(Pyr. 808, 1723).

nounced or stressed, it is often clear that the texts make strong use of rhyme, meter and alliteration; they are poetic by nature. In many cases, word play is so powerful that the spoken text would amount to incantation.

As is generally recognised, even modern poetry cannot be satisfactorily translated from one language to another. If the literal sense of the words is adhered to, then the rhyme, meter and word play is lost. If rhyme and meter are retained, then the sense of the words is distorted. With Egyptian the problem is compounded.

Following is a brief passage from the Bremner Rhind Papyrus, a typically verbose New Kingdom text which, rendered into modern language, becomes an interminable and exceedingly tedious mumbo jumbo. It is mainly concerned with a sequence of maledictions directed at the serpent fiend, Apop, but it also includes a fascinating incantatory paragraph of cosmology, which by shifting tenses (all based upon the same word), deals with the perennial problems of time, timelessness and creation, a device that in the Old Testament is employed in the famous phrase, 'Before Abraham was, I am.'

Egyptian, like Hebrew, is written without vowels. But unlike Hebrew, Egyptian has disappeared as a spoken language, and the pronunciation of the vowels is guesswork. Even so, the incantatory nature of the following text is obvious. (I have inserted vowels — following usual orthodox custom — in the attempt to make the text pronounceable; instead of writing *hpr-i*, I have written *kheper-ee*.)

Rendered phonetically, the text (Bremner-Rhind 28,20) reads:

Neb djer djed-ef:
Kheper-ee kheper kheper-oo,
Kheper-kooie em kheper-oo en khepree, kheper em sep tepi,
Kheper-kooie em kheperoo en khepree kheper-oo
Kheper kheper-oo poo,
En pea-en-ee yoo pea-oot-yoo ir-en-ee
Pea-en-ee em pea-oot-yoo
Pea eren-ee yoo-essen ir-ee pea-oot pea-oot-yoo

If, in trying to twist your tongue around the unaccustomed sounds, you decide it is all abracadabra, you could well be right. Though the dictionary declares the origin of familiar Cabbalistic formulae 'uncertain', Harold Bayley, in *The Lost Language of Symbolism*, Williams and Norgate, 1951, says this incantation may be one of the names of the sun god, Mithras. If so, then this is probably derived from the Egyptian, *kheper*, the scarab beetle, which is the symbol and name of the morning sun, the sun as transforming principle.

The above text, rendered into English, reads:

The Master of the Universe declares:
When I manifested myself into existence, existence existed. I came into existence in the form of the Existent, which came into existence in the First Time. Coming into existence according to the mode of existence of the Existent, I therefore existed. And it was thus that the Existent came into existence, for I was anterior to the Two Anteriors that I made, for I had priority over the Two Anteriors, for my name was anterior to theirs, for I made them thus anterior to the Two Anteriors . . . *

Literature

Most of the hieroglyphic texts are theological or commemorative. There is little 'literature', but what there is is not devoid of interest. Stories have been discovered dating from the Middle Kingdom. In content, impact and style (insofar as so delicate a matter as style can survive the hazards of translation), these stories are reminiscent of stories from the *Arabian Nights*. In certain cases the correspondences are close enough to suggest that the Egyptian original was handed down through the ages, more or less intact.

These Egyptian stories prove that a lively literary tradition, even a sense of humour, existed in ancient Egypt. They may also be used to illustrate the theme of secular versus esoteric literature. Though this is the most important literary distinction there is, literary authorities and most contemporary writers do not realise the distinction exists. Therefore, all of us go through the educational system fed upon literature that, from the point of view of esotericism, is not literature at all but journalism, or worse. Egyptologists cannot be expected to show keener literary sensitivity than anyone else; therefore, the point of these ancient stories has been missed.

Esoteric literature resembles initiatic teaching in that both proclaim the same message: that man is not as he could be, not as he should be; that man contains within himself the spark of divinity; that his destiny and proper task is to kindle that spark into a flame.

But initiatic teachings are directed at those who are consciously disciples. The Sermon on the Mount and much of the Gospels were not preached to the masses (the Bible is explicit on this point). These teachings were directed at Christ's disciples; to the people He spoke in 'parables'.

The parable offers the same pill but with a suitable sugar coating, and it is directed at the public. It is not to be confused

* Translated from the French version given by Sauneron and Yoyotte in *La Naissance du monde*, Sources Orientales, Editions du Seuil, p. 49.

with allegory, which is a rational and intellectual personification of abstractions such as 'truth' or 'morality' — an attempt to disguise the familiar Sunday school sermon. Allegory is always obvious; esoteric literature is never obvious. Its meaning is veiled in symbols. But these symbols are chosen from the exoteric world, the world of everyday life; and it is a characteristic of esoteric literature that it can be read and enjoyed without its inner meaning ever becoming apparent. Yet the power and validity of the symbolism is such that it sets up a ferment subliminally, subconsciously; true esoteric literature is almost immune to changes of literary fashion or the passage of time.

There is practically no contemporary adult esoteric literature. The whole of Western literature has scarcely produced half a dozen genuinely esoteric works. But if we were lucky, as children, amid the social-oriented banalities and the TV propaganda, we came into contact with fairy tales. Many of these are esoteric, or must have been esoteric initially. This is the source of their power, their longevity, and the peculiar quality they have of sticking in the mind. The esoteric tale has a 'flavour', an 'atmosphere'. We cannot 'prove' it; to 'explain' it is to kill it. But we can feel it. And once we come to understand that it is the tale's unrealised but experienced inner meaning — its esoteric heart — that is responsible for its power, we can distinguish between the esoteric, the exoteric and the pseudo-esoteric with some confidence. (*The Frog Prince, Snow White, Rumpelstiltskin, Moby Dick* and *The Brothers Karamazov* are esoteric; *Portnoy's Complaint* is exoteric; *Siddhartha* is pseudo-esoteric.)

The symbolic themes of esoteric literature are found the world over; like gesture they seem to be universal. Esoteric literature ultimately concerns man's quest for the divine within himself. Often the quest is explicitly a search — for the grail, for treasure — either hidden or inaccessible. Often the treasure is guarded by monsters or enemies who must be overcome by a combination of courage and guile. All of this symbolizes the struggle of man against his own nature — the archetypal struggle between Horus and Set, between the Old Adam and the New Man, between David and Goliath, between Sinbad and the Old Man of the Sea who will not get off Sinbad's back.

Sometimes the prize is a beautiful princess or handsome prince; to attain the prize tasks must be performed, and courage, determination and often cunning are required. Sometimes the prince or princess is disguised as a frog or a beggar, or he or she may be asleep or enchanted. Successful completion of the quest is rewarded by inheriting the kingdom and 'living happily ever after', i.e., in 'eternity'.

Some Egyptian tales are esoteric, others are not. I shall examine briefly one example from each category.

By common consent, the most powerful of the Egyptian

tales is that of Sinuhe. This is datable precisely because it incorporates an historical event; the death of Amenemhet (first pharaoh of the Twelfth Dynasty) and the accession to the throne of his successor Sesostris. This historical event has prompted scholars to regard the story as embellished biography. It is not. Even if it had an historical basis, that is not the point of the story; its detail discloses its true nature, and its true nature is in the grand tradition of esoteric literature.

The Story of Sinuhe is a tale about exile. Sinuhe, a courtier to Amenemhet, is away on a campaign. While away, he hears that the king is dead and the new king has assumed the throne. For no good reason (the story makes this clear) Sinuhe becomes frightened, and he flees. His travels take him out of Egypt (out from within himself) into increasingly remote and barbarous lands. He does not know where he is going, or why — an aspect of his flight powerfully and economically conveyed by the author in a few details. For example, it is specified that Sinuhe crosses the river in a boat without a rudder. Travelling into exile in a boat without a rudder is a powerful literary description of a psychological state. Sinuhe, blown by the winds, ends up in Asia, the Egyptian equivalent of Siberia. But coming to his senses, he decides to do the best he can under the circumstances, while cherishing within his heart the dream of returning to Egypt. He ingratiates himself with the barbarians and rises to be a man of power in their midst. At a certain point, though already old, he defeats (in what is described as physical combat) the awesome adversary of his hosts. This is a clue to the un-historical intentions of the author. How can an old man, near death, physically become the champion of the barbarians?

At long last, word of Sinuhe's virtue reaches the court of the pharaoh himself, Sinuhe is forgiven, invited home and received in the spirit of the returning prodigal.

Despite the usual pidgin quality of the translation, despite the alien nature of much of the detail (the supplications to the pharaoh, etc.), it is surprising how much power Sinuhe still exerts across the ages. It may also be significant that the historical event featured in the story is the death of Amenemhet and the accession of Sesostris. It is difficult to pinpoint the passing of a precessional age and the beginning of the next; but it is certain that the age of Taurus passed and the age of Aries began right around this time — a change distinctly mirrored in the symbolism of Egyptian art with the accession to power of the ram of Amon. It may be that Sinuhe's fear is intended to symbolise the fear, quite natural to man, of the new and unknown age just dawning. But until a translation upon symbolic principles is available, this is conjecture.

The second story is called *The Eloquent Peasant*. This story is not esoteric; it is cautionary. That is, like Aesop's fables, it

J. W. B. Barns
'Sinuhe's Message to the King: A Reply to a Recent Article'
Journal of Egyptian Archaeology, 53, p. 14

This flight which this humble servant did, I did not foresee it; it was not in my mind; I did not plan it; I know not what parted me from my place. I was in the condition of one in a dream. . . . I did not take fright; none pursued me; I heard no reviling utterance; my name was not heard in the mouth of the reporter (informer?) excepting only those things whereat my flesh crept (?), and my feet taking control of me, the god who ordained this flight drawing me on . . .

does not touch upon spiritual truths, but makes a point that is psychological.

The Eloquent Peasant is about a farmer who believes he has been wronged by a neighbour. He seeks redress, and ultimately ends up before the viceroy or Nomarch. The remainder of the story is taken up by the peasant's long-winded grievances; a display of inexhaustible variations upon a single theme. Here is the eighth petition; following seven others of equal length, with one still to follow.

The Eloquent Peasant

Eighth Petition

Then this peasant came to make petition to him (The High Steward, Rensi) an eighth time and said: 'O high steward, my lord! Men suffer a far fall through greed. The rapacious man lacks success, but he has a success in failure. Thou art rapacious and it beseems thee not; thou stealest and it benefits thee not; thou who shouldn't (?) suffer a man to attend to his own right cause. It is because thy sustenance is in thy house; thy belly is full; the corn measure flows over and, when it shakes (?) its superfluity is lost on the ground.

O thou who shoulds't seize the robber, and who takest away the magistrates, (they) were made to redress troubles; they are shelters for the indigent; the magistrates, (they) were made to redress falsehood. No fear of thee causes me to make petition to thee. Thou perceivest not my heart; silent one, who turns him ever back to make reproaches to thee. He does not fear him to whom he makes his claim; and his brother is not to be brought to thee from out of the street.

Thou hast thy plot of ground in the country, and the guerdon is in thy domain. Thy bread is in the bakery, and the magistrates give to thee. And (yet) thou takest! Art thou a robber? Are troops brought to thee to accompany thee for the divisions of the ground plots?

Do justice for the Lord of Justice, the justice of whose justice exists. Thou reed-pen, thou papyrus, thou palette, thou Thoth, keep aloof from the making of trouble. When what is well is well, then it is well. But justice shall be unto everlasting. It goes down into the necropolis with him who doeth it; he is buried and the earth envelops him; and his name is not obliterated upon earth, but he is remembered for goodness. Such is the norm in the word of god. Is he a balance? It does not tilt. Is he a stand-balance? It does not incline to the one side. Whether I shall come or another shall come, do thou address (him); answer not as one who addresses a silent man, or as one who attacks him who cannot attack. Thou dost not show mercy; thou dost not weaken (?); thou dost not annihilate (?); and thou givest me no reward for this goodly speech which comes forth from the mouth of Ra himself. Speak justice and do justice; for it is mighty; it is great; it endureth long, its trustworthiness (?) is discovered, it bringeth into revered old age. Does a balance tilt? (If so), it is (through) its scales which carry all things. No inequality is possible to the norm. A mean act attaineth not to the city; the hindermost (?) will reach land.

Ninth Petition

Then this peasant came to make petition to him a ninth time, and said: 'O high steward, my lord! The tongue of men is their stand balance . . . ,

Egyptologists do not like *The Eloquent Peasant*. Sir Alan Gardiner comments: 'But whereas the simplicity of the story of Sinuhe, its conciseness, its variety of mood and its admirable felicity of expression make it a great literary masterpiece, the same praise cannot be given to the tale of the Eloquent Peasant . . . the nine petitions addressed to Rensi are alike poverty stricken as regards the ideas, and clumsy and turgid in their expression. The metaphors of the boat and of the balance are harped upon with nauseous insistency, and the repetition of the same words in close proximity with different meanings shows that the author was anything but a literary artist.'

These strictures typify the attitude of Egyptologists who cannot understand the popularity this story enjoyed in Egypt.

Yet to appreciate *The Eloquent Peasant* as literature, sophisticated modern man need make no concessions, as long as three factors are borne in mind.

The first is that, though it comes to us in writing, like fairy tales, epic poems and all other ancient literature, it was meant to be told aloud.

The second is that with Egyptian, the problems of translation are always greater than with other ancient languages. The gaps and queries are unavoidable where words and phrases cannot be deciphered. Apart from this, all stylistic efforts cease as soon as the given sentence or paragraph begins to approach coherence. No translator would dream of serving up a Greek tragedy in this kind of English, but with Egyptian, it is standard practice.

The third is that dramatic literature is not the only kind of literature there is, or was.

The astute reader may have already perceived the story's true nature through the quoted passage. If not, then the end will give the game away.

With his nine interminable, repetitious petitions unanswered, the eloquent peasant storms off, determined to bring his suit before Anubis himself, the ultimate adjudicator. At this point, he is brought back by the servants of the high steward. He fears he will be punished for his insolence, since his harangues have degenerated from pleas for mercy and justice into open abuse of the high steward and of authority in general.

In one sense his fears are ill-founded. Ultimately he obtains redress and is awarded the goods and possessions of the neighbour who had robbed him. But in another sense, his fears are justified. The end of the story is actually anti-climactic. The eloquent peasant is indeed punished and his punishment is the point of the whole story. For prior to his reward, he is forced to sit down and listen to his nine endless petitions read back to him word for word by the scribes of the high steward.

If, up to this moment, difficulties of translation concealed the true nature of the story from scholars, the point should now be clear even to the most scholarly. Evelyn Waugh could not have thought up a more fitting finale.

Exaggeration, endless harping upon the same metaphor, manifold nuances of meaning given to the same expression, fatal as they might be to dramatic literature, are the foundations of another equally time-honoured form of literature — comedy.

The Eloquent Peasant makes elaborate use of comic methods later exploited by figures such as Rabelais, Cervantes, Shakespeare (e.g. in drawing Polonius), Sterne and Ionesco to name but a few. It is true that it is almost unreadable, but it was never meant to be read — certainly not by the general public. Given a translation based upon an understanding of the story's intent, and told by a skilled raconteur, it is probable that even today *The Eloquent Peasant* would reduce an audience to helpless, exasperated hilarity. It is the world's oldest shaggy dog story.

Sir Alan Gardiner
Journal of Egyptian Archaeology 9, p. 6
To those without a knowledge of the Egyptian language some explanation why texts of this sort occasion so great difficulty may be of interest. The meaning of a large majority of the words employed is either known already, or else can be elicited through comparison with other examples; but not the precise nuances of meaning, only the kind of meaning, its general direction, and its approximative emotional quality. Taking into consideration the further facts that the absence of any indication of the vowels makes the distinction between the various verb forms very difficult, and that the Egyptian dispenses almost entirely with such particles as 'but', 'because', 'when', 'through', it will become evident that texts of a purely moralising character, where there is no concrete background against which the appropriateness of this or that rendering shows up unmistakably, must present extraordinary difficulties. . . .
Nevertheless the number of moralising texts which we now possess is not inconsiderable. . . . Some confidence that we have succeeded in fathoming an old Egyptian sentiment may often be gained by noting how well the same sentiment, expressed in different but similar words, fits into other contexts. By slow degrees we are acquiring a fair working knowledge of the psychology of these ancient folk.

The Temple of Man

Marcel Griaule
Op. cit.

In his account, Dogon civilisation appeared in the likeness of a huge organism, every part of which had its own function and its own place as well as contributing to the general development of the whole. In this organism, every institution was integrated; none was outside it; and however divergent it might seem and however incompletely understood, was found to fit into a system whose structure revealed itself day by day with increasing clarity and precision.

E. Drioton
Pages d'Egyptologie
Cairo, 1957, pp. 111-112

Historians of Egyptian Religion ... have cast light, often sagely, upon the different levels of particular cults, their development, their combinations, but without successfully providing a view of the whole which supports it.

Max Guilmot
Le Message Spirituel de l'Egypte Ancienne
Hachette, 1970, p. 21

The illustrious Belgian Egyptologist, Jean Capart, told me at the end of his life, 'One knows everything about Egyptian Religion, everything except the essential: its Soul.'

Schwaller de Lubicz began his work at Luxor on the hunch that the Great Temple there was the Parthenon of Egypt — that is, a sacred structure built according to strict harmonic proportions. If this hunch could be proven, it would mean that knowledge of harmony and proportion existed some fifteen hundred years before their alleged invention by the Greeks. This in turn would necessitate a drastic revision of widely-held opinions of human social evolution.

By the time he had finished his fifteen-years' work at the site, the nature of the revelations forced upon him by the Temple had led Schwaller de Lubicz to reinterpret the whole civilisation of ancient Egypt.

This interpretation sees Egypt as an organic whole, no one part of which can be legitimately abstracted and studied without at least tacit reference to the manner in which that part interacts with the whole. The analogy of a civilisation and its various aspects with the various organs of the human body is to be taken symbolically, if not actually literally — it is more than a mere figure of speech. Egyptian civilisation must be regarded organically as existing and passing through its various life phases in time. Whatever the political vicissitudes of Egyptian history, the Temple, which was responsible for the religious, artistic, philosophical and scientific life of society, performed its task in full consciousness and deliberation. Egyptian civilisation is itself a gigantic gesture, an organised sacred dance whose execution spans four millennia.

The Temple at Luxor, which Schwaller de Lubicz calls 'The Temple of Man', is the perfect example of this symbolic understanding in action. It is a vast stone symbol, the greatest achievement of New Kingdom Egypt, incorporating within it — or utilising — the totality of Egyptian wisdom: science, mathematics, geodesy, geography, geometry, medicine, astronomy, astrology, magic, myth, art, symbolism. All of these contribute to the Temple, and all can be reapproached, studied and (within the limits of our own understanding) resuscitated as we discover the roles these various fields play within the Temple's structure.

The Temple tells, in stone, in its proportions and harmonies, its art and sculpture, the story of the creation of man; it signals his development, stage by stage, and it recreates in artistic form man's relationship to the universe.

This kind of aim has never entirely vanished in the West. Followers of Rudolf Steiner have attempted to build upon similar principles, and at the moment, the center being built by followers of Sri Aurobindo at Auroville in India also makes use of cosmically significant harmonies and proportions. But these are notable exceptions. As a general rule, it is safe to say that the planning of a structure as complex and subtle as Luxor is beyond our present capacities, and alien to our way of thinking as well. It is difficult to imagine generating sufficient interest in such a project to set it in motion, and equally difficult to imagine successful designing upon an equivalent scale.

Perhaps because of its inherent strangeness, this aspect of Schwaller de Lubicz's work — which is its culmination and central theme — has been the target for the most impassioned criticism, ranging from open abuse to admonitions to regard his conclusions with 'extreme caution'.

Possibly caution is called for. Yet, as I have indicated over the course of this book, even without Schwaller de Lubicz, a gradual process of upgrading and reinterpretation of the various aspects of Egyptian civilisation has prevailed in orthodox circles for decades. It is just that to date no one has tried to re-examine Egypt as a whole in the light of this revised opinion.

But Schwaller de Lubicz's documentation supporting his explanation of the Temple is as thorough and as elaborate as the rest of his work; the same formidable array of measurements, diagrams and closely reasoned argument is provided. Nowhere is there argument or evidence that contradicts him. The academic admonishment to caution is no more than a way of dismissing a theory without going to the trouble to actually disprove it.

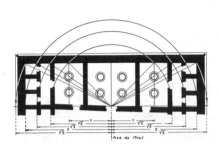

Schwaller de Lubicz's analysis of the top sanctuary of the Temple shows it constructed upon solid and rigorous geometric play. The correspondences shown are exact to a millimeter or so. Again, it is not my intention here to go into the significance of the geometry, but simply to show the undeniable fact of its existence. The proportions of the inner chamber are in the ratio 8:9 — musically, the tone.

J. Yoyotte
Dictionary of Egyptian Civilisation
Ed. G. Posener, Methuen, 1962, p. 276

Symbolism

As a result of an incorrect understanding brought about by a mixture of Greek idealism, Babylonian astronomy and Egyptian natural physics, the Graeco-Roman philosophies, particularly hermetic literature, propounded the astonishing theory that the old Pharaonic religion concealed in its hieroglyphs purely mystical ideas.

There is much argument over the latest development of these composite theories. 'Symbolistic Egyptology', bearing the stamp of Adamistic occultism and overlaid with literary mysticism, postulates the astrological infallibility of the 'sages', reduces any historical fact to something subsidiary and, manipulating in turn the rules of Cabbala, arithmetic juggling and general assertions of the positive sciences, selects as *keys* certain features of the plan and decoration of temples in order to demonstrate that any Egyptian monument conceals absolute Knowledge, and in an esoteric way symbolises the perfect concord between the world, the earth, and the human body in cosmic rhythm, etc.

This system has nothing to do with a new method of historical research as is sometimes believed; it only offers the barely renovated theories of mediaeval alchemists which the laborious arguments endeavour to project backwards some thousands of years. This mode of thought is a variant of the old European occultism and transcends in principle all philosophical conceptions, all scientific progress and all religion. Its . . . popularity with some educated men is explained by the aura which surrounds Black Magic and by the instinctive desire of modern people to regard ancient civilisation in a way which would conform with their sentimental opinions. But it would only be for the sake of being different that one would pursue such theories — it would be extremely difficult to defend a science belonging to the *Djahiliya* when the 'Revelation' has come about through Champollion. [The careful reader will notice in this long tirade the absence of a single fact. Author's note.]

Personal note from Lucie Lamy

... I enclose as well, two pages of extracts from P. Barguet, so that you see, (*Revue des Conférence Français en Orient*, Dec. 1948) regarding the sacred animals: The Bull prior to 2000 BC and the Ram after 2000 BC.

The following, from p. 287 of the above, that I cannot help but put in parallel with the phrase from M. de Lubicz (Le Roi de la Théocratie Pharaonique, p. 260):

'Osiris, signifying in general, *renewal...*'

And above all, notice the titles:

'Cosmic aspects of the Temple', Barguet

'The Temple as Microcosm', Derchain

'The Symbolism of Light in the Temple of Dendera', Daumas

'Thus penetrating mystically through the temple entrances up to the hidden statue, within the dark of the sanctuary, the sun is united with the divine image and *the cosmic return of the light*, within the grandiose order of the world.... The illumination of the sanctuary by the sun is therefore, in its own turn, a symbol of the rite.... There is between the formalities of the cult and *the rhythm of the universe* a profound and necessary bond which, for once, the texts and the images have generously conserved....

(Interesting to remember that Barguet and Daumas were at Luxor at the same time as ourselves.)

And there is, besides, a series (of plaquettes) by Drioton, dedicated to M. de Lubicz, in which he treats of the *philosophy* underlying Egyptian Religion; it's *monotheism*, which he shows to have been there from the earliest epochs, and he finishes one of these many articles by saying,

'It is certain that the Egyptian teachings on Divinity were the precursors of the Christian Revelation in a certain sense; and although, in telling the peasants, "Your ancient gods themselves were preaching Christianity to you" the Christians of Alexandria were materially wrong, spiritually they were speaking the truth.'

Do you not find Drioton a curious character?

Why did he oppose us so strongly? When, at heart, even before knowing us, he already *knew* there was far more to the 'Egyptian Religion' than that which classical Egyptologists wanted to see....

(Etienne Drioton, apart from being an eminent Egyptologist, was also a Catholic Canon.)

There is an amusing story relating to the original appearance of *Le Temple de l'Homme* in 1957, and its official reception. Rather than try to summarise this, which would mean deleting all the funny bits, a short personal experience will capture the essence of the situation.

Early on in my research, before I had studied *Le Temple de l'Homme* in depth, I was granted an interview with a high-ranking official of the Egyptological Department of the British Museum. He assured me that in his opinion, and in the opinion of all other Egyptologists, Schwaller de Lubicz was mad. His work was repudiated in its entirety.

I replied that I realised this, yet that to me, a layman, it all seemed backed by exhaustive documentation — documentation, moreover, that had been checked and supervised on the

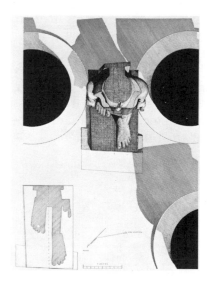

This colossus of Rameses II (carved from a single block of granite) gives the unmistakable impression of 'advance'. The impression is particularly strong on site when the statue is seen in conjunction with the somewhat ruined colossi flanking it: they distinctly do not advance. But the camera refuses to capture what the eye easily perceives in this case. A study of the colossus revealed it based upon a rigorous symmetry from every angle except when viewed from above. The illusion of 'advance' is created solely by the twist of the supporting dorsal stela and the positioning of the feet — an instance of the astonishing command of technique common in Egypt.

The high-ranking official was T. G. H. James, then curator of Egyptian Antiquities.

site by an orthodox Egyptologist converted to the Symbolist school, Alexandre Varille, and by an architect, Clement Robichon, chief of excavations for the French Egyptological team in Egypt. Was there, I asked, any disproof of the documentation?

The official admitted there was not, but assured me that if Egyptologists should trouble themselves to furnish themselves with disproof (which they were too busy to do), that disproof would soon be acquired.

It was impossible to argue effectively against this conviction. I asked if he might furnish me with an instance where, even without formal disproof, he could substantiate an error. He admitted that he had not actually read through *Le Temple de l'Homme*, nor did he know of any other Egyptologist who had.

I was, at the time of the interview, acquainted with the controversy surrounding the appearance of the book. I pointed out that there was at least one respected orthodox Egyptologist in a responsible position, Arpag Mekhitarian, secretary of an Egyptological institute in Brussels who, without espousing Schwaller de Lubicz's views, had committed himself on record to say that the work demanded serious study and the courtesy of formal disproof if that were possible.

'Ah, yes,' replied my high-ranking official, 'Mekhitarian is something of a mystic. He might well say that.'

Arpag Mekhitarian
Cahiers du Sud, No. 358
December, 1960, pp. 335, 346

Each of us [orthodox Egyptologists], within the little sphere of his specialty, must have the courage to verify the elements with which he is most familiar; he must check, on the site if necessary, the assertions made by M. de Lubicz and must call unselfconsciously for help from colleagues and technicians able to throw light upon domains which formerly have been closed to him; above all, he must not reject *a priori* as inconceivable that which exceeds his understanding. . . . The symbolism of M. Schwaller de Lubicz . . . is not a simple personal and fantastic interpretation of facts, but conclusions drawn from precise and objective evidence which up to now has escaped the acumen of Egyptologists.

The axes

The Temple of Luxor is a perfect example of art as a deliberate manipulation of harmonic phenomena whose end result is magic.

This enormous asymmetric structure, over eight hundred feet long, was built in stages to a design unique in sacred architecture. Prior to Schwaller de Lubicz no one could satisfactorily account for this strange plan. Some thought it caprice, others thought perhaps the Temple was meant to follow a curve of the nearby Nile, and still others thought that because the Temple spanned over a thousand years from its beginning to the completion of the forecourt, the alignments shifted according to some astronomical plan — a not unreasonable notion.

But Schwaller de Lubicz was able to show that the plan in its entirety was complete at the very beginning. This curiously skewed complex is strictly aligned upon three separate axes. Without exception, every wall, colonnade, hall and sanctuary is rigorously aligned upon one or the other of these axes.

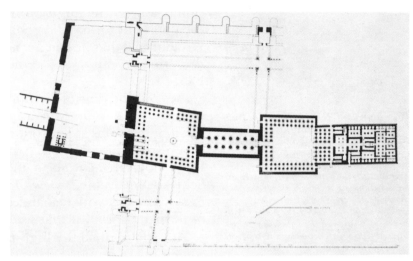

Schwaller de Lubicz found the two principal axes of the Temple of Luxor chiselled into the subfloor, beginning with the Holy of Holies. Our photo, taken some twenty-five years later, shows the same axes — much trodden out by multitudes of visitors but still visible. The presence of the graven axes is unarguable. Schwaller de Lubicz found that all colonnades and all walls of the Temple were aligned to these axes or to an angle derived from them (and to a third, hidden, or 'occult' axis never actually graven in, but complied with nonetheless). These axes constitute one of the most important pieces of evidence. For while the thinking underlying the choice of these axes is extremely complex, the fact of the axes is there for all to see. And if, as Schwaller de Lubicz claimed, the whole of the Temple is constructed to align to these axes, then it is obvious that the plan of the Temple is deliberate in its entirety, and it is up to Egyptologists to furnish an explanation if they object to the one put forward by the Symbolists.

In 1993, the axes are no longer visible. They have been covered over with gravel, as part of the general temple tidying-up program.

The manner in which these axes are obtained and the harmonic considerations that dictated their choice are too complex to go into here. But the axes are chiselled into the sandstone floor of the Temple and obviously served as a guide for the earliest stage of construction. Thereafter, this floor was covered over in white limestone, but the subsequent construction continued to be rigorously aligned to the invisible axes!

The nature of the Symbolist thesis is such that certain aspects lend themselves better than others to ironclad documentation. As courtroom evidence to set before a jury of uncommitted readers, the question of the axes is important; indeed, it is possible to use it as a fulcrum upon which the whole of the case may rest. The meaning of the axes is a very delicate affair, but there is no need to go into the complexities of art, magic, harmony, myth and symbolism to establish the factual existence of these three axes. Either they are there or they are not. As the photos show, these axes are chiselled into the floor of the Temple. To prove or disprove Schwaller de Lubicz's claim that all walls, colonnades and halls are aligned to these axes would not waste all that much of orthodox Egyptologists' valuable time. If Schwaller de Lubicz's claim should be substantiated, then it would be up to orthodox Egyptolo-

156

The 'Holy of Holies', Sanctuary of
Amon, and the 'Reflection of Amon'.
The upper sanctuary corresponds in role
and in location to the pituitary gland.
The Axis of Amon runs exactly from its
center to the exact center of the curious
sanctuary that is almost a mirror image
of the first. The symbolism involved is
too complex to touch upon here. It is the
geometry of the plan that strikes the eye,
and that underlines the importance of
Schwaller de Lubicz's discoveries. He
found the position of the reflection of
Amon determined to the millimeter by
the hypoteneuse of a 1:7 triangle. If this
finding is correct, then it is a powerful
evidence of the kind of sophisticated
geometrical and harmonic knowledge
that de Lubicz claims for the Egyptians;
for there can be nothing fortuitous about
the choice of the 1:7 triangle.

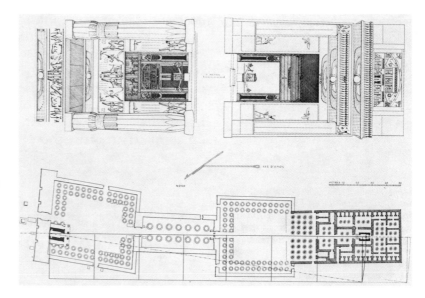

gists to find some alternative explanation of the meaning of
the axes should they continue to find the Symbolist explanation unacceptable.

Until the existence of the axes is disproved or satisfactorily
explained away in some other fashion, Schwaller de Lubicz's
evidence, to the layman, looks like very good evidence indeed.
And it becomes difficult not to follow him in his subsequent
interpretation — no matter that it takes us into a totally alien,
but fabulous realm of sages and magicians.

Because there is nothing in our own society that remotely
corresponds to a Temple of Luxor, it is difficult to understand
why Egypt should have exercised such infinite pains and
genius on what is ultimately a symbolic gesture. It is even
more difficult for us to understand the uses to which it was put
and the effect it must have had on those exposed to it. We can
only say that it was such a gesture, and following Schwaller de
Lubicz we can see how the design was organised.

Schwaller de Lubicz calls the Egyptian philosophy the
Anthropocosm, the Man Cosmos, a concept whose subtleties
are not easily grasped. It has found its way into two familiar
sayings, the Hermetic ('As above, so below') and the Biblical
('God fashioned man in His image'), but both these sayings,
while true, incline to misleading interpretations. The first
lends itself to too sharp a distinction, while the second lends
itself to too close a commingling. Man is not exactly a little universe to be regarded as distinct from a greater universe. On the
other hand, the Biblical phrase lends itself to pictures of a mus-
cular God with a long grey beard, which is not right either.

It is easier to say what the Anthropocosm is not than to say
what it is. Taoism and Zen take negative explanation as the saf-
est way out and leave it at that. But the rational Western mind

does not take readily to this kind of approach, and Schwaller de Lubicz takes pains to deal with the concept of the Anthropocosm as well as language will allow. Actually, the Anthropocosm may be found underlying all initiatic philosophies, but differently expressed in different philosophies. Man is not a 'product' of the universe nor a 'scale model' of it; he is to be regarded as an embodiment, its 'essence' incarnated in physical form. If an artist succeeds in putting all that he knows,

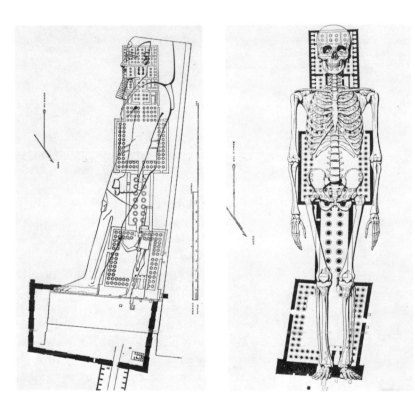

Schwaller de Lubicz prepared a skeleton according to the latest biometric researches and found it corresponded closely to the proportions employed by Egypt in the colossus of Rameses II (one of several in the courtyard of the Temple of Luxor). The only striking discrepancy, the size of the head in proportion to the body, is no doubt due to artistic considerations outweighing the biological. If the head were true to scale, the enormous statue would appear pinheaded when viewed from the ground. Both colossus and skeleton were then superimposed upon the independently prepared plan of the Temple. Note the close accord between human joints and Temple separating walls.

The Temple of Luxor is a planned, wholly conscious embodiment of the laws of creation. The symbolism of the various halls, chambers and sanctuaries strongly supports Schwaller de Lubicz's theory. Can it be accident that on the architrave corresponding to the site of the umbilical cord, the birth of the king is announced? Is it chance that in the sanctuary corresponding to the vocal cords, the names of the king are written, and that on the west wall is pictured the 'theogamy', the king born of the Neters — that is to say, the mystical creation through the Word, which is the 'Virgin' birth or Immaculate Conception?

J. L. DeCenival
Living Architecture, Egyptian
Oldbourne, 1964, *passim.*

A single feature could evoke a multiplicity of forms, myths or spiritual forces . . . so it [the temple] became a microcosm of Egypt and the entire cosmos where this encounter of god with man actually took place. . . . Each feature of a temple was conditioned and explained by an entire network of symbols. . . . For the Egyptians, the

feels, believes and understands into a work of art, that work is not a scale model of the artist yet it is more than a 'product'; it is not to be understood as distinct from the artist (as a child from its mother), yet it is not identical to him either. It is an 'embodiment' of the artist, an artistic expression of all that he is. The Anthropocosm bears an analogical relationship to the universe that created man.

The Temple of Luxor is not a scale model of creation; it is not a stone equivalent of the laboratory skeleton. Rather it is a symbolic model which conforms to scale. In one sense it is a library containing the totality of knowledge pertaining to universal creative powers. This knowledge is not set down explicitly in books, but is embodied in the building itself. In another sense the Temple is in the nature of a magic rite, extending over two millennia, designed to evoke in the beholder an under-

essence of a being resided in his name; what to us is no more than a fairly bad pun was, for them, a theological explanation!

From the ancient temple the new one inherited part of the ritual of mythological cycle on which the symbolic program had to be based.... If we try to make the temples into idealisations of the human form ... we are completely on the wrong track.

standing of creation and creative power. The proportions of the Temple are those of Adamic man, man before the fall, and of perfected man, man who has regained his cosmic consciousness through his own efforts. The Temple excludes the crown of the head, seat of the intellectual faculty. The cerebral cortex dualises, permits distinction, creates the illusion of separateness. Adamic man cannot distinguish, cannot choose between good and evil, and perfected man has reconciled Set and Horus

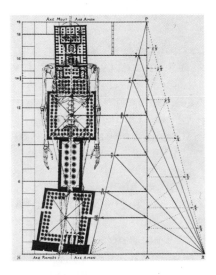

Schwaller de Lubicz discovered a method of geometrically obtaining harmonic intervals and projecting them upon a plan. The harmonic intervals for strings are based upon the division of the string fundamental in half initially. The harmony for brass is based upon division of the fundamental in a 4:1 ratio. This diagram combines both harmonic systems, and when projected against the plan of the temple, determines practically all of its major architectural features.

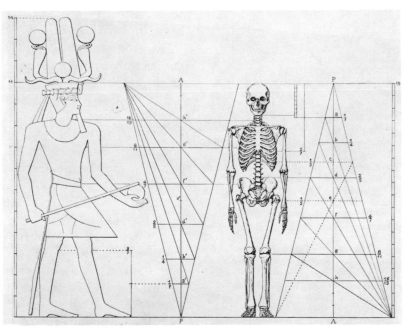

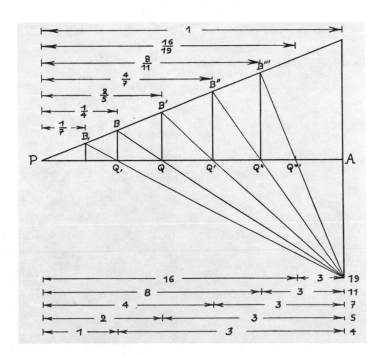

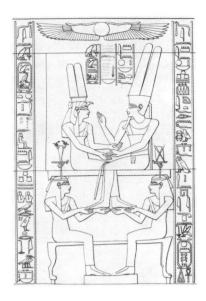

Scene of the 'theogamy' or marriage to the gods. The direct correspondence between fundamentals of Christian theology and ritual and ancient Egypt is clear in the intricate symbolism of this Luxor relief which, in Egyptian terms, portrays the Annunciation and creation through the Verb.
Amon and the queen, Mut-m-ouia, are seated on the symbol for the sky, supported by Selkit (scorpion emblem) and Neith (crossed arrows), whose own feet also do not rest upon the ground, denoting the wholly spiritual nature of the scene. On the right, the first of four columns upon which are written 'words spoken by Amon'. On the left, the first of columns on which are written the exclamations of the queen and Amon's reply.
The scene is found in the center of the west wall of the sanctuary corresponding to the vocal chords.

within himself. The walls, colonnades and sanctuaries all correspond to the siting of various vital centers.

Schwaller de Lubicz examines in detail contemporary studies of biometrics (the study of human measures) and finds these correspond very closely to the measures consistently employed in Egypt. These measures he shows conforming to a formal canon; proportion was never a matter of individual artistic preference.

These proportions are in turn commanded by the interplay of harmonic series (a fact unknown to biometricians, who operate empirically and statistically), the first with a root of two, the second with a root of four.

Thus the various sections of the human body stand in complex but always harmonious relationship to each other. And the discrete phases of growth also stand in harmonious relationship to earlier and later stages. These relationships are incorporated in the proportions of the Temple itself, in the proportions of the various wall paintings and statues. And the symbolism of each section corresponds to the organic vital center represented by that section. Sometimes direct and unmistakable, sometimes extremely subtle, this symbolism takes many forms, all of which are intended to evoke in the beholder a living understanding; nothing is the result of arbitrary choice, individual caprice or even aesthetic preference.

At the site of the umbilical cord, an inscription on the architrave between two columns announces that here takes place the birth, growth and coronation of the king.

At the mouth are written all the names of the Neters — i.e., the Grand Ennead creating through the Word.

In the hall corresponding to the centers of perception, the emphasis is on time and measure, orientation and the 'cross-

On the architrave corresponding exactly to the site of the umbilical cord according to Schwaller de Lubicz's superimposed skeleton and colossus, the birth of the king is announced.

The superimposition of the skeleton over the plan of the temple was another exciting time. I had to measure the pavement stone by stone, then months went into surveying the temple with the aid of the tacheometer, more months to get the plans exactly right. . . .

At the same time, I had to learn the laws of human biometry, the proportions of each bone down to the smallest detail, in order to establish a flawless skeleton. Then, designing the skeleton to the same scale of the temple, and superimposing it. . . . That provided us with more than we dared expect . . .

One day, I asked Varille, as I showed him the architraves at the court of Amenophis III, what was written exactly at the point where the projection placed the navel.

'It is here, the true site of the birth of the King, where he passed his infancy, and from whence he departed, crowned,' Varille replied.

Sir Alan Gardiner
Egypt of the Pharaohs
Oxford, 1961, *passim*.

True history is unthinkable without knowledge of personal relationships and in Egypt itself the chronicles of Arab times offer an almost continuous spectacle of bitter animosities. . . .

In the Pharaonic Age it cannot have been otherwise, or at all events, we must largely discount the unruffled narratives

ing' or inversion characteristic of this center. The hall contains twelve columns, one for each hour of the day, and is twelve fathoms long. East, the rising sun, represents the forces of creation; West symbolises completion. Therefore, the vulture on the wall to the East is carefully and deliberately left unfinished; in the same scene to the West, the vulture is finished. And the sacrificial animals are depicted front forward to the East, but with backs showing to the West.

At the site of the thyroid gland, which controls growth, there are scenes of childbirth and nursing.

Under the chin, at the vocal chords, the king is baptised and given his name. In this hall there is also the scene of the theogamy or marriage to the god, which is in effect the 'Immaculate Conception'.

Outside the Temple are the famous engravings of the victorious Rameses and the battle of Kadesh, a scene puzzling to Egyptologists: there was a historical battle of Kadesh but it was not a particularly important battle, and there were others reflecting to a far higher degree the military prowess of the pharaoh. As for pharaoh demolishing the entire enemy singlehanded, that is attributed to the usual Egyptian vainglory and left at that.

Schwaller de Lubicz insists that the scene in its entirety, though it uses the actual battle of Kadesh as a reference point, is symbolic. Even the immodest Ramesside kings would not expect the populace to swallow the single-handed defeat of a powerful enemy, or to believe that these enemies could be vanquished by the king seated upon his golden throne in the midst of the enemy camp. The purpose of this complex relief is the depiction of the battle between the forces of light and darkness.

of positive exploits which are so nearly invariable. It is more by inference than by explicit statement that we become aware of the conflict between Queen Hatshepsowe and her younger consort, Tuthmosis III. . . . In general it may be said that anything sinister or unsuccessful in the careers of the Pharaohs is carefully suppressed, thus depriving us of just the information which gives history its colour and complexion. It is a piquant fact that while individual character and fortune were so carefully concealed we still possess the mummified bodies of a number of the monarchs. In one case only, that of Akhenaten toward the end of Dynasty XVIII, do the inscriptions and reliefs bring us face to face with a personality markedly different from that of all of his predecessors, but the much varying estimates of this religious innovator only confirm the point which is here sought to drive home, namely the essentially one-sided and unreal picture of the rulers which emerges from the records they left behind them. . . . What is proudly advertised as Egyptian history is merely a collection of rags and tatters. In the Middle and New Kingdom the general aspect of such records as may strictly be called historical remains the same; unchanged is the self-satisfaction of the writers, the obvious predilection for the picturesque, the suppression of everything except isolated incidents — all these things invariably accompanied by the stringing together of titles and laudatory epithets.

Ibid., p. 61

If is be asked where our best historical material is to be found, our answer may seem to be almost a contradiction in terms; it is to be found in Egyptian fiction, where the authors were able to depict existing conditions and to vent their feelings with a freedom impossible when the predominant intention was that of boasting.

Ibid., p. 85

No doubt these new enthusiasts for the solar cult felt unequal to honouring their chosen god with the magnificence that the Dynasty IV rulers had bestowed upon the glorification of themselves, for they removed the scene of their building activities some miles to the south of Giza where an invidious comparison would be less practicable.

Having vanquished the enemy, the king can enter the Temple; to enter the Temple, all obstacles in the external world must be overcome. This is why the battle scenes are all on the exterior of the Temple walls.

The siting of the Temple, its exact orientation, its foundations and the manner of construction of the foundation — all are dictated by symbolic considerations, not by economy. Egypt transported granite obelisks a thousand miles down the Nile in order to conform to the fire symbolism of the obelisk. The coursing of the stones itself, the placing of the joints and the size and shape of the blocks employed were part of the grand symbolic design. The bizarre, time-consuming and structurally unnecessary stone masonry has long puzzled Egyptologists, for there is no logical, practical or economic explanation to account for this consistent practice.

Meanwhile, the dimensions of the Temple resolve themselves into fractions of terrestrial and cosmic measures (as do the pyramids). Because the whole of the Egyptian system of weights and measures was based upon terrestrial and cosmic considerations, the dimensions take on different significance when calculated according to the different measures, such as the span (our fathom), the royal cubit and other cubits. No doubt the total volume of the Temple had some cosmic significance as well.

The Temple of Luxor is designed to evoke understanding of the creative power of the Absolute through a strict imitation of its creative processes.

The Temple is 'alive'. Though obviously it has no power of self-replication, nor physical autonomy, as far as our sensory apparatus is concerned it is in constant motion; its intricate alignments, its multiple asymmetries, make it oscillate about its axes. (This secret was either handed down or rediscovered by the builders of the Gothic cathedrals, which incorporate similar asymmetries.) The Temple 'grew' in discrete stages; symbolically, it grew from a 'seed'.

L. C. Stecchini
Appendix to *Secrets of the Great Pyramid*, by Peter Tompkins
Harper & Row, 1971, pp. 338, 343

Akhenaten intended to cut at the root the power of the priests of the Temple of Amon. . . . The temple of Amon was the geodetic center of Egypt, 'the navel'.

The new capital . . . was set . . . at the middle point between the northernmost point Behdet and the southern limit. . . . The new city . . . was planted in a position which seems most undesirable. . . . Even the climate was inferior. . . . Unless one assumes there was a compelling mathematical reason for choosing this location . . . one must

agree that . . . 'The Tell el-Amarna Revolution' was the product of a playful young man, or a religious fanatic, or a degenerate obsessed with his sex problems. . . .

Akhenaten wanted to prove that Thebes could not properly claim to be the geodetic center of Egypt and that he had chosen the geodetic center conforming to an absolutely rigorous interpretation of *maet*, the cosmic order of which the dimensions of Egypt were an embodiment. . . . One should reevaluate the entire historical role of Akhenaten, taking as the starting point what he himself considered the initial step in his program.

The old as 'seed' of the new. From the Temple of Luxor. A striking example of the common Egyptian practice of re-employing significant features of an older temple in a newer construction. Quite obviously, this example cannot be motivated by economic considerations. The example is typical of thousands of others, but in most cases the reemployed blocks have fallen out or been stolen by souvenir hunters, leaving only telltale gaps.

Schwaller de Lubicz claims that Egyptian temples were constructed and demolished according to astrological plan, and never according to the whim of a pharaoh. Powerful evidence can be marshalled in support of this claim.

Certain temples of Egypt have been partially or nearly totally ruined due to natural causes. Others have been deliberately dismantled. It is fairly easy to distinguish between the two types of destruction. Temples destroyed by nature (earthquakes, for example) present the archaeologist with a site in which vast amounts of rubble have been covered over by sand. Napoleon's drawings, and early photos, show the state of these

163

sites as they were found originally. After excavation, the typical result is that most or much of the fallen stonework is still on site, sufficient in certain cases to make restoration feasible.

By contrast, temples that have been dismantled deliberately are found practically clear of rubble. There is nothing there except what has fallen through natural means. After the site is cleared there is nothing remaining that would make restoration possible.

A

B

C

Schwaller de Lubicz claimed that the life span of Egyptian temples and monuments was known in advance, and based upon symbolic and astrological considerations. Temples were not torn down and replaced to assuage the ego of a new pharaoh, but were dismantled and as it were annulled by the Sages of the Temple when their symbolic time had been served. The truth of this claim is easily proved.

Temples not deliberately dismantled but destroyed by natural causes (earthquakes, etc.) presented Egyptologists and archaeologists with a totally different aspect from those deliberately dismantled. Luxor and Karnak have been destroyed by time. Drawings by Napoleon's savants show the state in which the temples were found. After excavation, the site contained vast amounts of rubble, in certain cases enough to make reconstruction possible in principle.

By contrast, Kom Ombo was carefully dismantled. C is a photograph taken in the late nineteenth century prior to excavation. Note the fallen architraves but the absence of other rubble. Upon excavation, apart from the fallen architraves the site was free of rubble.

D

E

Outer pylon of the Ramesseum of Thebes (Luxor). There is no mistaking the site of a temple that has fallen from natural causes, as opposed to one that has been dismantled.

165

It might be argued that the stone was pillaged by the Christian and Arab civilisations following Egypt, for it is well known that the limestone casings of the pyramids were removed by the Arabs to build much of Cairo.

But the Egyptian demolition experts left contrary evidence.

The Egyptian temple was regarded as an organic, living unity. Tearing the walls down and effacing certain of the reliefs was not in itself enough to destroy the 'life' of the building, just as cutting down a tree will not necessarily prevent it from sending up new shoots.

The 'nerves' of the temple had to be severed. And since the 'nervous system' of the temple was carefully thought out to begin with, and executed at considerable time, trouble and expense, a reverse process was called for.

The temples of Egypt were built upon symbolic as well as architectural considerations, and many of these symbolic considerations served no architectural purpose whatsoever. One striking example is the practice of cutting into each block of stone a symbolic mortice that linked this stone with the stone adjacent to it. As far as I was able to gather, this practice prevailed in every Egyptian temple from the Old Kingdom on. (Exceptions are the granite temple attributed to Chephren and the so-called Oseirion of Seti I at Abydos. In the next chapter it will be argued that these two temples antedate Dynastic Egypt.)

Egyptologists have sometimes questioned these mortices in which no binding material is ever found, and have assumed that at one time they had wooden tenons inserted in them which subsequently rotted away. But there would be no purpose whatsoever in linking huge stone blocks with light wooden tenons. If the blocks were subject to stress, wooden ten-

ons could not hold. And since the blocks are not subjected to lateral stresses, the mortices are architecturally meaningless.

These mortices link one block to another symbolically: they make a kind of nervous or arterial system running throughout the whole of the temple. When the temple had served its predetermined purpose, it was taken down (it would be interesting to study the considerations that led both to the timing and to the extent of demolition); at this point, the 'nervous system' of

Economic factors may have determined the size and scope of any given temple or monument, but in the construction they played no part whatsoever. The system of inverse quoins prevailed from the beginnings of Dynastic Egypt (and perhaps before, if the so-called Chephren temple is, as I suspect, much older) and was a consistent architectural feature to the end. Nothing could be less economical than this time-consuming and totally unnecessary architectural device, which involves cutting away the entire surface of a block of stone in order to produce a small return that serves no constructional purpose.

These corners are symbolic, and typify the organic thinking of the sages. The temple is a unity, and a corner corresponds to an articulated organic joint which does not oppose one face flat against another, but overlaps and interlocks.

Symbolic mortices also serving no architectural purpose. There are no lateral or torsional stresses on these walls, and if there were, the little tenons that would fit these mortices could not counteract the enormous weight of the stone blocks. The mortices link the blocks; they are the nerve fibres of a symbolic organic structure.

167

KOM OMBO
*A column built of semi-circular blocks
(expressing duality) truncated and annulled
with a cross rather than a circle.*

the temple was cut. Following along the walls, a neat band of hammer marks cancels out or annuls the symbolic mortices.

The procedure was systematic, and can be observed in all those temples that have been dismantled (Kom Ombo, the Late Kingdom temple at Edfu and many others), while it is absent in temples that have fallen naturally (Luxor, Karnak). The same practice applied to dismantled columns. Across the top of each neatly truncated column there is a circle or cross of neat hammer marks. The choice of cross or circle itself was apparently determined by the construction of the columns. Columns made of single, circular blocks are cancelled with a circle; columns built with semicircular blocks are cancelled with a cross — an interesting instance of the meticulousness of Egyptian symbolic thought!

Since it is clear that the normal Egyptian method of dressing stone does not entail a neatly hammered band down the center, and since it is inconceivable that these bands could have been hammered in by the Christians or the Arabs, it must stand as proven that the temples were deliberately dismantled by the architects of Egypt, and the band of hammer marks across the mortices can only be interpreted as the symbolic sacrifice of the building.

Deliberate effacement of reliefs and inscriptions

Many of the temple sites of Egypt were subjected to repeated sequences of construction and destruction. Some, such as Saqqara, were in continual use from the beginnings of the Old Kingdom throughout the whole of Egyptian history. Temples were built and destroyed. Others were added to or subtracted from. Often the dictates of the ever changing symbolism of the times required the effacing of one set of symbols and the placement upon the same wall of another set. Sometimes reliefs and inscriptions that had served their time were effaced and nothing new added.

Egyptologists have explained this, not illogically, as a result of the desire of one pharaoh to obliterate the memory of his predecessors while inflating his own image. A second explanation sees the systematic final effacement of reliefs as the work of Christian zealots subsequent to the downfall of the Egyptian religion.

As is so often the case, closer scrutiny reveals the inadequacy of academic thinking when applied to Egypt.

Schwaller de Lubicz discusses in detail the significance of a number of reliefs which were partially effaced and then recarved. It is enough to point out that if self-glorification were the motivation of the practice, there was nothing stopping any given pharaoh from totally obliterating the work of

The effacement of alien or pagan gods by devotees of an opposing religion is a reasonable assumption, but it will not stand up to scrutiny in Egypt. These details show carefully hammered-out rows of hieroglyphs as well as effaced figures. Note the depth to which some of these have been removed — not a task casually undertaken. Those who would support the theory of defacement by Coptic Christians must say why the Christians who could not read the hieroglyphs should go to the considerable trouble of removing certain inscriptions but not others, meanwhile leaving certain images of the alien gods completely untouched.

A Kom Ombo. A row of hieroglyphs carefully hammered out. The rest of the wall left intact.

B Kom Ombo. A column neatly truncated. A hammered-out circle annuls it.

C Kom Ombo. Symbolic mortices join the blocks. A row of hammer marks follows the nerve system, annulling it.

A

B

C

his predecessors. But this demonstration is a matter of some delicacy and cannot be discussed at length here.

The proof of the deliberate replacement and effacement of reliefs and inscriptions is quickly established on the basis of the Ptolemaic temple at Kom Ombo.

Here, as elsewhere, only certain figures have been effaced. Why were some 'gods' effaced and not others? Zealots are seldom selective. When Cromwell's Puritans went idol-hunting,

A

A The Battle of Kadesh; Ramesseum, Luxor. The face, arms and bow of the king have been effaced as well as specific details and the head of his horse. What religious interest could the king's horse have held for the Coptic Christians?
B Kom Ombo. Neatly truncated columns, found in this condition upon excavation. It is hard to imagine an earthquake or other natural cause responsible.
C Kom Ombo. A figure left entirely intact except for the right knee.
D The head but not the headdress of the King is effaced, but attributed to religious zealots.
E A row of obliterated Hathors, the headdresses all left intact.

Further research and some rethinking inclines me to think my symbolic mortices and tenons are in fact structural after all. Once the temple is built they serve no purpose, but in the process of building, the tenons would keep the courses lined up as the next course of blocks was slid into place on top. The neat rows of hammer marks would provide a purchase for a skim of mortar. There are, however, instances where mortices have been cut in across the cracks in riven collosal statues, and these may well be purely symbolic.

I also think the idea of deliberately dismantled temples is mistaken. The neat look is the result of clearing, excavating and repair by Egyptologists over the past two centuries. But the effacement of reliefs by the ancient priests of the temple, rather than by later Christian fanatics is definitely correct.

B

they chopped the heads off all the statues they could get at; they broke all the stained glass they could reach.

Hammering out figures cut into stone is deep relief is not a task undertaken lightly. If Christian zealots really were responsible for the systematic effacement of the 'pagan' gods, then it would be reasonable to expect the job to be done in its entirety, or at least to be carried out systematically up to a point and then, at a definite, detectable point, abandoned for some rea-

C

D

E

171

son or another. Perhaps we might expect to find reliefs in the upper registers untouched because of difficulty of access. This is not the case.

By Christian standards, all the gods of Egypt were pagan, and all were equally unacceptable. The assumption that the effacement of the Egyptian reliefs was performed by Christians, reasonable as it may sound, is contradicted by the evidence. It is clear that some method of selection guided the practice. Some reliefs are hammered out, while others right alongside, depicting gods and scenes no less 'pagan', are left untouched. In many instances the effacing itself is carried out in an inexplicable manner. Sometimes the whole figure is hammered out, sometimes just the face. Sometimes the face is left alone and a specific area of the body or of the costume is effaced and the rest untouched. Religious zealots, as history shows, have never behaved in this manner on any other occasion. If Egyptologists wish to go on believing the Christian zealots responsible for the effacement of the reliefs, they will have to find evidence to account for their bizarre and unique behaviour.

A quick look at the manner in which the hieroglyphic inscriptions have been effaced makes the finding of such evidence highly unlikely. The same selective obliteration has been practiced on the hieroglyphs, and this obviously cannot be the work of the Christians. The reading of the hieroglyphs was always a privilege of the Egyptian priesthood. It is nearly inconceivable that the Christian Copts should have been party to their secrets. As our photographs show, in some cases it has been necessary to cut a channel a foot deep into the stone in order to remove the incised hieroglyphs, while inscriptions immediately adjacent are left untouched. Only the Egyptians themselves could have done this, and for symbolic reasons alien to the kind of thinking prevailing today.

The evidence that the temples of Egypt were torn down and rebuilt according to plan, and the evidence of the deliberate effacement of reliefs and inscriptions constitutes a proof of the existence of the body of sages de Lubicz calls 'the Temple'. It was this institution or secret society that made the decisions — not the reigning pharaoh, no matter that his face may adorn a thousand reliefs and colossal statues.

There can be no doubt that political exigencies dictated the scope and timing of construction to a degree. Obviously, in a time of anarchy and chaos, temples cannot be systematically torn down on schedule, much less constructed. But it can now be asserted without fear of contradiction that construction and destruction followed a preordained plan. Though we cannot yet say with certainty precisely the factors that dictated the plan, there are sufficient hints to convince us that these factors were astrological, and it remains for scholars capable of think-

'. . . and then these hippies of the new faith (ces hippies de la foi nouvelle) streaming out of their distant hermitages, would consummate their colossal and fanatical work and destroy the damned reliefs . . . Only then (with the fall of Philae) did they attempt to relentlessly eliminate every sign of this beauty — in their eyes perverse — that adorned the great Temple of Isis. And few were the reliefs that would escape — by what miracle — this iconoclastic fury.' Serge Sauneron, *Les pretres de l'ancienne Egypte*, tr. John Anthony West.

So furious were these iconoclasts that on the fifty-foot-high facade of the second pylon at Philae, the figures on the left, or west have been meticulously hammered out in their entirety, while to the east, or right, the huge figures have been left virtually untouched.

172

ing symbolically to resolve the mysteries.

With the demonstrated existence of 'the Temple', the rest of Schwaller de Lubicz's many heretical observations now follow, consistently and coherently.

The old as 'seed' of the new

It is well known that material from old temples was used in the construction of the new. Schwaller de Lubicz shows that neither economy nor expediency was responsible for this practice. Material from the old temples was employed symbolically. 'Seeds' of earlier constructions were embedded ('planted') in the walls and columns. The nature of the seeds makes it clear that the act was intentional, for they are gener-

A Medinet Habu, built by Rameses III, apparently following a period of (undetermined) disorder. The outer wall is entirely constructed of blocks from an earlier temple placed in no apparent order. Attributing this to economic considerations seems reasonable — until the rest of the temple is studied in this light. B shows a wall of reliefs typical of Medinet Habu, with hieroglyphs carved in extraordinarily deep relief — as much as four to six inches deep. If the Egyptians were eager to save money by re-employing old blocks for their walls; why then go to such astounding lengths to carve these deep inscriptions? Consider that it takes four times as long, and costs four times as much, to carve an inscription four inches deep as an inch deep, which is more than ample to ensure legibility. Clearly, economics is not the motivating factor.

A

B

ally reversed, the inscription face down, the symbolic 'root' growing down.

A similar practice was often applied to wall friezes. Key pieces from older works were systematically employed in the new for symbolic purposes.

What Egypt actually achieved by such a practice is hard to say: the art or science or magic of architectural 'genetics' is unknown to us. But the evidence leaves no room to doubt that

These drawings are exact representations of typical Egyptian foundations, showing the placing of material from old, superannuated temples as seeds from which the new was to grow. It is unlikely that the choice of 'seed' was arbitrary; a study of the inscriptions relating to specific columns, walls, sanctuaries and temple foundations might provide some interesting insights into the symbolic thinking underlying these structures.

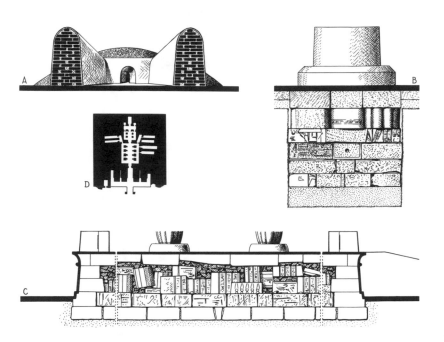

the reemployment of old material was deliberate, systematic and directed to a symbolic aim.

Le Temple de l'Homme, Schwaller de Lubicz's principal work, falls into three main sections. The first develops the theological and philosophical theme of the Anthropocosm. The second includes a study of the Golden Section, a detailed resuscitation of Pythagoreanism, analyses of harmony as the basis of the physical universe, and a study of Egyptian mathematics. The third is a step-by-step inquiry into the Temple of Luxor, in which the Anthropocosmic and mathematical concepts are applied.

Having reformulated the thinking of Egypt, Schwaller de Lubicz then elaborates, step by step, the sophisticated geometrical and symbolic procedures that must have taken place in order to arrive at the visible, measurable results.

It is difficult to summarise this step-by-step process without making it incomprehensible, but I will try to describe certain chief aspects employed and, hopefully, convey an idea of what the Egyptians did, if not how they did it. I will also select those pieces of evidence which, like the axes of the Temple, are categorical in nature: either they are there or they are not. If they are there, nothing in classical Egyptology can account for them. If they are not there — if even in a single instance Schwaller de Lubicz's evidence should prove false — then his whole interpretation may be called into question. Those who champion the Symbolist school would welcome an independent check upon the documentation. Egyptologists have consistently declined to provide one.

The grid

Else Christie Kielland
Geometry in Egyptian Art
Alec Tiranti, 1959, p. 4

On a number of Egyptian works of art, geometric marks are to be found, and for about 100 years Egyptologists have tried to explain them.

It is well known and accepted that all Egyptian art and architecture was set out upon a grid of squares (our graph paper is an equivalent) which allowed the precise determination of proportions and scale, matters never left to the whim of the artist. But whereas we work according to a metric, decimal system, or in standard English measures of quarters, eighths,

Limestone plaque from the First Dynasty. The grid is drawn on the back, but is here superimposed to show the system of proportion employed and already fully developed at the very beginnings of Dynastic Egypt.

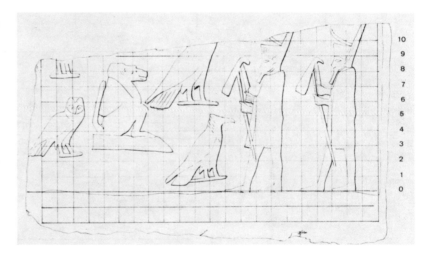

sixteenths and so on, Egypt through the Old, Middle and New Kingdoms operated on a grid of nineteen squares. The Late Kingdom switched to a grid of twenty two squares.

Now, these are very curious numbers to have chosen. If chosen purely arbitrarily, it is difficult to imagine a rationale, even a superstitious rationale, to justify such a choice. And without some sort of rationale it is even more difficult to understand why this choice should have prevailed over the centuries. The customary explanation — Egypt's 'extreme conservatism' — explains nothing, and is merely a label applied to a mystery. If Egypt was so conservative, how did it acquire its admittedly sophisticated architectural and medical techniques? Somewhere along the line, someone must have been willing to experiment, to use individual initiative. The cubit, the standard Egyptian measure, consists of seven palms of four digits each. Since everything else but art and architecture is measured out in such units, why a grid of nineteen squares for them? 'Extreme conservatism' is not good enough.

Schwaller de Lubicz demonstrates the remarkable Pythago-

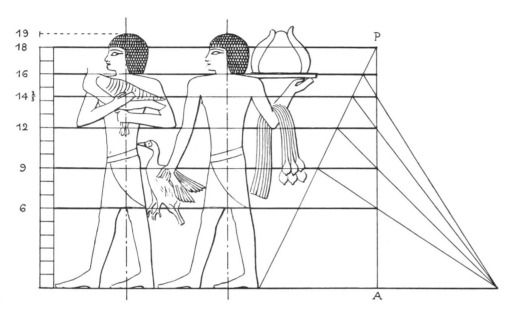

The system of proportion based upon a grid of 18:19 was in use at the very beginnings of Dynastic Egypt. This Old Kingdom tablet has the grid drawn upon its back. It is superimposed here to show its relationship to the actual drawing. The line drawn at 14 2/5 is proof that the grid is based upon harmonic considerations, for only a knowledge of harmonic considerations could produce a grid with lines falling at 6, 9, 12, 14 2/5, 16 and 18.

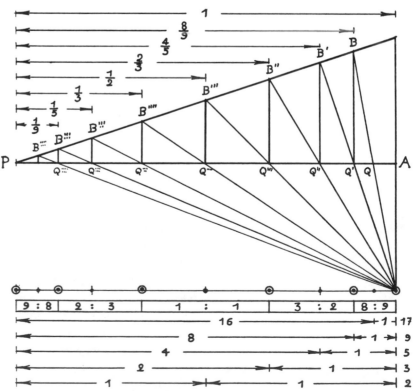

rean properties of the number nineteen, and particularly of the fraction 18/19, in biometry; nineteen also relates to cosmic measures, to the cycles of time, and to the twelve signs of the zodiac.

Knowledge of the peculiar significance of nineteen was not confined to Egypt. In Babylon, the nineteenth day of the month was particularly taboo, so much so that nineteen was counted as twenty minus one. Schwaller de Lubicz found that

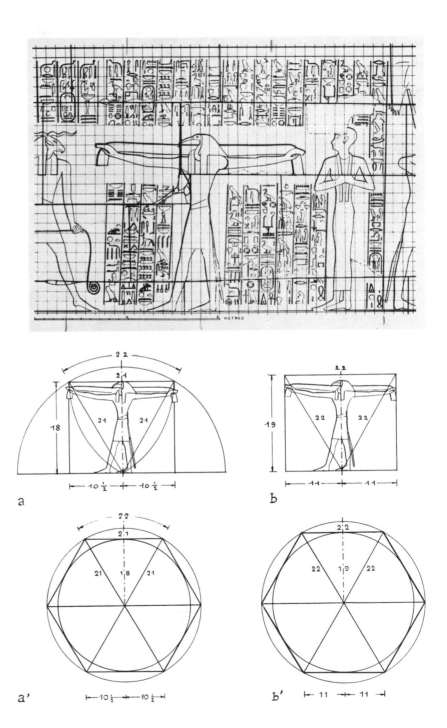

The ibis-headed Thoth is master of measures, and Schwaller de Lubicz found that successive hexagons circumscribed about the 18:19 grid determined Thoth's unusual dimensions.

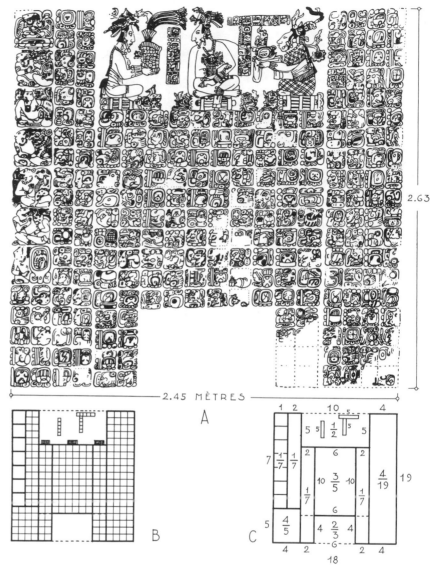

Many people have tried to find links between Mayan and pre-Mayan cultures and ancient Egypt, but without unanimously accepted conclusive proof. Schwaller de Lubicz subjected this famous Mayan text (to date untranslated) to a mathematical analysis and found it based upon complex numerical considerations strikingly similar to those of Egypt, including a grid of 18 upon 19 squares and an emphasis upon harmonic fractions: 2/3, 4/5, 1/7.

This is not in itself conclusive proof of a cultural link, since a Pythagorean approach to number might well lead independent thinkers to similar, even identical conclusions. But the similarities between the two systems are certainly striking, and ought to be studied in detail.

Mayan art was also laid out on a grid of nineteen squares. Scholars have always resisted efforts made to relate the civilisations of ancient Central America to Egypt. Though there are striking superficial resemblances between the hieroglyphic systems employed, the evidence has always been regarded as circumstantial. While the Mayan grid of nineteen does not necessarily prove a physical connection between the two cultures, it lends weight to the hypothesis. At the very least, it suggests a similar preoccupation with Pythagorean ideas.

The Royal Apron

This curious device is characteristic of Egyptian art. Its geometric configuration is obvious, yet no one prior to Schwaller de Lubicz seems to have asked if the apron had special significance.

Schwaller de Lubicz carefully measured seventy two of these aprons — almost all of them within the covered Temple of Luxor — and found in every single case that the aprons were constructed according to precise mathematical considerations. In each case, these proportions corresponded in some way to the mathematical relationships of the mural of which the royal personage was a part.

These aprons provide another test case. Either Schwaller de

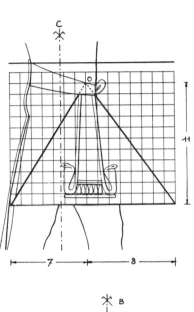

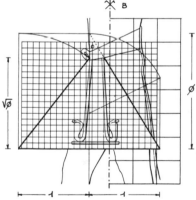

Some of Schwaller de Lubicz's studies of the geometrical properties of the so-called Royal Apron. In every case the apron was found to be generated by a geometrical scheme bearing some relationship — geometric, proportional or symbolic — to the scene or hall in which it was found.

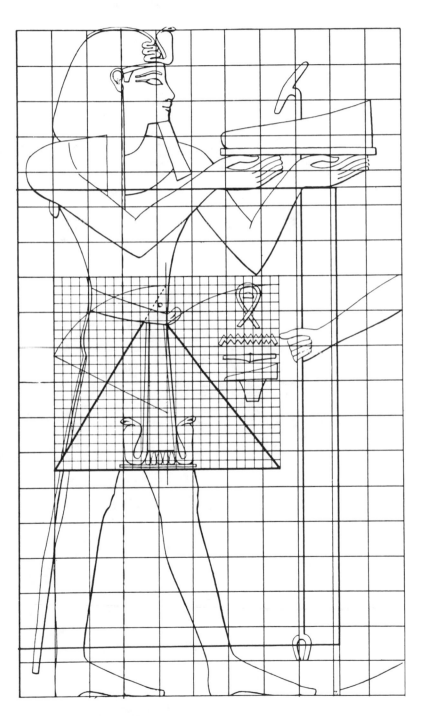

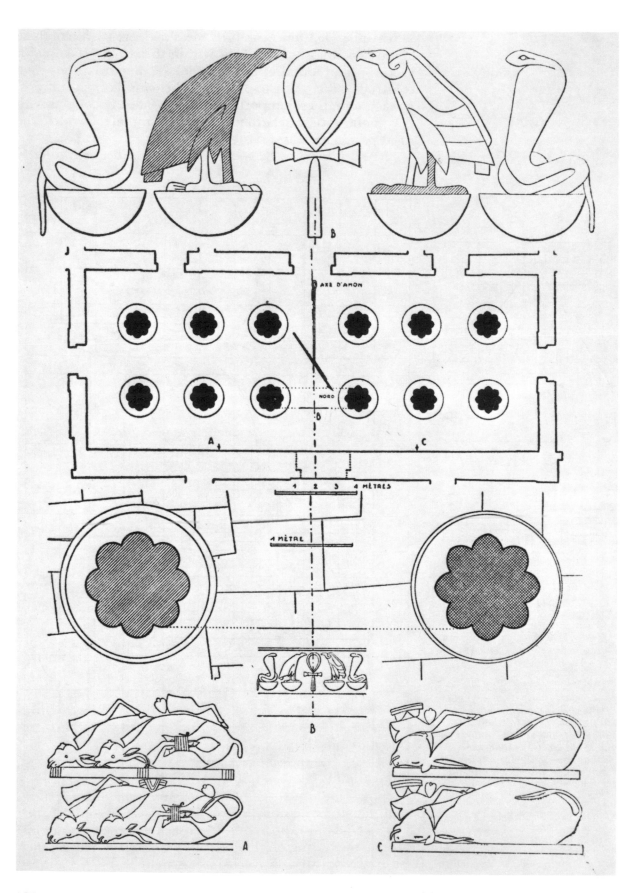

Lubicz's measurements are correct or they are not. The matter is easily checked on site. If correct, then there cannot be the slightest doubt of the Egyptian knowledge of geometry and of irrationals. And from that basic knowledge devolves the corpus of myth, the Anthropocosm, etc.

Meaning of the axes

I have mentioned the fact of the three axes of the Temple, but not the significance of that fact. An axis is an imaginary and ideal line about which a moving body revolves; in geometry, an axis is equally imaginary, a line without thickness, an abstract moment. The axis is 'occult', immaterial, a mental point of reference. It is an invention of man designed to make the principle of the axis comprehensible to our reason. Esoterically, the axis represents the Absolute, the still center of all movement throughout the universe, from atoms to galaxies.

The primordial impulsion of phi, generative power behind the created universe, provokes the fundamental asymmetry reflected in shifts of the axes themselves. Nature could not tolerate an actual fixed axis — that would be a perpetual motion machine. Life, all life, is a moment — more or less extended — of dynamic equilibrium between the forces of chaos and the forces of cohesion. Death is that moment when the forces of disequilibrium overpower the cohesive, harmonic forces of equilibrium. The 'wobble' of the earth about its own axis (responsible for the precession of the equinoxes) is a result of this natural, invariable law.

The three axes of the Temple of Luxor are mathematical and magical expressions of the law. On paper the axes appear as fixed lines. But put into practice, in the living architecture, they are vital channels animating the whole of the structure; the Temple's animation communicates itself to the beholder in harmonics, and in the form of visual vibrations. No doubt it communicated itself in sound as well when the Temple was in operation.

The lengths to which Egypt went to conform to these basic vital laws is astonishing. In taking his measurements of every possible aspect of the Temple, Schwaller de Lubicz and his team learned to expect the unexpected, but even fully awake to the situation, serendipity played an important part in their discoveries. For example, once when working in the hall of twelve columns corresponding to the centers of perception, one of the team leaned against the columns that formerly supported the roof, and noted something almost invisible to the naked eye and only apparent to the touch. On the East side of the room, the fluting on the columns was semicircular; on the West, it was ogival; constructed as an arch.

The Hall of Twelve Columns, Luxor (see arrow in large plan) corresponds to the centers of perception, and the twelve columns represent the twelve hours of day. The fluting of the eastern columns is semicircular — based upon one center. The fluting to the west is ogival — based upon two centers. East symbolises inception, beginning; west symbolises completion. The vulture on the east wall is left unfinished, the vulture on the west wall is finished — and the vulture symbolises assimilation. The sacrificial bulls to the east are trussed facing into the hall; the bulls to the west are trussed backs to the hall. To attribute such facts to 'coincidence' suggests a faith of such intensity in this Rationalist Neter that the poor mystic cannot but envy, beset as he may be by inner doubts and questions.

East represents unity; West represents duality. The semicircle is constructed about *one* center; the ogive is constructed about two centers.

This is another instance of categorical evidence: either the one side is semicircular and the other ogival, or they are not. If they are, it is inconceivable that this detail is an accident; the Egyptian quarrymasters were not likely to wrongly hew to order half a dozen forty-ton stone columns. It is therefore only reasonable to assume that there is some reason for placing semicircular columns to the East and ogival columns to the West. The reason can only be symbolic, and Schwaller de Lubicz's explanation is in perfect accord with his overall interpretation of Egyptian knowledge.

If both Schwaller de Lubicz's measurements and his explanation are correct, we may well ask what difference a detail of this order makes to the finished Temple. The answer can only be that this, and a thousand other minute details, taken together, contribute to the overall effect — just as a composer may score minute variations for his strings, undetectable as such to all but the most highly trained musicians, yet communicating to the ordinary listener an inexplicable shimmer, a subtle polish on the finished product.

The five kings of the Holy of Holies

The sanctuary Schwaller de Lubicz calls the 'Holy of Holies' may be regarded as a germ or seed whose dimensions, proportions and symbolism contain in résumé the finished product.

On the West wall of this sanctuary (which once contained a gold statue of a ram-headed Amon), there are five kings drawn, each portrayed in the presence alternately of Amon and Min-Amon (Amon as fecundating principle).

Measuring these kings, Schwaller de Lubicz found them gradually increasing in size. Each king measures exactly seventy-two digits, the digits being fractions of the different values of cubit, each of which is founded upon exact geodesic considerations: the difference between them is determined by the degree of latitude to which the measure pertains.

Schwaller de Lubicz then shows how the relationships between these different measures are connected to the notes of the musical scale, to the axes of the Temple and to the fundamental grid based upon nineteen squares.

Either these measurements are correct or they are not.

Special cubits were also designed to overcome problems posed by the square roots of two and three, permitting resolutions always in whole numbers. Prior to Schwaller de Lubicz conventional Egyptologists have generally ascribed the difference between the various Egyptian cubits to pharaonic inexactitude. Schwaller de Lubicz shows them to be based upon geodesic principles and then shows the manner of their application — proving both a rhyme and a reason for the whole system.

The Temple of Luxor is itself an initiatic text, an expression of a total understanding of the creation of Adamic man. It embodies the teaching and it is the teaching. McLuhan's famous phrase, 'The medium is the message' (inapplicable, in fact, to the areas McLuhan intended) applies perfectly to the Temple of Luxor and to the art of Egypt.

Given the wealth of documentation, the scholarly credentials of Varille and Robichon who supervised the measurements and plans, the systematic development of that evidence by Schwaller de Lubicz, the panoramic and yet coherent view of ancient Egypt that emerged, and the elegant manner in which this interpretation accounts for so much that was formerly paradoxical or inexplicable, the blank incomprehension of specialists and the deliberate decision to evade putting the documentation to the test is mystifying, even making allowance for the natural human unwillingness to change deeply held convictions.

Schwaller de Lubicz evidently felt his evidence had been presented in such a way as to force that desired confrontation. And with the evidence verified — in astronomy, mathematics, medicine, geodesics, geography and architecture — the importance of this interpretation would make itself felt beyond the confines of academic Egyptology. Schwaller de Lubicz therefore never developed the implications of his work, beyond a single remark to the effect that Egypt might serve as the most marvellous source of instruction for the world to come — or it might remain an occupation for the excavators and plunderers of tombs.

Alexander von Humboldt, quoted by G. Santillana and H. Dechend In *Hamlet's Mill*, p. xii

First people will deny a thing; then they will belittle it; then they will decide that it had been known long ago.

Egypt:
Heir to Atlantis

T. Eric Peet
Rhind Mathematical Papyrus
Hodder and Stoughton, 1923, p. 9

Surely the complicated fabric of Egyptian mathematics can hardly have been built in a century or even two, and it is tempting to suppose that the main discoveries of Mathematics should be dated to the Old Kingdom. There is a very definite tendency among Egyptologists to put this period down as the Golden Age of Egyptian knowledge and wisdom. There can be little doubt that some of the literary papyri have their roots in this era, as for example the Proverbs of Ptahhotep, and the antiquated constructions of the medical papyri make it possible that the science of medicine, such as it was, had its spring in the old Kingdom. . . . By the beginning of the First Dynasty the system of notation was complete up to the sign for 1,000,000. . . . In the Fourth Dynasty . . . land measures . . . are already in full development. . . . There appears to be no early evidence with regard to measures of capacity.

Dictionary of Egyptian Civilisation
ed. G. Posener
Methuen, 1962, p. 125

Hieroglyphic writing first appears in the beginning of the First Dynasty. . . . Almost from its inception it gives the appearance of being fully developed. . . . All the elements appeared together at the same time.

The origins of Egyptian civilisation

The origins of ancient Egyptian civilisation are a mystery. Though Egyptologists ignore Schwaller de Lubicz's picture of a grand, interrelated and complete system of knowledge, it is agreed that the salient features of ancient Egypt were complete by the First Dynasty, or were brought to completion with astonishing rapidity between the First and Third Dynasties, a period supposed to span but a few centuries.

Egyptologists postulate an indeterminate (and indeterminable) period of 'development' prior to the First Dynasty. This assumption is supported by no evidence; indeed the evidence, such as it is, appears to contradict the assumption. Egyptian civilisation, taken field by field and discipline by discipline (even according to an orthodox understanding of its achievement), renders unsatisfactory the assumption of a brief development period. The much vaunted flowering of Greece two thousand years later pales into insignificance in the face of a civilisation which, supposedly starting from a crude neolithic base, produced in a few centuries a complete system of hieroglyphs, the most sophisticated calendrical system ever developed, an effective mathematics, a refined medicine, a total mastery of the gamut of arts and crafts and the capacity to construct the largest and most accomplished stone buildings ever built by man. The cautiously expressed astonishment of modern Egyptologists hardly matches the real magnitude of the mystery.

W. Emery
Archaic Egypt
Pelican, 1961, p. 192

Even the earliest texts show that the written language had gone beyond the use of purely word signs which were pictures of objects or actions. There were also signs used to represent sounds only, and a system of numerical signs had also been evolved. Apart from the fact the hieroglyphs are already stylistic and conventionalised, a cursive script was also in common use. All this shows that the written language must have had a considerable period of development behind it, of which no trace has yet been found in Egypt. . . . Therefore until word to the contrary is forthcoming we must accept the fact that concurrent with the appearance of a highly developed monumental architecture, there is a fully developed system of writing.

A. Lucas
Ancient Egyptian Materials and Industries
Edward Arnold, 1962 (fourth ed.), *passim*

(Inlaid eyes, Class X) This kind of eye is known from the Fourth Dynasty.... It is an admirable imitation of the natural eye, of which it reproduces all the essential features ... and it is very much better than the eyes made at any other period, or by any other ancient people.

Egypt is the home of stone working and possesses both the oldest and the largest stone buildings in the world.... The ancient Egyptian stone statues, particularly those in such hard materials as diorite, granite, quartzite and 'schist', have long been a source of admiration on account of their excellent workmanship, and of wonder and speculation as to the nature of the tools used.

Ancient Egyptian linen varies considerably in texture, from the finest gauze to a canvas-like coarseness, and several different kinds of linen are distinguished in the linen lists of the Old Kingdom.

The Egyptians at an early date became very expert in the art of working copper on a large scale.... Perhaps the most remarkable examples ... are the large statue of Pepi I (Sixth Dynasty) and the accompanying small statue.

That the Egyptian goldsmiths were craftsmen of a very high degree of skill is shown by many examples.... Among the most outstanding may be mentioned the four bracelets from Abydos and that from Naga ed Der (First Dynasty); the gold foil and the gold brads or rivets from Saqqara (Third Dynasty); the gold bracelets and beads and gold cosmetic receptacle from the pyramid of Sekhemket (Third Dynasty).... Even as early as the Fourth Dynasty the ancient goldsmiths were manifestly able to manipulate comparatively large amounts of gold at one time.... The ancient gold leaf, however, was not nearly as thin as the modern ... though it was as thin as any produced in Europe until as recently as the Eighteenth Century.

The stone vessel industry reached its zenith during the early dynastic period and nowhere has there been found such a wealth of beautifully made, handsome stone vessels as in Egypt.

As early as the First Dynasty the Egyptians were able to carve wooden statues of near life-size, and during the Old Kingdom reached a high degree of skill, as is proved ... by the carved wooden panels with relief decoration from the tomb of Hesire and the six-ply wooden coffin from Saqqara, both of Third Dynasty dates.

A realistic approach to the mystery suggests alternatives that are unacceptable to the orthodox mind. The first is that Egyptian civilisation did not develop *in situ* but was brought to Egypt by hypothetical conquerors. This alternative simply translates the mystery of a period of development to the as-yet-undiscovered homeland of these conquerors. The second alternative is that Egypt did not 'develop' her civilisation, but inherited it.

Ruins of the Sphinx temple. The granite Chephren temple is out of camera, to the left. Note striated weathering as on the Sphinx itself, and elaborate jointing and dressing of these gigantic blocks.

Directly behind the Sphinx, a causeway leads to still another ruined temple just in front of Chephren's pyramid (in background). This temple, built of similar gigantic blocks, displays the same type of weathering, not found anywhere else in Egypt.

I believe this entire complex is of a piece. The granite casing is an addition, and may itself predate Dynastic Egypt. In other words, the Sphinx complex may contain evidence of two waves of civilization prior to Egypt.

The implications of this alternative are obvious. If the coherent, complete and interrelated system of science, religion, art and philosophy of Egypt was not developed by the Egyptians but inherited (and perhaps reformulated and redesigned to suit their needs), that system came from a prior civilisation possessing a high order of knowledge. In other words, this alternative brings up the old question of 'Atlantis'.

Despite ingenious cultural and philological arguments put forward by supporters of 'Atlantis', the scholarly consensus at the moment is that evidence for its existence is circumstantial and inconclusive. But a single remark made by Schwaller de Lubicz takes the Atlantis question out of philology and into geology, where, in principle, verification should pose fewer problems.

Sir Alan Gardiner
Op. cit., p. 41

Nowhere in the world have there ever been more skilful stoneworkers than the Egyptians, and the perfection of the innumerable vases, jars, plates and so forth found in the Step Pyramid (III Dyn.) is as much a wonder as the Great Pyramid itself.

T. R. Owen
Geology Explained in South Wales
David and Charles, 1973, p. 10

We all inevitably become Sherlock Holmes when we pick up a geological specimen and we ask ourselves the questions 'when', 'how' and even 'why'. Geology is therefore a cultural as well as a practical subject.

The mystery of the Sphinx and the riddle of 'Atlantis'

Schwaller de Lubicz observed that the severe erosion of the body of the great Sphinx of Giza is due to the action of water, not of wind and sand.

If the single fact of the water erosion of the Sphinx could be confirmed, it would in itself overthrow all accepted chronologies of the history of civilisation; it would force a drastic re-evaluation of the assumption of 'progress' — the assumption upon which the whole of modern education is based. It would be difficult to find a single, simple question with graver implications. The water erosion of the Sphinx is to history what the convertability of matter into energy is to physics.

The evidence: two approaches

Proof of Schwaller de Lubicz's observations lends itself to two approaches which may be taken independently but which must ultimately be complementary.

The first is positive: it involves proving that the agent responsible for the erosion of the Sphinx was in fact water.

The second is negative: it involves proving that the erosion of the Sphinx cannot be due to wind, sand, chemical action or the effects of expansion and contraction due to daily temperature changes.

Though the first, positive approach may be emotionally more satisfying, from a scientific point of view, negative evidence may be equally commanding. For if all known erosional agents can be effectively discounted except for water, then the only possible conclusion will be that water is the agent responsible.

In principle, there can be no objection to the water erosion of the Sphinx, since it is agreed that in the past, Egypt suffered radical climatic changes and periodic inundations — by the sea and (in the not so remote past) by tremendous Nile floods. The latter are thought to correspond to the melting of the ice from the last ice age. Current thinking puts this date around 15,000 BC, but periodic great Nile floods are believed to have

New Scientist
Feb. 10, 1977, p. 30

First, the great North American ice-sheet, melting and retreating fast after the last glaciation, suddenly did a *volte face* 14,000 years ago and readvanced to cover some 500,000 sq. km. of the continent. There are some hints from Europe, New Zealand and Patagonia of a similar readvance. Secondly, between 13,000 and 14,000 years ago the steadily rising world sea level abruptly dropped some 9 to 12 m., implying the locking up of sea water as some four million cubic km. of ice. And, thirdly, the then severely desiccated Nile *suddenly underwent a drastic flooding* about *13,500 years ago*. . . . The Gothenburg excursion has now been recognised at eight or ten localities around the world and so seems to be definitely a global phenomenon. Could its climatic effects have brought about the downfall of Neanderthal man? [Author's italics.]

taken place subsequent to this date. The last of these floods is dated around 10,000 BC.

It follows, therefore, that if the great Spinx has been eroded by water, it must have been constructed prior to the flood or floods responsible for the erosion. Moreover, the temple adjacent to the Sphinx and another temple up the hill from the Sphinx and connected to it by a long causeway show identical erosional effects. They must date from the same period. Those temples, in ruins today, are mentioned only in passing in popular accounts of ancient Egypt. Even within Egyptological circles, little attention has been paid to them. And yet these temples are as unique in Egypt as is the great Sphinx itself. They demonstrate an architectural mystery unequaled by and distinct from all the rest of Egyptian architecture, and they contain a number of stylistic features found nowhere else. The idea that the Sphinx is older than Dynastic Egypt is not original to Schwaller de Lubicz. The Theosophists, Gurdjieff and many unorthodox scholars have held this idea. But to date no one has thought to look to geology for proof.

How 'hard' is geology?

In geology, as in so many scientific and scholarly disciplines, popular works intended for the general reader convey an impression of serene scholarly unanimity; it is as though all fundamental issues were long since settled and agreed upon, and current work involved no more than sorting out and fitting into place minor pieces of the puzzle. But deeper research into specialised works discloses areas of conflict over details and broader issues. At the level of articles in geological journals, unanimity all but disappears, while persistent groups of dissidents challenge basic assumptions taken for granted by the majority. Few chemists will today support Cavendish's phlogiston theory, but there are a number of geologists, members of the American Creation Research Society armed with impeccable qualifications, who support a literal interpretation of the Biblical deluge, and even its chronology.

The state of controversy bears upon the geological inquiry into the Sphinx.

The nature of the erosion of the Sphinx

The accompanying photographs show clearly the nature and extent of the erosional damage to the Sphinx and its adjacent temple. This damage is visible to the naked eye of scholar and layman alike. In all of Egypt (with one intriguing exception) it is unique to the Sphinx and the complex surrounding it. Nowhere in Egypt was I able to find anything — man-made or natural — exhibiting closely comparable natural damage.

187

The evidence: positive approach

Normally, geologists are not required to make the choice between water erosion and the various agents of atmospheric weathering; the answer is usually obvious.

Erosion is rarely a factor considered in geological events with time scales measured in millions of years. The climatic conditions that determine the short-term nature of surface ero-

Cliff face behind the temple of Hatshepsut, west of Luxor. Geologists agree that this is originally water erosion, subsequently roughened and flaked away.

sion are usually sufficiently well established to admit of little doubt. No one thinks the white cliffs of Dover have been subjected to action by wind and sand in the measurable past; no one looks for evidence of water erosion on the mesas of the American desert. The climate and geology of these regions has been sufficiently stable for a long enough time for the present weathering agents to have obliterated evidence of the past.

Egypt presents an exception with its (still controversial) record of periodic severe floods, and a climate which — though relatively stable desert since about 8000 BC — was subject to periodic eras of rainier climate believed measurable in terms of millennia rather than centuries.

Geologists at the University of Wales and at Oxford have assured me that under such circumstances, positive corroboration of the water erosion of the Sphinx may not be easy to obtain. I suggested to them that careful chemical analysis of the stone surface might show evidence of chemical reactions that could only be the result of submersion in water, and also that concerted probing into the deep fissures running vertically down the sides of the Sphinx might uncover shells and other remains of fresh-water organisms commonly found strewn over the Egyptian sands. If such evidence were found, it might be in a better state of preservation than the shells that have been blown to and fro by the winds for fifteen thousand years. This would suggest that it had been there from the time of the subsidence of the waters, and not blown in along with the encroaching sands. My geologist friends expressed doubt

Rock face cut away to form the hollow in which the Sphinx was carved. The deep, smooth erosion is identical to that on the body of the Sphinx. Obviously, both the rock face and the Sphinx were carved before this severe weathering took place. Note the roughening of the upper layers, identical to that on the matching layers of the Sphinx. Excepting the rock face abutting the mysterious and atypical Oseirion at Abydos, no Egyptian monument or site shows weathering remotely akin to this.

that these methods would produce the positive evidence required. At the present moment, all that can be said is that the Sphinx awaits a team of qualified scientists willing to put the theory to the test.

All geologists I consulted agreed that, from the photographic evidence, the damage was typical of water-eroded surfaces, although I was cautioned that, in many cases, erosion by wind and sand could be strikingly similar to erosion by water.

The evidence: negative approach

But erosion by wind and sand can be ruled out for a very simple reason. The great Sphinx was allegedly constructed by the pharaoh, Chephren, successor to Cheops, around 2700 BC. For most of the past five thousand years it has been buried up to the neck in sand, and therefore completely protected from the effects of wind-blown sand. Within broad limits, it is possible to calculate the amount of time the Sphinx has been buried. This calculation has more than casual significance.

The Sphinx and the sand

When Napoleon arrived in Egypt he found the Sphinx buried to the neck in sand; the temple adjacent to it was invisible. Caviglia finally excavated the Sphinx in 1816. Under normal conditions, the *khamsin*, the fierce desert wind blowing from the South in the month of April, deposits sand gradually against any obstacle in its path, and hundreds of years may be

From the Description d'Egypte, *commissioned by Napoleon. Detail of head of Sphinx gives an idea of the slope running from the Sphinx to the pyramids, but foreshortens the distance. Note details of headdress and erosion lines which are no longer visible due to recent resurfacing of this area.*

necessary before it reaches its maximum level. Therefore, under normal circumstances any given monument or temple will be subjected to the erosional forces of wind-blown sand for long periods of time.

The Sphinx, however, is carved out of a single ridge of rock, only the upper portion of which is above the otherwise level ground. In order to carve the Sphinx, the builders had to hollow out a basin around the rock ridge deep enough to allow work on the monument. As might be expected, sand blows into and builds up in a hollow much faster than it does against an obstruction on the level surface, and by 1853, the Sphinx was again buried to the neck. This time it was excavated by Mariette. In 1888, Maspero had to dig it out again. And in 1916, Baedeker wrote in his guidebook that it was again covered. In twenty to thirty years, then, the hollow in which the Sphinx rests will fill up with sand. This means that without constant attention, the Sphinx swiftly becomes insusceptible to erosion by wind-driven sand.

There are some specific historical clues to dates during which the Sphinx was free of sand, which permit further deductions to be drawn with greater or lesser certainty.

There are no Early or Middle Kingdom references to the Sphinx. It first comes to historical prominence with a stone tablet erected between its paws by Tuthmosis IV around 1400 BC. The inscription on the stela tells how, in a vision, the Sphinx appeared to Tuthmosis, promising him the crown of

Egypt if he would see to removing the sand that covered it. Tuthmosis undertook the task and subsequently became king.

This proves that in Tuthmosis's time the Sphinx was buried; it also indicates that excavating was not a common occurrence. If it had been, Tuthmosis would not have called such elaborate attention to his deed.

If we now go back into Egyptian history to the date of the Sphinx's alleged construction by Chephren in 2700 BC, we find that Egypt remained politically stable for about four centuries following Chephren, after which it entered a period of chaos known as the First Intermediate Period, lasting about three centuries. This was followed by the renaissance of the Middle Kingdom, which lasted about four centuries and was followed by another period of chaos, the Second Intermediate Period. This ended with the establishment of the Eighteenth Dynasty and the New Kingdom.

It is reasonable to suppose that following Chephren (who has a connection with the Sphinx but did not construct it), the Sphinx and its temple might well have been tended through the period of stability, and equally reasonable to suppose that with the onset of the First Intermediate Period, it was left untended as was everything else in Egypt. Since nothing has ever been found around the Sphinx relating it to the renaissance of the Middle Kingdom, it is a fair guess that during these centuries it was left in the sand undisturbed, and remained so until Tuthmosis excavated it. So, of the thirteen hundred years between Chephren and Tuthmosis, the Sphinx was probably buried for a thousand.

In front of the Tuthmosis stela there was another stone tablet erected by Rameses II two centuries later, indicating that during his time, the Sphinx was consistently kept clear of sand. Thereafter, it disappears from the record. When Herodotus visited Egypt in the fifth century BC, he spoke of the pyramids at length, but did not so much as mention the Sphinx. This cannot be an oversight. The Sphinx, at some two hundred and forty feet long and sixty feet high, is the most spectacular single sculpture on earth. Failure to mention it can be due to only one cause — all but the head was buried in the sand. Given the architectural marvels of Egypt (in Herodotus's time in far better condition than they are today), the sight of a single colossal head in the sand would not necessarily deserve mention. And the location of the Sphinx is such that a visitor standing at the pyramids would probably overlook the head altogether.

At some time between Rameses II and Herodotus the Sphinx was left untended and covered in sand. Again a reasonable guess is possible. Another period of chaos, the Third Intermediate Period, began in 1085 BC. At or around this time we may reasonably assume the Sphinx was left to the mercy of the ele-

Sphinx stela erected by Thutmosis IV. Arrow points to lower registers that have flaked off since excavation, making the controversy over the presence of Chephren's name unresolvable.

E. A. Wallis Budge
Egypt and her Asiatic Empire
Kegan Paul, Trench, Trubner, 1902, pp. 80, 86

One of the works which he [Thutmosis IV] undertook will, however, keep his memory green . . . the clearing away of the sand from the Sphinx at Gizah. We have already mentioned . . . that the early history of this remarkable object is unknown, and that different views as to its age exist. . . . The lower portion of the stele is broken away, and the last few lines are in a very fragmentary state, but a few legible words in line 14 tell us that the Sphinx was made by King Khaf-Ra [Chephren]. . . . This piece of information . . . proves that in the XVIIIth Dynasty the priests . . . believed that it was fashioned by Khaf-Ra, the builder of the second pyramid at Gizah about two thousand years before.

ments, was covered swiftly by sand, and remained so until dug out by the Ptolemies.

Though no inscriptions exist to pinpoint the date, it is known that the Sphinx was again excavated, and during Ptolemaic or Roman times the rather clumsy repair work to the front paws was undertaken. From the remaining courses of stone about the lower portion of the body, it would appear that originally a fresh carapace must have been provided for the

whole of the body.

Allowing for maximum (and probably overly generous) possibilities, we can say that the earliest date for the excavating of the Sphinx would be around 300 BC. The latest date at which it might still have been tended would be 300 AD, since in 333 Christianity was declared the official and exclusive religion of Rome and the ancient religion of Egypt was made illegal. In any case the Egyptian religion had been languishing for centuries; it is most unlikely that attention was still being paid to the

Sphinx as late as 300 AD.

But if we allow that it might have been, we may be absolutely certain that the Christians and the Moslems who supplanted them three centuries later evinced only a destructive interest in the monuments of Egypt. From 300 AD to 1800 AD the Sphinx was indubitably buried in sand. Give or take a few centuries, I do not think any Egyptologist would seriously dispute this reasoning. The resulting figures give us:

		Sphinx buried
Chephren-Tuthmosis IV	ca. 1300 yrs.	1000
Tuthmosis IV-Ptolemies	ca. 1100 yrs.	800
Ptolemies-Christianity	ca. 600 yrs.	0
Christianity-Present Day	*ca. 1700 yrs.*	*1500*
Chephren-Present Day	ca. 4700 yrs.	3300

These somewhat laborious calculations are not undertaken in a spirit of idle curiosity, though in one sense they are superfluous. In assuming that wind and sand are responsible for the weathering to the Sphinx, Egyptologists overlook several other factors. The first is that geologists agree that only wind of a sufficient velocity to carry sand with it can produce noticeable erosion. In other words, the normal winds of Egypt, prevailing for eleven months of the year, produce negligible effects. It is only in the month during which the *khamsin* blows (and then only intermittently) that wind-sand erosion can occur. The *khamsin* blows only from the South, and on its South and East sides the Sphinx is effectively protected from the force of this wind by its temple complex, as well as by the hollow in which it rests. This means that if the Sphinx had been kept clear of sand for the whole of the last forty-seven hundred years, the effects of wind-sand erosion would be minimal, and one would expect the outer walls of the temple to exhibit the worst effects. They do not. Apart from this, due to such factors as turbulence, severe erosion by wind and sand commonly produces uneven and often spectacular effects like the weird, almost extraterrestrial figures in the American mesa lands. And because of the weight of the driven sand, geologists reckon that no matter what the force of the wind, erosion is largely confined to six feet above ground level. It is this that is responsible for those spectacular balancing towers of stone, hollowed out and scooped away at the base, but untouched above.

The Sphinx and its temple complex show no evidence of these typical effects. The weathering is severe and, to the naked eye, uniformly even. Only in one place is there evidence of typical wind-sand erosion, and that is in the one area where it

Why Herodotus failed to mention the Sphinx. This drawing, made by Napoleon's scholars, shows the Sphinx as they found it, and in the distance it is hardly impressive. This drawing is taken slightly south and east of the Sphinx, with the Cheops pyramid in the background and only the corner of the Chephren pyramid visible at the far left. This is a rather peculiar angle at which to view the Sphinx, and even today it involves a trek over desert to attain this particular vantage point. The Sphinx would be even less impressive (indeed almost invisible), from the pyramids themselves, unless one climbed part of the way up one of the eastern faces, which Herodotus probably could not have done very easily, since the smooth limestone facing stones were then intact.

F. W. Hume
Geology of Egypt
Egyptian Survey of Egypt, 1925-48, pp. 3, 27

In the wildest part of the desert ... it is possible to wander over plains strewn with the shells of innumerable oysters ... and to see in vision a surge of tumbling waters where now all is silent, rockbound, and utterly devoid of movement and life.

Where the ancient monuments are attainable by Nile floods, the effect of salt solutions will be very marked, and will be indicated by weathering of the lower part of the monument.

Karl W. Butzer and Carl L. Hansen
Desert and River in Nubia
Wisconsin, 1968

Totality of geomorphic change has been small since the early Pleistocene. Denudation of older gravels, dissection of wadis, and backwearing of slopes have taken place, but at rather slow rates. Chemical weathering, other than salt hydrations, has been almost insignificant from the geomorphic point of view.

The valley in the West side of the Nile at Luxor containing the tombs of the

Kings appears to be a water-eroded valley, but the tombs themselves show no sign of destructive water action. This means that water action of any significance probably ceased at least 4000 years ago.

B. W. Sparks
Geomorphology
Longmans, 1972, p. 254

It seems easier to relate landforms in many deserts to earlier water periods than to present conditions. Hume gives photograph after photograph of steep-sided valleys in limestone and sandstone country which are obviously water-cut forms.

Ibid., p. 334

Problems arise because of the great difference of distribution between erosion surfaces of various types, the poor state of preservation of many of them, and the possibility of other explanations.

might be reasonably anticipated: the nape of the neck. For, left to the elements, as we have seen, the body of the Sphinx and the temples around it swiftly vanish under sand. Only the neck and head remain exposed. Since wind-sand erosion is confined to the six feet above ground level, it is the neck and only the neck that would be expected to show the effects of this type of weathering. Indeed the neck, particularly the back of the neck, appears hollowed out, scooped away — the typical result of exposure to the driven sands of the *khamsin*.

This effect is hardly obvious, either to the naked eye or in a photograph. Compared to the dramatic damage to the rest of the body, it seems insignificant, and becomes noticeable only when one looks for it. When it is realised that this is the result not of five thousand years of constant exposure to the *khamsin*, but to more than double that amount (i.e., since Egypt became desert), it both corroborates the relatively minor effects of wind-sand erosion and makes much more inexplicable the damage to the body, exposed for only fourteen hundred years out of the last forty-seven hundred.

This brings us to the second crucial conditioning factor. If in only fourteen hundred years the wind and sand had reduced the Sphinx to its present condition, then we should expect to find evidence of similar or at least comparable damage to other Egyptian monuments built of similar materials and exposed to the *khamsin* for a similar length of time.

A

B

196

C

A, B, and C Details from old photos (around the turn of this century) show the head of the Sphinx prior to resurfacing of headdress, repair to the ear, and other works. Weathering is layered, as on the body and adjacent rock face, but much less severe. Yet it is the head that has never been buried and therefore has taken the full brunt of wind and sand. The colour of the stone is also distinctly different, and may be a natural outcrop of a harder stone.

C Also shows top two rows of deeply weathered blocks of the Sphinx temple.

D Modern photograph showing detail of smoothly polished surface of the face (plus artillery damage to nose and eyes).

D

Erosion damage to other Egyptian temples and monuments

While little remains in Egypt from Chephren's time, Middle Kingdom, New Kingdom and Ptolemaic relics abound. Due to its peculiar siting conditions that allow the Sphinx to become buried in sand in but twenty to thirty years, these other, later monuments have been exposed to the same kind of erosional effects for at least as long. Commonly, the topmost sections of

the temples have never been completely buried. This means that even Ptolemaic temples such as Denderah, Kom Ombo and Edfu have been exposed to wind and sand for five hundred years *more* than the Sphinx though they were built twenty-five hundred years after Chephren's time. The pylons and architraves of New Kingdom works such as Luxor and Karnak have been exposed for about three thousand years, more than twice as long as the Sphinx.

The photographs show the minimal effects of wind-sand erosion. In the older monuments successive *khamsins* have done little more than scour clean the surface of the dressed stones. The outlines of reliefs and hieroglyphs are somewhat blurred, and the wind and sand has worked into the joints between the blocks, rounding the perfect right angles of the corners. That is all. Nowhere in Egypt is there a statue or temple exhibiting weathering similar to the Sphinx and its temple

Butzer and Hansen
Op. cit., p. 77

Rock drawings cut into massive sandstones near Gebel Silsila in late prehistoric times are remarkably well preserved. . . . This all suggests that recent backwearing has been, in fact, very slow.

198

These drawings by Napoleon's scholars are recognised as authoritative and sufficiently accurate to serve as documentation (give or take the odd decorative Arab in the shadows, puffing on his hookah). They show the levels of sand on various temples, as found by Napoleon. All that is above the level of the sand may be assumed never to have been buried since no excavation had been undertaken during the past two thousand years. Note the conspicuous absence of severe erosion. Recent photographs taken expressly to demonstrate this point corroborate the accuracy of the drawings.

The severe damage to the huge Middle-kingdom colossi of Memnon is attributed chiefly to chemical action. The rising flood plain of the Nile has placed the colossi in the path of the annual inundation, and water rising by capillary action has reacted with salts in the stone destroying the surface. The colossi have never been buried in sand and therefore have caught the brunt of the elements for three thousand years; much longer than the Sphinx. Though severe, the damage to the colossi is not as severe as that to the Sphinx, and manifestly different in appearance.

complex. (The only exceptions are the colossi of Memnon, but their weathering is easily accounted for. These huge sandstone statues have fallen victim to the rising ground water level of the Nile. Water has risen by capillary action and reacted with salts in the stone, and the stone has crumbled away, almost destroying the outline of one of the statues. But the same conditions do not apply to the Sphinx, and the outward effects of the weathering are totally different.)

For the reasons outlined above, I believe it safe to maintain that the surface damage to the great Sphinx of Giza cannot be due to the action of wind and sand. Only one faint doubt remains, which applies as well to arguments against weathering by chemical action and expansion and contraction: that the stone from which the Sphinx is carved is of a radically softer nature than the stone used in all other Egyptian structures; a possibility easily checked, but which, to my knowledge, has not yet been done. The possibility must remain open until verified but I find it most unlikely that the Sphinx should be carved out of a stone so soft that in only thirteen hundred years, the weather could cut ridges two feet deep into it, while harder varieties, exposed for double that length of time, do not even show damage to their incised reliefs and hieroglyphs.

Chemical weathering and insolation

The negative approach to the evidence requires the elimination of all known erosional agents except water. If the Sphinx cannot have been eroded by sand and wind, it might still be expected to show the effects of insolation (interception of solar energy) and chemical action.

The smaller pyramid of Mycerinus is dressed in rough granite but polished around the entrance. Choice of type of stone was generally dictated by symbolic considerations (granite, a volcanic rock, was a 'fire' stone). To date, the symbolic meaning of the Mycerinus pyramid is unknown.

The northwest corner of the Mycerinus pyramid. A good example of the actual effects of wind erosion, and perhaps condensation and chemical action. Easily discernible on the corners are the points of maximum turbulence. Compare to erosion effects on the Sphinx and Sphinx temple.

Though differing in action, the visible effects of insolation and chemical weathering are somewhat similar and difficult to distinguish. In the former, the surface of the rock expands and contracts, eventually breaking up as chips and flakes of stone fall away. In chemical weathering moisture or rains soak into the surface, setting up chemical reactions with salts in the rock, and the surface tends to crumble, flake or chip away. The results differ according to the kind of rock and the prevailing weather conditions.

In time, detritus builds up and around the base of the rock, forming a protective mantle and preventing further weathering to the surface.

Insolation and chemical weathering tend to fracture, pit and roughen the surfaces they work upon. In the desert geologists agree they tend to work slowly over the course of thousands of years. Examination of Egyptian monuments suggests that dressed and polished surfaces are much less susceptible to their action than undressed surfaces. The columns, walls and architraves of the temples seem little damaged even if they have been fully exposed. In a relatively short time, on the other hand, both insolation and chemical weathering seem to have affected the undressed interior blocks of the pyramids once the smooth casings were removed.

In any case, the smooth, deep, polished weathering of the Sphinx is most uncharacteristic of insolation and chemical action, and it is inconceivable that these processes could produce such severe effects in the thirteen hundred years that the Sphinx has been fully exposed to them.

But closer examination reveals the presence of these processes just where they should reasonably be expected — adding still further support to Schwaller de Lubicz's observation. The upper layers of the back of the Sphinx and the corresponding upper ridges of rock face cut away when the hollow was formed to receive the Sphinx are visibly rougher than the lower portions. These areas have been exposed for a much longer period of time, and the roughened appearance is exactly what might be anticipated.

The huge blocks of the Sphinx temple give corroborative evidence. There appears to be an underlying, overall deeply stratified and initially smooth pattern of erosion, identical to that of the Sphinx, except that the grooves do not match up since the blocks are obviously quarried from the living rock and then placed out of their original position. On top of this underlying erosion, wind, sand, temperature and probably moisture and rainfall have roughened and blurred the original pattern. This combination of processes is particularly noticeable on the almost totally ruined temple at the top of the causeway leading from the Sphinx. Here, the effects of wind and weather have all but obliterated the underlying pattern of water erosion, and it

B. W. Sparks
Op.cit., p. 37

There may be a limit to the action of weathering unless the products of weathering are continuously removed.

F. W. Hume
Op.cit., p. 13

The final result ... from the actions of diurnal variations of temperature on a bare rock-plateau is a breaking up of the superficial layers into flakes of various sizes, which is in fact what we commonly observe in the Egyptian deserts. Once such a cover of flakes is produced, it acts as a blanket to prevent the alternations of temperature affecting the more solid rocks below.

can only be seen from a distance.

This effect I believe to be convincingly matched by many of the Egyptian cliffs (now miles away from the normal flood plain of the Nile) which geologists agree to have been water eroded in the past. From the distance, these cliffs give the appearance of smooth, stratified erosion similar to that of the Sphinx. But up close, it is found that the surface has been fractured and roughened by exposure to the elements, often to such an extent that the stratified appearance so visible from afar nearly disappears. The Sphinx is as smooth and unaffected as it is simply because it has been buried, not for the last five thousand years, but for much longer.

Everything falls into place. The closer one looks into Schwaller de Lubicz's observation, the more conclusively it is substantiated. Always allowing for the possibility that the Sphinx and its temple complex are constructed of a miracle rock that erodes ten times as fast and in quite a different way from all the rest of the stone in Egypt, the case for the water erosion of the Sphinx is a strong one. The erosion is typical of water erosion elsewhere, and the possibility of other forms of weathering and erosion can be eliminated, particularly if they are supposed to have been operative over the past five thousand years.

Two problems remain. The first is to explain how and why Egyptologists attribute the building of the Sphinx and its temple complex to Chephren. The second is to try to answer the questions arising in the minds of those sharp-eyed readers who have noticed differences in appearance between the head of the Sphinx and the rest of its body.

Chephren: non-builder of the Sphinx

The Sphinx and its temple complex are attributed to Chephren on the basis of three pieces of evidence, each indirect and circumstantial. They can be accepted as valid, moreover, only by ignoring the existence of another piece of evidence that directly mentions the existence of the Sphinx in the time of Cheops — i.e., prior to Chephren.

1 The stela of Tuthmosis IV: When it was first excavated, the bottom registers of Tuthmosis's stela were already flaked away. In the last line that was legible, following a lacuna of several words, the hieroglyph for the first syllable of Chephren's name (*khaf*) was decipherable. But there is no direct or indirect reference to Chephren as builder, and controversy soon arose over whether or not the still legible *khaf* was part of Chephren's name or of some other word: *khaf* is an element common to many Egyptian words. The controversy will never be settled, since the register in which *khaf*

J. H. Breasted
Ibid., Vol. II, p. 323

The stele [reign of Tuthmosis IV, Sphinx stela] records the words of the Sphinx as heard by Tuthmosis in his dream: '. . .The sand of this desert upon which I am has reached me. Turn to me, to have that done which I desired. . . . When he had finished this speech, this king's son [awoke]. . . . He understood the words of this god. . . . He said: Come, let us hasten to our house in the city . . . and we shall give praise [to] Wennofer, Khaff[re], the statue made for Atum-Harmakis. [This mention of King Khaffre has been understood to indicate that the Sphinx was the work of this king — a conclusion which does not follow; Young has no trace of a cartouche. Breasted's note.]

G. Maspero
Histoire Ancienne des Peuples de l'Orient Classique
Paris, 1895, Vol. I, p. 366

The Sphinx stele shows, in line 13, the cartouche of Chephren in the middle of a lacuna. . . . I believe that to indicate an excavation carried out by that prince, following which, the almost certain proof that the Sphinx was already buried in the sand by the time of Cheops and his predecessors.

appeared has subsequently flaked away. What is certain is that there is no mention of Chephren as builder of the Sphinx.

2 Statues of Chephren. Buried in pits dug into the floor of the Sphinx temple, a number of magnificent statues of Chephren were found, one in the form of a Sphinx. There are, however, no inscriptions anywhere in the temple, and therefore nothing to give a clue to its builder. Temples were commonly appropriated by successive pharaohs, then added to, worked upon, revised and revamped, and there is no reason to attribute the actual construction to Chephren or to any other known pharaoh. Digging pits into the floor of an already existing temple was a task well within the capacities of Chephren's architects.

3 Statues of Chephren resemble the face of the Sphinx. The reader may judge the extent to which this putative resemblance exists. From the Third Dynasty on, the sculptors of Egypt were masters at reproducing the faces of the pharaohs exactly and in every medium. While it is clear that Chephren bears a closer resemblance to the Sphinx than he does to Akhenaten, the likeness is hardly exact. Perhaps a detailed physiognomic examination would answer the question one way or the other. In any case, as evidence for Chephren as builder of the Sphinx, it is purely circumstantial.

Detail of statue of Chephren, found in a pit dug into the floor of the temple alongside of the Sphinx. The reader is free to decide if the claimed likeness to the head of the Sphinx is obvious or not. One aspect of Egyptian art that is incontestable was the Egyptians' ability to exactly reproduce a likeness regardless of the size or medium employed. The countless unmistakable portraits of Rameses II attest to this capacity, meaning that dozens or hundreds of sculptors and painters must have trained themselves to this degree of mutual precision. Fourth Dynasty artists were in no way inferior to those of the New Kingdom. It may be reasonably asserted that if the head of the Sphinx and that of Chephren were meant to be the same, that resemblance would be striking and unmistakable. Poses, stances and gestures may be ritualised in Egyptian art, but individual faces never are. Compare Chephren to the First Dynasty Menes.

J. H. Breasted
Ancient Records of Egypt
University of Chicago, 1906, Vol. I., p. 85

Live the Horus: Mezer, King of Upper and Lower Egypt: Khufu (Cheops) who is given life. He found the house of Isis, Mistress of the Pyramid, beside the house of the Sphinx of (Harmakhis) on the north-west of the house of Osiris, Lord of Rosta. He built his pyramid beside the tomb of this goddess, and he built a pyramid for the king's daughter Henutsen beside this temple.

4 The inventory stela. This interesting, possibly crucially important, stone tablet was discovered by Mariette in the mid-nineteenth century. It dates from the Twenty-sixth Dynasty, in the late Dynastic Period, but the inscription describes in some detail actions taken by Cheops (precursor to Chephren), during which a temple of Horus was discovered in the vicinity of the Sphinx; i.e., *the Sphinx was already there.*

The late date of the inventory stela has never been in doubt. But it was originally believed that the inscription was a copy of a much earlier text — which, if dating from the actual time of Cheops, would of itself overthrow the attribution of the building of the Sphinx to Chephren.

On the basis of internal textual and linguistic evidence, Egyptologists decided that the wording belonged to the late date of the stela itself, allowing the attribution of the Sphinx to Chephren to stand. Yet the Twenty-sixth Dynasty is famous for its concern with the Old Kingdom. It was during this period that exact copies of Old Kingdom architecture were undertaken (possibly for symbolic and astrological reasons). It is a commonplace of Egyptology that over the long course of Egyptian history, copies of old documents were made, and those copies in turn copied again, with textual differences arising over the course of time. (The Ba-bi text translated earlier is a case in point.) Egyptologists are now beginning to acknowledge that late inscriptions referring to very early actions (e.g., the dedicatory inscription over the crypt at Denderah) are not to be dismissed as inventions. Upon known and acknowledged scholarly bases, then, there is every reason to accept the possible validity of the inscription on the inventory stela.

The riddle of the face

Researches subsequent to the completion of this book effectively refute the one remaining argument by which Egyptologists might hope to substantiate their belief that the Sphinx (and its temple complex) was built by Chephren in 2700 BC: that it is constructed of stone so much softer than all the other monuments of Egypt that it has eroded to its present condition in the 2000 years it has been exposed to the winds and the sands.

Selim Hassan, the Egyptologist in charge of extensive excavations carried on at the site of the Sphinx in the 1930s, observes: 'So far as we can tell, the actual amphitheatre of the Sphinx was formed when Khufu (Cheops) was quarrying stone for his pyramid. We can deduce that from the fact that *the stone surrounding the Sphinx is of the same*

The weathering of the face of the Sphinx is strikingly less severe than that on the rest of the body. The head and headdress are not worn at all, because they have been resurfaced recently. The original level of erosion can be seen in photographs taken at the turn of the century. Though less severe, it clearly follows the stratification lines common to the body, which I take to signify that the initial eroding agent was the same.

Perhaps the most satisfactory explanation of the discrepancy is that the whole of the head and face consists of a harder outcrop of rock than the body. This is a common enough geological occurrence, and seems indicated by the fact that in order to lay bare the ridge of rock from which the Sphinx is carved, its builders had to hollow out virtually the entire depth of the body. In other words, the scene confronting the original

excellent quality as that of which the Great Pyramid is built.'

Selim Hassan
The Sphinx: Its History in the Light of Recent Excavations
Government Press, Cairo, 1949

A corroborating statement is made by scientists from a Stanford University Research team carrying on sophisticated electronic experiments on the Sphinx, its temple complex and the pyramids, in 1977. Their report notes that the Sphinx is carved from 'competent limestone', i.e. there is nothing that dramatically distinguishes the limestone of the Sphinx from other Egyptian limestones.

Joint A.R.E-U.S.A. Research Team
Electronic Sounder Experiments at the Pyramid of Giza
Office of International Programs, Washington, D.C.

Both Selim Hassan and the Stanford team also provide further support for the other argument developed here: that other Egyptian monuments, allegedly coeval with the Sphinx and built of similar materials, should show similar erosional effects.

Selim Hassan's team uncovered a large limestone stela near the Sphinx erected by Amenhotep II (1448-1420 BC). He notes: 'Only the rounded top of the monument, which had apparently been long exposed to the elements, has suffered erosion but even here enough remained to show that it had originally borne a double representation of the King presenting offerings to the Sphinx.' (Ibid. p. 37). In other words, long exposure to wind and sand had done no more than blur the surface inscriptions on this tablet — corroborating observations made by geologists studying Egypt as to the extremely slow erosional effects observable in the desert.

This conclusion is borne out by the Stanford Research team who found painted quarry marks on the stones in and around an entry into the Mycerinus pyramid that had been forced by Arabs around 1200 AD. After 700 years even these painted markings were still visible, although much blurred. (Ibid. p. 84)

Thus repeated observations testify to the minimal effects of protracted exposure to the desert winds and sands. The Egyptologist in charge of excavations at the Sphinx specifically remarks upon the high quality of the stone from which it is carved. And this observation is corroborated by contemporary scientists, using the most sophisticated modern techniques. Meanwhile, the erosional channels cut into the Sphinx are nearly two feet deep. There is nothing in Egypt that remotely resembles such weathering; except for the ancient cliff faces, untouched by

builders must have been a level plain broken by a single big lump of rock, and perhaps a slight ridge that subsequently became the back of the statue. The fact that this single outcrop existed on the plain suggests that it is formed of a more durable rock than the plain. In the photographs the face (all that is left that is original to the head) shows up a different colour, which is still more apparent to the naked eye, and the close-up taken with the telephoto lens suggests that the texture of the stone comprising the face is finer and closer grained than that of the rest of the body. But until actual tests are made, the relative hardness of the stones cannot be known.

The heavy damage to the face and the pockmarks visible in the close-up are not due to natural causes but to the fact that the Sphinx served the eighteenth-century Mamelukes as an artillery target.

Another possibility that presents itself, but that is difficult to prove, is that the whole of the face and head was resurfaced in Dynastic times, perhaps by Chephren, who obviously took an interest in the Sphinx complex even if he did not construct it. The buried statues prove a valid connection between this pharaoh and the Sphinx. It has been suggested that Chephren might have undertaken the work of resurfacing the original, ruined head and that in doing so, he might have cut away the damaged stone. But he still would not have been able to efface all evidence of erosion without destroying the proportions of the whole. If this were the case, we should expect to find the head of the Sphinx slightly small in proportion to the rest of the body; but photographic evidence cannot be relied upon to verify the possibility, since all depends upon the angle of the shot and the Sphinx is so big that it is impossible to find a vantage point that would allow a decision one way or another.

To the naked eye, the Sphinx is a miracle of harmonic proportion. It is possible that careful measurements of the Sphinx and a subsequent harmonic analysis would reveal the plan the original builders must have followed. It would then be possible to ascertain whether or not the proportions of the head were in keeping with the rest.

If a reworking of the head could be demonstrated, it might also explain the resemblance of the statues of Chephren to the head of the Sphinx. This resemblance is too close to ignore, but not close enough to prove Chephren was builder. (There is nothing ruling out the possibility of Chephren's ordering his sculptors to make him as Sphinx-like as possible.)

Though problems posed by the head of the Sphinx complicate matters, they do not mitigate the strength of the arguments put forward. The weathering to the face, and particularly to the back of the head, as shown in the old photographs and in the drawing commissioned by Napoleon, indicate that the original weathering agent was the same, and its

man, and conceded by all geologists to be the result of ancient water erosion (overlaid by some 12,000 years exposure to wind and sand).

Given this further evidence, the argument developed in this chapter now seems to me irrefutable: the Sphinx and its temple complex are vastly older than all the rest of Dynastic Egypt; the weathering is due to the action of water — of a flood, or floods currently dated at 10,000 BC and earlier. Obviously, for the Sphinx to be eroded by water, it must antedate the flood, or floods, responsible for the erosion. And history as it is presently taught is in need of serious revision.

lesser severity due to a harder consistency of the stone of the head, to its being resurfaced, or possibly to a combination of both factors. Despite its lesser severity, it is still unlike the weathering of any other monument of ancient Egypt, and insofar as these old photographs and drawings can be used as concrete evidence, they seem to corroborate other observations made in the course of this inquiry. The back of the head, particularly, is characterised by a roughened and broken surface, especially along the edges of rock strata. This is an effect noticeably dissimilar to the smoother appearance of the body, and it is in keeping with what might be expected, since this portion of the Sphinx and only this portion has borne the full brunt of the normal desert weathering since Egypt became desert. In other words, insolation, chemical weathering and to some degree wind and sand have worked upon the exposed head of the Sphinx producing characteristic crumbling, flaking and roughening of surfaces originally eroded by water. This effect is similar to what is found on the admittedly water-eroded cliff faces of Egypt, but on no Dynastic monument.

A question of style

Though we do not commonly think of artistic 'style' as a scientific subject, in recent years it has become one. If a Giotto fresco were found in a tenth-century church, art historians would have little difficulty showing that it was not original to the building. If a lost manuscript attributed to Dickens were found, scholars using computers to analyse rhythms, punctuation and the use of key words in particular situations would be able to verify or dismiss the alleged authorship with some assurance.

When we come to Egypt, where all architecture and art followed a canon and was subject to a theological imperative, the study of style becomes a rigorous discipline, as Schwaller de Lubicz demonstrated. If detailed analyses of style allow experts to make positive distinctions concealed from the naked eye, then glaring differences readily apparent to anyone must be taken into serious consideration.

The Sphinx and the complex surrounding it are stylistically as distinct from other Egyptian temples as a Cluniac abbey is from a Wren cathedral, as a Byzantine painting is from a Botticelli. By Egyptian standards, the temples are small, yet there is an air of massive, almost inhuman assurance to these structures, quite unmatched even by the prodigious ruins of Karnak. The builders of the Sphinx temple imposed upon themselves architectural and engineering problems of a magnitude encountered nowhere else in Egypt, not even in the pyramids.

Writers commonly use the word 'cyclopean' to describe the individual blocks of stone used in building this temple, and then go on to other subjects. But the use of cyclopean blocks raises questions rather more important than the number of asps responsible for Cleopatra's death.

One large block in the West wall measures approximately 18 feet x 10 feet x 8 feet and would weigh somewhere between fifty and seventy tons. For no conceivable rational architectural or engineering reason, it is elaborately dressed and slotted into place as if it were no more than a piece of a jigsaw puzzle. It is typical of the stones in this Sphinx temple complex, and quite atypical of all the rest of Egypt.

The use of blocks of this size raises interesting questions. Firstly, how did an ancient civilisation, apparently devoid of an advanced metallurgy, work and handle blocks of stone weighing as much as two fully-loaded trailer trucks? Secondly, why, if Dynastic Egypt was responsible for the Sphinx and its temple complex, did it never build in this style or to this scale again? Lastly, what could be the motive for men, ostensibly not so different from ourselves, to devise a project so arduous and, from an architectural and engineering standpoint, so irrational?

Suggestions and one answer

1 As far as I know, no architect or engineer has set himself to solving the specific problems involved in the Sphinx temple. A considerable amount of time and effort has been spent trying to solve the equally difficult but different problems raised by the construction of the pyramids, and many questions still remain. (D1, 2, 3, 4). Engineers and architects I consulted informally claim that surprisingly large and heavy objects can be handled by an ingenious use of levers and other primitive devices. But all agree that the lifting into place of a finely dressed, extremely dense and extremely heavy block of stone poses a different kind of problem. This question, too, must remain open for the present.

2 The architecture and art of Dynastic Egypt, from the First Dynasty on, reveals a consistent pattern, particularly when seen in terms of the 'flow' of the symbolic directives underlying changes in style. (Even the reforms instituted by the 'heretic' Akhenaten can be incorporated into this pattern when the symbolism of Akhenaten's peculiar and exceptional age are understood.) In no large sense is this pattern what we would call 'development' (as the modern racing car is a 'development' from the horseless carriage), and the one exception to this overall picture supports rather than undermines the hypothesis that Egypt inherited her wisdom from

an earlier civilisation.

From the First Dynasty to the Fourth, sculptors and painters show an increasing mastery over their materials. The canon of proportion already existed in the First Dynasty, but the ease with which artists and sculptors created within the limitations imposed by the canon increased dramatically during the four centuries allotted to these dynasties. This is exactly what might be expected in a situation in which the body of sages or initiates comprising 'the Temple' knew exactly what they wanted to achieve from the start, but in order to achieve it had to train a corps of artisans, more or less from scratch, to the necessary degree of expertise.

From the Fourth Dynasty on, there is nothing that can be called 'development'. In painting and sculpture, a degree of increased sophistication was purchased at the price of decreased purity and power. Egyptian history is a succession of periods of alternate decadence and renewal, with each peak less high than the peak preceding, like the waves of a dying storm.

In architecture, immediately following the period of the mastabas — which I take as a period of training rather than development — the Egyptian achievement was at its height, never again to be equalled. Zoser's Third Dynasty complex at Saqqara, the first major stone complex attempted by Egypt, is also the biggest and in many respects the most skillfully executed. In the century following Zoser, all the great pyramids were allegedly constructed with their vast, now mostly vanished funerary complexes.

Nothing in Middle or New Kingdom Egypt, including Luxor and Karnak, compares with this activity, or with the finesse of its accomplishment: Egypt never again worked to the kind of tolerances used in the many thousands of casing stones covering the Great Pyramid. The Ptolemaic temples are small, slapdash and decadent by comparison.

The message is implicit, if impossible to prove: Egypt at every stage imposed tasks upon herself commensurate to her ability to realise them. Edfu is not Karnak because Ptolemaic Egypt had sunk far below the level of Ramesside Egypt. Though Old Kingdom mortuary temples share features in common with the Sphinx temple, they are dramatically different in execution. The scale of the Sphinx itself dwarfs anything else Egyptian. The average building blocks used in the Great Pyramid weigh two and a half tons. Many of the blocks in the Sphinx temple weigh fifty tons or more.

Egypt always took the hard way out. If she had been able to deal with fifty-ton dressed blocks in the normal course of construction, she would have done so elsewhere, possibly everywhere.

The unasked question

Why should pre-Egyptian builders of the Sphinx employ fifty-ton dressed blocks to build a temple wall?

If the art and architecture of Dynastic Egypt represents an organised exercise in consciousness — if the task itself was so designed as to 'initiate' the artists and artisans engaged on the project into recognition of the cosmic truths enshrined in the

Rear or western wall of the Sphinx Temple. Note irregularity of erosion — exactly what would be expected with blocks cut out of the living rock. I think the water has eroded away the softer strata, producing this higgledy-piggledy effect.

Notice the deliberate coursing. The photo forbids appreciation of the magnitude of the task. One large block measured roughly by us was 18 feet x 10 feet x 8 feet and would weigh over 50 tons. While Dynastic Egypt handled larger single blocks than this (e.g., the fallen Colossus of Rameses II in the Ramesseum weighs a thousand tons), they did not regularly employ such blocks in construction. How the builders handled such stones and why they built with such gigantic single blocks are questions Egyptologists cannot answer, and therefore do not ask.

design, proportions and symbolism of the given temple or monument — then we may have an insight into the otherwise unfathomable motives for imposing such irrational hardships.

Technology is not an end in itself, even to modern man. We are curious about the mysteries of outer space, and therefore we develop space ships. We don't just go into orbit for the hell of it. And it is hardly likely that an ancient race, famed among scholars for its conservatism, lack of inventiveness and unscientific attitude, should go to the trouble of developing a rope-and-lever technology capable of handling fifty-ton blocks just to see if it could be done.

It is well known that ordinary men in a state of crisis can perform feats thought impossible by even the strongest men under ordinary circumstances. Human muscles of a person under hypnotism respond readily to suggestion and can be subjected to pressures unthinkable in a waking state. Women have been known to lift automobiles in order to rescue a trapped child. Is it not possible that the builders of the Sphinx temple (perhaps of Dynastic Egypt as well) provoked such superhuman conscious states *deliberately*? Is it not possible that the temple of the Sphinx was to its builders what a Dervish dance is to a modern Sufi — an initiation?

Details of granite temple adjacent to the Sphinx, attributed to Chephren on the basis of statues found buried in pits dug into the floor. There is no inscription or other evidence indicating Chephren as builder.

The monolithic simplicity of the style is most untypical of Egypt, similar only to the Oseirion at Abydos attributed to Seti I (also upon less than satisfactory evidence).

The Sphinx temple may contain the clues that lead to a final chronological solution. To me, it appears that a granite shell has been constructed as both an inner and outer lining to the already extant and deeply weathered sandstone ruins of the original temple. Note the striated erosion on the blocks behind the granite facing.

Summary

Schwaller de Lubicz's documented interpretation of ancient Egypt, his observation regarding the water erosion of the Sphinx and the train of deductions following upon that observation throw open the old question of Atlantis. The case for Atlantis, if not incontestable, is powerful, consistent and supported from a number of independent but complementary angles. Here are the salient points:

1 Egyptian civilisation was complete at its beginning. There is no sign of a period of 'development'.

2 Weathering on the body of the Sphinx is typical of water erosion elsewhere.

3 It is almost impossible to attribute this erosion to wind, sand, insolation or chemical reaction, since the Sphinx was buried in sand for most of its putative history.

4 There is a complete lack of similar erosional effects on other Egyptian temples and monuments exposed to the elements for as long or longer.

5 The attribution of the Sphinx to Chephren is based upon flimsy, circumstantial evidence.

6 The architectural style and building scale of the Sphinx and Sphinx temple complex are unlike anything else in Dynastic Egypt.

Atlantis: a brief recapitulation

It is beyond the scope of this book to examine in detail the myths and legends referring to vanished civilisations, golden ages, world floods and catastrophes, or to try to sort out the science from the pseudoscience in the considerable modern literature upon the subject. But a résumé will at least call attention to the principal problems and directions of research.

The Oseirion at Abydos, attributed to Seti I (ca. 1300 BC). The only other instance (along with the so-called Chephren temple) of monolithic granite architecture. The gradual rising of the water table (due to annual deposition of alluvial sediment and, with it, the gradual rise of the bed of the Nile) now makes it impossible to keep the Oseirion from being flooded. Calculations have shown that at the time of Seti, the water level would already have been at floor level of the temple.

Detail of weathering of rock face behind the Oseirion. Obviously, this has taken place since the rock was cut away to make room for the temple. Though the surface is rougher than that of the Sphinx, the stratified appearance is similar.

I believe this to be the action of wind, sand and possibly condensation and chemical action upon earlier water erosion. The top of the back of the Sphinx and the upper portion of the cutaway rock face adjacent to the Sphinx show similar roughened surfaces, while the lower portions — those buried in the sand for the longest period of time — are relatively smooth. Apart from the Sphinx and the Oseirion, I was unable to find similar weathering anywhere else in Egypt.

The orthodox view

The legend of Atlantis is based chiefly upon Plato's account in his *Timaeus*, which supposedly came to him from Solon — who had learned it in Egypt. To date no Egyptian text or reference has ever been found to corroborate Egypt as the source. Scholars have tended to dismiss the legend, but a few have believed that it must have some sort of historical basis.

The recent discovery of the island of Thera, near Crete, destroyed by an earthquake around 1500 BC and sunk beneath the Mediterranean Sea, has led a number of scholars to attribute the legend to the memory of this disaster. They think Plato added an extra zero to the date of its sinking, accounting for his 10,000 BC date.

But the civilisation described by Plato was infinitely more sophisticated than anything current in his own time. It is difficult to see how or why, in the full flower of Middle Kingdom Egypt, the demise of an insignificant little island should give rise to the legend, and equally difficult to see how it should give rise to the legends of flood and catastrophe elsewhere in the world.

Though not implausible, the Thera theory is hardly commanding . . . and there remains the water erosion of the Sphinx to explain away.

Egyptian chronological accounts

The archaeological record for the period preceding Dynastic Egypt is confused and incomplete. A number of neolithic cultures are thought to have existed, more or less simultaneously, from about 6000 BC onwards. These cultures built nothing permanent, apparently, and their arts and crafts were simple and rudimentary: there is no archaeological evidence that would support the notion of a prior great civilisation — with one possible exception.

These simple cultures had cultivated cereal grains and domesticated animals. The manner in which wild grains were originally cultivated and wild animals permanently domesticated is one of those questions that cannot be satisfactorily answered, but a period of long development is assumed. The fact is that throughout recorded history, no new animals have been domesticated; our domestic beasts have been around since the beginning, and no new grains have been cultivated.

The cultivation of grain and the domstication of animals probably represent — after the invention of language — the two most significant human achievements. We can fly to the moon today, but we cannot domesticate the zebra, or any other animal. We do not know how the original domestication was done, we can only guess. To attribute these immense achievements to people who could only chip flint and work crude mats and pottery is perhaps premature. It is plausible to suggest that, like the Sphinx and its temple complex, these inventions dated from an earlier and higher civilisation.

Following these neolithic cultures there is an almost equally hazy period called pre-Dynastic, yielding artifacts far superior to the earlier cultures. In some ways, this civilisation seems to lead to Dynastic Egypt — e.g., certain signs and symbols painted on crude pottery later became signs and symbols of the nomes of Egypt. In other ways, the culture seems distinct: the style of the sculpture is different, the people seem to belong to a different race, they dress differently, and the rigorous adherence to a canon of proportion, typical of all of Dynastic Egypt from the beginning, is absent. But there is little from pre-Dynastic Egypt either that specifically supports descent from 'Atlantis'.

On the other hand, there is the chronological account of the Egyptians themselves.

Egyptian chronological tables have been found in the course of excavation which date the founding of Egypt much earlier than the Dynastic record. All the writers of antiquity who had any contact with Egypt related tales of such tables. Unfortunately, there is no tablet or papyrus that is complete upon these crucial earlier periods, and there are many inconsistencies among the sources.

Nevertheless, there is agreement in a very broad sense. The various sources postulate a long period during which Egypt was ruled by the Neters and then another, almost equally long, period during which it was ruled by the Shemsu Hor, (the 'Companions of Horus'). The chronology is impossible to disentangle, and in some cases it depends upon the manner of calculation chosen, but the earliest calculation would place the founding of Egypt around 30,000 BC, the latest around 23,000 BC. Though the discrepancy is obviously very large, it is at least worth remarking that while the sources are independent, the discrepancy lies within a single order of magnitude.

Herodotus quotes one of his guides as saying that in Egyptian history, 'the sun had twice risen where it now set, and twice set where it now rises'. This remark Schwaller de Lubicz interpreted as a description of the passage of one and a half precessional cycles. This would place the date of foundation around 36,000 BC, a date in broad agreement with the other sources.

To this evidence must be added the ubiquity of legends of catastrophes and floods; the arguments put up by 'catastrophists' within geological and other scientific circles; the cultural, scientific, linguistic and mathematical correspondences found between the civilisations of Central America and Egypt;

217

Peter Tompkins
Mysteries of the Mexican Pyramids
Harper & Row, 1976, p. 176

Fired by Brasseur's books, Thompson argued that although there was no proof of the Atlantis theory, a tradition so widespread and a legend so persistent must have some basis in history. . . .

Thompson pointed to the traditions of widely separate peoples concerning a mysterious appearance on the shores of the Gulf of Mexico of the People of the Serpent, or Chanes. . . . Thompson pointed out that the leaders of the 'Ulmecas' were known as Chanes, or among the Mayas as Canob, 'Serpents', 'Wise Men' or Ah Tzai, 'People of the Rattlesnake'.

and the latest results in archaeology, which invariably push the beginnings of civilisation further and further into the past and upgrade the extent and sophistication of the scientific knowledge possessed by ancient humanity. Given all this evidence, 'Atlantis' can no longer be ignored by anyone seriously interested in the truth.

The implications

The simplistic view that sees history as a gradual but inexorable 'advance' is today losing ground to 'cyclical' theories which, if corresponding closer to historical known facts, are nevertheless simplistic in their own right. They substitute a mechanism of ebb and flow, of alternation between periods of 'scientific' and 'religious'dominance, for the mechanism of

John Greaves
The Enduring Mystery
Pyramidographia, 1646

The Arabian writers, especially such as have purposely treated of the wonders of Egypt have given us a more full description [of the Pyramids]: but that hath been mixed with so many inventions of their owne, that the truth hath been darknd and almost extinguished by them. I shall put downe that which is confessed by them, to be the most probable relation, as is reported by Ibn Abd Alhokm, whose words out the Arabick are these.

The greatest part of Chronologers agree, that he which built the Pyramids was Saurid Ibn Salhouk, King of Egypt, who lived three hundred years before the flood. The occasion of this was because he saw in his sleep, that the whole earth was turned over, with the inhabitants of it, the men lying upon their faces, and the stars falling downe and striking one another, with a terrible noise, and being troubled with this, he concealed it. Then after he saw the first stars falling to the earth, in the similitude of white fowle, and they snatched up men, and carried them between two great mountaines, and these mountaines closed upon them, and the shining stars were made darke. And he awaked with great feare, and assembled the chief Priests of all the provinces of Egypt, an hundred and thirty priests, the chief of them was called Aclimun. He related the whole matter to them, and they took the altitude of the stars, and made their prognostication, and they foretold of a deluge. The king said will it come to our country? They answered yes, and will destroy it. And there remained a certain

number of years to come, and he commanded in the mean space to build the Pyramids, and that a vault (or cisterne) should be made, into which the river Nilus should enter, from whence it should runne into the countries of the West, and into the land Al-Said.

And he filled them (the Pyramids) with talismans, and with strange things, and with riches, and treasures, and the like. He engraved in them all things that were told by wise men, as also all profound sciences, the names of alakakirs, the uses, and hurts of them. The science of Astrology, and of Arithmeticke, and of Geometry, and of Physicke. All this may be interpreted by him that knowes their characters, and language. After he had given orders for this building, they cut out vast columnes, and wonderful stones. They fetched massy stones from the Ethiopians, and made with these the foundations of the three Pyramids fastening them together with lead, and iron. They built the gates of them 40 cubits under ground, and they made the height of the Pyramids 100 royall cubits, which are 500 of ours in these times. He also made each side of them as hundred royall cubits. The beginning of this building was in a fortunate horoscope. After that he had finished it, he covered it with coloured Satten (marble), from the top to the bottome and he appointed a solemne festivall, at which were present all the inhabitants of his Kingdome. Then he built in the Westerne Pyramid thirty treasuries, filled with store of riches, and utensils, and with signatures made of precious stones, and with instruments of iron, and vessels of earth and with a mes which rusts not, and with glasse which might be bended, and yet

not broken, and with strange spells, and with severall kinds of akakirs, single and double, and with deadly poisons, and with other things besides. He made also in the East Pyramid, divers celestiall spheres, and stars, and what they severally operate, in their aspects; and the perfumes which are to be used to them, and the books which treat of these matters.

He put also in the coloured Pyramid (the third), the commentaries of the Priests, in chests of black marble, and with every Priest a booke, in which were the wonders of his profession, and of his actions, and of his nature, and what was done in his time, and what is, and what shall be, from the beginning of time, to the end of it. He placed in every Pyramid a Treasurer: the treasurer of the westerly Pyramid was a statue of marble stone standing upright with a lance, and upon his head a Serpent wreathed. He that came neare it, and stood still, the Serpent bit him of one side, and wreathed round his throat, and killed him, and then returned to his place. He made the treasurer of the East Pyramid an idoll of black Agate, his eyes open, and shining, sitting upon a throne with a lance; when any lookt upon him, he heard of one side of him a voice, which took away his sense, so that he fell prostrate upon his face, and ceased not till he died. He made the treasurer of the Coloured Pyramid a statue of stone, called Albut, sitting. He which looked towards it was drawn by the statue, till he stucke to it, and could not be separated from it, till such time as he died.

Thus farre the Arabians: which traditions of theirs are little better than a romance.

Lewis Mumford
Review of *The Myth of the Machine Time*, June 9, 1969

Mumford's profoundly reactionary answer to the megamachine is to throw a monkey wrench into it and send it down a time tunnel. Go back to Benedictine monasteries, where work was a 'byword for zealous efficiency and formal perfection'. Discover new prophets of 'modest, humane disposition' like Jesus and Confucius. Establish new routines, such as the Hebrew Sabbath that 'found a way of obstructing the megamachine and challenging its inflated claims'. Abandon the modern constitutional equivalents of ancient kingships and revert to Neolithic culture. In other words, Mumford would perfect man with weaving, pottery and thatched village anarchy.

To a few modern Luddites, this may sound like an attractive idea. But man had that chance 5000 years ago and muffed it. Mumford may as well forget that fantasy and address himself to the real problem: how to plug the megamachine into the circuitry of 20th century hopes.

J. G. Bennett
The Dramatic Universe
Hodder & Stoughton, 1956, Vol. I., p. 29

The faith that technology or some form of social revolution could liberate man from the need to work and suffer is in its essence indistinguishable from the crudest beliefs in the efficacy of magic.

Ibid., p. 29

Whitehead reminded us that narrowness in the selection of evidence is the bane of philosophy. Any system can be made to appear plausible, so long as we reject and ignore those elements of experience that have no place in it. . . . The scientific method of observation and experiment cannot take account of the unrepeatable and the exceptional, which occupy so great a place in our aesthetic experience.

Ibid., Vol. I, 1956, p. 30

Quality is an authentic element of all experience, but it cannot be known in the same manner as quantity is known. Our intuitions of quality are different from those of quantity and they cannot be expressed in the same language, and yet all experience, whatever its nature, is an awareness of qualities. No system of thought can ignore quality without incurring the risk of a sterility that is all the more deadly for being often self-satisfied and blind to its own limitations.

'progress'. These theories fail to take into account the laws of genesis.

According to Schwaller de Lubicz, all phenomena are subject to the laws of genesis. The principles of conception, birth, growth, senescence, death and renewal are universal and apply to everything: to the individual human being, to civilisations, to the human race taken as a unity, to planets, stars and galaxies.

When the laws of genesis are applied to history, the subject may become more complicated, but it begins to correspond to the picture of history in front of our eyes. It is a form of lunacy to maintain that the chaos of the twentieth century has 'evolved' from the 'primitive' civilisation responsible for the Sphinx, or to claim that we have 'progressed'.

We do not say that the diseased and neurotic adolescent has 'evolved' from the healthy infant he once was. Rather, the inexorable workings of the laws of genesis have given him access to powers he did not formerly possess, but he has lost certain other capacities and powers — and something has gone terribly wrong in the process. The cure, if the case is not beyond hope, is to use those capacities still in working order to find out what went wrong, to determine the factors responsible for that earlier state of health, and possibly even to try to recover certain of the powers and capacities lost because of education rather than cosmic law.

A cycle comes to an end, a new cycle begins — simultaneously.

In a park full of stricken oaks, it takes sharp eyes to spot the newly sprouted seedlings, but they are there. The organic, vital view of history allows us to look into the future realistically. There is no guarantee of the glorious future envisaged by ecstatic Aquarians; but there are possibilities that do not show up in the computerised fumblings of the doomwatchers and the futurologists. Nothing can be done to save the dying oak, but the tender seedlings can be trampled into the ground by any wandering jackass.

We have no civilisation of our own. Those cultures of the recent past worthy of being called civilisations (Vedic India, Tibet, Celtic Ireland, and to a certain extent early medieval Europe, Moslem Spain, Mayan and pre-Mayan America) are strangely less accessible to us than ancient Egypt.

At present, Schwaller de Lubicz's interpretation of Egypt provides us with the only coherent, consistent and structurally complete picture of a civilisation in action.

All esoteric doctrines teach that death is not an end, but a point of transformation. Throughout the ages, masters, saints, wise men, yogis, have terminated their lives in a state of serene accomplishment. What applies to the individual applies to

Time, Aug. 16, 1976
The devastating earthquakes in China, the Colorado flood, the mysterious ailment that struck the American Legionnaires in Philadelphia — all suggest a more fundamental and realistic perspective. It would be banal to say that such demonstrations of nature's awesome force restore man's humility. Still, it is worth repeating the thesis of French biologist Jacques Monod that events — and mostly the events of life itself — are profoundly random.

society as a whole, and a successful civilisation, in principle, should end on a similar note of serenity. That history provides precisely contrary evidence is simply a reflection upon the level of civilisation collectively attained. And there is not the slightest doubt of our present state: the deluge is once again upon us.

Yet our situation is richer in potential than any in the known past; and it is equally rich in irony. For the very forces responsible for bringing on the rains have inadvertently provided the material for building the vessel that can see the flood through.

However mistaken the spirit in which it has been performed, however perverted the conclusions commonly drawn from it, it is modern scientific scholarship that has made possible both access to the high wisdom of ancient Egypt (which is the wisdom of 'Atlantis') and the capacity to study and understand it.

Schwaller de Lubicz's interpretation of ancient Egypt, understood in all its potential, in all its implications, is no less than the blueprint for an ark.

Appendix I:
The Gauri/
Lehner survey

Since the last chapter of this book was written, an archeological and geological survey of the Sphinx has been undertaken. The project was carried out by Mark Lehner, Field Director for the American Research Center in Egypt, and Dr. K. Lal Gauri, Director of the Stone Conservation Laboratory at the University of Louisville, Kentucky. It was funded by a grant from the Edgar Cayce Foundation (strange intellectual bedfellows, indeed!). The results were published in the *American Research Center in Egypt Newsletter* (nos. 112, 114).

The survey was not designed to test for the possibility of a drastically altered chronology, and the conclusions put forward by Lehner and Gauri avoid any mention of such a revision. Nevertheless, in essence and detail, the published findings support the argument developed in my final chapter. Alternative explanations for the weathering to the Sphinx, advanced by Dr. Gauri in order to preserve the accepted chronology, are in my view utterly unconvincing and are contradicted by the very facts he himself revealed. But since my letter to Dr. Gauri designed to challenge his conclusions remains unanswered, 'official' endorsement has not yet been granted. Readers who have been following the scholarly reaction to Schwaller de Lubicz's meticulously documented theories throughout the course of this book will not be surprised by this latest show of scholarly incuriosity.

Though the published reports are somewhat technical, the issues at stake are easily explained and perfectly comprehensible to the alert reader. Here are the main points, and I will elaborate further below:

1   The standard explanation—that the weathering to the Sphinx is due to wind and sand—has been abandoned.

2   Mark Lehner finds that there has been not one, but three separate major repair campaigns carried out on the Sphinx. The dating of these campaigns poses perhaps insoluble

problems. Lehner provisionally dates the earliest campaign to the New Kingdom (1550–1070 BC).

3   Lehner notes that, *until the past few decades, no substantial weathering has taken place on the Sphinx since the first repair campaign was carried out.* This is perhaps the most crucial point in the argument for a revised chronology and must be emphasised.

4   Lehner goes on to deduce that this leaves only ±500 years for the Sphinx to have eroded from its original to its present condition—with channels worn two feet deep into its limestone walls.

5   Tests by Dr. Gauri prove that the weathering is due to water reacting with the natural salts in the limestone; in other words, that the damage to the Sphinx is due to water erosion.

6   However, he insists that this is due to ground water leaching into the body of the Sphinx from below. He does not elaborate on the mechanism theoretically responsible. Neither he nor Lehner seem troubled by contradictions implicit in their conclusions.

But these contradictions are both manifold and glaring and, short of some kind of geological miracle manifesting itself at the Sphinx and nowhere else in the world, Dr. Gauri's reasoning will not suffice to explain the erosion to the Sphinx.

The key to the fallacy is Lehner's discovery that no substantial erosion has taken place since the earliest repair campaign was undertaken. At the same time Lehner claims that, given the orthodox chronology, only ±500 years can be allowed for the erosion to have occurred.

Where then was Dr. Gauri's underground water at this time? And how did it leach up into the body of the Sphinx, eroding channels two feet deep into its sides in only ±500 years, then ceasing such destructive action for the remaining ±4000 years?

It might be argued, perhaps, that the various repair campaigns effectively prevented further erosion by protecting the surface of the Sphinx. But this argument will not do. The walls of the hollow, carved out to free the body of the Sphinx, have never been repaired (see photo, p. 201), and these show an erosion pattern absolutely identical to that on the Sphinx itself. Since Dr. Gauri's explanation calls for erosion taking place at the unthinkable rate of ±4 inches per century, the walls of the hollow, never having been repaired,

should show more severe erosion than the body of the Sphinx itself. Yet, they do not.

The questions raised by Dr. Gauri's explanation are further compounded by the peculiarities of the Egyptian ground-water level. This, until the recent disturbing factor of the Aswan High Dam, has been tied to the annual flooding of the Nile and can be easily calculated and demonstrated. Over the millenia, the Nile floods have gradually deposited successive layers of silt, raising the floor of the floodplain at roughly the rate of 10 feet per 1000 years. The underground water table has risen accordingly. This means that when the Sphinx was built, allegedly just short of 5000 years ago, the ground-water table level was some 50 feet below its present level (reckoning at 10 feet per 1000 years).

Following Dr. Gauri's explanation, this means that underground water, 50 feet lower than at its present level, seeped upward into the body of the Sphinx around the time it was carved, eroding away the surface stone at the rate of ±4 inches per century. And thereafter *ceased eroding altogether as the water level continued to rise over the ensuing 4½ millenia*—for as Lehner insists, all weathering to the Sphinx had virtually taken place by the time of the earliest repair campaign.

This, short of that geological miracle postulated earlier, seems impossible. And if it is in principle possible to raise impossibility itself to exponential levels, evidence exists to perform that feat.

The first bit of evidence concerns the curious Valley Temple discussed at some length in my final chapter. All arguments advanced there still hold, but further conclusions can be drawn from the existing data vis-a-vis Dr. Gauri's hypothesis.

As I pointed out earlier, the agent responsible for weathering the Sphinx was also responsible for weathering the mighty core blocks of the Valley Temple. On this basis as well, Dr. Gauri's hypothesis must be rejected, since water seeping upward through capillary action cannot traverse the breaks in the individual courses of stone. In other words, even if there were no commanding reason to disqualify Dr. Gauri's theory when applied to the Sphinx, it would be disqualified on the basis of the erosion pattern on the Valley Temple—since the same weathering agent has to be responsible for both, and that agent cannot have been water leaching up from underground in the case of the Valley Temple. A somewhat similar argument may be drawn from the erosion pattern found in the so-called Mortuary Temple connected to the Sphinx by the causeway and also discussed at some length in my final chapter.

This temple was built on the plateau more than 150 feet above the level of the Sphinx, but its erosion pattern is similar to that of the Sphinx (allowing for the rather drastic ravages resulting from its higher, more exposed position on the plateau). If water seeping up from underground were actually responsible for the erosion to the Sphinx, then that same water would have to have seeped still another 150 feet upward to weather away the Mortuary Temple. Also, it would have to have done so selectively, since it is only the Mortuary Temple amid the myriad mastabas and other structures built on the plateau in Old Kingdom times that displays that typical water erosion pattern. This is as inconceivable as the rest of the Gauri/Lehner hypothesis.

Thus the pieces already in place in the earlier argument now seem firmly cemented there. There seems to be no way in which water seeping from underground could have eroded away the Sphinx, the Valley Temple, *and* the Mortuary Temple. Yet all must have been eroded by the same weathering agent.

Mark Lehner's work reinforces all the arguments laid down above. Though his report is scrupulously devoid of any suggestion of controversy, it is clear that he has certain misgivings about his own attributions. If there were not something distinctly peculiar in allotting only ±500 years for the Sphinx to weather from its new to its final, eroded state, he would not have called attention to it in the first place.

Moreover, over the course of several pages too technical and lengthy to quote, Lehner puzzles over the provenance of the earliest repair campaigns, carried out with large blocks typical of Old Kingdom masonry. He first postulates that the original Sphinx had a surface screed of such shaped blocks, rather than a surface carved from the actual bedrock—the usual unspoken assumption. This might have explained the Old Kingdom style of these large blocks, but internal evidence—lack of rough quarrying marks on the actual surface of the Sphinx—forced him to reject this view. However, to persist in attributing the early repair campaign to the Old Kingdom would have upset the standard attribution of the Sphinx to Chephren, since *all* substantial erosion took place *prior* to the earliest repair campaign. Therefore, in order to preserve this standard attribution, he postulates a later, New Kingdom repair campaign even though, archeologically, the masonry style is anomalous.

All of these anomalies and contradictions disappear once the true, vast antiquity of the Sphinx is acknowledged. Of course this means totally rewriting the accepted chronology of the evolution of human civilization. Even more to the point, it means rethinking the whole notion of 'progress' as a linear process beginning with putative ape-like ancestors and proceeding in a smooth crescendo up to ourselves. This should prove a welcome challenge to scientists and scholars interested in the objective truth.

Appendix II: Sphinx update

I can think of no major valid scientific or scholarly theory in place today that has not undergone a long process of development, involving correction, winnowing, refining and revision. The quest to redate the Sphinx is no different.

Without a geological specialist to look into the details of the theory I'd pieced together, I could claim with assurance that the Sphinx had *not* been weathered by wind and sand (even Gauri/Lehner were agreed on that point). By pointing out the glaring inconsistencies in the Gauri/Lehner report, I could present a solid case for overthrowing the attribution to Chephren and for acknowledging the need to accept a much earlier date for its carving. If the science of geology had never been developed, or if reason and logic were determining factors in accepting or rejecting a theory, in principle the new theory could have established itself without the need for outside 'expert' help. But in the real-life, late twentieth century, a geologically-based theory needed geologists to confirm it before anyone within the academic establishment would take it seriously. (This is not to be taken to mean that the academic establishment has a monopoly on scientific or scholarly truth in any sense. But without some sort of academic backing, the media will not involve itself. And without the media, it is extremely difficult to get a new idea or theory out to the mass audience.)

In 1989, a friend at Boston University aroused the interest of a geologist colleague, Dr. Robert M. Schoch. A stratigrapher and paleontologist, Schoch was a specialist in the weathering of soft rock (such as the limestone of the Giza Plateau). He had exactly the kind of expertise needed to confirm or rebut the theory once and for all — there are thousands of geologists, but probably only a dozen or so sufficiently specialized in these areas to pass authoritative judgment on the theory's various elements.

Though Schoch could readily see the holes in

the Lehner/Gauri explanation, and though my photographs looked to his practiced eyes like typical water weathering, he was still deeply skeptical, mainly, because it looked too obvious. Schoch found it difficult to believe that in two hundred years of studying, excavating and restoring the Giza Plateau, no one prior to Schwaller had noticed that the weathering on the Sphinx was water weathering, and no one prior to me had noticed that this was peculiar to the Sphinx (and its immediately associated structures). His initial conviction was that, as an amateur, I must have overlooked some crucial piece of evidence that would allow the accepted dating and attribution to stand.

A brief, informal inspection trip to Egypt in June, 1990, provisionally convinced Schoch otherwise. There was no doubt in his mind that the Sphinx had been weathered by water. The pattern of weathering was such that it could not have been water leaching up from underground as Lehner/Gauri were claiming. But it also wasn't the floodwater that I had been postulating. According to Schoch, the weathering was typically precipitation-based; in other words, rainwater was responsible for weathering the Sphinx, not floods.

This turned out to be the one serious mistake I had made in putting together my own argument, but it answered a major reservation that been nagging me from the beginning. The geological literature I had used to develop the theory talked about immense floods in Egypt over the long millennia following the breakup of the last Ice Age and prior to the Sahara becoming desert. This seemed to me the only plausible source for the water that had weathered the Sphinx.

The problem is that the Sphinx is deeply weathered up to its neck. This necessitated 60-foot floods (at a minimum) over the whole of the Nile Valley. It was difficult to imagine floods of this magnitude. Worse, if the theory was correct, the inner limestone coreblocks of the so-called Mortuary Temple at the end of the causeway leading from the Sphinx had also been weathered by water, and this meant floods reaching to the base of the pyramids — another hundred feet or so of floodwaters. A number of critics had ridiculed that idea, though without ever addressing the anomalous weathering in the first place, or any of the other supporting pieces of evidence I'd put together.

Precipitation-induced weathering took care of the problem in a single stroke. The sources I was using for reference talked about these floods in conjunction with long periods of heavy rains, but it hadn't occurred to me, as a non-geologist, that the rains, rather than the periodic floods, were the actual weathering agent. In retrospect, it would not have taken a major stroke of genius to make that connection myself. But nothing in the literature I had consulted triggered it. Since dozens of scholars, including geologists, had devoted whole lifetimes to the Sphinx and pyramids, and none prior to Schwaller had ever noticed that it was water weathering to begin with, nor that the weathering to the Sphinx was both striking and unique, unlike anything else man-made in Egypt, I confess that I wasted little time in self-recrimination.

Unfortunately, without official access to the Sphinx enclosure, Schoch could not examine the limestone of the actual Sphinx firsthand. Privately he was convinced, but publicly a number of key questions had to remain open, pending an officially-sanctioned examination. We had to be able to get up close to make absolutely certain the weathering was precipitation induced. We also had to be able to say with certainty that the anomalous and unique weathering to the Sphinx was not a feature of anomalous and unique geology; in other words, if the Sphinx was carved from a different strata or type of rock than the rest of the plateau, that perhaps might account for its unique weathering pattern. Our public-access vantage point just outside the Sphinx hollow made this seem unlikely, but the possibility could not be dismissed.

On the basis of Schoch's provisional professional support, a Sphinx team began to form. By this time it was absolutely clear that establishing the Sphinx theory called for a master game plan. The actual science was only one factor. We also needed permission from the Egyptian Antiquities Organization to be allowed to do our work in the first place. The Giza Plateau is probably the most sensitive political/academic area in all Egypt; even with a theory much less incendiary than ours, it was difficult to get permission to work. Our financial backing had to come from private sources. And finally, since we could expect nothing but opposition from academic Egyptologists and archeologists, a way had to be found to get the theory to the public, if and when Schoch decided the evidence warranted full geological support. Otherwise it would simply be buried, possibly for good. We decided to record the on-going work in a video documentary, which would have wide public appeal. (The details of this complicated story will be fleshed out in our book, *Unriddling the Sphinx*, coauthored by myself and Robert Schoch.)

With the backing of his Dean, Schoch presented a proposal to carry on our work to the Egyptian authorities. Eventually permission was granted. Creative shoestring financing underwrote the enterprise. Operation Desert Storm forced a postponement of our time schedule, but by April, 1991, we were prepared for our first 'official' survey.

We had two main objectives. The first, of course, was to determine, definitively if possible, if the water-weathering theory held up upon close inspection. The second, which followed, was to see if all the other pieces of the theory fit together. This required the expensive but indispensible services of a geophysicist and state-of-the-art seismographic equipment.

One objection thrown back at me by the establishment (on those rare occasions when I could get any response at all) was a question: How could the Sphinx be the only relic of this postulated vanished civilization? Of course, I had never said that it was. There had to be more. If the Sphinx predated the formation of the Sahara, other structures must be buried somewhere, probably deeper than anyone had looked previously. In mapping the subsurface geology, we hoped our seismographs would turn up something.

Our team now included geophysicist Dr. Thomas L. Dobecki, an associate with a respected Houston firm McBride-Ratcliff & Associates, and, unofficially, an architect and highly skilled amateur photographer; two other geologists; and an oceanographer. An old friend, Boris Said, ex-race driver for Ferrari, ex-Captain of the U.S. Olympic bobsled team and now a producer of unusual documentary films, signed on to oversee the project as a whole and the video that we intended to make as part of our overall end-run strategy. (See the Afterword for more on this theme.)

With legal access to the Sphinx enclosure, Schoch was swiftly dropping conditionals. The deeply weathered Sphinx and its ditch wall and the relatively unweathered or clearly wind-weathered Old Kingdom tombs to the south (dating from around Chephren's period) were cut

from the same member of rock. In Schoch's view it was therefore geologically impossible to ascribe these structures to the same time period. Our scientists were agreed. Only water, specifically precipitation, could produce the weathering we were observing. Upon examination, the wall of the Sphinx ditch was even more crucial to our case than the much repaired, and now partially covered-over Sphinx. Only running water, coursing down the plateau and cascading over the walls of the ditch at low or weak spots could have created those deep vertical fissures and scooped out those shallow scalloped coves (see photo p. 189 and diagram below).

Preliminary readings of Dobecki's seismo-

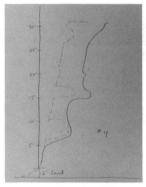

Sphinx Ditch Wall Profile. The solid line shows the actual profile of the weathered limestone rockface. The rolling contours are typical of precipitation (rain)-induced weathering. The broken line shows a hypothetical wind-weathered profile. In other words, if wind and sand had been responsible for the weathering to the Sphinx and its ditch wall, the broken line shows more or less what the ditch profile would look like. Notice that the wind would pick out the softer layers quite deeply but would leave intact the flat profile of the harder layers. This corrected an earlier observational error of my own (see Appendix I). I thought initially the ditch wall and the core body of the Sphinx showed virtually identical weathering. Close-up inspection revealed that the ditch wall was actually more deeply weathered. This proved to be easily explained, once we realized that the weathering was precipitation-induced. Whereas the body of the Sphinx was subjected only to the actual rainwater falling on it, the ditch-wall was subject to the much greater volume of run-off water from the whole of the plateau. Drawing: Robert M. Schoch.

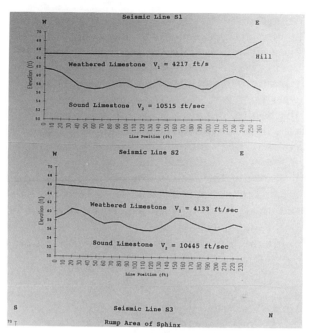

Seismic Refraction Profiles. Figs. S1, S2 and S4 show subsurface weathering profiles on either side and in front of the Sphinx. S3 shows the profile behind the Sphinx. The upper band in these figures shows the depth of the upper, weathered and deteriorated layer of limestone. This band averages 6-8 feet in depth on the sides and front of the Sphinx but only about half that behind the Sphinx.

graph readings also produced tentative gold. We were picking up 'anomalies' or 'cavities' deep in the bedrock between the paws and along the sides of the Sphinx.* In the area in front of the Sphinx, we found what appeared to be a set of deep channels or quarry features cut into the bedrock of the cliff that slopes off in front of the Sphinx temple (see diagram). If, eventually, these prove to be man-made, it could be a major archeological find.

We extended our inquiry into some of the pieces of corroboratory evidence I'd pieced together earlier but which needed geological expertise to back them up. In Saqqara, seven miles south of the Sphinx, there are mudbrick royal tombs dating from First Dynasty Egypt (ca. 3000 BC, or five hundred years before Chephren's

* According to Edgar Cayce, the famous 'sleeping prophet' (whose 'readings' received while in trance contained voluminous references to 'Atlantis' and earlier civilizations), the so-called 'Hall of Records' dating from the time of the fall of Atlantis, telling the story of early mankind was supposed to be located beneath the left paw of the Sphinx.

time). The soft mudbricks are still in stable and recognizable condition. Was it possible that the limestone Sphinx could sustain three feet of weathering to its body, while a few miles away, the mud bricks in tombs supposedly older could still be used in construction today? Schoch thought not, and he was now willing to go on record that the Sphinx was older than dynastic Egypt.

Months later, Dobecki's processed geophysical data turned up important new surprises (see diagram). The limestone bedrock floor immediately behind the Sphinx showed only half the depth of weathering of the sides (approximately four feet in back and eight feet along the sides). Since the stone of the floor is the same all around, and sides and back have been subjected to identical weather conditions since dynastic times, Schoch and Dobecki took this to mean but one thing: the back area of the Sphinx must have been cut out at a later date. Nothing else could account for the difference in weathering depths. Given the Old Kingdom style of the earliest repairs, and the near certainty that the Pharoah Chephren was intimately connected with the Sphinx as an early restorer, it seemed fair to postulate that this rear

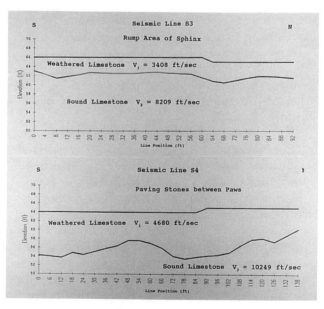

Robert Schoch and Thomas Dobecki, who carried out these studies, feel that the only plausible explanation to account for this disparity is that this portion to the rear (S3) of the Sphinx must have been cut out of the bedrock at a much later date than the sides and front; perhaps to facilitate one of the early repair campaigns. Diagram: Thomas Dobecki.

portion had been cut out *no later than* Chephren's time, some 4500 years ago. If the bedrock had weathered down approximately four feet in 4500 years, this meant that the deeper weathering along the sides had taken commensurately longer.

This evidence provided Schoch with hard quantitative data to support his geological diagnosis. Now he could put forward a very tentative date for the carving of the Sphinx: 5000 to 7000 BC as a minimum. 'Minimum' must be stressed, since weathering does not proceed in linear fashion. As the weathering gets deeper, it goes slower, since it's protected by the rock on top. (Moreover, for reasons too complex to broach here, it is conceivable that Chephren was not the first restorer of the Sphinx, either.)

Here Schoch and I disagree, or rather interpret the same data somewhat differently. Schoch very deliberately takes the most conservative view allowed by the data. Over the past couple of decades, there has been a general archeological revision and upgrading of our opinions of the civilizations that flourished between 10,000 BC and the rise of the civilizations of Egypt and Mesopotamia around 3000 BC. Jericho, dating back to 8000 BC, already featured massive stone walls; Catal Huyuk in Anatolia shows a full-fledged, sophisticated city culture. The hunter-gatherer Neolithic image for this long period has been much revised. Schoch thinks it possible that the Sphinx was produced by an Egyptian equivalent of these cultures. Even though the Sahara was already desert by this time, it was not as dry as it was in dynastic Egyptian days, and there were periods of increased rainfall during these millennia. Schoch thinks it possible that these rains may have weathered the Sphinx.

However, I remain convinced that the Sphinx must pre-date the break up of the last Ice Age. The technology involved in the Sphinx and its adjacent temples is of an exponentially higher order than anything in Catal Huyuk or Jericho. If technology of that order had been available in Egypt, I think we'd see evidence of it elsewhere in the ancient world. The drastic precipitation induced weathering, and the fact that — as our opponents interminably point out — we *don't* have evidence of anything else from the Sphinx era, makes me think that the more outrageous scenario is actually the more plausible one. (That missing other evidence is, perhaps, buried deeper than anyone has looked and/or in places no one has yet explored — along the banks of the ancient Nile perhaps, which is miles from the present Nile, or even at the bottom of the Mediterranean, which was dry during the last Ice Age.) If the Sphinx was as recent as 5000-7000 BC, I think we probably would have other Egyptian evidence of the civilization that carved it. Only further research will resolve the question.

An abstract of our team's work was submitted to the Geological Society of America, and we were invited to present our findings at a poster session at the GSA convention in San Diego in October 1992 — the Geological Superbowl. Geologists from all over the world thronged our booth, much intrigued. Dozens of experts in fields relevant to our research offered help and advice. Shown the evidence, some geologists just laughed, astounded (as Schoch had been initially) that in two centuries of research, no one, geologist or Egyptologist, had noticed the obvious — that the Sphinx had been weathered by water.

Our-end run strategy had been in place since the first official survey in April, when Schoch publicly acknowledged that the theory was geologically sound. Without exactly sending out press releases, we were looking to put the story before the public. An article in *Akbar el Yom*, an important Egyptian weekly, published predictably adverse comments from a battery of eminent Egyptologists but presented our own geological argument fairly and coherently. We took this as a good omen — alas, prematurely! We fared rather less well in English. In a wire service piece, Mimi Mann, AP archeological correspondent in Cairo, portrayed us as a bunch of loony Atlantis hunters (despite three hours of personal interview largely devoted to sidestepping the loaded 'A' word). Dr. Zahi Hawass, Director of Antiquities of the Giza Plateau and Sakkara, our most virulent critic to date, derided the entire exercise. 'American hallucinations! West is an amateur. There is absolutely no scientific base for any of this. We have older monuments in the same area. They definitely weren't built by men from space or Atlantis. It's nonsense and we won't allow our monuments to be exploited for personal enrichment. The Sphinx is the soul of Egypt.' Other no less hostile authorities were also quoted at length. Schoch's geology was allotted two lines.

But the reaction at the GSA Annual Meeting was more considered. Having seen our presentation, science and mainstream journalists now

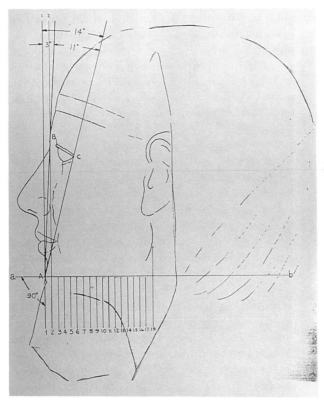 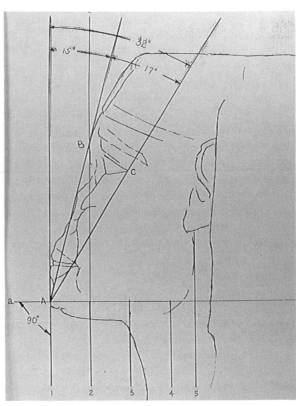

(D1)

Detective Frank Domingo's comparative studies of the Chephren statue in the Cairo Museum and the Great Sphinx. D1 compares the facial structure of both statues in profile. Despite the damage to the Sphinx, it is clear that these two faces are structurally radically different.

sought reactions from Egyptologists. 'There's just no way that could be true. The people of that region would not have had the technology, the governing institutions or even the will to build such a structure thousands of years before Khafre's (Chephren's) reign,' said Carol Redmount, an archeologist at UC Berkeley and world authority on prehistoric willpower. Our conclusions flew in the face of 'everything we know about Egypt' (*Los Angeles Times*, Oct. 23, 1991).

'That's ridiculous,' scoffed Peter Lecovara, assistant curator of the Egyptian Department in Boston's Museum of Fine Arts (*Boston Globe*, Oct. 23, 1991). 'Thousands of scholars working for hundreds of years have studied this topic and the chronology is pretty much worked out. There are no big surprises in store for us.' Ptolemaic Astronomers confronted by Galileo's evidence for a heliocentric solar system had once raised exactly

that objection. Out of dozens of 'experts' consulted, only two, Lanny Bell at The University of Chicago and John Baines at Oxford noticed that geology introduced a new element into the question of the age and attribution of the Sphinx. But both dismissed our conclusions without further ado.

Happily, the press was less dismissive. By the time the GSA conference was over, major stories had appeared in hundreds of papers around the world; we were on CNN, network news programs and radio. We were over the fifty yardline and heading downfield.

But suddenly we had to call time out and deal specifically with that alleged Sphinx/Chephren resemblance. (See p. 205) Only to Egyptologists has the ravaged face of the Sphinx *ever* looked like Chephren. To the practiced eyes of professional sculptors, painters and photographers on my frequent Egypt trips, the Sphinx and Chephren had little in common beyond their shared humanity. But in a *National Geographic* article (April, 1991), Mark Lehner 'proved' via computer imaging that the ravaged face of the Sphinx and the face of Chephren were one and the same. To arrive at his conclusion, Lehner acknowledged he had used the face of Chephren as his model.

Since the computer does as it's told, a Chephren-headed Sphinx was a foregone conclusion. Lehner's 'proof' was a technological tautology. The same computer technique could be used to 'prove' the Sphinx was really Elvis Presley.

Unfortunately, in a six column article, *The New York Times* accepted Lehner's reconstruction at face value, and so did England's prestigious *New Scientist*. In an age besotted by technology, who

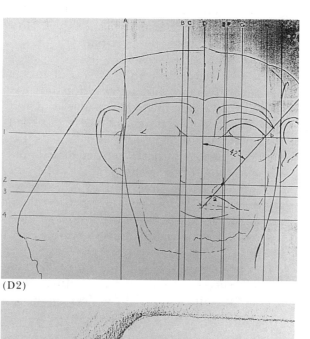

(D2)

(D3)

(D4)

D2 compares the statues full face. D3 and D4 are Domingo's artist's impressions of the face of the Sphinx as it might have looked before it was damaged — a very different face from that of Chephren.

231

would take the professionally informed opinions of sculptors and artists over spuriously-generated computer graphics? Widely disseminated disinformation is as good as information until discredited. It was now incumbent upon us to prove academic malpractice. Who might provide an expert, informed opinion that would stand up in court against Lehner's computer?

Who but the police? Boris Said, our executive producer and project director, came up with the inspired idea of putting the problem to a police forensic artist, whose daily job it is to reconstruct faces from partial or fleeting or remembered evidence. A sequence of phone calls led us to Detective Frank Domingo, senior forensic artist with the New York Police Department. Domingo agreed to come with us to Egypt on our next trip to make sure he got the precise photographs and measurements of both the Chephren statue and the Sphinx he needed to carry out his work.

Months later, Frank Domingo's completed report corroborated the obvious. 'After reviewing my various drawings, schematics and measurements, my final conclusion concurs with my initial reaction; i.e., the two works represent two separate individuals. The proportions in the frontal view and especially the angles and facial protrusion in the lateral views convinced me that the Sphinx is not Chephren. If the ancient Egyptians were skilled technicians and capable of duplicating images then these two works cannot represent the same individual . . .'

The face of the Sphinx was never that of Chephren. Whose it might have been becomes another big, unanswered question. (The Sphinx has by no means run out of riddles.) Chephren did not carve the Sphinx. Schwaller de Lubicz's casual observation is now backed by geological expertise and solid geophysical evidence. The Great Sphinx is much older than dynastic Egypt. How much older remains to be determined.

A new sophisticated technology is under development that will measure the effects of cosmic ray bombardment upon isotopes within the rock. From this data, scientists will be able to determine when the rock was first cut free from its bed and exposed to the air. Within broad limits that should give us a scientifically verified date for the original carving of the Sphinx. Meanwhile, our team will be looking underground with seismographs, perhaps radar and other new technologies for further evidence of the lost civilization responsible for the Sphinx and its temple complex.

My (now-informed) intuition tells me that when we finally succeed in scientifically putting a date to the Sphinx, that date will be so deep in the distant past it will be quite literally mind-boggling.

Afterword: Ringing out the old

Overthrowing and replacing the old order, any order, is risky business. Revolutionaries lead notoriously dangerous lives.

'There is nothing more difficult to carry out, nor more doubtful of success, nor more dangerous to handle, than to initiate a new order of things. For the reformer has enemies in all those who profit by the old order of things and only lukewarm defenders in all those who would profit by the new order, this lukewarmedness arising partly from fear of the adversaries who have the laws in their favour and partly from the incredulity of mankind, who never believe in anything new until they have had experience of it. Thus it arises that on every opportunity for attacking the reformer, his opponents do so with the zeal of partisans, the others only defend him half-heartedly, so that between them he runs great danger. It is necessary, however . . . to examine whether these innovators are independent, or whether they depend upon others, that is to say, whether in order to carry out their designs they have to entreat or are able to compel. In the first case, they invariably succeed ill, and accomplish nothing; but when they can depend on their own strength and are able to use force, they rarely fail. Thus it comes about that all armed prophets have conquered and unarmed ones failed . . .' wrote Machiavelli, with characteristic blunt acumen.*

We are all familiar with the problems innovators have experienced throughout history, from Galileo to Stravinsky. In virtually every sphere of human activity — intellectual, political, economic, philosophical — anything new is resisted (technology may be the only exception). In the arts, though regrettable, that resistance is understandable, sometimes even excusable (ears accus-

---

* *The Prince*, Chapter 6: 'Of New Dominions Which have Been Acquired by One's Own Arms and Ability,' tr. Luigi Ricci.

233

tomed to Brahms do not quickly attune to *The Rites of Spring*!).

But in science this situation should not prevail. Science — as scientists never tire of telling us — is the search for 'objective truth.' In theory, a scientific breakthrough stands or falls upon the quality and quantity of the evidence supporting it. In practice, change in science is resisted as ferociously as change in any other area.* Nobel Prize-winning physicist Max Planck spelled out the situation in a much quoted passage: 'Great scientific theories do not usually conquer the world through being accepted by opponents who, gradually convinced of their truth, have finally adopted them. It is always rare to find a Saul becoming a Paul. What happens is that opponents of the new idea finally die off and the following generation grows up under its influence.' Alexander von Humboldt, the great nineteenth-century naturalist, was equally caustic, 'First they will deny a thing, then they will belittle it, then they will decide that it had been known long ago' (see p. 183).

Innovation in the arts outrages sensibilities; innovation in science outrages belief. Scholarship occupies an ill defined, shifting middleground between science and art, and breakthrough scholarship is subject to the hostility that confronts innovation in both art and science. Scholarship usually concerns the *interpretation* of 'objectively' observed facts. The interpretation that best fits the facts is the preferable one. As in science, new facts may necessitate new scholarly interpretations. For example, the indisputable fact that the Temple of Luxor is an exercise in harmony and proportion necessitates such a new interpretation. But in scholarship it is impossible ultimately to 'prove' scientifically the validity of one interpretation over another.

Consider this analogy: Martian scientists land on Earth and take an interest in baseball. Over the years, a store of precise verifiable information (facts) would accumulate. The materials and official sizes of ball and bat, the different roles of the players, the intricacies of the scoring, even the complex rules of the game — all would yield to careful scientific observation. But if games were unknown on Mars, it would all seem point-less and not a little ludicrous — a curious religious rite, perhaps, performed by superstitious Earthlings and eliciting from us Earthlings a quite incomprehensible emotional response.

However, if, through some stroke of genius, one of these Martians acquired an insight into the nature of a game, all that otherwise baffling baseball information would transform itself into understanding. Our Martians might not necessarily share the Earthlings' enthusiasm for baseball, but baseball would suddenly make sense. Even so, it would still be impossible to 'prove' that baseball is a game! Or even that games exist in the first place — no matter that the pieces all now fall into place. If, for psychological reasons of their own (it makes them feel superior, more advanced, for example) the Martians prefer to go on regarding baseball as the Earthlings' religious superstition,# nothing can compel them to think otherwise.

Some scholarly disciplines recognize their own interpretive nature. Historians rarely pretend to be scientists. But in others, passionate allegiance is pledged to the flag of science — for in the Church of Progress, (the covert pseudo-religion that has reigned over the Western world for three centuries), it is only the imprimatur of 'scientific proof' that confers validity upon *anything*, with the possible exception of the arts. But in the Church of Progress, the arts don't really count for much that is serious. In the *New York Times*, the section devoted to the arts is called 'Arts and Leisure.' Imagine the ruckus that would ensue if the sciences were consigned to a section called 'Science and Tinkering.'

It is the prestige of science that most academics covet. Thus the pledge to the flag of science is often taken by people with no understanding of what science is, what its limitations are, or what scientists actually do. Egyptologists and archeologists are probably the worst among a battalion of academic offenders. Candidates for Ph.D.'s in archeology or Egyptology are not required to take a single course that would be called 'science' by a physicist, geologist or biologist. They have never been taught (and obviously have never learned for themselves) that science advances through experiment, in which measurement, replicability and predictability are essential com-

---

* See the chapter 'Heresy in the Church of Progress' in my book, *The Case for Astrology*, (Arkana/Penguin, 1991) for a thorough discussion of scientific objectivity.

A point that could perhaps be argued effectively by baseball-phobes but that is not the issue here.

ponents for the testing of theories. An Egyptian temple can be measured, but it cannot be repeated or predicted; an Egyptian text cannot be measured, repeated or predicted. In other words, by its very nature Egyptology *cannot* be a science, in the sense that physics or biology or geology are.

Egyptologists and archeologists operate under the mistaken conviction that a systematic method for acquiring data is enough in and of itself to make science. If that were the case, phrenology and astrology would also be sciences*

In real life, Egyptologists go at their jobs about as scientifically as Jackson Pollack but talk as though they were Einstein. So it is that the most common and loudly trumpeted objection to the Sphinx theory — now supported by geology and geophysics (sciences as hard-nosed as any in the world) — is that it has 'no scientific basis'# or that it is 'pseudoscience.'△

The evidence for Schwaller de Lubicz's symbolist interpretation has been laid out over the course of this book. But readers must still answer the central question for themselves: Were the temples of Egypt built by accomplished but superstitious primitives as academic Egyptologists insist? Or were they built by enlightened sages and artists in command of a highly sophisticated Sacred Science?

Thirty-five years have now elapsed since the publication of *Le Temple de l'Homme*; fifteen since the first publication of this book. It would be refreshing to report that Schwaller's thinking has made inroads into the Egyptological establishment. Unfortunately, even that normal painfully gradual Planckian process seems to have aborted. Over the years, many of Schwaller de Lubicz's original Egyptological opponents have retired or gone off to face the forty-two assessors in the judgment hall of Osiris. But with them went the few who were, at least in private, to some extent open to his ideas. They have been replaced by an even less receptive younger generation of academics.

When writing *Serpent in the Sky* originally, my intention was to include a chapter on the problems already experienced in disseminating Schwaller's work and ideas. But I was then working closely with Schwaller de Lubicz's stepdaughter, Lucie Lamy. Mlle. Lamy maintained cordial relations, on a personal level, with at least a few French Egyptologists. It was always her hope and belief that, eventually, the weight of the evidence would make itself felt. Antagonizing Egyptologists with an account and analysis of their own behavior (as of 1978), she felt, would only impede acceptance. In deference to her wishes I left the story untold.

But time has passed. Lucie Lamy died in 1984. Through those of his books, now in English, and through my own efforts, Schwaller's ideas have made modest inroads into a segment of the public consciousness. Artists, writers, creative people generally, architects in particular accept and appreciate the symbolist interpretation instantly, once it is laid out for them. They know firsthand what goes into creativity — and therefore know that masterpieces are not produced by superstitious primitives. Psychologists, teachers, engineers, lawyers, doctors and other professionals, some scientists — people accustomed to assessing evidence in one way or another — also find it convincing, as long as they are not Church of Progress Fundamentalists at heart, as many are. The symbolists are still few; the process is slow. It is now clear that neither time nor evidence will ever oblige Egyptologists to rethink the premises upon which their entire discipline is founded.

A brief account of the actual reception accorded symbolist Egypt is overdue. Through it readers may understand how academic Egyptology has managed to maintain its position in the face of such powerfully documented heresy.

La Querelle des Egyptologues

In 1949, the appearance of Schwaller de Lubicz's first book, *Le Temple dans l'Homme*, (a brief precursor or preview to the later, massive *Le Temple de l'Homme*) caused an uproar within French Egyptological circles. Though ordinarily such a dispute would never find its way into the public do-

* Actually, astrology is considerably more scientific than contemporary academic Egyptology, since it is at least based upon certain quantitatively verifiable premises. But there is no time to develop that thesis here.
# Dr. Zahi Hawass, Director of the Giza Plateau and Sakkara, in *Akhbar El Yom*, a respected Cairo weekly, April 20, 1991.
△ Dr. Mark Lehner, *New York Times*, February 9, 1992.

main, this was an exception. Over the years, working on site at Karnak and Luxor in Egypt collecting their evidence, Schwaller and his team had the opportunity to explain the symbolist approach firsthand to interested visitors.

Among these was Andre Rousseaux, an eminent French literary critic. Rousseaux had become a staunch advocate of the symbolist interpretation and had been following the academic dispute closely. Finally, enraged at the treatment the new interpretation was being accorded, he presented his view of the matter to the literary audience of the review, *Le Mercure de France* (July, 1951) in a long article called 'La Querelle des Egyptologues.'

As a philosopher, orientalist and mathematician (without formal credentials in any case), Schwaller had no direct access to the specialized journals of Egyptology. However, for a number of years, the symbolist case had been advanced for him by Alexandre Varille, a highly regarded young Egyptologist who'd become convinced of Schwaller's interpretation but who had, in effect, to throw over his entire career in order to espouse it openly.

Concentrating upon the running battle between Varille and his orthodox colleagues, Rousseaux summarized the symbolist approach and its potential importance for all Western thought. Supporting his essay with extracts from numerous letters and documents Rousseaux claimed that:

1 Varille adhered rigorously to every scholastic convention in presenting his evidence, and the evidence was in fact assailable. Nevertheless, he was dismissed by his colleagues as a 'fantasist.' The justification for this was that all Egyptologists agreed he was a fantasist, therefore he had to be one. (A similar scientific argument was advanced three centuries earlier in England by the notorious 'hanging judge,' Chief Justice Jeffries. The question then raging was whether or not there really were witches. There had to be witches, Judge Jeffries ruled, since there were laws against them.)

2 Varille insisted that de Lubicz's evidence *proved* Egyptology was in need of total revision. It was not that academic Egyptology was specifically wrong; it was that it was in its entirety superficial. Texts deciphered according to standard procedure appeared illogical and inconsistent, qualities then happily ascribed to the authors of the texts. But when interpreted symbolically, the same texts made perfect sense, and were consistent with a world view that had links to early Christianity, Hindu and other esoteric traditions.

Varille maintained that Egyptian texts could not merely be translated literally; they had to be *interpreted*. This, said the experts, was absurd, since the texts as they were currently translated did not disclose any such need for interpretation (A parallel process would be Biblical scholars translating the New Testament parable of the sower and the seed and insisting that it was simply inept agricultural advice.)

3 Rousseaux claimed that academic journals consistently refused to publish Varille's dissertations, all submitted according to standard procedures. Varille was then accused by opponents of failing to produce 'evidence' to support his case. Rousseaux cited several specific criticisms levelled at the symbolists and published Varille's answers. He proposed a confrontation on site at Luxor and Karnak, where Egyptologists would have the chance to review the evidence firsthand and discredit it.

Rousseaux's article drew furious rebuttals from two eminent French Egyptologists, Etienne Drioton, the target of much of Rousseaux's criticism, and Jean Sainte-Fare Garnot. Both insisted there was no real 'quarrel' between Egyptologists since all Egyptologists agreed Varille was wrong. Drioton expressed open approval of 'the common front of silence' erected by Egyptologists to withstand the symbolists' attack, citing the unanimity of opinion as evidence for the unsoundness of the opposition view. Drioton then raised a few other Egyptological objections, and declined the offer to meet at Luxor. Egyptologists had too many important things to take care of to waste time discrediting a few cranks (the question of how many asps killed Cleopatra had not yet been settled). But, he said, the symbolists were welcome to present papers at forthcoming Egyptological conferences in Istanbul and Amsterdam.

Now, in a second article, Varille was given space (denied him in his own Egyptological journals) to answer objections point by point. (Much of this argument has been incorporated into the main text of *Serpent in the Sky*, so there is no need to elaborate here.) But he declined the counter-invitation to come to Istanbul and Turkey, evidently feeling that neither the Turkish Egyptian ruins nor the Dutch Egyptian ruins were proper settings for the on-site examination of the evidence the symbolists sought.

Unfortunately, by the time the second article appeared, Varille had been killed in a car crash. The symbolists had lost their only official spokesman. Virtually the entire stock of *Le Temple dans l'Homme* was destroyed in the early fifties in an earthquake, effectively concealing symbolist Egypt from public view. As far as I know, no academic attention was paid to Schwaller's work until the publication, in 1957, of *Le Temple de l'Homme*.

Rousseaux now re-opened the subject, this time in the literary and philosophical quarterly *Les Cahiers du Sud* (#358). He resummarized the evidence and the issues and invited comments by specialists. Among the contributors to this article was Dr. Arpag Mekhitarian (quoted on p. 155), the only Egyptologist willing to violate the 'common front of silence.' But no one within Egyptology took up Mekhitarian's challenge then, nor had anyone as of the writing of *Serpent in the Sky* — though as we have seen (p. 154-155), in France at least, some of Schwaller's ideas were percolating into Egyptological thinking, without reference to their source and without recognizing that the rest of the symbolist interpetation must necessarily follow if these individual points were acknowledged. From an outsider's vantage point, that deliberate 'common front of silence' was successful. One of my aims in writing *Serpent in the Sky* was to break that common front.

Schwaller had treated his opponents with ceremonious Old World courtesy, inviting them to discussion and debate. All he got in return was neglect and abuse. It was clear that no combination of documented evidence, lucidity and reason would get a hearing within the Egyptological establishment. Patience would not further, nor civility. But a polemic that advanced the symbolist argument while exposing in specific, unarguable detail the nature of the opposition could cause something of stir—if it ruffled the right feathers. With brevity and ominous irony, Planck, Machiavelli and Von Humboldt had spelled out the problems of establishing a new order.

It was a daunting prospect, certainly; but to-day's innovators have recourse to a potential ally undreamed of prior to this century, the media. Generally, the media sticks to its job of spreading Church of Progress gospel, and the Church of Progress is every bit as intolerant and dogmatic as the Church of Rome ever was. But it does not (usually) have power over the physical life and death of heretics, and the media make unruly Jesuits. Sensing a 'story,' the media may publicize challenges to dogma that would otherwise be silenced for generations or even for good by the College of Cardinals of the threatened discipline. But because the quality of the evidence and the ultimate significance of the issues have little or no bearing upon the ultimate exposure the story will get, courting the media is a wild-card, dangerous procedure in its own right, like trying to befriend a tiger by hand-feeding it steaks. And yet, if the gods are smiling and the stars are right, it's sometimes possible to smoke the incumbents out of their ivory towers and provoke the desired confrontation, or put another way, to execute an end-run around the establishment.

In retrospect, my chosen strategy was only marginally successful. Predictably, *Serpent in the Sky* was completely ignored by academic Egyptological journals, but mainstream reviews were not abundant, either. A few editors reported back to me that the book had aroused the interest of a reviewer, but it had then been sent on for a second opinion to a local 'expert' (Egyptologist or archeologist), who had invariably advised against reviewing it. (I hadn't considered that possibility! But it's certain a less incendiary approach would have been equally unwelcome.)

Rather than risk offense or review favorably a book that challenged an entire discipline, the 'expert' advice was generally heeded. Without an audible media outcry, the end-run strategy was foredoomed.

Prophets on Hold

Serpent in the Sky gradually found its way to an audience over the years; however, its publication did nothing to breach the academic 'common front of silence.' According to Dr. Arpag Mekhitarian, still at Brussels,* to the best of his

* Private correspondence with Charles William Horton.

knowledge, no Egyptologists had taken up his 1957 challenge (see p. 155), though a few stray references (invariably pejorative) over the years suggest that academics at least have not totally ignored symbolist Egypt.

Michael von Haag, (*Travelaid Guide to Egypt*, 1981), printed a clumsily drawn version of the skeleton superimposed over the plan of the Luxor temple and supplied a similarly clumsy commentary on this most incendiary aspect of Schwaller's work: 'He [Schwaller] spent years measuring and drawing the position of the paving stones in the temple and then by shading in some but not others was able to "prove" that they formed a pharaonic profile with the top of the skull sliced off; and also he superimposed a skeleton on the temple plan to demonstrate a close similarity in its proportions to the human frame. Certainly Schwaller de Lubicz proves that if you have enough dots, and spend enough time connecting them, you can come up with any picture you like. [Jean] Cocteau, however, was very impressed when he met the archeologist whose mathematical interpretation of the temple launched Cocteau on a poetic and more perceptive vision' (p. 204).

Von Haag then quotes Cocteau at some length. Since Cocteau* is doing no more than paraphrasing Schwaller's symbolist Egypt into his own words, von Haag's admiration for these passages undercuts his own immediately preceding disparaging remarks. Elsewhere Mr. von Haag talks about 'the mumbo jumbo of solar boats' and finds Hathor's cow ears a subject for derision — a symbolic attribution that even the most literal-minded Egyptologist can satisfactorily account for. Among Hathor's roles is that of provider of divine or cosmic nourishment. Since the cow is an animal chiefly associated with providing nourishment, the cow is assimilated to Hathor, and Hathor is often portrayed as a cow or as a woman with cow's ears.

Schwaller also surfaces briefly in the *Journal of the American Research Center in Egypt* (Vol. XXVII, 1990), in a long lead article 'Restricted Knowledge, Hierarchy and Decorum: Modern Perceptions and Ancient Institutions' by Egyptologist John Baines. In this densely argued, densely written scholarly treatise, Dr. Baines cites Schwaller as an example as he briefly confronts his academic colleagues with the faint possibility that their refusal to examine alternative approaches to Egypt might be somewhat restrictive.

'An example may illustrate problems of legitimacy faced by work on abstruse topics and materials. Rene Adolphe Schwaller de Lubicz used methods that have not gained general acceptance to hypothesize an Egyptian anthropocentric mystic science, and disciples like John Anthony West have disseminated his views. The work of West was reviewed negatively by the classicist Peter Green, and West replied that the reviewer did not know the material. ("Tut-Tut-Tut," *New York Review of Books*, October 11, 1979. Correspondence: December 20, 1979) Green responded by saying that nothing in the Egyptian texts he knew fitted with the views of Schwaller de Lubicz; this is true, but does not answer the question. Egyptologists did not enter this fray, but Schwaller de Lubicz knew more about the Egyptian temple than either his disciple or his critic. I agree with Green with being suspicious of Schwaller de Lubicz's method, but the only possible reason *a priori* for this suspicion is that Schwaller's strategy of imposing images on ground plans can prove almost anything' (p. 3).

Baines does not elaborate further upon Schwaller de Lubicz, and it is, of course, absolutely true that Schwaller knew more about the Egyptian temple than I do. It is also true that Schwaller knew more about the Egyptian temple than Baines does. But I know more about Schwaller de Lubicz than Baines does, so I also know that the superimposition of the skeleton on the temple is just one *result* of Schwaller's method and not the method itself — and readers who have read this book up to this point also know that. If Baines had read me or Schwaller with attention he would know that, too.

Schwaller's 'method' was to measure accurately. From the measurements he derived the geometry and the proportions of the temple. The geometry and proportions proved incontrovertibly the existence of a mystical mathematical science, based upon a profound knowledge of cosmic principles and functions (the *neters*, or gods). It was this science that, ultimately, informed Schwaller's reinterpretation of the totality of Egyptian civilization. The correctness or otherwise of the skeleton/temple demonstration is not central to Schwaller's hypothesis, nor is it

---

* Cocteau's intention was to make a film about symbolist Egypt. But at some point he made disparaging remarks about then-King Farouk and became persona non grata in Egypt and the plans were abandoned.

the basis of his method. *Even if it is wrong* * it does not affect the overall validity of the symbolist interpretation. If, as a responsible scholar, Baines wants to retain his 'suspicions' of Schwaller's method, then he should begin with refutations of the proportions and the geometry (no one argues with the accuracy of the measures) of the temple and/or provide alternative explanations for the geometry and proportions that would retain intact his belief in an ancient Egypt devoid of real science or philosophy.

For example, he might start with the central triple chamber at the southernmost end of Luxor Temple (see p. 153) and show that it is not really proportioned 8:9, the proportions of the first note of the musical scale or, alternatively, that somehow these proportions are an accident resulting from the similarly meaningless and accidental geometric play responsible for the rest of this chamber. Following that, he might, after this decent lapse of four decades, perhaps take up that gauntlet originally thrown down by Mekhitarian and disprove those assertions that, according to Mekhitarian, are drawn from 'precise and objective evidence' (p. 155). Or perhaps he should rethink the basis of his suspicions.

The rest of Dr. Baines's article suggests rethinking is unlikely. His theme is, first, the putative existence of ancient Egyptian restricted or secret knowledge and second, the motivation for it. Referencing extensive Egyptological sources and many Egyptian texts referring to such knowledge, Baines concludes secret knowledge must have existed. As for motivation, he concludes that initiation into secret knowledge conferred 'prestige' upon the Pharaoh or priest made privy to it. That was the reason for keeping it secret.

There is no Egyptian text suggesting such a motivation. The texts make it clear that to the Egyptians, secret knowledge was a matter of profound importance (see margin note, p. 82). Rather than entertain the possibility that perhaps the Egyptians had some good reason for keeping knowledge secret, Baines concludes it must have been a kind of ritualized egotism.

So, while it is refreshing to see Schwaller's name pop up in an academic Egyptological journal, it is unlikely that the reference will impel Dr. Baines's even more dismissive colleagues to start reading Schwaller to see what they've missed. Within academia 'the common front of silence' holds.

Are the symbolists, then, classic examples of Machiavelli's 'unarmed prophets,' and destined to fail? Or, at some belated point, does the Planckian process finally start to apply? There are now, suddenly and unexpectedly, some reasons for hope, though the obstacles remain formidable. Establishing a new symbolist order involves difficulties over and above those confronting innovation in other disciplines — Max Planck was not thinking of Egyptology when he made his famous observation.

Fortress Egypt

A tacit territorial agreement prevails throughout all Academia. Biochemists steer clear of sociology; Shakespearean scholars do not disparage radio astronomy. It's taken for granted that each discipline, scientific, scholarly or humanistic, has its own valid self-policing system, and that academic credentials ensure expertise in a given field.

With its jealous monopoly on the impenetrable hieroglyphs,# its closed ranks, restricted membership, landlocked philosophical vistas, empty coffers, and its lack of impact upon virtually every other academic, scientific or humanistic field, Egyptology has prepared a near-impregnable strategic position for itself — an academic Switzerland but without chocolate, cuckoo clocks, scenery or ski slopes, and cannily concealing its banks. Not only is it indescribably boring and difficult to attack, who'd want to?

But if Swiss financiers suddenly decided to jam the world's banking system, Swiss neutrality and impregnability might suddenly be at risk. That is

---

* In academia, the rules vis-a-vis mistakes change according to location. Only those within the establishment are allowed to 'make mistakes.' Everyone else is a 'crank,' 'crackpot' or 'charlatan,' and entire lifetimes of work are discredited or dismissed on the basis of minor errors.

Who will claim authority to challenge the accepted translations of the texts, even when these read as nonsense?

Actually, a number of independent scholars have learned the hieroglyphs for themselves and produced alternative, less insulting translations of some of the texts. But since these are either ignored or dismissed out of hand by orthodox Egyptologists, there is no way to know if these translations come closer to the real thinking of the ancients or if they are themselves no more than figments of the translators' imaginations, and in consequence no more representative and satisfactory than the standard translations.

partially analagous to the situation of Egyptology. The gold is there, but its existence is denied, and no one is allowed to inspect the vaults except those whose credentials make them privy to the conspiracy and guarantee their silence. To date, only a handful of astute but powerless outsiders have recognized that the situation poses real danger. But it's not easy to generate a widespread awareness or appreciation of that danger.

If you think of Egyptologists at all, the chances are you conjure up a bunch of harmless pedants, supervising remote desert digs or sequestered away in libraries, up to their elbows in old papyrus. You don't think of them as sinister, or dangerous. The illuminati responsible for the hydrogen bomb, nerve gas and Agent Orange are dangerous; if you reflect upon it you see that the advanced beings who have given us striped toothpaste and disposable diapers are also dangerous . . . but Egyptologists?

Possibly they are the most dangerous of all; dangerous because false ideas are dangerous. At any rate *some* false ideas are dangerous. Belief in the flat earth never hurt anyone though it made navigation problematic. Belief in a geocentric universe held back advances in astronomy but otherwise had certain metaphysical advantages. Academic Egyptology is dangerous because it maintains, in spite of Schwaller de Lubicz's documented scholarly evidence, and the obvious evidence of our own eyes and hearts when we go there, that the race responsible for the pyramids and the temples of Karnak and Luxor was less 'advanced' than ourselves. As long as academic Egyptology prevails, children will be brought up with a totally distorted view of our human past, and by extension, of our human present. And millions of tourists will continue to visit Egypt every year, and have the experience of a lifetime vitiated* and subverted by a banal explanation that ascribes the greatest art and architecture in the world to superstitious primitives.

So the fabulous metaphysical gold of Egypt remains hidden; it's existence stridently denied. For orthodox Egyptology is really little more than a covert operation within the Church of Progress. Its unspoken agenda is to maintain the faith; not to study or debate the truth about Egypt.

---

* 'How can people come back from Egypt and live lives the way they lived them before.' Florence Nightingale, *Letters from Egypt 1849-1850, A Journey on the Nile.*

What might happen if the gold of Egypt were ever to become common knowledge? It's hard to say exactly. But it's just possible that there would be a public outcry to substitute it for the counterfeit coinage of the Church of Progress. Though this has been the benchmark standard for three centuries, it never bought anything much beyond Wonderbread and circuses. Today, it no longer even buys time.

But the practical questions remain: Can this knowledge be made common? Can people be induced to care? If, between them, Planck, von Humboldt and Machiavelli had summed up the situation in its entirety, the prospects would not be bright. But there are other factors that can now be brought into play.

Laying Siege to Switzerland or: Prophets with Firepower

As Victor Hugo remarked, 'There is one thing more powerful than all the armies in the world, and that is an idea whose time has come.' Over and above the cautionary lessons of Planck, Machiavelli and von Humboldt there is that mysterious and overriding *zeitgeist*. A cycle ends; a new one begins; no one can really say what brings down the old, what initiates the new, or what it is that determines when an idea's 'time has come.' All we know is that, historically, it has happened often; there is every reason to believe it will happen again; indeed, that it is already happening. But what will be Egypt's role?

Under any circumstances, symbolist Egypt on Schwaller's own level is for the few, like astrophysics or advanced mathematics or any other highly specialized discipline. At the 'appreciation' level, it is accessible to many more, but it is still not a subject with mass appeal. But the proven and prodigious antiquity of the Great Sphinx of Giza is a subject everyone seems to respond to. The geological evidence is so clearcut it can be satisfactorily explained for a mass readership. Though very complicated and sophisticated science will be needed to put dates on the Sphinx and carry the various elements of the theory forward, the significance of an older Sphinx can be made obvious to everyone.

The media response to the theory so far is proof of its appeal. Something about the notion of a provable 'lost civilization' seems to strike a deep chord within the human psyche; almost as though it were a distant memory. The academic 'common front of silence' cannot shut out the Sphinx theory from public consciousness. For the time being it can keep symbolist Egypt out of the universities, but even the universities are ultimately responsive to public pressure. *

In the late twentieth century, as the Church of Progress loses its grip, an alternative medicine, alternative psychology, even an alternative technology can take root and flourish outside and largely independent of the mainstream, and without much connection to the educational establishment. In medicine, public demand and the testimony of thousands of patients healed by alternative practices has forced doctors to reconsider their position. But even as the battle was underway, alternative practitioners could earn livings from their knowledge, (as long as they weren't witch-hunted out of business). No establishment affiliations were needed in order to learn or to practice (though many astute practitioners went to the trouble of acquiring mainstream medical credentials of one sort or another to smooth the way). The same applies to alternative psychology or technology (and to astrology, psychic readings, palmistry, tarot cards and other systems or practices totally unacceptable to the Church of Progress).

An alternative Egyptology is less easily managed. Almost no one can earn a living from it. Serious research is difficult to accomplish on a spare-time basis, and research requires access to the few major Egyptological libraries scattered around the world. In Egypt itself, excavation and all work on or in the pyramids, temples and tombs is controlled by the Egyptian Antiquities Organizations. No one without academic credentials can expect to obtain permission to carry out original work.# Infiltration from within is also peculiarly difficult. At least a few people I know personally have set out to acquire degrees in Egyptology, hoping to devote themselves full time to Egypt and ultimately to legitimize the symbolist interpretation. So far, none have been able to stick out the boredom or dutifully parrot the party line for the years necessary to get the diploma, knowing better from the onset.

It seems unlikely that symbolist Egypt will ever establish itself from within its own ranks. But pressure from outside Egyptology but within academia could force a change. Academics with an interest but no personal stake in the matter must sooner or later realize that the support of highly qualified geologists (of a fundamentally geological theory) must overrule either the clamor or the silence of the Egyptological/archeological establishment. At some point they must express those views.

Though the antiquity of the Sphinx does not of itself prove the validity of the symbolist interpretation, it opens the door to it in a way that no amount of carefully documented evidence could do. As Church of Progress thinking loosens its stranglehold on university intellectual life, students, faculties and trustees will grow increas-

---

* The lead article in the October 4, 1992 *New York Times Good Health Magazine* by Douglas S. Barasch, is called 'The Mainstreaming of Alternative Medicine.' Several weeks earlier in the *New York Times Sunday Magazine* section there was a long and balanced article on homeopathy. Universities are beginning to offer courses in alternative therapies; the National Institutes of Health has established an office to investigate unconventional medical practices. Though predicted long ago (see *Serpent* p. 118), this has been a gradual, often bitterly contested process.

For years the medical profession has routinely employed strongarm tactics against alternative medical practitioners, usually seeking to enforce antiquated laws to legally ruin the lives of homeopaths, chiropractors and others — and of course to deprive patients of help, (most of whom only tried alternatives because they could not be cured by orthodox methods). These inquisitorial methods are still very much in force whenever the A.M.A. or other bastion of orthodoxy thinks it can get away with it. The medical profession as a whole has certainly not undergone an overnight conversion.

Nevertheless, in principle, symbolist Egyptophiles may take heart from articles like these, especially when they show up in the *New York Times*, and not just the *New Age Journal*. For if sufficient numbers within the medical profession find themselves obliged to reconsider basic premises — then why not Egyptology? In practice, the situation is more difficult and less clearcut.

#Prior to the development of modern day Egyptology by the western nations, native Egyptians showed little regard or respect for their distant dynastic ancestors; the temples were quarried for stone, anything movable was cheerfully sold to antiquities dealers. Islam, along with Christianity and Judaism, tended to regard ancient Egypt as pagan and idolatrous. But today, at least in private, Egyptian Egyptologists often display a much higher degree of understanding and sensitivity toward the Pharaonic achievement than their European and American colleagues. It would not surprise me to find some closet symbolists among them. Egyptian licensed tour guides (a much coveted job) must have degrees in academic Egyptology and pass an exacting test to qualify. Over the course of years of research and leading tours myself, at least a few dozen have approached me, eager to learn more about symbolist Egypt. But within the closed ranks of practicing, professional Egyptology, academic prestige (such as it is), is still wielded by the major European and American Universities. So even though all ancient Egyptian sites are now entirely under Egyptian control, an Egyptian Egyptologist would be as unlikely to try to break the 'common front of silence' as anyone else, whatever his or her private convictions.

ingly unwilling to allocate ever-tighter university funds to a modern day equivalent of Ptolemaic astronomy. Sooner or later academic Egyptology will go the same way. With Schoch and the geologists finally carrying the ball, the end-run strategy is working. The prophets are in the process of acquiring firepower.

Church of Progress dogma insists civilization goes in a straight line from cavemen to our advanced selves. The antiquity of the Sphinx invalidates that conceit in a single stroke. Whoever carved the Sphinx and built the incredible temples alongside with carefully fitted two hundred ton blocks of stone were not 'hunters and gatherers.' Everything we have been taught to believe about our distant human past must be rethought. Progress itself is a matter of perspective: the maggot sees its world as a boundless field of seething, purposeful activity; the falcon flying above just sees a dead horse.

Who knows what a return to the gold standard of ancient Egypt — in some appropriately modern coinage — might bring?

Selected bibliography

Rather than simply list the many sources from which
material for this book was drawn, I have cited only those I
consider genuinely useful to the reader interested in
verifying or contesting the ideas put forward, or in looking
deeper into areas only touched upon in this necessarily
introductory volume.

Concerning Egypt, an unbridgeable gulf separates
popular accounts and the Egyptological source material
available only in major libraries and the Egyptological
departments of a few universities. Popular accounts are
catechistically repetitive, both in information and
conclusion. By contrast, source books and Egyptological
journals are nearly opaque to the non-specialist. My list of
both is accordingly brief.

As this goes to press, the works of R. A. Schwaller de
Lubicz, formerly available only in French, and in many cases
out of print, are in the process of translation into English,
and will soon be available. These are:

A Works by R. A. Schwaller de Lubicz and the Symbolists

1 *Le Temple de l'Homme (The Temple of Man)*, Translated by
   Robert and Deborah Lawlor. To be published by
   Autumn Books (USA).
   This is the cardinal work, to which all the others lead or
   refer. Though not intended for specialists, the sheer
   complexity and magnitude of the work makes it
   accessible only to those willing to devote the necessary
   time and effort to it.
2 *Le Temple dans L'Homme (The Temple Within Man)*,
   Autumn Books, U.S.A. 1977.
   Written prior to *T. de H*, this book contains in embryo the
   ideas later explored in detail.
3 *Le Roi de la Théocratie Pharaonique (The King of the
   Pharaonic Theocracy)*, Inner Traditions International.
4 *Le Miracle Egyptienne (The Egyptian Miracle)*, Inner
   Traditions International, New York.
   Both the above consist of essays probing deeper into

aspects of Egypt treated in *T. de H*. A prior grounding in the source work is an advantage.

5 *Propos sur Esoterisme et Symbole (Concerning Esotericism and Symbol)*, La Colombe, Paris, 1960.
A slender volume defining the precise manner in which Schwaller de Lubicz treats these generally woolly and ill-defined subjects.

6 *Symbol et Symbolique (The Symbol and the Symbolic)*, Le Caire, Cairo, 1957.
A useful essay comparing modern rationalism to the symbolic thinking of the ancients. Later developed in a different form in *T. de H*. But for those frightened off by the cost and size of the key work, this provides a useful, relatively accessible introduction.

7 *Rebel In the Soul*, Bika Reed, Inner Traditions International, 1978.

8 *Egyptian Mysteries*, Lucie Lamy, Inner Traditions International, 1981.

9 *Sacred Geometry*, Robert Lawlor, Crossroad, 1982.

10 *The Traveller's Key to Ancient Egypt*, John Anthony West, Alfred Knopf, 1985.

B Gurdjieff and His Followers

Gurdjieff, G. I.

1 *ALL & Everything*, Routledge & Kegan Paul (UK), 1949.

2 *Meetings with Remarkable Men*. Routledge & Kegan Paul (UK), 1959.

Ouspensky, P. D.

3 *In Search of the Miraculous*, Routledge & Kegan Paul (UK), 1950.

4 *A New Model of the Universe*, Routledge & Kegan Paul (UK), 1931.

5 *Tertium Organum*, Alfred A. Knopf (USA), 1947.

Nicoll, Maurice

6 *The New Man*, Stuart & Richards (UK), 1952.

7 *The Mark*, Stuart & Richards (UK), 1954.

8 *Living Time*, Vincent Stuart (UK), 1952.

Bennett, J. G.

9 *The Dramatic Universe*, 4 vols. Hodder & Stoughton, 1956-63.

Excepting their views on Time and Re-incarnation, the work of Gurdjieff and his followers corresponds to or complements Schwaller de Lubicz's ideas. Reading Gurdjieff himself requires an unflagging sense of humour, a degree of humility and a determination to surmount the innumerable exasperating obstacles deliberately set in the path. The reward tends to be commensurate to the effort expended.

Ouspensky expounds Gurdjieff's system with precision and clarity. Bennett is particularly valuable for his philosophical exposition of number mysticism. Nicoll provides a key to the inner, esoteric meaning of Christianity, and in *Living Time* develops upon Ouspensky's theory of recurrence.

C Esotericism and Anti-Materialism

1 Aurobindo, Sri, *The Life Divine*, Sri Aurobindo Lib. (New York), 1951.
2 Berdyaev, Nicolas, *The Meaning of the Creative Act*, Gollancz (UK), 1955.
3 Burckhardt, Titus, *Alchemy*, Stuart and Watkins (UK), 1967.
4 Capra, Fritjof, *The Tao of Physics*, Wildwood (UK), 1975.
5 Castaneda, Carlos, *The Teachings of Don Juan*, Penguin (UK), 1970.
6 Castaneda, Carlos, *A Separate Reality*, Penguin (UK), 1973.
7 Castaneda, Carlos, *Journey to Ixtlan*, Penguin (UK), 1975.
8 Castaneda, Carlos, *Tales of Power*, Bodley Head (UK), 1976.
9 Eckhardt, Meister, *Selected Treatises and Sermons*, Fontana (UK), 1963.
10 Evans-Wentz, *The Tibetan Book of the Dead*, O.U.P. (UK), 1968.
11 Griaule, Marcel, *Conversations with Ogotemmeli*, Oxford (UK), 1965.
12 Guenon, Rene, *The Reign of Quantity*, Penguin (UK).
13 Guenon, Rene, *The Symbolism of the Cross*, Luzac (UK), 1958.
14 Huxley, Aldous, *The Perennial Philosophy*, Chatto (UK).
15 Kenton, Warren, *The Tree of Life: Introd. to the Kabbala*, Rider (UK), 1972.
16 Mead, G. R. S., *Fragments of a Faith Forgotten*, University Books (UK), 1960.
17 Merton, Thomas, Tr. *Chuang-Tzu*, Allen & Unwin (UK), 1972.
18 Neihardt, J., *Black Elk Speaks*, Paladin (UK), 1970.

19 Reps, Paul, *Zen Flesh, Zen Bones*, Penguin (UK), 1971.
20 Santillana, G. & von Dechend, H., *Hamlet's Mill*, Gambit (USA), 1969.
21 Shah, Idries, *The Sufis*, Doubleday (USA), 1960.
22 Sheldrake, Rupert, *A New Science of Life: The Hypothesis of Formative Causation*, (London) Blond.
23 Sheldrake, Rupert, *The Presence of the Past*, (London) Collins, 1988.
24 *Tao Te Ching*, tr. Gia Fu-Heng & English, T., Wildwood (UK), 1975.
25 Waddell, Helen, *The Desert Fathers*, Fontana (UK), 1962.

The above is an idiosyncratic and abbreviated list representing a cross-section of books in the mystical tradition. Guenon's *Reign of Quantity* is an erudite onslaught upon the spurious metaphysics of Materialism, perhaps the best single book upon the subject. Griaule's *Conversations with Ogotemmeli*, a little-known work of anthropology is particularly interesting in the light of Castaneda's work, demonstrating a mystical tradition based upon a recognizable number mysticism within an African tribe.

D Egypt and Egyptology

The Pyramids

1 Tompkins, Peter, *Secrets of the Great Pyramid*, Harper & Row (USA), 1971.
   Solidly researched. Full accounts of the theories, orthodox and unorthodox that have raged upon the subject.
2 Edwards, I. E. S., *The Pyramids of Egypt*, Pelican (UK), 1963.
   Orthodox viewpoint, excellent detail on the problems, many unsolved, attendant upon construction.
3 Mendelssohn, Kurt, *The Riddle of the Pyramids*, Thames & Hudson (UK), 1975.
   Convincing demolition of the orthodox 'tomb' theory, but the one substituted by the author is no better.
4 Smyth, Charles Piazzi, *Life & Work at the Great Pyramid*, Edmonton & Douglas (UK), 1867.
5 Smyth, Charles Piazzi, *New Measurements of the Great Pyramid*, R. Banks (UK), 1884.
6 Davidson, David, *The Great Pyramid, Its Divine Message*, Williams and Norgate (UK), 1932.
7 Lauer, J-P, *Le Probleme des Pyramides d'Egypte*, Payot (Paris), 1948.

E General and Popular Works

1 Clark, R. T. Rundle, *Myth and Symbol in Ancient Egypt.* (London) Thames and Hudson, 1959. Orthodox but perceptive and erudite, a valuable reference work.

2 De Cenival, C. B., *Egyptian Architecture*, Oldbourne, Living Architecture Series (UK), 1964. Excellent and unusual photographs. The author, with the help of several well-known Egyptologists, has used some of de Lubicz's ideas without giving him credit, and then condemned the whole of the 'symbolist' school without supplying a bibliographical reference allowing the reader to form an independent opinion.

3 Desroches de Noblecourt, C., *Tutankhamen*, Penguin (UK), 1965. Excellent illustrations, valuable detail.

4 Erman, Adolf, *A Handbook of Egyptian Religion*, Constable (UK), 1907. A standard work. Useful information.

5 Gardiner, Sir Alan, *Egypt of the Pharaohs*, Oxford (UK), 1961. Strictly orthodox, along with Montet, listed below, particularly valuable as a demonstration of the gulf between the orthodox and the symbolist interpretation.

6 Lefebvre, G., *Romans et Contes Egyptiennes*, Adrien-Maisonneuve (Paris), 1949. Preferable to the available English renderings of the same material.

7 Maspero, G., *Popular Stories of Ancient Egypt*, Tr. by C. H. W. Johns, H. Grevel (UK), 1915.

8 Masters, Robert, *The Goddess Sekhmet: Psycho-spiritual Exercises of the Fifth Way*, Llewellyn Publications, 1991. A lucid study of the baffling 'spiritual bodies' of ancient Egypt.

9 Montet, Pierre, *Eternal Egypt*, Mentor Books, 1964. Orthodox interpretation. De Lubicz criticised, but no bibliographical reference or names mentioned.

10 Morenz, Siegfried, *Egyptian Religion*, Methuen (UK), 1973. Has had some impact in orthodox circles and represents a step forward. Interesting as an illustration of the difference a point of view makes when considering identical material.

11 Nightingale, Florence, *Letters From Egypt: A Journey on the Nile 1849-1850*, Ed. A. Sattin, (New York), Weidenfeld & Nicholson, 1988. The best and most sensitive early travel account of Egypt I know.

F Specialized Books

The titles listed below largely describe the contents of the works. Intended for specialists, a quick glance through is enough to demonstrate both the painstaking work that has gone into Egyptology and the large number of open questions in every field.

1 Antoniadi, Eugéne Michel, *L'astronomie égyptienne depuis les temps les plus recules*, Gauthiers-Villars (Paris), 1934.
2 Badawy, A., *Ancient Egyptian Architectural Design*, University of California Publications, Near Eastern Studies (USA), 1965.
3 Borchardt, Ludwig, *Die Annalen und die Zeitlichen Festlegung des Alten Reiches der Aegyptischen Geschichte*, Verlag Von Behren (Germany), 1917.
4 Breasted, James Henry, *Ancient Records of Egypt*, Russell and Russell (UK), 1962.
5 Breasted, James Henry, *The Edwin Smith Surgical Papyrus*, Chicago (USA), 1930.
6 Champollion, M. le Jeune, *Lettre a M. Dacier relative a l'alphabet des hieroglyphs phonetiques*, Firmin Didot (Paris), 1832.
7 Clarke, Somers & Engelbach, R., *Ancient Egyptian Masonry*, Oxford (UK), 1930.
8 Faulkner, R. O., *Ancient Egyptian Pyramid Texts*, Oxford (UK), 1969.
9 Gardiner, Sir Alan, *Egyptian Grammar*, O. U. P. (UK), 1950.
10 Gillain, O., *La science égyptienne*, Brussels, 1927.
11 Hume, W. F., *Geology of Egypt*, Ministry of Finance, Egyptian Survey of Egypt, 1925-48.
12 Hayes, William C., *Most Ancient Egypt*, Chicago (USA), 1965.
13 Kielland, Else Christie, *Geometry in Egyptian Art*, Alec Tiranti (UK), 1959.
14 Lefebvre, G., *Essai sur la medicine égyptienne*, Presses Universitaires de France, 1956.
15 Lucas, A., *Ancient Egyptian Materials and Industries*, Edward Arnold (UK), 1962.
16 Mayer, Eduard, *Chronologie égyptienne*, Annales de Musee Guimet, 1912.
17 Peet, T. Eric, *The Rhind Mathematical Papyrus*, Hodder and Stoughton (UK), 1923.
18 Tannery, P., *Memoires Scientifiques*, Gauthiers Villars (Paris), 1915.
19 Weill, R., *Chronologie égyptienne*, Geuthner (Paris), 1926.

G Pattern, Proportion, Number

1 Albarn, Keith, *The Language of Pattern*, Thames & Hudson (UK), 1974.
2 Critchlow, Keith, *Order in Space*, Thames & Hudson (UK), 1964.
3 Doczi, Gyorgi, *The Power of Limits: Proportional Harmonies in Nature, Art & Architecture*, Shambhala, 1981.
4 Gardner, Martin, *The Ambidextrous Universe*, Penguin (UK), 1970.
5 Gardner, Martin, *Mathematical Puzzles and Diversions*, Penguin (UK), 1970.
6 Gardner, Martin, *Further Mathematical Diversions*, Allen & Unwin (UK), 1970.
7 Ghyka, Matila, *Le Nombre d'Or*, Gallimard (Paris), 1930.
8 Ghyka, Matila, *Essai sur le Rhythme*, Gallimard (Paris), 1938.
9 Ghyka, Matila, *The Geometry of Art and Life*, Sheed & Ward (USA), 1948.
10 Jenny, Hans, *Cymatics 1 & 2*, Basileus Press, Basil, 1967, 1972.
11 Michell, John, *The Dimensions of Paradise: The Proportions and Symbolic Numbers of Ancient Cosmology*, Harper & Row, 1988.
12 Stevens, Peter S., *Patterns in Nature*, Penguin (Peregrine) (UK), 1976.
13 Thompson, D'Arcy, *On Growth and Form*, 2nd ed., Cambridge University Press, 1942.
14 Young, Arthur M., *The Reflexive Universe*, Delacorte, 1976.

H Atlantis and Lost Civilizations

1 Braghine, Col. A., *The Shadow of Atlantis*, Rider (UK), 1938.
2 Clube, Victor & Napier, Bill, *The Cosmic Serpent*, Universe, 1982.
3 Cohane, John, *The Key*, Turnstone (UK), 1973.
4 Donnelly, Ignatius, *Atlantis: The Antediluvian World* (UK), 1889.
5 Lee, J. Fitzgerald, *The Great Migration*, Skeffington & Son (UK), 1933.
6 Mavor, James, *Voyage to Atlantis*, G. P. Putnam's Sons (USA), 1969.
7 Temple, Robert, *The Sirius Mystery*, Sidgwick & Jackson (UK), 1976.
8 Tompkins, Peter, *Mysteries of the Mexican Pyramids*, Harper & Row (USA), 1976.

James Mavor develops the currently-favoured scientific view equating Atlantis with the Greek island of Thera, and carefully avoids mention of the body of contradictory evidence. The other books on the list try to cope with that evidence, with varying degrees of success.

I Astrology

1 Addey, John, *Harmonics in Astrology*, Fowler (UK), 1976.
Results of the author's search to re-discover and reestablish the harmonic and numerical basis of astrology.
2 Gauquelin, Michel, *Cosmic Influences Upon Human Behaviour*, Garnstone Press (UK), 1974.
Results of a lifelong statistical study proving correspondences between human personality and the positions of the planets at birth.,
3 Jerome, Laurence B., *Objections to Astrology*, Prometheus Books (USA), 1976.
4 Musaios (Dr. Charles Muses), *The Lion Path: You* Can *Take it with You*, Golden Scepter Press, (Berkeley, CA.) 1987.
5 West, John Anthony, *The Case for Astrology*, Viking/Arkana, 1991.
Studies the accumulated evidence from all scientific fields supporting the astrological premise. Examines and attacks the many misconceptions prevailing amongst scientists and scholars.

J Progress, Darwinian Evolution and Other Fantasies

1 Ayer, A. J., *Language, Truth and Logic*, Gollancz (UK), 1936.
2 Bronowski, Jacob, *The Ascent of Man*, BBC (UK).
3 Crick, Francis, *Of Molecules and Men*, University of Washington, 1968.
4 Haldane, J. B. S., *Science & Life: Essays of a Rationalist*, Humanist Library (UK), 1968.
5 Medawar, P. B., *The Art of the Soluble*, Methuen (UK), 1967.
6 Morris, Desmond, *The Naked Ape*, Cape (UK), 1968.
7 Monod, Jacques, *Chance and Necessity*, Collins (UK), 1972.
8 Russell, Bertrand, *Wisdom of the West*, MacDonald (UK), 1969.
9 Orgel, L. E., *The Origins of Life*, Chapman & Hall (UK), 1973.

10   Skinner, B. F., *Beyond Freedom and Dignity*, Cape (UK), 1972.
11   Toffler, Alvin, *Future Shock*, Random House (USA), 1970.

A much-abbreviated, entirely arbitrary list. Individual titles have been chosen for their profoundly transparent absurdity and arrogance, and for the fact that each has achieved a measure of renown in either scholarly or popular circles; in itself a depressing comment upon the quality of the modern educated mind.

Index

NOTE: *mn* references are to marginal notes; *fn* references are to footnotes; *illus.* references to illustrations and their captions.

QUEST BOOKS
are published by
The Theosophical Society in America,
Wheaton, Illinois 60189-0270,
a branch of a world organization
dedicated to the promotion of the unity of
humanity and the encouragement of the study of
religion, philosophy, and science, to the end that
we may better understand ourselves and our place in
the universe. The Society stands for complete
freedom of individual search and belief.
In the Classics Series well-known
theosophical works are made
available in popular editions.